HSIN-PAO CHANG (1922-1965) was educated in China and at Washington State University and received his Ph.D. from Harvard in 1958. At the time of his death he was associate professor of history at the State University of Iowa.

Commissioner Lin Tse-hsü

*Courtesy of Lin Ch'ung-yung, fifth-generation descendant
of Commissioner Lin*

COMMISSIONER LIN
AND THE OPIUM WAR

Hsin-pao Chang

The Norton Library
W · W · NORTON & COMPANY · INC ·
NEW YORK

Books That Live

The Norton imprint on a book means that in the publisher's
estimation it is a book not for a single season but for the years.

W. W. Norton & Company, Inc.

FOR GLEN W. BAXTER

FOREWORD

THE Opium War, generally taken as the opening event of China's modern history, has embittered Chinese patriots and embarrassed conscientious Westerners for more than a century. In mainland China it is used today not only as evidence of inveterate Western iniquity, but specifically as proof of the Marxist-Leninist theorem that free-enterprise capitalism leads to aggressive "imperialism" which allies with reactionary "feudalism" to the detriment of the common people everywhere. The modern Chinese sense of grievance over the war is reinforced by the plain facts that opium smoking was pernicious and that Commissioner Lin's effort to suppress the opium trade was the immediate occasion for hostilities.

It would be hard to devise a more stark and simple, black and white, story of Chinese victimization than the facts of history seem to portray. In comparison, the wrongs suffered by the American colonists, which led them to rebel against British tyranny, sink into insignificance. Indeed, the question is unavoidable: why was the Chinese reaction to the opium evil not more vigorous?

The inquiring scholar finds the Opium War less starkly black and white: he may conclude that Anglo-Chinese hostilities would have occurred even if there had been no opium trade, that other Western powers would have aggressed against China even if Britain had not, and that Chinese patriots today would have a sense of grievance even if Sino-Western relations had avoided warfare. These suppositions follow from the basic fact that Chinese civilization had developed its own distinctive ways, different from Western ways, but that by 1840 it had lost the power to sustain itself vis-à-vis the expanding West. The rule of a million or so Manchus over some 300 million Chinese was a symptom of the institutional distinctiveness of the Chinese empire, which made it behave quite differently from a modern nation-state or from the China of today, where a late-maturing nationalism now views the past with a considerable feeling of shame.

The traditional Chinese sense of cultural superiority, or culturalism, intensifies the modern sentiment of nationalism and nationalistic grievance. The adjustment of modern China to the multi-state system, her proper functioning as part of the world community, will remain incomplete until this sense of grievance at her modern history is exorcised by a rational perspective on it. I am not certain this can ever be achieved, for the decline and fall and revolutionary transformation of the old Chinese civilization has been an unprecedented tragedy for the participants, and it is still unfolding. But the need for the historian's rational analysis and dispassionate understanding of events is plain. Naturally, this must be a work of individual judgment, an effort not to sit as a judge only but to be a witness for all sides of the argument and to recapture the circumstances, the moods, and the beliefs of the protagonists. To do this for the Opium War is an exacting task.

Hsin-pao Chang has brought to this work many years of careful self-training in the historian's craft, an unusual grasp of the materials in Chinese as well as in English, and a thorough devotion to seeking the truth of history without *a priori* interpretations. He has used the newly published diary of the protagonist on the Chinese side, Imperial Commissioner Lin Tse-hsü, and has had access to British and American business archives, including the monumental repository of the papers of the leading firm in the China trade, Jardine, Matheson and Company, at Cambridge University. While these Western records generally confirm aspects of the story already known, Dr. Chang's penetration of hitherto unused Chinese materials gives us a more balanced account of the origin of the Opium War than has ever been available in any language. Taken as a whole, his work can contribute to building a common understanding of this early conflict between China and the West and of the heritage of ideas and emotions that it bequeathed to us.

John King Fairbank

Francis Lee Higginson Professor of History
Harvard University

PREFACE

THE importance of the Opium War in modern Chinese history has not been disputed. Whether Chinese or Western, radical or conservative, scholars have invariably taken it as a starting point in the study of modern China. Since the Communist revolution of 1949, research workers and popular writers in China have laid more emphasis on this war than ever before. Their yields on the subject in the last decade are truly impressive. Apart from more serious works, a historical play entitled *Lin Tse-hsü* appeared in early 1958 which was soon made into a film.

In 1954, *Ya-p'ien chan-cheng*, a monumental collection of Chinese materials on the Opium War, was published under the able editorship of Professor Ch'i Ssu-ho. This was followed, three years later, by another significant compilation — *Ya-p'ien chan-cheng wen-hsueh chi* (A collection of Opium War literature). In these volumes, and in several newly established museums and archives, materials of the greatest importance were rescued from obscurity, a great part of which had never before been available to the public. Indeed, these materials are so interesting and valuable that they have induced Arthur Waley to digress from his more purely literary pursuits and to produce a book on the Opium War.

In the West, no less massive and important collections have become accessible in recent years. The famous Jardine Matheson Archives, the Forbes and Heard collections at Baker Library (Harvard), the Latimer papers at the Library of Congress, the Carrington manuscripts at the Rhode Island Historical Society, and a host of other archival sources await exploitation by historians of the present generation. These new materials and the increasing emphasis which Communist writers have placed on the subject have made a new historical study of the Opium War possible and necessary.

The Opium War, like most other historical events, was not brought about by a single factor; it had a wide range of causes. In abstract terms, it was a clash between two different cultures. When two mature cultures, each possessing its own peculiar institutions and values, come into contact, conflict of some kind is bound to arise. It was commerce which brought the English and the Chinese together, and the most important aspect of that commerce in the decade prior to the war was the opium trade.

Chinese efforts to stop this trade were the immediate cause of the war.

Many writers insist that the traffic in opium provided nothing more than the spark that set off an explosion whose origin lay entirely in cultural differences. This position is not invalid from the long-term point of view. But historians must also consider other factors, the immediate precipitating causes. The historian who has not studied these causes is invited to examine the massive records alluded to above, which give a new picture of the activities of the opium traders and the counteractions of the Chinese officials. He is asked to think along hypothetical lines and to assume for a moment that the opium trade was carried on in another country — one with a culture analogous to England's — in obstinate violation of the laws of that country. In such a case could war be avoided?

Let us also ask whether it was simply a coincidence that the war broke out in 1839–40, after the phenomenal growth of the opium trade had alarmed the Chinese into enforcing the prohibition laws strictly. Why not in the previous two centuries, during which crises of other kinds could well have touched off a war? It was the stagnation of the opium trade that led to the visit of Admiral Maitland to Chinese waters in 1838. It was William Jardine who almost single-handedly drew up the plans for the English expedition in 1839. In the famous letter that Viscount Palmerston wrote to the emperor's minister, the opium question was a major theme. The close and concrete connection between the opium trade and the war of 1839–1842 cannot be denied, and there is nothing unfitting about the term "Opium War," which has been disavowed by many as being unjustifiably pejorative.

I readily admit the great importance of cultural differences; I do not overlook the imperfect condition of the old Canton system, the inertia resulting from a long and weighty tradition, and the inability of Chinese officials to cope with the ever-expanding British trade. These aspects have been well studied by other writers and their significance duly appreciated. Here I am placing special emphasis on the opium traffic as an immediate cause of the war because it has not received adequate attention.

The opium question itself is not a simple one. It had intricate legal, moral, political, economic, and administrative aspects. It is not the primary interest of this study to trace the increasing importation of opium each year or the amount of treasure that flowed out as a result. The subject is treated from a broader approach, and an attempt is made to assess the issues and to outline the succession of events that made armed conflict unavoidable. Opium, in terms of its far-reaching and enduring effects, has probably touched the lives of more Chinese than any other single article has ever done. Throughout my life in China, I witnessed hundreds of my countrymen and my closest relatives become its victims. In pursuing this study, it was of no use to deny or suppress my own feelings. The goal of the Ranke school, "objective writing," has been generally considered impossible of attainment, for in selecting his material from the massive repertory of sources, the historian has already relied on subjective criteria. I have written the following pages as a Chinese, but in the course of my research and presentation I have tried to avoid any knowingly biased or partial approach and to observe the discipline of the historian's craft as I know it. I have been conscious of the lack of an up-to-date monograph on this subject that fully employs Chinese materials. It is therefore a satisfaction in itself to tell the story from the Chinese as well as from the English side.

This study has been facilitated not only by the publications in Chinese mentioned above, but also by the enlightened policy of Matheson and Company, Ltd., in permitting qualified students to conduct research in the important early records of the firm, deposited at Cambridge University. I greatly appreciate their kindness in extending this courtesy to me. In a period of world-wide tension, this action by the leading firm in the China trade sets an outstanding example in support of the cause of mutual understanding. The facts of the historical experience of the Chinese and Western peoples must be seen in realistic perspective by all sides before we can expect any degree of international harmony. I hope that this exploration of events of more than a century ago, at the commencement of China's first important relations with the West, can give us all a better understanding of one early source of Sino-Western friction.

I most gratefully acknowledge my indebtedness to Professor John K. Fairbank, who generously helped me at every stage in the preparation of this book. My thanks go to the Harvard-Yenching Institute, which supported me while I was writing my dissertation, the forerunner of this volume, and joined with the East Asian Research Center in assisting to bring the work to publication. The interest my colleagues at the State University of Iowa have taken in my work is also greatly appreciated.

To the following archivists and librarians I am obliged for their cooperation and assistance: K. B. Gardner and Eric D. Grinstead of the Department of Oriental Printed Books and Manuscripts, and G. H. Spinney, State Paper Room, all of the British Museum; E. K. Timings of the Public Record Office, London; A. K. Ch'iu, Dorothea Wu, and K. H. Liu of the Chinese-Japanese Library of the Harvard-Yenching Institute; T. L. Yuan, Edwin G. Beal, K. T. Wu, Joseph E. P. Wang,

Patrick T. K. Tseng, and L. Hsü of the Library of Congress; and Walter M. Whitehall and Mary Hackett of the Boston Athenaeum.

Professors Franklin Ho (Columbia), S. H. Chou (University of Pittsburgh), and Robert Gillespie (University of Illinois) have kindly read the economic sections of the typescript; their criticism and advice saved me from many pitfalls. Professors Benjamin Schwartz of Harvard, K. C. Liu of the University of California at Davis, and T. Y. Kuo, Director of the Institute of Modern History, Academia Sinica, have also offered invaluable suggestions. I am especially grateful to Professor Kuo for his help in procuring copies of Lin's portrait and calligraphy.

While in London and Cambridge, I was fortunate enough to make the acquaintance of Clayton Bredt and Judith Forshew, both brilliant young scholars trained in the School of Oriental and African Studies, University of London. They and Edward Kaplan of the State University of Iowa helped assiduously with the final stage of revision. Barbara Robinson, a student at Oxford, helped me read several letters of Captain Elliot, whose handwriting required expert deciphering. Elizabeth Matheson of Harvard's East Asian Research Center provided invaluable editorial advice.

Professor Herbert J. Wood of Washington State University first led me into the field of Sino-British relations and has offered generous guidance in research. Professors Raymond Muse and H. Paul Castleberry of the same institution introduced me to the historian's craft; their encouraging concern has been warmly appreciated.

I am further indebted to Holmes H. Welch, who aided me during the planning stage; to Professor C. D. Cowan of the School of Oriental and African Studies for putting me in touch with the right persons in the right places during my search for materials in London; to Arthur Waley, who had just published his work on the Opium War and spent an afternoon discussing various problems with me, giving me the benefit of his insight; to Mrs. Averil Edwards of London and Professor T. K. Cheng of Cambridge for making my work there less of a drudgery.

Dr. Glen W. Baxter, to whom this volume is dedicated, did everything possible to facilitate my work during my years at Harvard. To Professor and Mrs. David M. Farquhar I owe an overwhelming debt. They read the manuscript several times and offered their expert advice on organization and style. A large part of the manuscript was written in their home, where I found the warmth, wit, and encouragement so conducive to work.

H. P. C.

CONTENTS

I. SINO-BRITISH CONTACT UNDER THE OLD ORDER   1

THE BRITISH TRADE. THE CANTON SYSTEM. THE BASIC CONFLICTS. THE CHALLENGE TO THE OLD ORDER

II. THE RISE OF THE OPIUM TRADE   16

THE INFLUX AND SPREAD OF OPIUM BEFORE 1830. THE GROWTH OF THE OPIUM TRAFFIC AFTER 1830. THE MARKET IN CHINA. ECONOMIC REPERCUSSIONS. VESTED INTERESTS IN OPIUM

III. THE DIPLOMATIC CRISIS   51

THE NAPIER MISSION. THE QUIESCENT INTERIM. CAPTAIN ELLIOT AND THE STRUGGLE FOR EQUALITY. THE FORWARD PARTY AND THE POLICY OF COERCION

IV. THE INTENSIFIED COMBAT OVER OPIUM   85

THE SHORT-LIVED LEGALIZATION MOVEMENT. THE GREAT DEBATE. NEW PROHIBITIONS AND THE MAITLAND AFFAIR. THE STORMY WINTER OF 1838–39

V. COMMISSIONER LIN AT CANTON   120

LIN THE MAN, THE OFFICIAL, AND THE SCHOLAR. PRELIMINARY INVESTIGATIONS. THE POLICY OF ADMONISHING THE BARBARIANS. THE DETENTION OF THE FOREIGN COMMUNITY

VI. OPIUM SMOKE AND WAR CLOUDS   161

CAPTAIN ELLIOT'S PREPARATIONS FOR EMERGENCY. THE MOTIVE FOR THE OPIUM DELIVERY. THE DISPOSAL OF THE SURRENDERED OPIUM. THE BOND PROBLEM AND THE AFTERMATH

VII. THE COMING OF THE WAR AND THE FALL OF LIN   189

THE BRITISH DECISION FOR WAR. THE CHIEN-SHA-TSUI AFFRAY AND EXTRATERRITORIALITY. THE KOWLOON CLASH AND THE CHUENPEE ENGAGEMENT. TINGHAI AND THE DISGRACE OF LIN. LIN'S ROLE IN CHINESE HISTORY

Appendices

     A. Principal Opium Edicts, 1729–1839   219

B. Opium Exported from Bengal and Bombay and Imported to Canton on British Accounts, 1816–1840   222

C. Statements of the British Trade at Canton, 1834–1836   224

D. The Incarcerated British in China
      (An Eyewitness Account of the 1839 Confinement at Whampoa)   229

Notes   233

Bibliography   273

Glossary   302

Index   313

MAPS

The Opium Trade in China, 1833–1839   25

The Canton Estuary (showing sites of major occurrences)   59

The Canton Factories at the Time of the Detention of 1839   152
      (based on Captain Elliot's plan sent to Lord Palmerston on May 29, 1839, *PP: China Corr.*, p. 416, and on a survey by W. Bramston, 1840, in Morse, *Chronicles*, vol. 3, facing p. 1)

COMMISSIONER LIN AND THE OPIUM WAR

NOTE ON
CURRENCY AND WEIGHTS

Currency

Other than copper, the currency of premodern China was not a coin, but a weight of silver. This weight was known to foreigners as the "tael," from the Hindu "tolā" through the Malayan word "tahil." Its exchange value varied from time to time and from place to place. During the period covered by this volume, the tael in Canton was worth 6s. 8d., or $1.388. The dollar was basically the Spanish dollar (see Chapter 1, note 32).

Weights

1 picul = 100 catties = 133 1/3 lb. avoirdupois
1 catty = 16 taels = 1 1/3 lb.
1 tael = 10 mace = 1 1/3 oz.
1 mace = 10 candareens

Indian and Turkey opium came to China in chests and cases, respectively, each containing a net weight of not less than a picul. When Commissioner Lin said that each chest weighed between 100 and 120 catties, he was obviously referring to their gross weights. See Chapter 6 below.

SINO-BRITISH CONTACT
UNDER THE OLD ORDER

THE Europeans who streamed to the East starting in the early sixteenth century were inspired by a variety of motives: some came for adventure or conquest; some came to save souls; and others came to make money. Undoubtedly the most important and persistent of these urges was the one for profit.

The first Europeans to trade with China were the Portuguese whose vessels plied the China coast without much competition during the whole century from 1517 on.[1] The British and Dutch made attempts to trade at Canton in the first half of the seventeenth century. In 1729 the Dutch began sending ships directly from Holland to Canton. Other seafaring European peoples followed these early traders, and during the greater part of the eighteenth century the companies of the Austrian Netherlands ("Ostenders"), Sweden, Denmark, France, and Prussia offered vigorous competition to the British in the tea trade.[2]

THE BRITISH TRADE

The British efforts to trade with China began long before tea had become an article of consumption in Europe and before the Honorable Company (officially "The Governor and Merchants of London Trading into the East Indies") was chartered on the last day of 1600. In 1582 a fleet of four English ships went as far as the coast of Brazil, being prevented from proceeding to China by want of provisions and by hostile Spanish warships. Another attempt was made in 1595–96, when three ships bearing Queen Elizabeth's letter to the emperor of China were sent out to trade; none of the three ever reached China.[3]

The East India Company was first granted a fifteen-year monopoly on trade east of the Cape of Good Hope as far as the Straits of Magellan in

1600, and in 1609 this monopoly was made perpetual.[4] From the outset the company showed great interest in seeking commercial relations with China. Sporadic and abortive attempts were made during the first half of the seventeenth century, but it was not until early in the following century, when a union with a competitive company was completed and the political situation in China stabilized, that British trade in China could be firmly established.[5]

Apart from the jealousy of the Portuguese, the main factors frustrating the company's hopes for trade were China's age-old policy of restricting foreign trade, the inflexible tribute system which was part of that policy, and the precarious conditions along the coast during the earlier period of the Ch'ing dynasty. Owing to China's geographical isolation from any power which could rival her size, wealth, and cultural accomplishments, ever since the Han and T'ang dynasties Chinese bureaucrats were firmly convinced of their national superiority. In accordance with the Confucian concept of interstate relations, China's contacts with her nomad neighbors in the north and the small states to the south were regulated by a master-tributary framework. China needed nothing from her neighbors; the emperor compassionately permitted barbarian tributary missions to visit Peking so that they could benefit from direct contact with the source of civilization and share China's abundant wealth.[6] The European traders in China were naturally expected to think and behave as had all other barbarians in the preceding millennium. They should respectfully carry on their mercantile activities under the strictly regulated tribute system. Failure to submit to the system constituted a challenge to the existing order. The inevitable clash between the Western concept of international relations and the traditional Chinese concept of a universal ethico-political system under the paternal and benevolent Son of Heaven forms the dominant theme of the history of China's relations with the West.

The European mercantile invasion of the China coast coincided with the collapse of the Ming and the rise of the Ch'ing dynasty. During the first four decades of the new dynasty, as the resistance of the Ming loyalists against the Manchu authority continued in the Amoy-Formosa area, not only was foreign trade along the southern coast prohibited by Peking; the pirates made it entirely unsafe.[7] The Manchus finally subdued Amoy in 1681, Formosa in 1683, and trade restrictions were subsequently lifted. Foreign ships were permitted to call at such ports as Canton, Amoy, Ch'üan-chou (Chinchew), Foochow, and Ningpo.[8]

The Yung-cheng Emperor, who acceded to the throne in 1723, was less in favor of foreign trade. He gradually restored the former restrictions. In 1755 the British attempted to establish certain privileges at Amoy and Ningpo, but their efforts precipitated opposition among Cantonese officials and merchants, who were able to exert enough influence in Peking to block the British aims.[9] Two years later, the Ch'ien-lung Emperor practically prohibited foreign trade at any port other than Canton.[10] Thus from 1757 until the opening of four other ports by the Treaty of Nanking in 1842, Canton remained the only legal trading place for foreign ships.[11] Although the East India Company resolved as early as 1715 to establish a factory at Canton and to dispatch its ships at regular intervals, not until 1770 was there a permanent staff; the earlier staff was made up of supercargoes of the ships of the season.[12] The history of the British trade in China from this time to the late 1830s is, therefore, essentially the history of the Canton factories.

THE CANTON SYSTEM

The trade at Canton before the time of the treaties is not an obscure subject. There are abundant materials left by contemporary traders and missionaries recording this colorful and hectic period, and modern scholars have quite thoroughly studied this phase of trade and diplomacy. Since the Canton trading system was the context in which the opium crisis arose, it may be helpful to outline some of its special features and to survey its growth and organization.

After a short period of trial and error in the 1770s, the English East India Company's organization at Canton was worked out in final form by 1786, when the Select Committee permanently superseded the council of supercargoes as a collective body superintending the company's affairs in China. The Select Committee commonly consisted of three seniors among the supercargoes, who carried out the orders of the Court of Directors in London.

The company maintained a strict monopoly on English trade between Canton and London, importing lead, tin, and copper from Cornwall, woolens from Yorkshire, and cottons from Lancashire.[13] The largest export from Canton was, of course, tea. In 1761 the company shipped 2,626,000 pounds (worth £831,000) out of Canton. This amount increased yearly, and by 1800 it was 23,300,000 pounds (worth £3,665,000).[14] For nearly two centuries — until opium shipments by private traders assumed importance — the balance of trade was always unfavorable to the

British. Nine tenths of the stock of each ship sailing to Canton consisted of bullion. Take the season of 1722–23, for instance: the company's stock on board the four ships dispatched to Canton amounted to £141,828, at least nine tenths of which was in silver.[15]

The situation was alleviated by the so-called country trade. This was a trade between China and India conducted by private British subjects licensed by the East India Company in India, and it constituted one important link in a triangular mercantile network. The country traders supplied China with cotton piece-goods, elephant teeth, and opium from India and competed with the Chinese junk trade in bringing in birds' nests, camphor, rattan, tin, and spices from the coasts and islands of Malaysia. The funds derived from this trade were paid to the company treasury at Canton in return for bills of exchange on London, and between 1775 and 1795 the company could already count on this source for over a third of its funds.[16]

The monopolistic counterpart of the East India Company on the Chinese side was a small group of merchants, the hong merchants, who in 1755 became the sole agents allowed to deal with foreign ships. This was one year after the security merchant system had been instituted and two years before the restriction of foreign trade to the port of Canton.[17] Apparently the hong merchants were officially organized in 1686, the year following the establishment of the office of Superintendent of Maritime Customs for Kwangtung in Canton. The institution may have been inspired by, but was not the direct descendant of, the thirty-six brokerage firms (ya-hang) employed as agents by the Canton Superintendency of Merchant Shipping in the late Ming period.[18]

In 1720 the hong merchants formed a monopolistic guild known as the Cohong (kung-hang) to regulate prices and to strengthen their position in dealing with Chinese authorities and foreign merchants. The Cohong was officially recognized in 1760, and in succeeding years it acquired increasing powers as the agent of the Chinese government. To tighten control over the foreign traders, in 1754 the Canton authorities had instituted the security merchant system, whereby each foreign ship was required to have one of the hong merchants assume responsibility for its conduct and duties.[19] As the Canton trading system fell into a more definite pattern, the hong merchants assumed heavier and heavier responsibilities, which have been well summed up by John K. Fairbank: "They not only settled prices, sold goods, guaranteed duties, restrained the foreigners, negotiated with them, controlled smuggling, and leased the factories to them; they also had to support the militia and educational institutions, and make all manner of presents and contributions to the authorities far and near." [20] With such enormous responsibilities, the merchants' fortunes naturally fluctuated radically. In 1781, for instance, only four survived; in 1790, only five; the others presumably disappeared through bankruptcy.[21] But those hong merchants who did survive commercial fluctuations, political crises, administrative exactions, and a host of other pressures were able to amass great wealth. Howqua, foremost among them, estimated his estate at $26 million in 1834. In the opinion of H. B. Morse, his was probably the largest mercantile fortune in the world at the time.[22]

The official authority to whom the hong merchants were directly responsible was the Superintendent of Maritime Customs for Kwangtung (*Yüeh-hai kuan-pu*), better known in the West as the "hoppo." [23] The first hoppo in Canton was appointed as part of the new national customs organization established in 1685. As a representative of the Imperial Household Department (*nei-wu-fu*), the hoppo was to collect and remit the duties on the foreign trade of Canton to the Board of Revenue (*hu-pu*) at Peking. Like other facets of the Canton trade, the supervision of customs underwent a series of changes, adjustments, and reforms, no doubt because of struggles between dynastic and provincial interests and among rivals on the local level. Before the hoppo was firmly established as the sole superintendent of customs in 1750, his office had been briefly abolished and re-established in the 1720s, and his job had been successfully but temporarily taken over by various other provincial authorities in the 1730s and 1740s.

After a period of trial and error, it appeared that the governor-general and the governor, as the highest civil authorities of the province, shared some jurisdiction over the management of foreign trade, but the hoppo alone was in charge of the collection and remission of duties. From 1750 on, the hoppo's report to the Board of Revenue was countersigned by the governor-general, and after 1792 the latter together with the governor prepared a separate secret report every month so that the board could check one source against the other at the year's end.[24] When more serious issues arose, such as the Napier and Maitland crises in the 1830s, the governor-general and the governor had more authority over these foreign affairs than the hoppo did.

As the routine gradually took shape under the Canton system from the 1760s to the eve of the Opium War, the legitimate trade at Canton (as distinguished from the illicit trade at Lintin and along the east coast) was carried on in an orderly manner. The trading season commenced in early October, when foreign ships arrived along with the southwestern monsoon. The earliest ships of the season were dispatched from Whampoa usually in November and the greater number by the end of the following January.[25] (After March, business, aside from opium transactions, became very dull.) Before entering the Bogue, the ship had to procure from the customs house at Macao a permit and a pilot,[26] who conducted the ship at once to the anchorage at Whampoa. Arrangements were then made for discharging and receiving cargo immediately after the ship had been reported officially and her owner or consignee had obtained a security merchant, a comprador, and a linguist. The comprador provided stores and all necessary provisions for the ship. The linguist looked after all the details at the hoppo's office, such as the application for a permit for discharging and receiving cargo and the payment of duties and other charges. But before any business could be transacted, the security merchant had to file a declaration to the effect that the ship had no opium on board.

These duties and charges fell into four categories: the measurement duty, the *cumsha* (present), the charge for the pilotage, and the fees. The measurement duty was determined not by the tonnage but by the length and width of the ship. It was calculated by multiplying the length between the mizzenmast and the foremast by the breadth at the gangway, and dividing the product by ten. Vessels were then divided into three classes on the basis of this measurement and calculation and duties levied in accordance with the unit rate for each class. The charges thus calculated for a vessel of three hundred tons roughly amounted to $650 and for a vessel of twelve hundred tons, $3,000.

The *cumsha* consisted of fees and percentage allowances for the differences in scales and purity of silver. Originally paid to different officers, it was gradually transferred to the account of the hoppo as part of the imperial revenue. It amounted to 1950 taels for each ship before the season of 1829–30, and thereafter, following some protests, was reduced to 1600 taels ($2,223), including a fee of 810.691 taels for port entry and 480.420 taels for port clearance. Vessels of France, Austria, and Prussia, however, were paying 80 taels more and those of Surat 80 taels less.[27]

The charge for pilotage was relatively small, $60 in and the same out. This did not include a still smaller compensation (varying from $10 to $50, determined by bargain) paid for the outside pilot who conducted the vessel from the ocean through the islands to one of the anchorages off Cabreta Point (Chi-ching-t'ou, beyond the shallows off Macao Roads) or off Lintin.

The fees were $400 for the comprador and $200 for the linguist to enable them to defray expenses, including some unauthorized exactions, while the vessel was at Whampoa. The remuneration for the linguist's services was not included in these fees. He received $75 from an English company ship and $50 or $60 more from her commander. His remuneration from a vessel of another identity, for example, a country ship or an American ship, varied somewhat in amount.

A ship could sometimes discharge its cargo and receive a new one in three weeks, but usually these tasks required not less than one or two months. (The outbound cargo was taken to the ship by the sellers at their own risk and expense.[28]) Before the ship could depart, a port clearance (*ch'uan-p'ai* or, colloquially, *hung-p'ai*) had to be obtained. This document, commonly referred to by foreign traders as the "grand chop," was granted only after the measurement and *cumsha* charges had been fully paid and often after additional money had been extorted from the security merchant.

Strictly speaking, the port clearance was a passport for other parts of the empire rather than a clearance for departure from Canton. The British Museum has preserved a port clearance issued to the ship *Juliet* (Captain Wilson) on December 14, 1836. It is an enormous and impressive document measuring 26.25 by 19.5 inches.[29] It states: "This European ship, having paid the duties and other charges, if by contrary winds or water should be driven to any other province, not with design of remaining there to trade . . . shall be immediately permitted to depart, without further exaction of charges." [30]

At the Canton factory complex, where the foreign mercantile companies leased their quarters from the hong merchants,[31] each establishment first had to engage a comprador, who supervised the domestic affairs of the house and procured provisions according to the orders of his employer. As head servant and steward, the comprador employed for the house its shroffs,[32] cooks, water carriers, laborers, and porters, and "secured" their good conduct. The compradors of various houses were recommended and guaranteed by the linguists, and the linguists were selected and guaranteed by the hong merchants. Despite this chain of responsibility both to the master and to the Chinese government, they also had to be investigated and licensed by the prefecture and district governments.[33]

The factories were situated in a compound in the southern suburb of the city, about three hundred feet from the bank of the Pearl River. They were built in a uniform row, all facing south, and their collective breadth from east to west was a little over a thousand feet. Each factory consisted of several buildings standing one behind the other, separated only by narrow courts.[34] The foreign residents found ample provisions of good quality and variety and, considering the latitude, the climate was agreeable and healthy. Their main complaints were against the lack of outdoor space and the restrictions on their activities.[35]

The regulations designed to ensure control over the foreign community caused much inconvenience. Some restrictions, such as those against the employment of Chinese servants, were so unrealistic that they gradually became dead letters. (But they were always revived during crises, as in 1814, 1834, and 1839.) Others, however, were strictly enforced: foreign warships were barred from entering the river; foreign women were not allowed to visit the factories.[36] The rule about women, although appalling to many, was enjoyed by a few. The unhappily married painter, George Chinnery, was ready to flee to Canton whenever his wife threatened to come from Calcutta to join him at Macao.[37]

New regulations were added from time to time, and those in force were read aloud by the linguist in the factories at irregular intervals. In general, foreign traders were not to have direct intercourse with the Chinese; all their transactions were to be handled through the hong merchants. Foreigners were also forbidden to remain at Canton out of season — after their goods were sold and ships laden, they had to return home or stay at Macao. A series of conflicts in the 1830s centered on the prohibition against foreigners' presenting petitions; their communications were to be transmitted by the hong merchants. If the hong merchants held back a petition unfavorable to themselves, according to a concession made in 1831, two or three foreigners might go to present it to the guard at the city gate, but they were not allowed to pass the gate.[38]

Despite these annoying restraints, the erratic behavior of some hong merchants, and the exactions of the government, the trade at Canton grew steadily. Employing annually about 150 first-rate vessels and an enormous amount of capital, during its halcyon days the Canton trade constituted an important portion of the world's commerce.[39] In the first ten years beginning with February 1750, 194 foreign ships called at the port, while in the one-year period from June 13, 1835, to June 8, 1836, 199 foreign ships called. In the next year (June 1836 to June 1837), this figure reached a peak of 213 incoming ships. (After this the legal trade sharply declined because of the political complications involved in the phenomenal increase of illicit traffic in opium.[40])

The commercial facilities at Canton were appreciated by some foreign residents, who claimed that Canton was unsurpassed by any other port in the world.[41] William C. Hunter, the American merchant in Canton who wrote so much about the trade, emphasized the safety of life and property enjoyed by foreigners in Canton. "In no part of the world," he maintained, "could the authorities have exercised a more vigilant care over the personal safety of strangers who of their own free will came to live in the midst of a population whose customs and prejudices were so opposed to everything foreign, and yet the Chinese government was bound by no treaty obligations to *specially* provide protection for them." [42] In 1910 H. B. Morse supported these views and held that the "Co-hong system, monopolistic though it was, was one which, on the whole, worked with little friction." He pointed out that for years the East India Company paid the dividends on its stocks solely from the profits of its China trade and that the discomforts of a foreigner's life at Canton "were as nothing to the prospect of accumulating a competency." [43]

Friendly personal relations existed between Chinese and foreign merchants, and both groups were known for their professional honor and integrity. Morse writes that "trading operations were entirely on parole, with never a written contract: and there was much help and sympathy from one to the other." There were many anecdotes — such as the story about a hong merchant's canceling the debt of a foreign trader who had fallen into difficulties — which the old China hands and Sinophiles loved to hear and repeat.[44] This agreeable state of affairs gave little hint of the storm that was soon to break.

THE BASIC CONFLICTS

If China had been able to limit her contact with Britain to the commercial level and confine foreign influence to the factories, the final armed conflict of 1839–1842 might have been avoided. But, in the nature of things, cultural intercourse could not be prevented. And Chinese and English values, stemming from totally different traditions, could hardly have made a sharper contrast. This was obvious in government structure, law and ideas of justice, social organization, economic thought, political institutions — indeed, in every facet of human activity. In the Confucian tradition, merchants were at the bottom of the social scale in terms of prestige, while the great mercantile houses of nineteenth-century Britain were the pillars of the empire. A Chinese youth, if he had ambition, prepared himself for the civil-service examination, which was the only path to the coveted and privileged official-gentry-scholar circle. His English cousins perhaps were busily plying the ports of Europe and Asia, seeking new sources of wealth.

The best minds and the greatest statesmen of China had no taste either for things un-Chinese or for things mercantile. What, aside from the classics, history, philosophy, and belles-lettres, was worth their time and attention? The Chinese with whom the foreigners came in contact were not the cream of the literati; the officials who came to manage foreign affairs in Canton were bureaucrats of doubtful integrity and scruples. The hoppo, for instance, always a Manchu appointed by the emperor for an invariable tenure of three years, was allowed to amass a fortune after he had satisfied his patrons in Peking. It has been satirically stated that "it took the net profit of the first year of his tenure to obtain his office, of the second year to keep it, and of the third year to drop it and to provide for himself." [45] These men were not the best representatives of Chinese culture; nor were they particularly interested in nurturing the good will of the foreign traders. Indeed, the whole Canton system was built on a central theme of contempt for foreigners and disdain for merchants.

There was no Chinese counterpart of the Royal Asiatic Society or the Oriental Translation Committee. A few eccentrics like Wei Yuan and Pao Shih-ch'en, who branched out into the fields of statecraft, world geography, agriculture, and other fields of practical study were no doubt regarded by their contemporaries as failures. On the eve of the Opium War, no high-ranking Chinese official had any conception of the way in which improvements in shipbuilding, artillery, and navigation had increased the strength of the European powers. In fact few, if any, had any inkling that England was not just another Siam. In 1816, the governor-general of Canton wanted "the English tribute bearer" (Lord Amherst) upbraided for refusing to perform the kowtow. If the tribute bearers from Siam had always done this to express their gratitude for the emperor's great compassion, why, he wondered, should not Lord Amherst do the same? [46]

The lack of mutual understanding was further aggravated by the language barrier. No educated Chinese knew even a smattering of English. Commissioner Lin in Canton recruited the best language talents available, but samples of their work read little better than the pidgin English which, after about 1715, had become the commercial lingua franca in Canton.[47]

The English were slightly better prepared to deal with the Chinese language. Robert Morrison, the first Protestant missionary to China, studied Chinese most assiduously, even though foreigners were forbidden to learn it. He had difficulty in engaging tutors and had to go about the task surreptitiously. But at the time of the Napier Mission, his dictionary had been published, and he was ready to act as interpreter. Morrison's son, John Robert, and several others followed in his footsteps. But throughout the stormy decade after Napier, we hear of only four interpreters employed by British commercial, diplomatic, and military establishments. The most competent among them were undoubtedly John Robert Morrison and Robert Thom. Young Morrison was an important member of the Committee of Communication, which served the whole foreign community on a subscription basis.[48] Robert Thom was the author of two sections, "Dialogue on Buying Woolens" and "Dialogue on Buying Piece Goods" in *A Chinese Chrestomathy in the Canton Dialect*, compiled by E. C. Bridgman.[49] His more important work was a translation of *Aesop's Fables*, published in four fascicles in 1837 and 1838. But the manuscript was not really prepared by him; he delivered the fables orally to his native teacher, who wrote them down in Chinese.[50]

Samuel Fearon, whose moral standards and linguistic ability were doubted by Thom, was not a full-fledged interpreter.[51] On Captain Elliot's recommendation, his appointment as temporary assistant in the Interpreters Department was approved by London in November 1840.[52] Pressed for more interpreters, Elliot recruited even the opportunistic Charles Gutzlaff into his service at an annual salary of £200.[53] These men, who at their best could handle only some commercial language and rudimentary diplomatic documents, did not even scratch the surface of China's splendid literary tradition. It is no wonder that high officials in Canton, whose respect for scholarship far exceeded that for navigation and commerce and whose criteria of judgment were taken from the classics, poetry, and calligraphy, should despise the European barbarians. It is equally natural that the Europeans, bred in the tradition of Western democracy and nurtured in the spirit of the new mercantilism, should consider the mandarins as bigoted and ignorant tyrants.

The Canton system was but the last phase of China's ancient tribute diplomacy. Until the nineteenth century, the foreign relations of the

empire, whether under Chinese or alien sovereigns, were limited almost
entirely to continental neighbors. Inner Asia had always been the main
source of invasion. The tribute system was the crystallization of the age-
old policy of force and appeasement (*chi-mi*).[54] When the danger came
from overseas, the Chinese were totally unprepared to cope with it. The
English, unlike the Tibetans, Mongols, Burmese, and Annamese, could
not acknowledge the cultural overlordship of China. The Macartney
Mission in 1793 and the Amherst Mission twenty-three years later both
planned to assert equality by establishing a resident minister at Peking.[55]

The East India Company was more tolerant of Chinese feelings than
London was, out of fear that existing trade privileges might be jeopardized.
After the company lost its monopoly, however, Britain stepped up her
struggle for diplomatic equality. Lord Napier vigilantly avoided any detail
of protocol that might suggest submission, and Captain Elliot spent nearly
all his energy during the first twenty months of his superintendency seeking direct communication with the Canton authority. Meanwhile, the free
traders were denouncing the tribute nonsense more loudly.[56]

The different concepts of law were a major source of friction between
the Chinese and the foreign community at Canton. The basic policy of
the Ch'ing rulers was to discourage lawsuits. Good citizens, as the K'ang-
hsi Emperor decreed, were supposed to settle their difficulties like brothers
by referring them to arbitration. The "troublesome, obstinate, and quarrel-
some" who went to court were to be treated without any pity.[57] One China
missionary observed: "The criminal laws of China operate very powerfully against the exercise of benevolence in cases where it is most needed.
Whatever crimes are committed in a neighbourhood, the whole neighbours are involved; and contrary to what is the case in most other civilized
countries, the law considers them guilty until they can prove themselves
innocent."[58] This difference in tradition led to dispute whenever a
foreigner was involved in a criminal case, particularly in the case of a
homicide.

The case of the *Lady Hughes*, a country-trading ship from Bombay,
may be cited as an example. In November 1784, when she fired a salute
for some guests who had dined on board, a Chinese was killed and two
others were wounded in the mandarin's boat alongside. Under strong
Chinese pressure, the unfortunate gunner was eventually given up to the
Chinese authorities for execution.[59] The gunner of the *Lady Hughes* was
the last Englishman surrendered to the Chinese for trial and execution.
It became a definite policy of the English not to turn men accused of
homicide over to the Chinese for trial.[60]

The lack of confidence in Chinese jurisprudence inspired long and earnest endeavors to establish some form of extraterritoriality. The task began with Lord Macartney, if not earlier, when his mission was instructed to obtain "one or two cessions of territory" in convenient locations where "English traders might reside and where English jurisdiction might be exercised." [61] The problem of jurisdiction over crimes committed on Chinese soil resulted in a series of crises between 1784 and 1842. Aside from opium, China's demand for the murderer of Lin Wei-hsi was the most decisive factor in bringing about the conflicts in 1839. The jurisdiction problem involved sovereignty and, like the issue of diplomatic equality, could not be solved short of drastic measures.

THE CHALLENGE TO THE OLD ORDER

The differences in culture and institutions, the problem of diplomatic equality, and the conflicts over judicial sovereignty would not have resulted in war had Sino-British contacts not increased so greatly. The Industrial Revolution predetermined the vast British commercial expansion, which brought traders with growing frequency and persistence to China's shores. The East India Company had performed its historical function, and by the turn of the century it had become conservative and chary of new demands and reform.[62] It was left behind in the age of the new mercantilism and eventually lost its monopoly. The chief role in the nineteenth-century British overseas expansion was taken over by the private traders, who began to appear in Canton as early as the late 1760s.[63]

The early private English firms in China were all known as "agency houses." Up to the 1820s, their job was selling and buying for firms mainly in London and India on commission, but eventually many houses took on some "speculation," especially in opium and rice, on their own account. Thus in the 1830s, Jardine, Matheson and Company, the most influential of the private firms, was trading successfully in these articles while also performing agency activities.[64]

William Jardine (1784–1843) joined Magniac and Company in 1825 after spending fifteen years as a company ship's surgeon and several years in Canton as a resident agent. James Matheson (1796–1878) began his career in a Calcutta firm. By 1820 he had become Danish consul in Canton and was soon trading with Manila and Singapore. A few years later he joined Magniac, which was under the charge of Jardine. In 1832 the firm took on the name, Jardine, Matheson and Company.[65]

Operating mainly with outside funds, the agency business required only a very modest amount of capital.[66] With the decline of the East India Company, the private firms grew both in number and importance. By 1834 they were handling more than half of Britain's trade with China.[67] They were indeed vanguards of the nineteenth-century British empire, funneling the resources of underdeveloped areas into its economic system and seeking new markets all over the world for its surplus industry. This rapid expansion almost immediately clashed with China's containment policy. Under the old Canton system, built on the doctrine that the "Celestial Empire does not value things brought from a distance," [68] there was no room for more trade.

Chinese government officials did not offer protection or assistance to trade. Instead, they drained it with ruinous rapacity. They exacted 100,000 taels from the hong merchants in 1832 to finance the campaign against the Lien-chou insurrection, and 120,000 taels in 1833 for public relief. Besides these emergency collections, the hong merchants paid out annual presents and contributions which in 1834, for example, amounted to 456,000 taels, breaking down as follows.[69]

Tribute to the emperor	55,000 taels
Repairs along the Yellow River	30,000
Expenses of an agent at Peking	21,600
Birthday presents to the emperor	130,000
Similar presents to the hoppo	20,000
Presents to the hoppo's mother or wife	20,000
Annual presents to various officers	40,000
Compulsory purchases of native ginseng	140,000
	456,600 taels

The hong merchants, entrusted with the management of the foreign community, were totally uninterested and incompetent in public affairs. They had the monopoly over foreign trade but lacked sufficient capital for large dealings. Although there was an official regulation forbidding them from going into debt to foreigners, the temptation was irresistible. They paid an interest of 1.5 percent a month, and the prospect of lending money at this high rate was what attracted the first private English trader to Canton in the 1770s.[70] In the 1830s the annual hong debts due foreigners were usually in excess of $3 million,[71] and we read much about the bankruptcies of the hong merchants.[72] Their position was so precarious that Beale and Company made it clear to its constituents that its "Agents in Canton are not responsible for the failure of Hong Merchants, to whom they may have disposed of goods on account of their constituents, as a commission of 3% cannot be considered likewise a premium against bad debts." [73]

Britain's economy was undergoing a great change, and British traders to China accordingly adopted a new outlook. But the Chinese refused to make any adjustment. After 1834 Britain opened her trade to all, but China clung to the monopoly of the hong merchants. The economic force behind the free traders was too great to be restricted or contained. They had a mission: to tear down the inadequate Canton system and to rebel against the outmoded tribute diplomacy.

In the broad sense, the Opium War was a clash between two cultures. One was agricultural, Confucian, stagnant, and waist-deep in the quicksand of a declining dynastic cycle. The Taiping rebellion was only a decade away, and the disintegrating economic, political, and social factors were already at work. The other society was industrial, capitalistic, progressive, and restless. When the two met, conflicts were inevitable, and the defeat of China was equally inevitable.

But the vital force that brought on the cultural conflict was Britain's commercial expansion. The friction that arose in the realms of diplomacy, law, and government was merely symptomatic of the basic problem — expansion versus containment. The opium trade was an indispensable vehicle for facilitating this expansion and the two could not be separated. Had there been an effective alternative to opium, say molasses or rice, the conflict might have been called the Molasses War or the Rice War. The only difference would have been a matter of time: in the hypothetical case, the major article of import being harmless, the lethargic Chinese would not have been alarmed into action so soon. The war could have been postponed, but not avoided.

THE RISE OF THE OPIUM TRADE

THE opium-producing poppy was first brought to western China by the Turks and the Arabs in the late seventh or early eighth century.[1] It was variously called *ying-su, mi-nang,* or transliterated as *po-pi* (poppy) and *a-fu-jung* (afion or ufyoon). The first known mention of the plant in Chinese occurred in the *Pen-ts'ao shih-i* (Supplementary herbalist), written in the first half of the eighth century by Ch'en Ts'ang-ch'i. The T'ang poet T'ao Yung of Szechwan province wrote the verse *Ma-ch'ien ch'u-chien mi-nang-hua* (In front of the horse I saw the poppy flower for the first time) in the closing years of the dynasty.

The Sung poet Su Tung-p'o said in a poem: "The boy may prepare for you the broth of the poppy." His brother Su Ch'e also wrote a poem on the cultivation of poppies for medicinal purposes. Another reference to the plant appeared at about the same time in *K'ai-pao pen-ts'ao* (The herbalist of the K'ai-pao period), compiled in 973 by Liu Han. Succeeding editions of similar works published in the Chin, Yüan, and Ming dynasties did not fail to include opium and describe its medicinal uses.[2]

Opium as a medicine in premodern China was always swallowed raw; however, in 1620, some Formosans began mixing it with tobacco and smoking it. This practice spread to the coastal areas of Fukien and Kwangtung in the 1660s. The Chinese eventually developed their own mode of consumption by burning opium extract, a refinement of the raw stuff, over a lamp and inhaling its fumes through a pipe. By the late eighteenth century, the habit had spread widely to other parts of the country. Its broad dispersion in China, so much more than in other parts of the world, is an anomaly awaiting further investigation. The existence of a well-to-do leisure class, living under alien regimes that stifled all creative activities, certainly helps to explain it. Throughout the nineteenth century and spanning well into the twentieth, the drug afforded the escapist literati much relief, reminiscent of the early Taoist hedonists who took a different kind of drug, and became the common man's favorite pastime as well as a status symbol.

The earliest record of opium duty collected by the Chinese customs is in 1589, when two mace of silver was imposed on every twenty catties of opium. In 1684, when the coastal uprisings were suppressed and maritime trade was again opened, opium was classified as a medicine and for each ten catties a duty of three mace was levied.

Opium is indeed a very useful therapeutic agent. Its principal alkaloid (morphine) relieves pain, allays emotional distress, and relaxes the mind. Thomas De Quincey, among other writers, did his best work under the influence of the drug. But opium consumption is accompanied by certain physiological effects: a slowing down of the heart and respiration, an irregularity of basic bodily functions, and a decrease in body weight and basal metabolism. The greatest mischief, however, seems to lie in its habit-forming nature. The addict becomes a complete slave of the drug, which becomes as much a necessity for him as water or food. When the drug is withheld, unbearable, even fatal, symptoms follow within four to twelve hours after the last dose. "These withdrawal symptoms . . . are extreme restlessness, chills, hot flushes, sneezing, sweating, salivation, running nose, and gastrointestinal disturbances such as nausea, vomiting, and diarrhea. There are severe cramps in the abdomen, legs, and back; the bones ache; the muscles twitch; and the nerves are on edge. Every symptom is in combat with another. The addict is hungry, but he cannot eat; he is sleepy, but he cannot sleep." As tolerance develops, the addict's dose constantly increases and his need becomes so great that he will do anything, lie, cheat, or steal, to obtain money for the drug. The loss of moral integrity and crime are the natural results.

These detrimental effects on the individual and on society became quickly known, and in 1729 the domestic sale and consumption of opium were prohibited by imperial edict. In 1796, the newly enthroned Chia-ch'ing Emperor prohibited its importation and domestic cultivation as well. Since then, opium has always been contraband in China.[3]

THE INFLUX AND SPREAD OF OPIUM BEFORE 1830

The Portuguese were the first to import opium to China in any sizable amount. The *Ming-shih* (History of the Ming dynasty) tells us that their merchants once presented the emperor with two hundred catties of opium and his empress with a hundred catties.[4] Recognizing the importance of the opium trade, the government of Goa attempted in 1764 to confine it entirely to Macao. For this purpose a prohibition was issued that Portuguese ships were not allowed to bring in opium belonging to other nationals and that their merchants should not buy any drug from foreign vessels lying in the neighborhood of Macao. These regulations were soon found troublesome, since the Portuguese merchants did not have the necessary capital to secure the supply for the Chinese market, and the shipowners had no way of getting a good freight. The English traders soon began to take advantage of this incapacity. They carried the drug in their own ships and were able to undersell the Portuguese.[5]

In 1773 the East India Company launched a small experimental venture into the opium trade. It proved quite successful, and the trade grew. In 1780 a depot for British-imported opium was established in Lark's Bay, south of Macao. Following the prohibition edict of 1796, the company refrained from taking a direct part in the opium trade, but the Select Committee did everything possible to assist the private traders.[6]

From the beginning of the nineteenth century, a great number of edicts were issued by various echelons of the Chinese government, reiterating old commands or promulgating new ones with regard to the prohibition of the import, sale, use, and domestic production of opium (see Appendix A). But the Chinese government was too weak to crush the illicit trade that was so lucrative to the smugglers and such a necessity to the large number of addicts. Effective enforcement of the regulations seldom lasted for any length of time.[7] The committee invariably transmitted the prohibition edicts to India, but usually added remarks to the effect that they foresaw no impediments to the continuance of the trade. The authorities in India also perfunctorily informed the opium purchasers at the public sales of the existence of the edicts in China, but frankly advised that there should be no undue alarm about them.

The position of the company was a delicate one. To the Chinese the company officials declared that they were not connected with the opium trade and that it was entirely up to the Chinese government to suppress the traffic. They cautioned the country traders to avoid referring to their product as "Company's opium," lest a harmful impression be made on the Canton authorities. On the other hand, the company inserted into its licenses issued to country ships a clause providing that the license would be void if opium other than that procured at the company's public sale in Bengal were taken aboard, and the Select Committee assisted in the enforcement of this provision by subjecting the ships to search.[8]

At the time of the first prohibition edict (1729), the annual importation of opium was about 200 chests, a chest being equal to approximately 140 pounds (varying somewhat from season to season and from type to type). Thereafter, it increased slowly, reaching by 1767 the annual total of a thousand chests. It was not until the end of the eighteenth century that the import of the drug substantially increased.[9]

From the turn of the century to the eve of the Opium War, the opium trade may be divided into three phases: 1800–1820, 1821–1830, and 1830–1840. During the first phase all opium imports on British accounts averaged less than 4,500 chests per year. For the first nine seasons, because of the prohibition orders at Canton, the trade was driven out of the Canton River and, as the Portuguese authorities relaxed their control over the trade in 1802, Macao became the emporium. In 1801 the Bengal opium known as Patna was being sold at Macao for $560 to $590 a chest, and Malwa, the Portuguese product, did not emerge in the Chinese market until 1805 and was "scarcely saleable at $400 per chest." [10]

In the season 1805–6 the trade suffered a serious slump. This may be explained by a number of factors, including disputes with the Portuguese, intensified activities of pirates around Macao, and competition from opium brought in by the captains of the company ships and the country-trading ships for quick sale at low prices. In 1809, as the enforcement of the prohibition edicts was relaxed, much of the trade returned to Whampoa and Canton, although a portion of it still continued at Macao.[11]

The spread of opium into provinces beyond Kwangtung and Fukien first came to the attention of the Chia-ch'ing Emperor in 1807, when a censor by the name of Cheng Shih-ch'ao complained about the laxity of the prohibition laws in Canton and the inroads made by the drug even in the capital. Although the emperor did not consider it a significant problem, he regarded opium smoking as detrimental and issued an edict in November enjoining the local authorities and the hoppo to take harsher measures against offenders of the prohibition laws. Six years later, in 1813, the emperor was greatly alarmed to find that quite a number of the officers of the imperial body guard as well as eunuchs at the court had become addicted to opium. At the emperor's command, new regulations concerning the punishment of smokers were enacted: officers convicted of opium smoking were to be cashiered, flogged one hundred strokes, and made to wear the cangue for two months; eunuchs who were found to be addicts were to wear the cangue for two months and be exiled as slaves to Heilungkiang; all military and civilian violators were to be beaten one hundred strokes and made to wear the cangue for a month. The emperor also repeated former prohibition laws and authorized the governors-general and governors to dismiss any superintendents of customs offices who were remiss in enforcing opium laws.

In April 1815 the emperor approved a joint recommendation from the governor-general of Canton and the hoppo that Portuguese ships arriving at Macao be inspected for opium. The local officials threatened to search not only the Portuguese ships, but every ship in the river. Under pressure from the mandarins, the hong merchants requested the captains of each ship to file bonds declaring that there was no opium in the cargo. But the British ignored the request and none of these threats was executed. In 1817, as a result of an incident involving the robbery of an American opium ship, the *Wabash*, the Chinese again pressed for the bonds. The Select Committee, still angry about the rude reception which the Chinese had given the Amherst Mission, ordered the *Orlando* to move up to the Bogue to intimidate the Chinese. At this the Canton authorities dropped their demands.[12] But each concession only served to add fuel to latent fires.

In 1821 Governor-General Juan Yuan adopted an unprecedentedly strict policy toward opium. Within a short period, sixteen opium dealers in Macao were arrested. One of them, possibly the main dealer, Yeh Heng-shu, known to the foreigners as Asee, apparently avenged himself by revealing the corrupt practices of the officials for whom he had acted as a bribe-collecting agent. "The same caitiff Asee, the late principal dealer at Macao, has received sentence of transportation to the cold country, but is still in prison here. He has it seems made representations to Pekin, laying open the venality and corruption of the Mandareens and offering proofs by the production of his book of accounts of the bribes he has been paying them for several years. . . . It is expected a special commission will be sent from Pekin to adjudge the matter." [13]

The Canton authorities put tremendous pressure on Howqua, the senior merchant. He was deprived of his third-grade official rank, which was to be restored only when the opium traffic had been eliminated. In November and December, the local officials issued strict orders that the opium ships were to leave the river, and the hong merchants refused to secure any ships carrying opium. The campaign was carried out with such vigor — the merchant Charles Magniac called the suppression "the hottest persecution we remember" — that the opium ships had to leave the Canton River. But they did not retreat very far; they anchored off the island of Lintin, at the mouth of the river, and there the trade continued to flourish until the 1839 crisis. The departure of the opium ships from the inner river marks the end of the first phase of the opium trade.

The second phase lasted for about a decade (1821–1830). The trade, with Lintin as the depot, increased from less than 5,000 chests a year to a phenomenal 18,760 chests. The annual average import by British merchants was 10,114 chests, well over half being Malwa, the opium produced in western India, which was not controlled by the East India Company at this time (see Appendix B).

The most remarkable event in the trade during this phase was the upheaval caused by the introduction of Malwa. Before 1815, Malwa was imported only in negligible amounts and was difficult to sell. In the season of 1815–16 a group of foreign merchants had forced the price of Bengal opium so high that the substitution of cheaper products was necessary. Thus the imports of Malwa by country merchants snowballed from 600 chests in 1816–17 to 1,150 in the next season, and 4,000 chests in 1822–23. The immediate effect was a decline in the price of Bengal opium. Selling for $1,300 in 1817, a chest of Patna could get only $840 in 1818 when Malwa was selling at $680.[14] The high profits to be made in the Malwa trade, as compared with those made in the monopoly-controlled Bengal trade, attracted numerous dealers, large and small. James Matheson sailed for India on the *Hooghly* in December 1819 with the idea of secretly bringing back to China supplies of Malwa. His attempt was thwarted by Portuguese officials at Daman and Goa who had been bribed by rival Portuguese opium traders; but less than a year later, the Magniacs, Davidson, and the Dent brothers formed a Malwa syndicate with their Bombay agents.

The East India Company faced the challenge of Malwa by adopting a policy of expanding its production of Bengal opium, thereby forcing the price down. At the same time, the company sought quicker means of ensuring the ascendancy of company opium in the China market; they tried to buy up the whole Malwa crop. In 1821–22 they bought 4,000 chests and sold it at public auction in Bombay. These tactics boomeranged as the enormous supplies of Malwa brought the volume of sales of Bengal opium from 2,910 chests in 1821–22 down to 1,822 chests in 1822–23, while Malwa rose from 1,718 to 4,000 chests. The surplus of Malwa also caused Bengal opium to fall $523 in price per chest (a drop from $2,075 to $1,552). In the next season, although the quantity of Bengal products sold was restored to the 1821–22 level, the price remained at a low $1,600, and even the price of Malwa dropped from $1,325 per chest in 1821–22 to $925 in 1823–24.[15] At the conclusion of the 1823–24 season, although the country traders sold the same amount of Bengal opium as in the 1821–22 season, their gross earnings from the sale were reduced by over 1.38 million dollars; they sold 172 more chests of Malwa than in the preceding season but got 1.3 million dollars less in return.

The company discontinued the policy of increasing production of Bengal opium and, in response to the request of the Select Committee, shifted to restrictionist tactics in 1824. They forced agreements upon certain Indian princes to curtail the production of Malwa opium. But by this time the majority of Chinese addicts had already developed a taste for Malwa, and the opium dealers speculated in it with confidence. With the exception of one season, the Malwa "smuggled" out through the Portuguese port Daman between 1826 and 1831 always exceeded the amount which was authorized by the company to be bought at Bombay.[16] Thus the same trend, more opium at lower prices, continued. The following figures show the state of the trade at the beginning and end of the second phase.[17]

Year	Patna and Benares			Malwa		
	Chests	Price	Value	Chests	Price	Value
1821–22	2,910	$2,075	$6,038,250	1,718	$1,325	$2,276,350
1830–31	6,660	870	5,789,794	12,100	588	7,110,237

THE GROWTH OF THE OPIUM TRAFFIC AFTER 1830

The 1830s saw a tremendous increase in the opium trade. There were several reasons: the end of the East India Company's monopoly and the rapid influx of British traders, the policy of expanding opium production in India, the new clipper ships which made speedier transportation possible, and the rapid extension of the traffic farther and farther east and north along the China coast.

In 1831 the company launched a new and lasting policy with regard to the Malwa problem. It announced that any amount of Malwa would be allowed to pass through Bombay provided a transit fee of 175 rupees per chest were paid. (The rate was later adjusted.) The dealers, happy to avoid the circuitous route via Daman, applauded the new policy.[18] The shipments of Malwa to China on the country traders' accounts immediately jumped to 15,403 chests in 1832–33, double the amount of the preceding season.

The expiration of the company's monopoly gave the trade a further impetus, as can be seen in a comparison of the first and second seasons of the free trade at the port of Canton.

	1834–35			1835–36		
	Chests	*Price*	*Value*	*Chests*	*Price*	*Value*
Patna	6,245	$576.75	$3,602,045	9,692	$744.82	$7,218,800
Benares	1,522	545.20	829,800	2,300	704.00	1,619,200
Malwa	8,749	596.99	5,223,125	14,208	601.81	8,550,622
Turkey	nil	—	—	911	566.00	515,626
	16,516		$9,654,970	27,111		$17,904,248

Such large quantities of opium flooded Canton that the traders felt an urgent need for new markets. Matheson experimented with dispatching ships up the east coast early in the 1820s, and other houses made similar attempts, but these first efforts met with little success.[19] By 1832, however, the traffic on the coast east of Canton began to be of some importance, and it soon exceeded that carried on at Lintin.[20] This spurt in the coastal traffic in the 1830s, by virtue of its far-reaching impact on China's attitudes toward the opium issue, warrants particular attention.

In October 1832, Jardine, Matheson and Company sent the clipper *Sylph*, with Charles Gutzlaff on board as interpreter, on a six-month northern voyage as far as Tientsin. Meanwhile James Innes was selling the Bengal drug at an average of $870 per chest on board the company's barque *Jamesina* in Chinchew Bay (Ch'üan-chou). An unexpected boom in Canton, however, induced Jardine in November to call both vessels back to Lintin, and Innes was instructed to pursue the *Sylph* as far as Ningpo to bid her return with her opium.[21] The chase was apparently not successful; the *Sylph* completed her voyage as planned and returned in April 1833.

During the year 1833, several vessels of Jardine, Matheson made voyages to the coast. By the middle of April, Captain John Rees of the brig *Kronberg* was able to give a precise account of his adventure, which won Jardine's warm appreciation.[22] On July 10, the *John Biggar* under Captain William McKay, with Gutzlaff aboard, left Lintin against an easterly wind and arrived at Chinchew Bay on the 15th. McKay's reports of his proceedings to the company are particularly vivid and detailed; they enable us to make a case study of the coastal operation.

On the 17th three boats came off and after much wrangling one of them took 9 chests [of] old Benares and 2 chests [of] old Patna @ $810. . . . Immediately after this the whole of the smuggling boats belonging to the port were seized. One of the merchants wrote to us on the 20th informing us of this circumstance[. He] noticed the great vigilance of the mandareens and many other difficulties and requested us to lower our prices. . . . The smuggling boats are however yet in limbo and we are told that the mandareens are making use of them to prevent smuggling with us. The merchants came off in small boats during the night. Their money is shroffed and the opium delivered to them during the following day and the next night they go on shore. . . . The mandareens are not troubling us much but in the harbour and on shore they are very vigilant. Shortly after we arrived a fleet of six of them anchored near us. The Doctor [Gutzlaff] (dressed in his best; which, on such occasions is his custom) payed them a visit accompanied by two boats made to appear rather imposing. He demanded their instant departure and threatened them destruction if they ever in future anchored in our neighbourhood. They went away immediately, saying they had anchored there in the dark by mistake. We have seen nothing more of them.[23]

In the early part of August, the mandarins were so vigilant that all the merchants completely deserted the *Biggar* and the trade was stopped. Captain McKay weighed anchor on the 13th and made sail for Mee-choo (Ma-tsu-po), where he stayed for a week. On the 20th he again made sail for Chinchew and anchored in the bay two days later. The mandarins had already left. A merchant came at once and purchased forty chests of old Benares at $775 per chest, putting down $2,000 as "bargain money" and promising to clear the whole in a fortnight. Twenty-two chests were delivered to the customer's doorstep when all but $500 had been received. "We assisted in landing the 22 chests and guarded it up to the old gentleman's door which was some distance from the landing place and in the suburbs of the Town. The old fellow was found in his office busy writing. The remainder will be landed tomorrow night."

From the 22nd to the 26th, Captain McKay sold "a good deal," but on the latter day, two mandarin boats appeared and went into the inner harbor. The trade was again entirely stopped, and McKay again had to leave the station for a few days.[24] The Bay of Chinchew offered no natural hiding place for the opium ships; so McKay worked out a system of regular cruises to embark upon whenever the mandarins stopped the trade. After the mandarins returned to their station at Amoy, he would come back to resume selling.

It appeared that Captain John Rees, now in command of the *Colonel Young*, was to take over the station at Chinchew in September, and McKay instructed him: "The mandareens are troublesome here at times, the only way to shake them off is to move off for a few days; or, if they

anchor near you threaten to cut their cables, &c." He recommended his
favorite anchorage for such cruises and suggested that after an absence

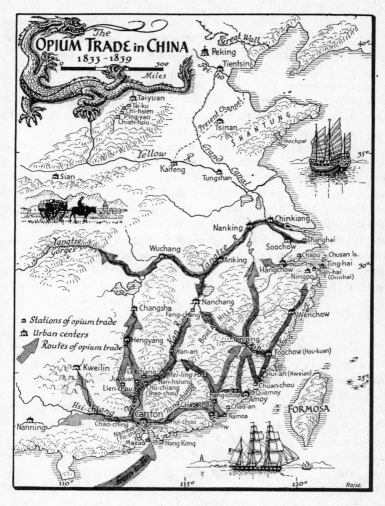

The OPIUM TRADE in CHINA 1833-1839

500 Miles

Great Wall

Peking
Tientsin
Pei-ho

Taiyuan
Tai-ku
Chi-hsien
Ping-yao
Chieh-hsiu

Present Channel

Tsinan

SHANTUNG

Kiaochow Bay

Yellow R.

Sian

Kaifeng

Tungshan

Grand Canal

Chinkiang

Nanking

Shanghai

Yangtze Gorges

Wuchang

Anking

Yangtze

Soochow

Chapu — Chusan Is.
Ting-hai
Chen-hai
(Chinhai)

Hangchow
Ningpo

Nanchang

Changsha

Feng-cheng

BOHEA HILLS

Yen-ping

Wenchow

Stations of opium trade
Urban centers
Routes of opium trade

Hengyang

Wan-an

Foochow (Hou-kuan)

Kweilin

Lo-chang

Hui-an (Hweian)

Juyuan
Lien-chou

Nan-hsiung
Chü-chiang
(Shao-chou)

Mei-ling Pass

Chuan-chou
Quemoy

Hsi-chiang

Chang-chou
Chao-an

Amoy

FORMOSA

Nanning

Chao-ching

Canton

Chaochow

Namoa

Nam-hoi
Fo-shan

Panyu

Hui-chou

Yellow

Macao

Hong Kong

Rajsz.

from Chinchew of at least five days, the mandarins would have gone, and
"if this be the case I feel confident your opium will be cleared out in two
days." [25] By October, Rees was well established at Chinchew Bay, and
until the eve of the Opium War he skillfully supervised Jardine's coastal

fleet. As the trade rapidly grew, more vessels were dispatched to the coast. The *Jardine* and *Harriet* stationed at Namoa (Namo, Nan-ao), the *Austin* north of Chinchew where the *Colonel Young* found a base of operation, and the *Governor Findlay* made voyages sometimes as far north as Ningpo,[26] while the *Lady Hays, Kronberg, Falcon,* and the *Red Rover* cruised from Calcutta and Bombay to Lintin and from Lintin to the stations on the east coast, fetching opium supplies and returning with treasure realized by the sale of opium.[27] The *Fairy*, which had arrived from Liverpool in November 1833 and was now commanded by Captain McKay, had become the most important of such communication vessels between the several bays on the coast and the depot at Lintin.[28]

The success of the coastal trade in the 1830s was attributable, among other factors, to the uncommon qualities of William Jardine and the zeal of his captains. Judging by the voluminous letters sent to the captains from Canton, Jardine no doubt won their trust and devotion by always taking care of their personal interests with the utmost care and generosity. With unusual vision and remarkable efficiency, he speculated in the opium market in Canton, supplied the ships with ample cargo, and directed the voyages of the fleet. Specific details, however, he was perfectly willing to leave to the captains. In a letter to Rees late in 1833, he stressed the futility of laying down any fixed plan of operations for the ships in Canton: "You must be guided by circumstances, after consultation with Mr. Innes and Mr. Gutzlaff — bearing in mind that money is always useful here a few days before the Chinese new year." [29]

The Reverend Charles Gutzlaff is something of an anomaly. He was born in 1803 to a Prussian tailor's family at Pyritz in Pomerania. Perhaps only to escape the drudgery of being a girdler's apprentice, young Gutzlaff managed to acquire training in schools for missionaries and was sent to Siam in 1824 by the Netherlands Missionary Society. Here for the first time he learned the Fukien dialect from Chinese settlers. In 1829 he was married to an Englishwoman whose death shortly afterward left him with a handsome fortune.[30] From the early 1830s on, he closely associated himself with affluent trading firms in Canton, served Her Majesty's Superintendent as an interpreter, distributed religious tracts while accompanying opium clippers on their coastal voyages, participated in the expeditions against China, and, for two decades, had a part in almost every major event on the China coast.

In the Chinese magazine he published, he vigorously denounced the evil effect of opium on man's health and morality and compared the drug to a deadly poison.[31] Yet Gutzlaff had a large role in the development of the coast traffic. It will be recalled that he was on board the opium clipper *Sylph* in her northern expedition of 1832–33. Over the next few years, he made numerous trips up the coast, acting as counselor and trouble shooter, occasionally selling some piece goods himself.[32] Time and again, Jardine urged his captains to ask Gutzlaff for advice. On July 3, 1834, he wrote to Captain Rees: "You will be pleased to consult with Doctor Gutzlaff on all points, connected with your change of destination, and avail yourself of his extensive knowledge of the language, and character of the Chinese, in forming your plans; and in carrying them into effect. We are well aware of the zeal of both partners for our interest." [33]

While the coast trade flourished, the threat from competitors and the vigilance of the mandarins became serious issues. Up to late 1834, when Dent and Company sent the *Aurelia* to the coast, Jardine, Matheson practically monopolized the coast trade. In the following March two more rival ships were reported to be ready to share the distant market.[34] Jardine at first attempted to induce the mandarins to attack the newcomers. This scheme failed and the mandarins became more persistent. He then thought about an alliance with his competitors to deal with the Chinese officials.

On March 9, Jardine suggested to Captain Rees: "If you could manage matters, so as to make the mandarins attack everyone but your own party it would have a good effect; and Mr. Gutzlaff having agreed to accompany Mr. Gordon to the Bohea hills, embarking in a few days in the *Austin*, you will have his aid in communicating with them." Meanwhile he reminded Rees that he had every advantage, "from your knowledge of the coast, and number of vessels placed at your disposal; while the quickness of our returns will enable us to sell cheaper than any of them." In the event of failure to make any arrangement with the mandarins, Jardine recommended a price war, a plan calculated to "sicken" the competitors off the trade by placing a vessel alongside each of the "strangers" and selling at a rate lower than the lowest rate that was to be paid to the other craft.[35]

The competition which so concerned Jardine, however, did not become severe until April 1836. Throughout 1835, the only vessel belonging to a rival firm actually stationed on the coast was Dent's clipper *Aurelia*; the *Water Witch*, which Dent had also intended for the voyage, had not yet arrived. The Parsee traders were determined to follow suit, but were not yet ready to dispatch a ship. Late in 1835 Jardine sought to make arrangements from the Canton end. On Decemebr 9, he informed Captain Rees, "a low Mandarin has left Canton for Amoy, or Chinchew Bay, to make an arrangement with the Admiral; for the easy carrying on the coast trade — he proposed excluding all other ships, having us in full possession of the market — but this is not to be expected. You may, however, encourage it, if proposed to you by the commanding officer of the Junks." [36]

Following the tightening of the prohibitions in Canton, Jardine was very much annoyed by the increased competition on the coast, and he complained in April 1836 of the "mean acts" of the captain of the *Lord Amherst* "for the petty consideration of selling a few additional chests." He emphatically instructed his captains that they could afford to sell as cheap as any of the newcomers and that they should not "allow them to steal out by any underhand, or concealed underselling." Once more he proposed to Rees: "As you have more vessels than your opponents, how would it answer to place one of them alongside the *Amherst*, and run prices down as low as they may think fit to go; while you keep prices up in the distant Bays?" [37] The shrewd Rees, however, managed to enter into an agreement with the *Amherst* which, contrary to Jardine's expectations, succeeded in staving off further difficulties with that vessel.[38]

The general problem of competition nevertheless continued to cause uneasiness. Writing to Captain Rees on June 4, 1836, Jardine complained bitterly: "Your energy and perseverance reduced the Trade to a regular system, in the Bays now generally frequented; and the less enterprising part of the Canton merchants, are now availing themselves of the market you opened for them." His "grand aim" now was to open new fields. The more effective suppression of the opium traffic at Canton made the need for expansion of the coast operation all the more urgent.[39]

As early as July 1834, Jardine pressed Rees to investigate the possibility of trade on the coast of Formosa. Two years later, he proposed another idea to the captain: "How would it answer to send a vessel to the Chusan group, there to remain for 3, 4 or even 6 months? Prices are high in that vicinity; and with perseverance and good management, not neglecting bribes, or fees, to the Mandarins, we must, I think, succeed, to some extent." In January 1838, he dispatched the *Governor Findlay*, commanded by Captain F. Jauncey, northeastward to thirty-two degrees latitude (around the Yangtze estuary) to deliver a large amount of Malwa on the account of a Chinese customer and with a view to opening the Chusan Islands "for the disposal of the drug." He was willing to make some sacrifices to accomplish this object and hoped to obtain raw silk in return. As the operation expanded, more small craft were needed to keep up the connection between the stations and to carry on the trade with the nearer bays at Namoa and west of Canton. To meet this need, early in 1838 the company bought the *Omega*, a fast vessel built on Java.[40] The *Coral* was bought the next summer; and the *Maria* and the *Hellas* were soon added to Jardine's coastal fleet.[41]

One story particularly worth telling in connection with the expansion of the coastal trade was the unhappy voyage of the *Fairy*. This voyage was proposed by Captain Rees, who, after Jardine's repeated requests for new plans, finally came up with a scheme in May 1836 for a north-ward trading trip along the coast. The *Fairy* got her instructions in July.[42] The brig never came back; she was plundered and carried off after the murder of her commander, Captain McKay.[43] Some of the crew landed on the islands off the China coast and were eventually sent to Foochow where, it was reported, they were well treated. The governor there wrote to the authorities in Canton asking for a linguist to ascertain whether the men were wounded by the mutinous part of the crew, or by the Chinese.[44]

Gutzlaff was subsequently sent to Foochow to inquire about the crew, but he came back with contradictory tales. Nearly a year after the loss of the *Fairy*, in 1837 Her Majesty's sloop *Raleigh* conveyed Gutzlaff from Macao to the Min River on the coast of Fukien, to obtain further information on the fate of the crew. In 1839 the Admiralty addressed a communication to the Foreign Office asking Lord Palmerston whether the expense of this passage should be paid by the public. The Foreign Office's reply was that "as Mr. Gutzlaff accompanied the 'Raleigh' on her cruise by the direction of Her Majesty's Superintendent at Canton, for the purpose of acting as Interpreter in the communications of the Commander of that vessel with the Chinese, Lord Palmerston is of the opinion that the expense of his passage should be paid by the public."[45]

The rapid growth of the coastal opium trade led to intensified inter-ference by the Chinese government. In dealing with this resistance, com-manders of the opium vessels invariably resorted to tactics of evasion, bribery, and intimidation. Before his death in 1836, Captain McKay seemed to excel in devices for escaping the mandarins' attention. He left several vivid accounts of how he kept away at sea during the day, coming in after dark to receive money and deliver the drug.[46]

No one doubts the incompetence of the Chinese water forces in suppressing the opium traffic. Nevertheless, an examination of the records concerning Jardine, Matheson's coastal operation in the late 1830s reveals numerous allusions to troublesome and strict mandarins. In the case of Chinchew Bay, we note that Captain Rees attempted to offer fees to the mandarins in conjunction with the *Lord Amherst* in early 1837, but the efforts were in vain and the brokers continued to be harassed.[47]

Perhaps a more effective method of coping with the mandarin problem was by a show of force, and it was not infrequently used. There is on record a letter of Jardine indicating that, as early as 1835, Captain Grant at the Lintin station was selecting "good steady European sailors for the coast vessels." In the summer of 1837, the *Amherst* struck and sank a junk (while the *Aurelia* was watching nearby), and several men lost their lives. As the mandarins received more frequent and more stringent orders to stop the traffic in opium, the number of such clashes increased. On May 3, 1838, Jardine praised Captain Rees, writing, "your proceedings on the coast have been rather of a violent description occasionally of late; but you appear to have got wonderfully well out of your scrapes."[48]

The opium trade in China had by this time reached such magnitude that it attracted the attention of merchants, economists, and other informed circles in all parts of the world. *Hunt's Merchants' Magazine* of New York commented that the sum paid by the Chinese for opium was probably "the largest sum given for any raw article supplied by one nation to another, if we except the cotton-wool exported from the U. S. to Great Britain; and it is a lamentable fact that the use of this narcotic, too, is constantly extending, and it is difficult to conjecture how it could be reduced." The contemporary compiler of commercial handbooks, John Phipps, held that the scale of the trade in opium "can scarcely be matched in any one article of consumption in any part of the world." Disinterested onlookers were also gravely concerned over the development of the traffic. The *Edinburgh Review* warned: "The importation of Indian opium into China has increased in an extraordinary manner since the expiration of the charter . . . We cannot make this statement without some feelings of regret, since a contraband trade in this drug, carried on with great obstinacy, is naturally calculated to increase the dislike of the Chinese government towards the strangers engaged in it."[49]

At this time it was widely believed that Americans had very little to do with the opium traffic. This idea was refuted by a contemporary

British journal, the *Quarterly Review*: "On the contrary, with one or two exceptions, every American house in China was engaged in the trade. There were American depot ships at Lintin, and on the coast . . . in fact, both in the act which originated the dispute [in 1839], and the insults and outrages consequent thereon, our transatlantic brethren have had their full share." [50]

The Americans dealt in both Indian and Turkish opium, but they so monopolized the Turkish product that many Chinese concluded that Turkey must be a part of the United States. As far as it can be ascertained, the Americans imported 2,924 piculs of opium to China in nine seasons between 1813 and 1826 (data for three seasons in this period are not readily available). In one extraordinary season, 1818–19, imports were as high as 818 piculs as compared with the 466 piculs, a more normal amount, in 1836–37. Although Turkish opium was quite negligible on the China market before 1828 and even in its good years (late 1820s and early 1830s) seldom amounted to more than 5 percent of the total opium shipments to China, American firms soon developed an interest in Indian opium. The Boston merchants began to deal in it after 1834, and in 1835 Russell and Company was able to report that its ventures in Indian opium for several American clients promised to yield a good profit. In 1839, the opium it surrendered to the Chinese was surpassed by only two firms, Dent and Jardine, Matheson; the amounts were 1500, 1700, and 7000 chests respectively.[51]

According to C. W. King, the Rhode Island merchant who resided in Canton at the time, the amount of opium shipped to China from 1800 to 1839 under the American flag totaled about 10,000 chests. The relative significance of the American share in the trade can be seen by a comparison with the figures in Appendix B. Moreover, during and after the hostilities, a considerable amount of the British opium traffic was continued with American help and protection.[52] The *Quarterly Review*'s comments cited above are therefore not invalid.

Nationalities aside, the opium traffic was so lucrative that almost every foreign merchant in China was involved in it. Writing in 1839, the widow of Reverend Robert Morrison stated that D. W. C. Olyphant, an American merchant whom Morrison had regarded as a "pious, devoted servant of Christ, and a friend of China," was the *only* foreign trader in Canton who did not engage in the forbidden traffic.[53] The *Chinese Repository*, with palpable uneasiness, summed up the rather anomalous commercial community at Canton:

The most eminent merchants engaged freely in the traffic; and no man received a less ready welcome to the highest ranks of society because his eastern fortune had come from the sale of opium. And up to the present day, throughout India and in China, many of the most distinguished merchants — men who would be slow to engage in any other than what they regarded as just and honourable pursuits — have been foremost in this traffic.[54]

The influx of opium into China on such a scale necessarily had far-reaching repercussions. It mobilized a large section of the population into active participation in law-defying pursuits: the grave social implications of this need no further comment. Economically, the most conspicuous effect of the opium trade was the drain of silver specie, then China's main currency. As a result, commerce and finance in China were seriously handicapped. Furthermore, it not only contributed to the corruption of local governments and police forces, but also sapped the energy of the army and made a useful and active life impossible for a great many merchants, sailors, laborers, and others in all occupations. More and more people were being drawn away from normal, socially productive careers.[55] In the end the Peking authorities could not help becoming alarmed. A great debate on how to cope with the situation was touched off, and the party that advocated a firm policy was put in power to crush the trade totally and forever.

THE MARKET IN CHINA

The most important Chinese links in the traffic were the several dozen wholesale or brokerage organizations, called yao-k'ou, in the Canton area. A yao-k'ou had capital of anywhere from twenty or thirty thousand to upwards of a million dollars, and it was composed of scores of individuals in partnership. The yao-k'ou, having paid for the opium at the Canton factories, fetched it from the receiving ships (ya-p'ien-tun) anchored at Lintin by means of "smug boats," as foreigners called the craft known to the Chinese as p'a-lung (scrambling dragons) or k'uai-hsieh (fast crabs). These boats, frequently described in memorials to the throne and in foreigners' accounts of the trade, were "of great length and beam, the latter increasing rather disproportionately abaft to give quarters to brokers' agents who always went with them."[56] With a crew of sixty to seventy "intelligent and very active sailors," and twenty or more oars on each side, the swiftness with which they moved about the creeks and rivers was "almost incredible." In most cases they were successful in eluding the mandarin boats. Fully armed, they were always ready to retaliate in case the forts had not been bribed successfully beforehand. In 1831 it was estimated by the Chinese authorities that between one hundred and two hundred of the smug boats were roving about the Canton waters, carrying opium to shore from some twenty-five receiving ships.[57]

There were three routes by which opium was distributed from the Canton area to other provinces. Westward, through Chao-ch'ing, it was shipped to Kwangsi and Kweichow. Eastward, it went to Fukien through Ch'ao-chou (Chaochow) and Hui-chou. The northern route was the most prosperous one; opium was concentrated in the shipping centers of Ch'ü-chiang (Kükong) and Ju-yuan and was relayed through Lo-ch'ang to Hunan and through Nan-hsiung (Namhung) to Kiangsi.

Before the foreign opium ships began to frequent their bay, the Chinchew merchants in Fukien came down to the Canton River every summer and brought back large amounts of opium. It was very much at their instigation that the foreign ships began sailing up to the Fukien coast to supply the brokers of the Chinchew and Hui-an area. In southern Fukien, the Chao-an dealers obtained their supplies through the very short inland route at Namoa (an island near the Kwangtung-Fukien border) and the Swatow area in Kwangtung. Thus the shipping centers of Fukien province were Chinchew, Chang-chou (Lung-ch'i), and Chao-an. From Chinchew, opium was transported northward through the provincial capital to Wen-chou on the southeastern coast of Chekiang. It was also shipped to the northwest, through Yen-p'ing to western Chekiang and eastern Kiangsi. From the Chang-chou and Chao-an area, dealers brought it northeastward to Yen-p'ing or westward to southern Kiangsi. From Hunan, Kiangsi, and Chekiang, it was further relayed to the Yangtze Valley, to the northern provinces, and into the interior. Thus, the governors of Anhwei, Shensi, and other provinces successively reported the penetration of opium into their territories.[58]

The trade was so lucrative that, according to a contemporary scholar, many propertyless people borrowed funds and well-to-do people sold their properties in order to engage in it. To protect themselves, these dealers often organized and associated themselves with the secret societies. According to a memorial of Chou T'ien-chueh, director-general of the grain transports, in the Hunan, Hupei, and Kiangsi area, where opium traffic was very heavy, hundreds of brigands banded together to pursue the trade. They carried weapons and belonged to secret societies.[59]

In the early years of the nineteenth century, consumers of opium were usually young men of wealthy families. But gradually people of every description — mandarins, gentry, workers, merchants, servants, women, and even nuns, monks, and Taoist priests — became addicted to the drug. In 1838 the emperor was informed by his officials that, in Kwang-tung and Fukien provinces, nine people out of ten had developed a habitual craving for opium (shih-jen chiu-yin).[60] It quickly spread to other parts of the empire. The well-known scholar Pao Shih-ch'en esti-mated that in 1820 the city of Soochow had more than a hundred thousand addicts, who spent upwards of ten thousand taels a day on opium. The population statistics of Soochow for the year 1820 are not readily available for comparison, but undoubtedly a very large section of the adult population in that city were opium smokers.[61]

These crude estimates can be somewhat corroborated by remarks made by foreign observers. It was pointed out by contemporary English authors that opium shops were as plentiful in certain towns in China as gin shops were in England. All classes of people, "from the pampered official to the abject menial, continually flocked to these shops despite the official prohibition." Opium pipes and other apparatus for smoking were pub-licly exhibited for sale in Canton, both in shops and among the wares of street hawkers. Lieutenant Ouchterlony, who was with the expedi-tionary forces to China and subsequently became the acting engineer at the new settlement of Hong Kong, maintained, "As the people of all the southern portion of the empire were known to be all more or less addicted to the use of the drug, in smoking chiefly, it was an evil of great magnitude."[62]

In late 1838 Lin Tse-hsü, still governor-general of Hu-Kuang (Hunan and Hupeh), wrote a memorial contending that opium addicts in China far exceeded 1 percent of the total population (400 million, according to the Board of Revenue). Pao Shih-ch'en estimated that the average smoker had to spend one mace (one tenth of a tael) daily on opium, and the market value of opium was four times as much as an equal weight of silver.[63] The average daily need of an opium smoker would then be 2.5 candareens (one fourth of a mace), or 1.7 candareens of the pre-pared smoking extract.[64] Thus the 40,000 chests imported in 1838–39 would supply eight and a half million smokers for that year.

An English medical man, Toogood Downing, who had been in Can-ton, estimated that 33,200,000 ounces (taels) of smoking extract were pre-pared in 1836 and supplied approximately twelve and a half million smokers.[65] In accordance with this estimate, the daily consumption of smoking extract would be 0.73 candareens. Another Englishman, speaking from the point of view of a resident opium merchant at Canton, in an open letter addressed to Lord Palmerston, maintained that in 1838–39 (the original has 1837–38, obviously a mistake), the 40,000 chests of opium imported yielded 2,400,000 catties of smoking extract and supplied 2,104,110 consumers out of a total Chinese population of 350 million. In other words, one out of every 166 persons was an addict. He held that "although many used less, five candarines of the extract was considered to be about the quantity consumed daily by the regular smokers. A good many smoked a mace. Three or four mace was considered a very large quantity, and it was said that but few could consume it." [66] In 1879 it was estimated that average smokers consumed two to five mace of the extract and heavy smokers consumed five to twenty mace each day. On this basis, Robert Hart two years later calculated that about 200,000 chests of unprepared opium were being consumed annually by two million smokers in China, only about two thirds of 1 percent of the population.[67]

The estimates of the total number of smokers in China were thus at great variance. It is impossible to determine with accuracy the total number because the exact daily consumption of an average smoker is not known and there is no reliable record of the total amount of opium supplied, for the Canton imports were supplemented by the domestic product and by supplies smuggled in elsewhere along the coast. The fact that opium smoking was concentrated in certain strategic areas (along the coast, in the cities, in the river valleys) and among certain sections of the population (young and middle-aged men, civil servants, soldiers) undoubtedly gave the illusion that the number of smokers was greater than it actually was. Dr. Downing reported: "The class of people who consume opium in China are those of the male sex, chiefly between twenty and fifty-five years old. It affects soldiers very much, rendered [sic] them weak and decrepit." [68] It was estimated by Chiang Hsiang-nan that opium smokers constituted 10 to 20 percent of the officials in the central government, 20 to 30 percent of those in the local governments, and 50 to 60 percent of the private secretaries (mu-yu) who handled law, punishments (hsing-ming), and taxes (ch'ien-ku); among the regular attendants (ch'ang-sui) and underlings of officials, the smokers were innumerable (pu-k'o-sheng-shu). In late 1838 Lin Tse-hsü stated frankly in a memorial to the emperor that opium smokers were most numerous among those affiliated with the yamen (government offices).

Eight or nine out of every ten private secretaries, relatives of officials, regular attendants, clerks, and orderlies, Lin reported, were opium addicts.[69]

Soldiers were even more generally addicted. Among the soldiers in the several coastal provinces, reported Hsiang-k'ang, the military governor of Kirin province (Chi-lin *chiang-chün*), those who did not smoke opium were exceptions. The degeneration of the Chinese armies owing to opium addiction was fully exposed in 1832 when Governor-General Li Hung-pin's troops suffered a great defeat in the war against the Yao rebels at Lien-chou. The emperor was enraged because Li Hung-pin had not eradicated the opium evil from among his troops, and as a result Li was exiled to Urumchi and Liu Jung-ch'ing, the provincial commander (*t'i-tu*), was sentenced to hard labor in Ili. Even though Liu Jung-ch'ing was over seventy years old and the law of the empire provided that, in all cases where the crime was less than capital, any offender who was under fifteen or above seventy was allowed to have his sentence commuted to an expiatory fine, Liu's appeal to the throne was refused, ample proof of the emperor's wrath.[70]

Early in 1833 a censor memorialized requesting strict measures to check the spread of opium among the troops. In response, the emperor issued an edict enjoining all the governors-general, governors, and provincial commanders of the empire to stamp out the evil. The effect of the drug on the army was undoubtedly one of the main considerations behind the Tao-kuang Emperor's determination to extirpate all traffic.

It goes without saying that the figures introduced here, all estimates made in the early nineteenth century, should not be taken as scientifically accurate. However, the simple fact that a regime as torpid and sluggish as the Manchu government of the 1830s could be jolted into action denotes the seriousness of the situation. Perhaps John McCulloch, the contemporary compiler of a commercial dictionary, was not exaggerating when he attested that in China the habit of smoking opium "has become almost universal." No one would question the Tao-kuang Emperor's sincerity when he complained that the ranks of opium smokers and dealers had swelled to such a measure that they were almost equal in number to those who dealt in and used tobacco.[71]

ECONOMIC REPERCUSSIONS

The immediate economic effect of the opium traffic was the eclipse of other lines of commerce. Reporting to the emperor in late 1838, Governor-

General Lin Tse-hsü revealed that from his own investigation in Soochow (when he was governor of Kiangsu) and later in Hankow, he had found that there was a depression in almost every area of trade. The merchants informed Lin that they could sell only half of the volume of commodities (presumably excluding staple goods such as rice) that they had sold twenty or thirty years ago; opium had taken the place of the other half. The daily cost of living of a poor man in an average year, according to Lin, was about four to five candareens (4 to 5 percent of a tael) of silver, and a mace (10 percent of a tael) would be plentiful for every need. But each opium smoker had to spend a mace a day for supplies of the drug. Thus these people spent over half of their income on opium.[72]

Another economic effect of the opium trade was its influence on the Shansi banks. These banks, founded and controlled by Shansi merchants of Ch'i-hsien, P'ing-yao, and T'ai-ku, played the most significant role in China's economic and financial network in the nineteenth century.

The first and most important of the Shansi banks was the Jih Sheng Ch'ang, which grew out of the Jih Sheng Ch'ang dye store. The dye store was founded by a P'ing-yao merchant at the end of the Ch'ien-lung period (1736–1795). Toward the end of the Chia-ch'ing period (1796–1820), it began to handle remittances on an informal basis. In 1831, it was formally changed into a *p'iao-chuang*, or Shansi bank.[73]

The second Shansi bank was the Wei T'ai Hou, also founded by a P'ing-yao merchant. It began as a silk and cloth store in 1814, but from 1831 on concentrated on remitting funds. In 1834 it formally became a *p'iao-chuang*. In the same year, three other silk and cloth stores in the area were transformed into *p'iao-chuang*. The main function of the *p'iao-chuang* throughout the nineteenth century was the transmission of funds from one place to another; they were different in nature from the native banks or money shops (*ch'ien-chuang*), which were mainly exchangers operating only in a limited locality. The principal cause for the rapid development of the Shansi banks in the 1830s was the increase in the number of bandits, which made the overland shipping of specie extremely risky.[74]

According to a study made by Kao Shu-k'ang, the opium traffic, which had reached new heights in the 1830s, contributed considerably to the prosperity of the Shansi banks.[75] Ch'en Ch'i-t'ien did not deal specifically with this question in his book on the Shansi banks, but statements which tend to support Kao's view are not lacking. First of all, Ch'en and Kao both maintain that the Shansi banks originated around 1830.[76] Secondly,

Ch'en points out that the Jih Sheng Ch'ang and Chih Ch'eng Hsin banks, among others, sought and gained the friendship of the hoppo at Canton and kept up good relations with the successive appointees to that office. The hoppo, we are told by many Western writers, derived a large income from the opium trade, and he frequently had to make large remittances to Peking.[77] Third, in discussing the role of the Shansi banks in foreign trade, Ch'en maintains that, since foreign trade was limited to Canton before the Opium War, Chinese merchants from Shansi or Hupeh who wanted to buy imported goods had to transport specie to Canton to make the payments, and agents for foreign merchants had to transport specie to silk and tea marts to purchase their cargoes. It was only natural that both parties made use of the remitting mechanism of the Shansi banks. According to Ch'en, the Shansi banks charged a commission of only 3 percent for bills on Shanghai sold at Canton. If the specie had actually been transported from Canton to Shanghai, the charge would have been above 20 or 30 percent.[78]

Until the 1860s, the Shansi banks were the sole medium through which money was remitted, and their services greatly facilitated the foreign trade at Canton. Since opium constituted more than half of the total imports at Canton from the time the Shansi banks began operating to the crisis of 1839,[79] the banks' fortunes were necessarily connected with the opium trade. Of the nine Shansi banks that maintained branch offices in Canton, seven were founded in the beginning of the Tao-kuang period (1820), at a time when the total value of imported opium began to increase substantially; two were of the T'ai-ku group and five of the P'ing-yao group.[80]

The Shansi merchants' interest in the opium trade developed fairly early. In 1820, Kuo T'ai-ch'eng, a censor, reported to the emperor that wealthy merchants and great traders from T'ai-ku (which produced many Shansi bank proprietors) and Chieh-hsiu were profitably pursuing the opium trade. The governor of Shansi memorialized late in 1830 that many merchants from T'ai-ku, P'ing-yao, and Chieh-hsiu who carried on trade in Canton and the southern provinces had become addicted to opium and were bringing supplies of the drug back with them. The opium trade soon took root in Shansi, and, in more modern times, Shansi, Szechwan, and Yunnan topped the list of provinces where the sale and smoking of opium were most prevalent. In 1910 the governor of Shansi stated that in his province poppies were cultivated everywhere and opium smoked by everyone.[81] It can therefore be safely concluded that the growth

of the Shansi banks was related to the opium trade, but just how much
of the banks' prosperity can be attributed directly to opium is a question
which awaits further investigation.

Another economic effect of the opium trade was the drain of specie
from China; this, probably more than anything else, made the country's
balance of trade unfavorable for the first time in its history.[82] The outflow
of silver precipitated a severe economic crisis. The market values of the
two mediums of payment — silver and copper — deviated greatly from
the official exchange rate.

Ever since T'ang times (618–906), the legal ratio of exchange between
gold, silver, and copper was 1:10:1000. In other words, one tael of gold
was equal to ten taels of silver or to one thousand taels of copper. The
statutory weight of a T'ang copper coin was one tenth of a tael, and this
weight continued to be the desideratum for Ch'ing copper coins. Thus
one thousand copper coins should have equaled one tael of silver. The
actual weight of the copper cash, however, was adjusted in the hope of
maintaining the legal ratio between silver and copper.[83] But the market
ratio seldom coincided with the legal ratio. Before the Chia-ch'ing period,
a tael of silver could often be exchanged for only seven or eight hundred
copper cash. But in the Tao-kuang period, the market value of copper
cash had depreciated considerably, as shown by the following statistics.[84]

Year	Number of copper cash exchangeable for a tael of silver
1644	700
1722	780
1740	800
1743	700–815 (Kwangtung)
1748	750 (Shantung)
1751	781 (Shansi), 820 (Peking)
1760	880
1766	1,100 (Yunnan)
1770	1,150 (Yunnan)
1775	955 (Peking)
1779	880 (Peking)
1794	2,450 (Yunnan), 1,400 (Fukien, Chekiang)
1800	1,450–1,650 (Shantung)
1822	2,000–3,000 (Peking)
1828	2,600 (Shantung), 1,300 (Soochow, Sungkiang), 2,500 (Chihli)
1830	2,700 (Shantung)
1832	1,250 (Chekiang)
1838	1,650

    1842   1,650 (Chekiang)
    1846   4,600 (Chihli), 1,500 (Kiangsu, Anhwei, southwest Shansi)
    1847   2,000 (Hunan, Hupeh)

The radical appreciation of silver was naturally accompanied by in-creasing fiscal difficulties at every level of the government and by economic hardship among the people. The censor Huang Chung-mo complained as early as 1822 that people who had to exchange copper cash for silver to pay their taxes were suffering greatly.[85] In 1838, another official pointed out that most taxes were collected in copper cash in the various districts, and, before being remitted to Peking, they had to be converted into silver at a great loss. The salt merchants had to pay levies with silver while receiving copper cash for their sales; consequently the lucrative privilege of selling salt under the government monopoly system became a burdensome penalty. Should this situation continue for a few more years, the memorialist asked, how could taxes be collected? [86]

The pressure of the demand for silver began to be felt long before the Tao-kuang period. In 1814 Su-leng-e, who as hoppo at Canton had re-ceived the Macartney Mission, stated that for the past several years over a million taels of silver had been smuggled out of Canton each year. In 1822, Huang Chung-mo wrote that the outflow of silver from China must be stopped and that the barter system should be the sole pattern of foreign trade in Canton. Three years later, another censor, Chang Yuan, pointed out the effect of the opium trade on the drain of silver. This is believed to be the first instance of a Ch'ing official's seeing some connection between the opium traffic and the shortage of silver. By 1836, every statesman, whether in favor of legalization or prohibition of the trade, agreed that the outflow of silver was caused solely by the import of the drug, and they were almost hysterically alarmed by the amount of money being spent on this article. Thus Huang Chueh-tzu, director of the Court of State Ceremonial, estimated that between 1823 and 1831 the Chinese people spent over 17 million taels each year for opium; be-tween 1831 and 1834 over 20 million taels; and between 1834 and 1838, over 30 million taels in Canton alone, while additional millions of taels worth of the drug were purchased on the coasts of Fukien, Chekiang, and Shantung. Lin Tse-hsü said that in the late 1830s Chinese consumers spent over a hundred million taels each year on opium.[87]

Until 1826 the balance of trade had always been favorable to the Chinese. In most of the trading seasons during the first two thirds of the eighteenth century, total British shipments to China consisted of not more than 10 percent in goods, as opposed to specie. From 1721 to 1740 British payment for Chinese goods was 94.9 percent specie and only 5.1 percent goods. A solution to Britain's problem of balancing the trade was eventually found in India's opium and cotton. Beginning at the close of the eighteenth century the trade between India and China, the country trade, developed rapidly, and after the mid-1820s the flow of specie began to reverse its direction.[88] This transformation is illustrated by the following figures.[89]

Periods	Flow of silver (outflows indicated by minus signs)
1681–1690	189,264 taels
1691–1700	139,833
1701–1710	769,665
1711–1720	6,312,798
1721–1730	2,287,676
1731–1740	2,528,338
1741–1750	642,000
1751–1760	412,800
1761–1770	3,411,453
1771–1780	7,564,320
1781–1790	16,431,160
1791–1800	5,159,542
1801–1810	26,658,835
1811–1820	9,932,442
1821–1830	−2,282,038
1831–1833	−9,922,712

With the rapid rise of the opium trade in the 1830s, silver began to drain out of China at an alarming rate.[90] In the eight-year period beginning with 1828, the treasure (silver dollars, sycee silver, and gold) exported from Canton on British accounts, not including that carried out by smugglers along the coast, amounted to 39 million dollars, breaking down as follows.[91]

Seasons	Brought in	Taken out	Net export
1828–29	$ 730,200	$4,703,202	$3,973,002
1829–30	1,158,644	6,755,372	5,596,728
1830–31	255,355	6,595,306	6,339,951
1831–32	683,252	4,023,003	3,339,751
1832–33	745,319	5,155,741	4,410,422
1833–34	703,019	6,731,615	6,028,596
1834–35	60,000	3,959,453	3,899,453
1835–36	71,211	4,468,411	4,397,200
	$4,307,000	$42,392,103	$37,985,103

In the year beginning July 1, 1837, the value of treasure taken out by the British increased to as much as $8,974,776, not counting a balance of $2,770,762, chiefly debts incurred by the hong merchants.[92]

During the early years of the nineteenth century, the Americans, three quarters of whose shipments were silver dollars, brought in a considerable amount of specie to offset the silver outflow on British accounts. From 1818 to 1834, for instance, British ships brought away $50 million worth of silver while the Americans were carrying in upwards of $60 million. But the situation began to change after 1826–27; as the American traders became more and more involved in the opium trade, their vessels shipped in less and less silver. In the six seasons from 1828 to 1833, the British collected a total of $29.6 million worth of specie from Canton, while the Americans in the same period brought in only $15.8 million worth of specie and bills on London.[93]

The edicts prohibiting the export of silver were never as clear-cut and vigorous as those prohibiting the traffic in opium. Moreover, they were often so mixed with absurd regulations (such as disallowing trade through the medium of silver and permitting only trade by barter) that their overall effect was much weakened. No statutory provisions were ever promulgated by the Board of Punishment to render them more effective, as in the cases of the prohibitions against exporting gold, iron, and copper, and the export of silver dollars was never prohibited. Of the total amount of silver dollars brought in, mainly by the Americans, much of it immediately found its way out again to India, through the hong and English merchants, without being circulated in Canton. Consequently, sycee silver was smuggled out regularly, and the Chinese officers did not interfere, provided ample "fees" were paid them and provided the smuggling took place at Lintin or Macao, instead of Whampoa or Canton.

Sycee silver was shipped out of China not only to pay for foreign imports but also by private English traders to supplement the insufficient and uncertain methods of remittance to India. Since the sycee were 15 percent purer than silver dollars and could be procured at a lower rate in China, the shipping of Chinese sycee to India was a very favorable form of remittance. On June 3, 1839, H. G. Gordon, chairman of the Bombay chamber of commerce, wrote to the various China and East India Associations in Britain, pointing out the importance of the outflow of Chinese silver, brought about chiefly by the opium trade, to the economy of India and the commercial soundness of Great Britain. He concluded: "Without the India trade the court of directors could not have so favourably conducted their large remittances for home charges, nor could merchants in England have purchased teas, to the amount they have done, without having sent remittances largely in bullion to that country." Gordon had offered many tabular materials to corroborate his statement. The following statistics, taken from his data, indicate that over 65.5 percent of the imports of treasure at Calcutta and Bombay in the two seasons from 1836 to 1838 were from China (value of treasure in rupees).[94]

	Year	Total imports	Imports from China
Calcutta	1836–7	6,448,475	2,339,469
	1837–8	10,841,609	5,509,393
Bombay	1836–7	13,478,368	10,074,238
	1837–8	14,650,829	11,849,508

Sycee silver was not only shipped out of China by private traders to India; the East India Company, especially during the last days of its monopoly, shipped considerable amounts of silver to London. Even in earlier years, when the balance of trade was not so overwhelmingly against China, the company had at times smuggled silver out of Canton. Herbert Wood has described the company's position in 1817: "Since the balance of trade between India and China was so much against China, and since the Committee could not use all of the surplus, the rest had to be shipped to India in spite of the Chinese regulation against the practice; the Committee itself had at times resorted to smuggling in order to export." [95]

China's monetary crisis was also hastened by the increase of copper cash in circulation, and the copper coins of the Tao-kuang period (1821–1850) were continually and drastically debased. The production of the Yunnan copper mines, which supplied most of the copper minting in the empire, had declined steadily since the 1790s, largely because of poor bureaucratic control, and after 1811 it dropped even more sharply.[96] Consequently smaller and lighter coins were made. In the early years of the Ch'ing period, a copper cash weighed 0.12 or even 0.14 taels and had a diameter of 1.1 inch, but at the end of the eighteenth century officially minted coins, not to speak of the numerous illicit issues, measured only 0.85 or even 0.80 inches in diameter and weighed no more than 0.075 taels. In 1807, a memorialist estimated that not more than 40 percent of the coins weighed the legal one tenth of a tael. Yet the workmanship in these debased coins was still up to standard. In the Tao-kuang period, however, poorly minted copper cash began to overwhelm the empire and the weight dropped to as low as 0.05 taels.[97]

Another factor in China's financial crisis was the general decline in the world production of silver. The following figures indicate that, in the decade beginning with 1821, silver production hit the lowest mark since 1741. (Silver imports to China during the two decades prior to the Opium War naturally dropped off.)

Period	Annual average (in fine ounces)
1741–1760	17,140,612
1761–1780	20,985,591
1781–1800	28,261,779
1801–1810	28,746,922
1811–1820	17,385,755
1821–1830	14,807,004
1831–1840	19,175,867
1841–1850	25,090,342
1851–1855	28,488,597
1856–1860	29,095,428
1861–1865	35,401,972
1866–1870	43,051,583
1871–1875	63,317,014

The price of silver during the 1833–1873 period showed little fluctuation; in London it remained at the level of 60 pence per standard ounce and in New York at a little over $1.30 per fine ounce.[98] The steadiness of the price of silver and the drop in its production, however, should not be interpreted as a sign of a corresponding decline in the demand for silver. During the first half of the nineteenth century, as a result of the Industrial Revolution, the volume of transactions increased and general prices fell steadily.[99] Thus the fact that the price of silver remained at a constant level while general prices declined suggests that the world demand for silver tended to increase, not to decrease.

The domestic supply of silver in China was always very limited.[100] Moreover, the silver reserve at Peking was greatly depleted by huge expenditures in military campaigns. In the middle of the eighteenth century, the vaults of the Board of Revenue had a deposit of over 20 million taels. It had mounted to 70 million taels in the 1790s. But in the course of the first two decades of the nineteenth century, a great amount was spent in the campaigns against the rebels in Yunnan, Kweichow, Hupeh, Szechwan, and Shensi, and by 1820 there was only a little over 10 million taels left in the treasury. In the 1830s, for the two campaigns

against the insurrections of the Moslems and minority races in the southwest, the imperial government spent more than 30 million taels, almost
three fourths of its regular annual revenue. Once the treasure was diverted to the frontiers in these military campaigns, it was difficult, with
premodern modes of transportation and remittance, to attract it back to
the localities where it was most needed. Meanwhile, replenishment of
government stores of silver was slow in coming; by 1820 a total of 26
million taels of land tax, salt gabelle, and grain tax owed the imperial
government by the several provinces had not been commuted, perhaps
mainly because of the high ratio between silver and copper cash.[101]

The effect of the silver shortage on China's currency was aggravated
by the constantly expanding supply of copper coins. In the first hundred
years of the dynasty, the coinage of copper cash was very limited; seldom
did the annual income issue exceed the two billion mark, and the average was about two to three hundred million coins. In the period 1800–
1830, however, the number of copper coins minted was two billion fifty
million every year. Furthermore, since the value of copper as money exceeded its value as a commodity for nonmonetary purposes, it became
profitable for private individuals to cast coins. From the latter part of
the eighteenth century, the country became increasingly flooded with
spurious cash.[102]

Between 1820 and 1850 numerous Japanese and Annamese coins found
their way into China, contributing further to the imbalances of the
currency system. The Japanese coins which circulated in China were
known as the Kan-ei *tsū-hō* (current treasure of the Kan-ei period).
Although the Kan-ei period lasted only twenty years, from 1624 to 1643,
the coins which appeared for the first time in 1626 continued to be cast
until 1859, and over a thousand varieties have been recognized by experts.[103] The Annamese coins which invaded the Chinese market, minted
in the Canh Hung (1740–1785), Quang Trung (1789–1791), and Gia
Long (1801–1820) periods, were all light, the last-mentioned weighing not
more than half as much as the standard Chinese coins.

The copper cash possessed only limited power as legal tender. The
government as well as the people preferred silver to copper, which was
practically useless in transactions involving large sums. Consequently,
bad money was created in the form of copper coins, and the monetary
authorities were not willing or able to pay out silver in exchange for
copper at the legal ratio. As long as no redemption facilities existed, the
operation of Gresham's Law was ineluctable: silver was driven out of

circulation by copper coins and Spanish dollars.[104] It should be pointed out in this connection that the hoarding of silver in premodern Chinese society was quite a common phenomenon, and the series of wars, natural calamities, economic instability, and famines which punctuated the unhappy Tao-kuang period no doubt encouraged hoarding among the people.

A currency system using two metals as mediums of payment depends on the determination and firm maintenance of a suitable ratio between the two metals. Any considerable fluctuation in the supply of one would upset the bimetallic parity. The monetary situation in the United States in the 1830s is somewhat reminiscent of what was happening at the same time in China. Before 1834 the mint ratio between silver and gold in the United States was 15 to 1. Because the market value of gold in terms of silver was higher, gold was driven out of circulation and silver became almost the sole monetary standard. In 1834 the ratio was changed to 16 to 1, but this placed silver too high, and it was subsequently driven out by gold.[105]

Despite the multiple factors contributing to the deviation of the copper-silver exchange rate from the legal ratio and the fact that the Ch'ing government had seldom been able to maintain a suitable exchange ratio between silver and copper even under better circumstances, Chinese officials and scholars unanimously attributed the trouble to the drain of treasure resulting from the import of opium. Instead of seeking other currency reforms, they held that the only way to alleviate the economic crisis was to stop the import of opium. Thus the demand for a new policy toward opium grew louder and louder.[106]

VESTED INTERESTS IN OPIUM

One may pause to ask why the opium trade could not be stoppped, since the emperor and his officials were so determined to put an end to it. It is generally assumed that the corruption of the Canton authorities and the persistence of the British traders made it extremely difficult to eliminate the traffic, but the extent to which this was so has not been fully appreciated.

Corruption among officials was generally tolerated and had become more or less customary in the last century of the Ch'ing dynasty.[107] At the downfall of the famous Ho-shen (1750–1799), the property confiscated from him was estimated by one modern historian as upwards of

800 million taels. This indicates that during the two decades he was in power the wealth he had amassed, apparently from illegitimate sources, was equal to four sevenths of the total imperial revenue for the same period. The cupidity of Ch'ing officialdom is also shown by the scandalous case of 1841, when it was discovered that a sum of more than 9 million taels of silver was stolen from the treasury of the Board of Revenue by none other than the officers who had been entrusted to guard it.[108]

It was well known that a great number of the Chinese entrusted with the responsibility for putting down the opium trade consumed the drug themselves.[109] It was also known that the Canton authorities were often paid to connive, although it is questionable whether men in the highest positions actually encouraged the traffic. The deep-rooted avarice of local Chinese officials led the editor of the *Canton Register* to conclude that they refused to take seriously the orders from Peking and that the trade at Canton was understood to serve as a supplement to their deficient salaries. The *Register* even accused the Chinese government of being the "universal smuggler," for it winked at the contravention of its own laws and encouraged the contraband trade not only by impossible and ridiculous restrictions, but by actually inviting its own officers to engage secretly in it.[110]

In 1826, Governor-General Li Hung-pin built a fleet of patrol ships (*hsun-ch'uan*) which were modeled exactly after the smug boats. But the better equipment merely caused the bribes for connivance in the traffic to increase; the smuggling was not checked — it thrived. In 1832 the fleet was abolished. Five years later, it was restored by Governor-General Teng T'ing-chen, who appointed Han Chao-ch'ing its commander. Han then made an agreement with the smugglers whereby he was regularly provided with a few hundred chests of opium which he could hand over to the higher authorities, claiming that they had been captured by his forces. By an imperial edict of 1815, public servants were to be promoted and rewarded if they captured a specified amount of opium. Consequently Han was promoted to the rank of brigade general (*tsung-ping*) and decorated with the peacock feather.[111] It was not until after Commissioner Lin's arrival in Canton that Han and his associates were removed. During the trial of these officers, by coincidence, Governor-General Teng came to call on Lin, and the latter refused to receive him until the trial was over — this to avoid the embarrassment that might arise should Teng ask for leniency toward the defendants.[112]

The wealthy Chinese merchants in Canton, Chinchew, and elsewhere, who had for many years derived a large profit from opium, no doubt co-operated with the foreigners to neutralize the government's efforts to suppress the trade. But virtually no reliable sources of information concerning the merchants' activities have been discovered, so we can only surmise that they were illegally involved.[113] The importance of their role is obvious, but any detailed treatment of it must await the appearance of fuller evidence.

The Chinese government, grown hopelessly incompetent and corrupt, had allowed the evil to spread to such an extent that it was too late to eradicate it by eleventh-hour policies. A few honest and industrious statesmen could not be expected to win a quick victory over widely ramified and obstinate vested interests and over the urgent needs of the large number of addicts.

Had the economic stake of the British government and merchants not been so immense, perhaps it would have been less difficult for the Chinese government to stop the opium trade. The Bengal government had a monopoly on the production of opium and derived an enormous profit from its sale.[114] The poppy was grown on the East India Company's lands for the company by the ryots, their peasant tenants. The produce was sold by the company for export to China and was consumed almost entirely by the Chinese.[115] In 1800 the company's net profit in Indian opium production was calculated at 2,370,772 rupees, and it rose to 8,144,178 rupees in 1815 (although in the following years it fluctuated). In 1832 the total revenue derived from this source rose to 10 million rupees; in 1837, to over 20 million; and in 1838, to nearly 30 million. While at the turn of the century opium provided less than 3 percent of the company's revenue in India, in 1826–27 it provided over 5 percent and two seasons later almost 9 percent. By the 1850s this figure was more than 12 percent, a sum close to four million pounds. Thus the Court of Directors wrote the Select Committee in 1818: "The profit derived from the opium trade with China has of late years proved a most essential aid to the Indian Resources." Fully recognizing this, the Select Committee of the House of Commons reported in 1830 and 1832 that "it does not seem advisable to abandon so important a source of revenue as the East India Company's monopoly of opium in Bengal." [116]

In addition to furnishing a most profitable source of remittances from India to London, opium financed Britain's China commerce, which was the most valuable trade the East India Company possessed.[117] Count Bjornstjerna, in his *British Empire in India*, pointed out: "Hence we find that England's gain from its East India possessions amounts to no less than 6,500,000 pounds sterling a year; a sum which would in the end completely ruin this colony if it were remitted in this form. But such is not the case; it comes to England in the following manner: — East India opium is sent to China, and is there exchanged for tea; this is taken to England, and covers all the exchange."

Had it not been for opium, bullion would have seeped out of Britain in exchange for tea, which in the 1830s furnished the Exchequer with three and a half million pounds sterling.[118] The significance of opium may be further illustrated by a dispatch from Captain Elliot to Lord Palmerston, from Macao on February 2, 1837, which states that the value of British imports of opium into China in the preceding year amounted to nearly $18 million, about $1 million in excess of the value of tea and silk exported during the same period on all British accounts. A keen and careful observer, Elliot was reluctant to see British commerce and capital become so heavily dependent upon "the steady continuance of a vast prohibited traffic in an article of vicious luxury, high in price, and liable to frequent and prodigious fluctuation." [119]

But the stakes involved were too high for the British to abandon the trade. The Duke of Wellington declared in May 1838 that, far from looking gloomily upon this opium trade, Parliament had cherished it, suggested its extension, and had deliberately looked for means of promoting it.[120] It is therefore not without justification that Jardine, the leading opium merchant, shortly before his departure from Canton on January 26, 1839, defended himself and his fellow traders:

I hold, gentlemen, the society of Canton high: it holds a high place, in my opinion, even among the merchants of the East; yet I also know that this community has often heretofore and lately been accused of being a set of smugglers. This I distinctly deny; we are not smugglers, gentlemen! It is the Chinese Government, it is the Chinese officers who smuggle, and who connive at and encourage smuggling; not we: and then look at the East India Company — why, the father of all smuggling and smugglers is the East India Company.

Similarly, *Blackwood's Magazine* concluded: "The sin of the opium trade, if sin there be, rests not with British merchants, but is divisible, in about equal proportions betwixt the Chinese and British Governments and the East India Company." [121]

The British government and the East India Company, for financial reasons, were bent on preserving opium production; the private British merchants, for reasons of profit, were obstinately determined to continue the traffic. Thus it is not surprising that when the Chinese government, compelled by economic crisis, finally decided to extirpate the traffic, conflict erupted.

THE DIPLOMATIC CRISIS

Uɴᴅᴇʀ the old Canton system, although foreign trade was carried on under severe restrictions, the East India Company was able to stave off many a potential crisis. But when the company's monopoly in China ended, the stability of the old order ended with it, and the trade at Canton was immediately put on a precarious footing. A new phase of Sino-British relations had begun.

The private traders in Canton and the owners of industries in Manchester, Blackburn, Glasgow, and other cities of Great Britain had striven for more than a decade to end the company's commercial privileges in China; and in 1833 the first reformed Parliament took steps to abolish its monopoly of the Canton trade. In March 1834, the *Canton Register* happily announced, "the British trade to China will be entirely free and unrestricted" after the following April.[1]

THE NAPIER MISSION

The Chinese governor-general at Canton, Li Hung-pin, was informed by the hong merchants as early as January 1831 that the charter of the East India Company was to expire in 1833 and that the British merchants would then become free traders. Li had the hong merchants enjoin the *tai-pan* (president of the Select Committee) to write home for a capable *tai-pan* to come to manage the British trade so that chaos would not follow upon the company's dissolution. In 1834 Lu K'un, the new governor-general, again told the hong merchants that someone should be made responsible for regulating the trade. It is significant that the Chinese governor-general was anticipating a type of manager of commercial affairs, not an official from England.[2]

On December 10, 1833, a Royal Commission appointed William John Napier, a Scottish peer of ancient lineage, as chief superintendent of the British trade in China. His duties were, among other things, to regulate, govern, and protect His Majesty's subjects in Canton by arbitration or mediation, and he was urged to conciliate the Chinese in carrying out these duties. One of his principal objects was to investigate the possibility of extending the trade to other ports of China. He was cautioned not to jeopardize what the British had already achieved and was instructed not to proceed to Peking without permission from the home government.

Lord Napier had entered the Royal Navy as a midshipman in 1803 at the age of sixteen. In 1814 he was promoted to the rank of captain and put on half pay in the following year. In this period of more than twelve years of active service, he participated in much hard fighting, including the Battle of Trafalgar. After his marriage in 1816, young Napier had settled in Selkirkshire, Scotland, and devoted himself to sheep farming. A man full of confidence and inclined toward innovation, he took part in an effort to extend roads into remote parts of the country and contributed a great deal to the introduction of a new breed of sheep into Scotland. In 1818 he was elected a fellow of the Royal Society of Edinburgh, and five years later he succeeded to the peerage.

Lord Napier and his suite sailed from Portsmouth in the *Andromache* on February 7, 1834, and arrived at Macao on July 15. Two days later he received a communication from John Francis Davis, the last president of the company's Select Committee in Canton, accepting his new appointment as second superintendent. Lord Napier arrived at Canton at 2 A.M. on July 25 and took up residence in the British factory. At daybreak the Union Jack was hoisted on the flagstaff.

On receiving a report of Napier's arrival in Macao, Governor-General Lu K'un sent two senior hong merchants on July 21, 1834, to ascertain the nature of this barbarian's business and to inform him that, if he wanted to proceed to Canton, he must first file a petition and wait for permission. When the merchants reached Macao, they found that he had already left for Canton.[3]

For some time the Chinese government at Canton had been issuing orders restating the regulations that forebade foreign merchants to communicate directly with Chinese officials; such communications were to be sent through the hong merchants. In 1810 the Chinese authorities notified the supercargo that foreign merchants were not allowed to ask others to render their petitions into Chinese; only if the petitioner himself were able to write the characters was a foreigner permitted to use Chinese. This rule had been reiterated recently by Lu's predecessor, Governor-General Li Hung-pin, in a set of regulations which provided that, if it were absolutely necessary for a foreigner to communicate with the governor-general on a matter of great importance, the petition should be presented through the senior hong merchants or security merchants. Only if the said Chinese merchants persisted in intercepting the petition were foreigners permitted to carry it themselves to the city gate and submit it to the officer on guard. In such circumstances no more than one or two foreigners were allowed to approach the gate.[4]

However, in conformity with his instructions, Lord Napier prepared a letter to the governor-general, had it translated into Chinese by his Chinese secretary, Dr. Morrison, and had Astell, his secretary, accompanied by a party of gentlemen from the factory, carry it to the city gate. Astell was specifically instructed to deliver it to a mandarin, not a hong merchant. This letter was refused.

Thus, Lord Napier, within two days of his arrival in Canton, had transgressed the Chinese regulations in six ways: he had proceeded to Canton without a pass, taken up residence there without a permit, attempted to communicate with the governor-general by letter instead of by petition, used Chinese instead of English, had his letter presented by more than two persons, and tried to communicate directly with a mandarin rather than through the medium of the hong merchants.

Confronted by this unprecedented situation, the governor-general put pressure on the hong merchants, who were the sole agents for managing foreigners. He issued three more edicts before the end of the month after his first proclamation of July 21, 1834, charging the merchants with the duty of notifying the barbarian chief that he was to leave Canton as soon as his business was completed and that thereafter he must not visit Canton without permission. They were to remind him that commercial affairs were to be directed solely by the hong merchants. In his last proclamation, Governor-General Lu directed the hong merchants to command Lord Napier to leave the port immediately. As long as the barbarian chief remained at Canton, he said, it would be a national disgrace, and he threatened to bring the hong merchants to trial.[5] His Lordship, however, remained adamant and refused either to leave Canton or to communicate through the merchants.

Pressed by the governor-general, the hong merchants brought pressure to bear on the British merchants. On the 16th, they stopped the shipment of cargo to British vessels, an action upheld and praised by the governor-general two days later in another proclamation. In this document, he admonished the barbarian chief to repent and answer through the hong merchants, so that commercial transactions could be resumed; otherwise trade with the British would be entirely cut off. His proclamation again produced no effect.[6]

In the initial stage of the controversy, the governor-general seems to have intended to solve it locally. On August 23 he compromised by dispatching three officials to call upon Lord Napier to settle the dispute. Much time was spent in bickering about seats and etiquette. Napier scolded them for coming late, sought to impress them with his rank, and added that Great Britain was "perfectly prepared" for war although she desired no war with China. The three officials learned nothing about the British objectives; nor did they learn when Napier would depart.[7]

On August 16, apparently inspired by a letter published in the *Canton Register*, Lord Napier suggsted at a meeting of the English merchants that a chamber of commerce be organized to strengthen the unity of the English community and to form a channel of communication between the hong merchants and the superintendent. He was successful, at least for the time being, in overcoming the dissension among the English merchants, and the participants declared their intention to act unanimously on all future occasions.[8]

Having rallied the British merchants behind him, Napier proceeded to launch a new offensive. He regarded the visit of the three mandarins as a strong indication of lack of determination on the part of the local Chinese authorities. His next move was entirely unexpected by the Chinese. On August 26, he issued a public statement entitled "State of relations between China and Great Britain at present," which was translated into Chinese, printed, and circulated widely among the inhabitants of Canton. In this document he declared that it was the former governor-general who had caused him to come to Canton, and he complained indignantly about the manner in which he had been received by the local government. He revealed the proceedings of the conference with the three mandarins, stridently accused the governor-general of "ignorance and obstinacy" and of allowing the hong merchants to suspend the trade, and declared that as a result of Lu's refusal to accept his letter, "thousands of industrious Chinese who live by the European trade must suffer ruin and discomfort through the perversity of their government." Finally he emphasized the ceaseless effort that he would make to extend the trade to all China on principles of mutual benefit. He cautioned that the governor-general would find it as difficult to stop this effort as "to stop the current of the Canton river." [9]

Lord Napier had been contemplating the use of propaganda even be-fore the middle of August. In his report to Viscount Palmerston on August 14, he mentioned the desirability of publishing statements among the Chinese people: "The Chinese all read, and are eager for information; publish among them, and disseminate, far and wide, your intentions, — that is, all your intentions both towards the Government and them-selves." [10] He did not realize, however, that such measures would only doubly irritate the Chinese without in the least benefiting his cause. Under China's paternalistic system of rule, the publication of statements attacking the government constituted an intolerable outrage.

In response to this public statement, the governor-general issued several edicts to the hong merchants: on August 27, he advised them to admonish Lord Napier to obey the law; three days later he reprimanded them for having failed to prevent Napier's arrival at Canton; on the 31st he ordered them to demand his immediate departure from the city.[11]

At this critical moment, two abortive peace overtures were made. On the 28th, Howqua and Mowqua, the two senior hong merchants, came to notify the chief superintendent that four mandarins would come for a conference provided that the Chinese seating arrangement was adopted. This was refused. On September 2 and 3, negotiations were carried on between the hong merchants and the influential William Jardine, and a tentative agreement was reached. But since the provisions were rather unfavorable to the Chinese, Governor-General Lu was advised by his lieutenants not to accept them.[12]

The negotiations finally broke down on September 4, when a joint proclamation by the governor-general and the governor was published, once more enumerating all the complaints against the barbarian chief and prohibiting all commercial transactions between the Chinese and the English. All Chinese employed by the English were ordered to leave their jobs. A copy of this proclamation was pasted on a thin board, sus-pended at the gate of the British factory, and guarded by some twenty soldiers. Lord Napier went down to the gate at once and removed the proclamation. A large number of Chinese soldiers assembled in the neighborhood of the factory, blocking all the exits. Napier applied to Captain Blackwood for a squad of marines to be sent to the factory, and at the same time requested the captain to proceed to Whampoa with both of the British frigates.[13]

Official proclamations, in the traditional Chinese concept of law and government, were looked upon with awe and respect; they were no less sacred to the Chinese mind than the union flag was to the English. In April 1831 reports reached Peking that a government proclamation posted near the English factory had been defamed by the barbarians and that the latter had posted their own statements. These incidents offered sufficient grounds for the imperial government to censure the local officials at Canton.[14] After Lord Napier had removed the governor-general's proclamation and had circulated his own statement, there was little reason to hope for conciliation.

All supplies to the British were now cut off. The prohibition was so complete that in the following days Napier and his suite were compelled to live on salt meat conveyed from the warship.[15] On September 6, the eleven hong merchants transmitted an order from the governor-general to the British merchants to the effect that the forts and guardhouses were to allow English ships to leave the port but not to come in.

Two days later, Lord Napier issued a manifesto directed at the governor-general through the medium of the British Chamber of Commerce, citing numerous cases from the past two hundred years in which British individuals had had direct contact with the Chinese local government. The governor-general was attacked for wantonly stopping the trade and was warned that the order prohibiting the entry of British ships was a preliminary to war: if the British flag were fired upon, their frigates would certainly take revenge. Napier threatened to circulate this manifesto among the people if he did not hear from the provincial authorities within a week.[16]

The marines now arrived at the factory, and early in the morning of September 7, as the frigates *Imogene* and *Andromache* passed the Boca Tigris, the fort began firing blanks which were soon followed by shot. When the balls fell near the British vessels, the frigates returned the fire.[17] Two days later the frigates approached Tiger Island and were again fired upon; they fired return volleys, causing some damage to the battery. Late on the 11th, the frigates reached Whampoa. During the clashes one man was killed on each vessel and several were wounded. In his memorial to the emperor, Lu mentioned only that some tiles of the roofs of the forts were shattered and that his forces had suffered no casualties.[18]

The frigates were called to Whampoa to intimidate the Chinese, although Lord Napier's avowed reason was to "protect the treasure of the East India Company, the British subjects at Canton, and their property," as he wrote the secretary of the Chamber of Commerce on September

5.[19] He was convinced that a show of force would compel the Chinese to alter their course of action. On August 16, in a general meeting of the British merchants, Lord Napier announced that he expected the coming of the two frigates to "operate" on the governor-general and the hong merchants. The British merchants were told that, "if necessary, His Majesty's ships should move up to Whampoa; and if their presence there was not sufficient protection, they should anchor under the wall of the town." Napier thought that the local government would then speedily come to terms.[20]

Lord Napier had not foreseen any resistance when he ordered the frigates through the Bogue. In his reports to his own government, he frequently cited the military weakness of the Chinese. He wrote Earl Grey of India on August 21: "What can an army of bows, and arrows, and pikes, and shields do against a handful of British veterans? I am sure they would never for a moment dare to show a front. The batteries at the Bogue are contemptible; and not a man to be seen within them." This strong conviction no doubt guided all his proceedings in Canton, and he ignored the instructions from Palmerston that he not violate Chinese laws and usages and not appeal for the protection of British military or naval forces.

In his contempt for Chinese military strength, Napier also ignored Palmerston's instructions that he should be assisted by company men who had had experience in China. He disregarded the advice of John Davis, now his second in command. Since August 7, 1834, Davis had suggested a policy of remaining "perfectly quiet" and had objected to taking a coercive attitude toward the local government. In the latter part of August, he was dispatched to Macao, where he remained through the most crucial and stormy period of the negotiations; he did not see Lord Napier again until the retreat of the Mission. He had no access to Napier's instructions until after the latter's death. Instead of seeking the assistance of men who had long been servants of the company, Napier associated closely with the private merchants, especially Jardine, who took some part in the negotiations with the hong merchants in the closing phase of the dispute. To Lord Napier, the company's policy toward the Chinese had been much too soft. He accused it of having taught the Chinese that England "depended upon them for food and raiment, and that the Emperor was the only Monarch of the universe." [21]

To a large extent, the crisis resulted from Lord Napier's unrestrained ambition and desire for glory. He attempted to do more than his government had asked of him. He had publicly avowed that he proposed "to hand his name down to posterity as the man who had thrown open the wide field of the Chinese Empire to the British Spirit and Industry." Contrary to instructions, on August 21 he requested military forces from India for the purpose of taking possession of Hong Kong.[22]

It is understandable that Napier might have underestimated the military strength at Canton. Unlike his predecessor, Li Hung-pin, who was exiled to Urumchi in 1832 for incompetence in military affairs, the new governor-general, Lu K'un, was both incorruptible and adept in military matters. Lu, a native of Hopei province, obtained his *chin-shih* degree in 1799 and had built up a remarkable reputation. During the campaign against the Moslem rebels in 1806, he had been placed in charge of finances and supplies for the more than 36,000 troops sent to Sinkiang. For managing this extremely difficult operation, which had cost more than eleven million taels, he was awarded the title of Junior Guardian of the Heir Apparent and the Button of the First Rank. In the war against the Yao rebels of Hunan in 1831–32, Lu again demonstrated his military talent. For this service he was awarded the double-eyed peacock feather and the hereditary rank of *Ch'ing-ch'e tu-yü* of the first class.[23]

The governor of Canton, Ch'i Kung, a native of Shansi, had earned his *chin-shih* degree in 1796 at the age of nineteen. He won the title of Junior Guardian of the Heir Apparent in 1832 for his efforts in the same war against the Yao rebels. In the next year he was appointed governor. Tseng Sheng, the provincial commander-in-chief, was also a veteran of this war.[24]

As governor-general, Lu K'un immediately took steps to strengthen the military establishment at Canton. At the end of 1832, the emperor approved Lu's request for Hupeh military officers to train his troops. Meanwhile Ha-feng-a, the Tartar general and veteran of the Moslem war of 1830 in Sinkiang, made one hundred huge cannons and selected five hundred good soldiers for maritime defense.[25]

The governor-general began to make special military preparations as soon as Lord Napier arrived at the end of July. By the beginning of September he had additional boats cruising off Macao and three hundred soldiers from his command had been dispatched to the Portuguese settlement. The entrance of the British vessels into Whampoa had caused the infuriated Canton authorities to reinforce defenses along the river on a large scale.[26] Chains and rafts, which had frequently been used to blockade the river against the entrance of foreign ships, were called into service once again. The Chinese used twelve barges, each weighted down

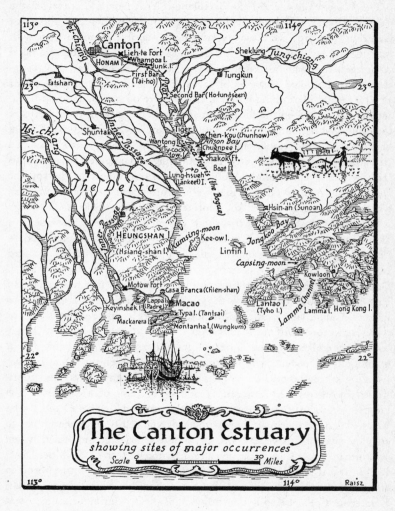

The Canton Estuary
showing sites of major occurrences
Scale 0 _____ 30 Miles

by one hundred thousand catties of rock, to block the Canton River at the fort of Lieh-te, about seven miles from the capital. They assembled twenty-eight craft from various districts as a cruising guard. Sixteen hundred soldiers were drawn from the forces of the governor-general, the governor, and the commander-in-chief and were dispatched to guard both shores of the river leading up to Canton.

The Chinese also barred the Ta-huang-chiao River, a tributary of the Canton River which leads to the city of Canton, with stakes and rafts. Guarding this area were twenty cruising boats, five hundred men with cannon, and one hundred men of the water forces, all from the command of the governor-general. Further down, near the second bar, at Ch'ang-chou-kang, they laid obstacles of rocks and stakes to cut off the exit of British vessels. Here three hundred troops were on guard, and additional forces were posted on the hills commanding Whampoa, in the suburbs of the capital, and around the factories, gates, and streets of the city.[27] More than twenty large vessels and over a hundred smaller boats equipped with firewood, straw, saltpeter, and sulphur, and manned by numerous soldiers and over a hundred divers, were in readiness to destroy the British ships by fire. These vessels were furnished with soaked mattresses, which the Chinese believed could protect them from shells.[28]

When it became apparent that there was no hope of peaceful settlement of the Napier affair, the Canton authorities dispatched a memorial to Peking on September 8, reporting all the events since the arrival of Lord Napier. The memorial was transmitted with such haste that it reached Peking on September 20, taking only thirteen days (normally it would have taken about twenty-two days). The emperor upheld the actions taken at Canton and cautioned the local authorities to be vigilant but not to resort to force without justification.[29]

On September 15, the governor-general and the governor jointly memorialized the emperor informing him of the entrance of the two frigates and of the military preparations. This document was also transmitted by express and reached Peking at the end of the month. The emperor was so furious at learning of the incident that on October 5 he wrote a rescript reprimanding the officials vigorously for their failure to stop the two British vessels. On the same day he issued an edict, which was dispatched to Canton at the extremely quick speed of 500 li per day,[30] reproving Lu K'un for neglecting defense work and permitting insult to the national pride. He ordered that the responsible officials be punished: Lieutenant-Colonel Kao I-yung, adjutant of the provincial naval force, was to wear the cangue in public; Li Tseng-chieh, commander-in-chief of the provincial water forces, though on leave during the crisis, was to be ousted; the governor-general himself was to be deprived of his title of Junior Guardian of the Heir Apparent and of the double-eyed peacock feather. At the same time, he ordered that the British be intimidated into submission; only if they bowed and acknowledged their misdemeanors should they be pardoned. If they remained stubborn, the emperor ordered, force must be used to drive them out.[31]

From the very beginning of the dispute, the Chinese had tried to divide and conquer by announcing that it was Lord Napier who had violated Chinese laws and that, as soon as he left Canton, trade would be resumed. This tactic began to bear fruit in early September when, without the knowledge of the superintendents, a group of English merchants, including members of such important concerns as Whiteman, Dent, and E. W. Brightman, petitioned the hoppo requesting the resumption of trade. In answer the hoppo promised that trade would be resumed as soon as the barbarian chief left Canton. Lord Napier, having lost the support of these people and under the governor-general's forceful threat of September 11, finally decided to retreat to Macao.

It was Dr. T. R. Colledge, Napier's surgeon, who negotiated an agreement with the Chinese whereby Napier was to leave for Macao on two Chinese government boats and the British frigates were to sail to Lintin. On the evening of September 21, Napier embarked on the slow and tedious trip to Macao, harrassed by the incessant beating of gongs and firing of firecrackers. When he reached Macao he was seriously ill, and at half past ten on the night of October 11, 1834, he died.[32]

The overriding reason for the failure of the Napier Mission was well summarized by the Duke of Wellington when he wrote that it was "an attempt made to force upon the Chinese authorities at Canton, an unaccustomed mode of communication with an authority, with whose power and of whose nature they had no knowledge, which commenced its proceedings by an assumption of power hitherto unadmitted."

Had Lord Napier been a man of more finesse, even though failure could not have been avoided, the relations of the two countries might not have become so precarious so quickly. A letter from an English reader had been published in the *Canton Register*, August 5, 1834, suggesting some alternative courses of action. Inasmuch as Napier was reluctant to communicate with the Chinese government through the hong merchants, it was suggested that a British chamber of commerce be formed as a medium of communication.[33] Could Lord Napier deliver a letter in English to the Chinese government and thus circumvent the issue of petition? Could he stay in Macao and have some British merchants negotiate through the hong merchants for his entry into Canton? Had he taken one of these measures, Napier might have had a somewhat better chance of establishing himself in Canton.

The Chinese, alarmed by the incursion of the British ships, now hastened to strengthen their maritime defenses. A brave and energetic officer named Kuan T'ien-p'ei replaced the old and ailing Li as the admiral of the Kwangtung water forces on October 10, 1834, and in the following year more cannon and forts were installed at the Bogue and other strategic places.[34] At the same time, new regulations were enacted and old rules were reiterated: foreigners were reminded that they were not to sail their men-of-war into the Bogue; that they were not allowed to bring firearms or women into Canton; and that they must hand in all petitions, except those which brought complaints against the hong merchants, through the latter group. In addition, the new regulations restricted the number of Chinese that could be employed by foreign houses. Each factory could hire only two Chinese watchmen and four Chinese water carriers; an individual foreign merchant could hire but one Chinese, a watchman. The employment of Chinese servants was prohibited.[35]

The "Napier fizzle," as it was locally called, was a wedge that cut deeply into Anglo-Chinese relations. It made the character of the "barbarian" more unfathomable to the Chinese and doubled the British merchants' disdain and distrust of the Chinese.

THE QUIESCENT INTERIM.

John Francis Davis succeeded Lord Napier as chief superintendent, and Sir George Best Robinson was moved up to the office of second superintendent on October 13, 1834. Davis had arrived at Canton in 1813 as a junior writer in the factory. He soon undertook an intensive study of the Chinese language, being relieved of all other duties at the time, and by October 1814 he was able to translate a document from the Hsiang-shan magistrate into English. In the following January, his translation of San-yu-lou (Three dedicated rooms), a Chinese tale, was ready for publication.[36] Davis rose rapidly. He was appointed one of the interpreters for the Amherst Mission and in 1825 was made Chinese secretary and deputy superintendent of imports of the company. Two years later he was put on the Select Committee and on January 17, 1832, with the departure of C. Marjoribanks, succeeded to the presidency.[37]

Davis' long association with the company and his prominent position on the Select Committee nurtured in him a conservative point of view that was quite out of sympathy with the new free-trade movement. His familiarity with Chinese customs and institutions prevented him from agreeing with Lord Napier's bombastic approach to handling the local government. Thus Davis found no red carpet rolled out before him as he started his duties as chief superintendent. The *Canton Register*, the vociferous organ of the free traders that owed its creation to Alexander Matheson, immediately responded. Its editors lauded Davis' "personal character for good sense, consistency, and moderation of conduct," recognized his literary accomplishments and knowledge of the Chinese language, but they could not forget his "unfriendly sentiments . . . recorded in his evidence before the House of Commons" and an even stronger stand expressed four years earlier in a *Quarterly Review* article that they assumed had come from Davis' pen. The *Register* did not mince words in its criticism of Davis' appointment: "One brought up in the late School of monopoly can never therefore be a fit Representative and controller of the free traders who . . . 'cherish high notions of their claims and privileges, and regard themselves as the depositaries of the true principles of British Commerce.' " [38] Since it was well known that Davis' expressed intention was to wait quietly either for overtures from the Chinese or for new instructions from his home government, the *Canton Register* editorial went on to warn him that if he undertook to negotiate on any terms but those Lord Napier had insisted on, namely "direct communication with the constituted Authorities and not with Hong merchants," he would betray British commercial interests in China. [39]

Meanwhile, toward the end of 1834, eighty-five British merchants, including Jardine and Matheson, petitioned His Britannic Majesty in Council to dispatch a diplomat with plenipotentiary powers (not one who had engaged in trade at Canton) in a ship of the line, accompanied by two frigates, three or four armed vessels of light draft, and a steamer, all fully manned to proceed up the east coast of China to a station "as near to the capital . . . as may be found most expedient," to demand ample reparation for the insults to Lord Napier and the expansion of trade to other ports. Writing to Viscount Palmerston on January 19, 1835, Davis denounced this petition as "crude and ill-digested," saying that it represented the opinion of only "a portion of the English traders at Canton (for some of the most respectable houses declined signing it)." Aware of his unpopularity, Davis now resigned in favor of Sir George Robinson under the technical arrangement of "absence on leave" and embarked in the *Asia* for England on January 21. [40] He had served as superintendent for only three months and ten days.

Before his departure, Davis had directed his colleagues to continue his unaggressive policy, and Robinson did his best to do so during his term as chief superintendent (January 21, 1835, to December 14, 1836). To those satisfied with the status quo and the lucrative trade that was being carried on so smoothly, "his skill, temper, and caution produced most excellent effects: everything seemed to have returned much to the old channel," and no complaints, either from the English or the Chinese, were heard.[41] But since this attitude was no longer the dominant one in Canton or in London, Robinson's subsequent resignation was accompanied by no official recognition.

Robinson was by no means a brilliant, shrewd, or vigorous man. Although he had joined the company as early as 1820, he was never prominent in the hierarchy of the Canton factory; in 1833, the last season of the monopoly, seven men ranked above him.[42] In 1828 he had been reprimanded by the president of the Select Committee for being remiss in obeying certain orders. He protested to the committee in a letter that closed: "Finding that my best endeavours have only exposed me to what I feel to be your very unjust censure, I must beg to decline an office the duties of which render me constantly liable to such vexatious and frivolous remarks." He was told that it was not up to him to decline an assigned duty and that he was expected to obey orders cheerfully. This episode, and his being heir to a baronetcy, led H. B. Morse to dub him "a bad case of swelled head."

In November 1828, after the reconstitution of the Select Committee, Robinson was transferred to other duties, and at this time he tendered an apology for his previous impropriety, assuring the committee that he would devote his utmost efforts to the new job. But on the same day he applied for leave to go to England, even though he had just returned nine months earlier. When this request was rejected, he applied for leave to go to Macao for a change of air. Receiving another rejection, he applied again in December and was finally granted a leave. Meanwhile he was severely censured for a letter he had written to the Select Committee in November.

After assuming the position of chief superintendent in January 1835, it did not occur to Robinson to ascertain the majority views of the British merchants in Canton or to learn which way the wind was blowing in London. His actions were based only on what he believed to be good for the trade. He was so naive as to have written Palmerston: "Whenever His Majesty's Government direct us to prevent British vessels from engaging in the [opium] traffic, we can enforce any order to that effect, but a more certain method would be to prohibit the growth of the poppy and manufacture of opium in British India." [43] This reads almost like a passage from an edict of Lin Tse-hsü. Robinson obviously believed that the British government was sincerely interested in discouraging the opium trade.

The immediate task that Robinson faced, like his predecessors, was to establish direct contact with the Chinese government and to assert the equality of British government representatives with the Chinese officials. The Chinese, on the other hand, repeatedly enjoined the English to send a letter home without delay "calling for the selection and appointment of a commercial man thoroughly acquainted with the great principles of dignified respectability, to come as a *taepan* [*tai-pan*] to Canton, to control and direct affairs of buying and selling." They particularly warned that in no circumstances should "an official chief be again appointed to come to Canton, — causing detriment to a right course of things." [44] Robinson made no endeavor to establish direct intercourse with the local government; he declared that he would follow Davis' policy until he received fresh instructions. But the instructions never came.

The majority of Robinson's dispatches to Viscount Palmerston and the Duke of Wellington were in the nature of defenses of his policies. In a dispatch to Palmerston dated from Macao, October 16, 1835, he outlined his intentions: "I trust your Lordship will approve of the perfectly quiescent line of policy I have considered it my duty to maintain under the present aspect of affairs. . . . My anxious endeavours will be used for the maintenance of tranquillity and the prevention of disorders and difficulties of any kind." He went on to contend that "the less we have to do with the Chinese authorities and people, save when appealed to in cases of aggression and injustice, which I trust will be rare and trifling, the less apprehension may be entertained of those perplexing difficulties in which we are liable to be involved."

Full of self-congratulations, at the end of the first year of his administration Robinson concluded a report to Palmerston: "It is with extreme satisfaction I assure your Lordship that I have never witnessed, during a period of sixteen years passed in the China service, a more quiet, regular, or I trust, prosperous season than the present; and I can only pledge myself, that I shall never wilfully incur any hazard or danger to the important trade confided to my care." Four months later he again boasted, "It affords me great pleasure to intimate to your Lordship, that, after one of the most active, and, I believe, successful seasons ever remembered in

China, there exists at the present period of relaxation the most perfect tranquillity and quiet."

The official status of Robinson's commission was not recognized by the Chinese authorities in Canton or even by the Portuguese government at Macao. Apparently to further avoid any contact with Chinese officials, Robinson conceived the idea of taking up residence on a ship. On November 25, 1835, he moved aboard the *Louisa*, a seventy-ton cutter, without waiting for permission from his home government, and at Lintin, among the receiving ships, he spent the rest of his term of office. He assured Palmerston that "a short period will exhibit how far the present plan of an authority established either afloat or without the river, will prove efficacious and beneficial." On April 18, 1836, he reported the result: "The Chinese are not . . . disposed to interfere with the exercise of our functions and powers outside the river, and, so long as we do not attempt to go to Canton, will take no notice whatever of our proceedings."

Robinson's two years as superintendent could indeed be summed up as a time of peace and tranquillity. He did little beyond the routine task of attesting the manifests of British ships at Lintin and issuing port clearances. His only outside work of any importance was to send to the Foreign Office the information about China gathered by Charles Gutzlaff, the official interpreter. These papers later became the substance of Gutzlaff's book, *China Opened*, published in 1838.

The only exciting moments in Britain's relations with China during Robinson's incumbency were caused by incidents involving the *Argyle* and the *Fairy Queen*, both of which entailed unavoidable contact with the Chinese. On January 22, 1835, twelve men in a boat belonging to the British ship *Argyle* were seized by some Chinese bandits forty miles west of Macao. They demanded five hundred dollars as ransom for their prisoners. The three superintendents jointly prepared a report (not a letter, since Napier's communications in letter form had not been accepted by the Chinese), requesting help in bringing about the release of the English captives. The document was presented at one of the gates of Canton by Captain Elliot (the third superintendent), the captain of the *Argyle*, and their interpreter, Charles Gutzlaff. They arrived at the gate on the morning of February 1, 1835, and were treated "with the greatest indignity" by the soldiers guarding it. A Chinese officer attempted to grasp the hilt of Captain Elliot's sword, and they struggled for several minutes until Elliot fell to the ground. They were then "forcibly dragged and pushed through two wicket gates," and soon a military mandarin, several linguists, and two higher mandarins came upon the scene. The mandarins contemptuously refused to accept the document because it was not a petition, in spite of Gutzlaff's loud announcement that Elliot was His Britannic Majesty's Officer. The linguists twice offered to accept the document, but the English would not give it to them. The upshot of the episode was that the British attempt to assert equality by direct communication failed; however, the twelve English captives were released on February 19.

The *Fairy Queen* affair well illustrates Robinson's policy of avoiding contact with the Chinese government and the divergence of opinion between him and the free-trade group of British merchants. Upon the arrival of the British ship *Fairy Queen* early in December 1835, her captain dispatched an officer in charge of the mails to Canton in a Chinese fastboat. Since the fastboat had been illegally hired, the officer was seized and detained by some minor Chinese officers. He later wrote a letter to his captain earnestly requesting the payment of five hundred dollars to the bearer of the letter for his release. On Robinson's advice the letter bearer was detained aboard the *Fairy Queen*. The next morning another letter came demanding a smaller amount.

The captain wanted to rescue his officer by force, but was dissuaded from this course by Robinson, who immediately forwarded a communication to T. A. Gibb, the consignee of the *Fairy Queen* in Canton. Before Robinson received Gibb's reply, the detained officer was released. In his report to Palmerston, Robinson explained apologetically that, even if he had been stationed in Canton, he could not have "prevented mischievous consequences until too late." He maintained that as an officer of the government, totally unconnected with the trade, his influence with the hong merchants "would have been secondary to that of Mr. Gibb, or any other guardian of commercial influence about to load the ship, — a prospective source of profit to them. In all cases of this sort, the officers of His Majesty's Government if at Canton, must be viewed by the Hong merchants, who derive no advantage from them, in a very insignificant light, compared to wealthy firms or individual British subjects largely engaged in commerce." [45] It is clear that Robinson had no intention of sending a protest to the Chinese government, and that even if he had been in Canton he would still have managed the affair through the hong merchants. In Canton, however, the British subjects took an entirely different view. The *Canton Register* published a special supplement covering the affair, and the editorial expressed growing impatience.[46]

Robinson's dispatches, constantly apologetic about his actions, seldom abusive of the Chinese, and occasionally grumbling about the meagerness of his pay, must have bored Palmerston considerably. Yet Robinson's repeated entreaties for new and clear instructions brought no results. Legally the power of the superintendent was very limited. Robinson had no criminal or admiralty jurisdiction over his countrymen. In dealing with the Chinese, as he pointed out himself, he was no better equipped than the supercargoes of the East India Company.[47] There was no reason to expect more from him.

Palmerston's reticence was by no means an indication of his lack of concern for the China problem. Bypassing the chief and the second superintendents, he had been gathering information from Charles Elliot, the third member of the Commission, for Elliot had been carrying on a private correspondence with Lennox Conyngham of the Foreign Office. In one of these letters, dated January 28, 1836, Elliot complained that Sir George Robinson "has virtually suspended the functions of his colleagues. The Chief Superintendent has only informed me of what he is going to do or not to do." He regretted that Robinson did not see clearly enough the strong necessity of "taking up the cautious and conciliatory instructions of the Government with an earnest spirit to give them effect." Elliot observed that Robinson's conciliatory policy was "not very generally approved" among the British subjects at Canton and added:

The plain truth is that we have "two Houses" here, and they are so desperately angry with each other that their feuds colour their opinions upon every subject under the sun. One set of gentlemen are *absolutely in a passion* with the whole Chinese government and people because they are very ill-inclined to another set of gentlemen who, they imagine, are willing to conciliate the Chinese and go on smuggling quietly. I wish I could add that the moderate party were the stronger, but that is not at all the case. The ardent gentlemen have it hollow in point of numbers.

Captain Elliot hoped that the government would make known its disapproval of the general temper of the majority of the British merchants at Canton. He had opposed the late Lord Napier's hard-headed approach and attributed Napier's failure largely to his personal pretensions. Elliot went on to say that he did not subscribe to any territorial designs on the Chinese, since they would jeopardize the existing prosperous trade; nor did he place much stock in the idea of making a commercial treaty with China. He even expressed grave doubts as to the advisability of dispatching a high official to China. It was his conviction that "the pervading principle of the Chinese policy in respect to the European governments . . . was to keep the peace." Once the provincial authorities were convinced of the English officers' desire to prevent difficulties, he believed, they would come to adopt a course of accommodation. He thought the office of the superintendent should be able to win the confidence of the Chinese government within the framework of the existing instructions if the British officers were cautious and conciliatory in their conduct toward the Chinese.[48]

CAPTAIN ELLIOT AND THE STRUGGLE FOR EQUALITY

After the failure of Lord Napier's policy of force and the loud protests against Robinson's undynamic policy of retreat to life on a ship, Elliot's middle-of-the-road proposal had a strong appeal. Elliot's letter was received on June 6, 1836, and on the 7th Palmerston removed Robinson from his post. On June 15 he appointed Elliot chief superintendent, and Elliot took office on December 14, when the order reached China.[49]

Charles Elliot, born in 1801, was the son of the Honorable Hugh Elliot, holder of several high offices, including the governorship of Madras. In 1815 young Elliot entered the Royal Navy as first-class volunteer on the *Leviathan* on the Mediterranean station, and in the next year he became a midshipman and served on the *Minden* during the bombardment of Algiers. He subsequently served with distinction in India, on the African coast, and in the West Indies. He attained the rank of lieutenant in June 1822 and was promoted to the rank of captain on August 28, 1828.

After a successful naval career, Elliot virtually retired from the navy in 1828, being actively employed in the service of the Colonial or Foreign Office. From 1830 to 1834 he was Protector of Slaves and a member of the Court of Policy of British Guiana.[50] In 1833 he was ordered home to put his knowledge of slavery to work — the government was then deliberating the issue of abolition of slavery in the colonies. He accepted the position of master attendant in the Napier Mission with reluctance, because he had hoped for higher authority and greater responsibility. Shortly before his departure from China, Davis had given full endorsement of Elliot's ability in a communication to the Foreign Office, stating that "the talents, information, and temper of that gentleman would render him eminently suited to the chief station in this country." [51] Thus Elliot's advancement to the chief superintendency was not a hasty or casual decision.

As chief of the commission, Elliot lost no time in trying to establish himself in the provincial capital. He saw an opportunity in the new governor-general, Teng T'ing-chen (Tang), who had assumed office only in February and was, compared to his predecessor, relatively free from suspicion and prejudice against the British. Elliot immediately announced his appointment to the governor-general by a notification dated December 14 and drawn up in the form of a *pin* (*ping*), or petition, in which he styled himself not *tai-pan*, but *yuan-chih*, "an employee from afar," a term apparently coined especially for this occasion.[52] The whole document was worded with meticulous courtesy. Elliot asked four leading British merchants to transfer the document to the senior hong merchant for transmission to the governor-general. The translation of this paper, Elliot wrote Palmerston, was handled in the manner that the Select Committee had been accustomed to use; it was superscribed with the Chinese character *pin*, carrying the meaning of a petition from an inferior to a superior. It was then placed in an open envelope addressed to the senior hong merchant. Realizing that such a procedure would be frowned on by Palmerston, Elliot defended his actions by maintaining that his willingness to respect Chinese customs was "the course at once most consonant with the magnanimity of the British nation, and with the substantial interests at stake, in the maintenance of peaceful commercial relations with this Empire."[53] He minimized the hong merchants' function, representing it as merely that of a messenger.

The governor-general, considering the phraseology of Elliot's communication sufficiently submissive, deputed two magistrates, a subprefect, and the senior hong merchant to investigate. The deputies found that Elliot was a "fourth-grade employee of Great Britain" and had been appointed to supervise British merchants and sailors. The Portuguese and other nationals at Macao had testified that Elliot was a peaceful man, and there were no other complications. His title was different from *tai-pan*, the one used before, but the governor-general thought that the difference was only nominal. He therefore memorialized the emperor recommending acceptance of Elliot. The emperor gave his approval on the condition that Elliot be subject to the regulations and terms which had governed the former *tai-pan*. He was to stay at Canton during the trading season and retire to Macao during the inactive months.

In the middle of March 1837, the emperor's approval was received at Canton, and on March 29 the passport issued by the hoppo for the superintendent reached Macao. Captain Elliott arrived at Canton on April 12, proud that "for the first time in the history of our intercourse with Canton the principle is most formally admitted, that an officer of a foreign sovereign, whose functions are purely public, should reside in a city of the Empire." Elliot's optimism was not really warranted at this stage, since the Chinese had not yet modified their views. The governor-general and the emperor had pointed out that "though the title is not the same as that of the *tai-pan*, the business of controlling does not differ," and Elliot's much-stressed statements that his functions were purely public and that he could not engage in trade were not correctly understood by the Chinese.

Apparently as a result of inaccuracies in the translation, the Chinese thought that Elliot's job was merely to control the merchants and sailors, and not to control trade (*pu-k̲uan mao-i*). As it later developed, after some effort on the part of Elliot, his communications to the governor-general were sealed before going through the hong merchants, but the same practice did not apply to communications going in the other direction. Official Chinese communications to Elliot were not addressed to him at all: "They speak of me, not to me." The communications were in the form of injunctions to persons with whom Elliot had "no congeniality of pursuit." The status of the captain, as far as the Chinese government was concerned, was still vague.

From the day he arrived in Canton (April 12, 1837) until the crisis brought about by the arrival of Lin Tse-hsü, Elliot faced two principal problems. The first was to establish direct communication with the Chinese government on terms of equality. This was no easy task, since it entailed nothing less than a revolution in China's age-old institutions for conducting foreign affairs. The second and perhaps more important problem was to secure and expand British trade, an inseparable part of which was the opium trade, and to cope wtih the rapidly increasing smuggling within the Bogue carried on by armed English boats. The distinction should be made, as will be shown later, between opium smuggled ashore from outside the Bogue by Chinese and similar smuggling done by Englishmen. The Chinese operations were carried out under Elliot's tacit protection, but smuggling by Englishmen alarmed him because he feared it might harm other branches of British trade.

In a dispatch dated July 22, 1836, Lord Palmerston had specifically prohibited Elliot from channeling his addresses to the Chinese government through the hong merchants, for this arrangement would imply that the commission was under the control of the hong merchants. Elliot was ordered to insist that communications from the governor-general come to him directly or through responsible officers of the Chinese government. Furthermore, Elliot's addresses to the governor-general were not to be superscribed with the character *pin*.

Before receiving this dispatch, however, Captain Elliot had already communicated with the governor-general. Unsure that his line of conduct would be approved by the home government, at the same time he wrote a private letter to the Foreign Office asking for "one line by the overland mail to Bombay just to tell me whether my movements are to be fatal to me or not." Upon receipt of clear instructions in Palmerston's dispatch, he realized that he would have to stiffen his approach to the Chinese authorities.

Shortly before his departure from Macao for Canton, Elliot received a letter from the government of Singapore informing him that seventeen Chinese sailors had been rescued from a sinking junk by an English ship and had been escorted to that port, where they were waiting for arrangements to be made for their return home. Seizing upon this opportunity, Elliot wrote a communication to the governor-general to be transmitted just one day before his scheduled arrival in Canton, so as not to give the governor-general time to reply before the official announcement of his arrival was received. This communication was designed to make it perfectly clear to the Chinese authorities that Elliot was an officer, not a merchant, and that he had far-ranging political connections. It was also hoped that the gratifying nature of the news contained in this document would ensure a favorable response to the announcement of his arrival.

The communication, which concluded with the phrase, "The interchange of these charities cannot fail to strengthen the bonds of peace and good-will between the two nations," surprised and alarmed the governor-general. He replied on April 19, 1837, in the usual form of an injunction to the hong merchants, saying that between "the Great Emperor and the small, the petty, how can there exist anything like 'bonds of peace and good-will'"? He chastised Elliot for deviating from the established rules, for using absurd phrases like "your honorable country" in place of "Celestial Empire," and he enjoined Elliot to have all further communications closely perused by the senior hong merchants to avoid similar errors in the future.

On receiving this edict, Captain Elliot at once ordered the senior merchant Howqua to appear in his office within one hour, or else he, Elliot, "would leave Canton in a few hours." Howqua came and found, much to his distress, that Elliot wanted to return the edict that Howqua had just forwarded to him. After some pleading, Howqua succeeded in persuading Elliot at least to explain the objectionable points contained in the paper. Elliot agreed to keep it for two more days, until the morning of the 22nd, when Howqua was to return and pick up both the edict and Elliot's explanations.

This agreement was carried out. In the note of explanation to the governor-general, Elliot protested that he was a foreign officer and that he could not therefore "submit his addresses to the Governor, to the knowledge and approbation of the Hong merchants, before they are forwarded." Moreover, he declared, in the future he could receive only sealed communications from the governor-general sent directly to himself, not to the merchants. At the same time, Elliot told Howqua that if the matter were not brought to a satisfactory conclusion within four days, he would leave Canton, taking the outer passage (the main channel) without bothering to ask for a passport. When Howqua pleaded for more time, the deadline was finally fixed at midnight on April 28.

Two days later Howqua came to inform Elliot that Governor-General Teng had declared that it was beyond his power to communicate with Elliot directly, but he admitted that the superintendent's objections were justified. The governor-general was willing to concede to Elliot the right to communicate with him by means of sealed documents sent via the hong merchants, and he was also willing to send his replies to Elliot through the three senior merchants, who held honorary official ranks, rather than through the Cohong as a whole. Not wishing to push the Chinese too far, Elliot agreed to accept Teng's edict provided the language were not disrespectful to the British government and that it met his government's final approval. Teng's edict was therefore delivered on April 25. A month later, writing to Lord Palmerston, Elliot presented his views that "if the actual manner of the intercourse, (direct with the Governor [the governor-general] — indirect from him) be not best suited to the condition of circumstances in this country, at least, its further modification had better be left to time and favourable opportunities." [54]

In his reply Lord Palmerston expressed the government's approbation of Elliot's actions, but at the same time urged him, "you will not fail, on every suitable opportunity, to continue to press for recognition on the part of the Chinese authorities, of your right to receive, direct from the Viceroy [governor-general], sealed communications addressed to yourself, without the intervention of Hong merchants."

Captain Elliot's next step was to secure some relaxation of the restrictions on his freedom of movement around the Canton-Macao area. Under the traditional system, servants of the company had to live in Macao during the off-season, they had to have a passport, and they had to travel through the inner passage on Chinese boats. This process usually entailed a delay of at least ten days. Elliot, mindful of this inconvenience, agreed to abide by the old rules simply because he feared that "if this point had been pressed at that moment, I should awaken the suspicions of the Gov't, and risk the success of the main object in view." Thus, when the trading season was over, he left Canton by the normal procedure. He did, however, harbor an intention to "seize the first favourable occasion for a return by the outer passage."

A few days after Elliot's return to Macao, he received a report from Whampoa that a minor mutiny was taking place on a British ship. He immediately boarded the *Louisa*, which had not passed the Bogue since the Napier dispute in 1834, and came up through the outer passage. At the same time, he notified Governor-General Teng that "sudden and urgent occasions for his immediate presence in the provincial city frequently occur" during the retirement at Macao, "both for the dispatch of public business and the quelling of disturbances on board the English shipping at Whampoa." The delay involved in getting the "chop" (an official document, in this case a passport) was a hindrance to the performance of his duties. He requested permission "to repair to Canton in his own boat whenever these sudden necessities present themselves," and promised to report his arrivals and departures.

By an edict of June 1, 1837, the governor-general granted Elliot's request: "The said superintendent's presentation, 'that if, during the period of his stay at Macao he should have affairs to attend to at Canton or Whampoa, he fears that to be required always to wait till his application for a passport is answered will be productive of injurious delays,' is a correct statement of the matter, and it is my duty to permit him from time to time, as business may occur, to come up and down in an European boat, not making it necessary to apply for a passport." The only condition was that, before his departure and return to Macao, he must file a report with the subprefect at Macao for the information of the hoppo and the governor-general. The edict was also, as usual, tempered with some celestial flavor: "But he must keep his station, and diligently attend to his official duties. . . . Let him, on no account presume, when without business, to frame pretexts for moving, lest he draw on himself investigation." The next day Elliot happily reported to London that this edict formally placed him "on a different footing from any foreigner who has ever yet resided in this country."

In the meantime the recognition of the superintendents by the Portuguese authorities at Macao was officially secured. In the course of 1836, Lord Palmerston had carried on negotiations with the Portuguese government, with the result that the local government at Macao had received instructions concerning conduct in all matters relating to the British Commission. These difficulties were thus smoothed over by early July 1837.

Elliot now found a new opportunity to argue for direct communication with the Chinese authorities in August and September when he received three successive edicts from the provincial government, asking him to report to the crown of England on the opium ships infesting the coast of Kwangtung and the eastern coast of China. The governor-general and governor both enjoined Elliot to have these opium ships removed. Elliot replied that the wishes of the Canton authorities, being expressed in edicts of "no more authentic and formal shape" than those addressed to native merchants, could not be submitted to his government. Knowing that the Chinese were most anxious to appeal the opium question to the British Crown, Elliot declared that, because of the improper mode of communication, no intelligence of the opium question had ever reached his government.

Elliot also informed the governor-general that a British warship had recently visited the coast of Fukien province. The governor-general stationed there had sent his instructions concerning the arrival of the ship to certain officers of that province, and his message was delivered to the British ship under their seals. Elliot now demanded the same manner of public intercourse. "If your Excellency, in your wisdom, shall judge fit to conform to this same practice, whenever it be desired to lay communications before His [Elliot was unaware that Victoria had acceded to the throne] Majesty, all difficulty upon the subject will be removed."

In replying to this address, the governor-general and the governor called it a "specious document" and asserted that the rules of the celestial empire required that all commands to foreigners be transmitted through the hong merchants. They did, however, yield on the point of the urgent opium question. They would "adapt their proceedings to the occasion" and instruct the prefect and the commandant of police of Kuang-chou prefecture to communicate their wishes to the superintendent. In return, the superintendent was asked to send away the opium-receiving ships and to report on the matter to his king, so that opium ships could be prevented from coming again. On the next day, September 29, 1837, the prefect and police commandant issued commands to Elliot as instructed.

The third round of the fight over modes of communication took place in November 1837 and led to a serious crisis. On November 21, Captain Elliot received instructions from Palmerston directing him to insist on more direct official communication and the elimination of the character *pin*. In a message of November 23, Elliot explained his government's position to the governor-general. He concluded by saying: "If your Excellency shall think fit always to forward your pleasure directly to the address of the undersigned, through the Kwang Chow Foo [the Kuang-chou prefect] and the Kwang Heep [the Kuang-chou commandant], as was lately done [referring to the communication of September 29, 1837], and will further consent to receive his respectful addresses in reply, without the specification of the character *Pin*, all difficulty will be removed."

The *pin* did not appear on this document; instead, the characters *ta-chien* and *ching-shang* were affixed after the names of the addressee and the sender, respectively. The new device, *ching-shang*, translated by Elliot's interpreter as "presented before his high place," had never been used in Chinese government documents and consequently would not arouse objections from Her Majesty's government. It was, however, used in informal correspondence among friends of equal status.

This document, transmitted through the senior hong merchants, greatly vexed the governor-general. After considering it, he instructed the merchants to return it to Elliot with his own marginal remarks, "Cannot be permitted." Following this rebuttal, Elliot prepared another note, dated November 25 and superscribed in the same new style, in which he stated that he had received a very strict order from his government containing new instructions with regard to the mode of communication, and he requested that the chief civil and military officers of the district be sent to learn the details and receive a copy of the letter. "The least mistake or omission in the communication of these instructions," cautioned Elliot, "might be attended with unhappy consequences."

This note was delivered at the city gate by Morrison and Elmslie, Elliot's interpreter and secretary. On the next day, the 26th, the hong merchants brought Elliot the governor-general's reply. Elliot declined to receive it, despite the merchants' assurances that the edict was a very courteous explanation of the difficulties involved in deviating from the ancient custom with respect to communicating with foreigners. At this point Elliot refused to discuss the matter with them, the merchants, any further; he handed them a third note that placed the responsibility for interrupting communications entirely on the Chinese side.

This third note was soon brought back unopened by the hong merchants, who explained that the governor-general had refused it because of the improper superscriptions. Elliot protested, that inasmuch as the governor-general had received two previous addresses in the same form, his refusal of the third would constitute a just ground of complaint against him by the British government to the emperor. He then gave them an unsealed copy of the third note, telling them to do with it as they saw fit — report it to the governor-general or not. At any rate, he told them, he was going to strike the flag and proceed to Macao in five days, on December 2. The merchants assured Elliot that the governor-general saw no insuperable objection to the idea of direct communication, but he was not able to sanction the new superscriptions used on Elliot's addresses. Elliot, however, remained adamant.[55]

After circulating a notice among British residents informing them that all communications between him and the governor-general had ceased, Captain Elliot proceeded to Macao. He had been in Canton for only seven and a half months. Although he left Canton in an abrupt manner, he felt contented. The establishment of direct intercourse with Chinese officials, in his judgment, was only a matter of time. Shortly after his arrival in Macao, Elliot wrote to Palmerston. He said that his official status was virtually recognized by the Chinese and that the governor-general would be willing to communicate with him if he did not insist on the point of superscription. The Foreign Office gave Elliot its full support. In a dispatch of June 15, 1838, Palmerston assured Elliot that the government considered him "perfectly right in retiring from Canton to Macao." [56]

In February, March, and April 1838, there was a vast increase in the number of English boats engaged in the illicit opium traffic inside and outside the Bogue, and these vessels frequently came into armed conflict with Chinese government junks. More drastic preventive measures, either on the provincial authorities' initiative or by order of Peking, were imminent. Elliot became anxious to resume contact with the Chinese government. On March 17 he prepared a statement declaring that the long absence of responsible authorities over his countrymen "may produce dangerous and deeply-rooted irregularity leading to violent modes of remedy: and in such proceedings it is to be apprehended innocent men might suffer to the great risk of the maintenance of peace between the two countries." He proposed, pending further instructions from England, that his addresses to the governor-general be directed to the Kuang-chou prefect and the commandant, who were to open them and lay them before the governor-general. The governor-general's commands were likewise to be transmitted to them to be copied and sent to Elliot. On the communications between the two officers and Elliot, no super-scriptures except their names and titles would be necessary, since they were all of the same rank, the fourth grade.[57] If the governor-general accepted this proposal, Elliot would return forthwith to Canton to resume his urgent duties.

Under Elliot's direction, Morrison showed this statement to Howqua and told him that he should feel free to make Elliot's opinions and position known to the governor-general. This Howqua did when Teng returned from an official tour in early April. Later Howqua returned the paper to Morrison with the message that the governor-general had seen the paper but could not agree to its terms. "Should any serious disaster ensue," Elliot wrote Palmerston afterwards, "threatening the lives of Her Majesty's subjects engaged in these pursuits [illegal traffic between Lintin and Canton], (and in my own judgment this result is perfectly probable,) I shall not fail to found the strongest remonstrances against such extreme measures upon the Governor's rejection of these last proposals."

At the end of May, Elliot's request that British men-of-war be sent to the Canton River area was granted, and he predicted that the problem of direct and equal communications with China would be solved with little difficulty when the ships arrived. When Rear-Admiral Frederick L. Maitland reached Macao, Elliot took care to caution him never to forward or receive any communication to or from the Chinese authorities except on an equal basis. A few days following Maitland's arrival, Elliot received a document from the subprefect of Macao (*chün-min-fu*). Because the inside of the document bore the character *yü* (command), Elliot returned it unread with a written remark that he would only read it after the mistake was corrected. Soon Elliot received an edict from the governor-general, drawn up in the old form and addressed to the hong merchants, from whom it was transmitted to Elliot through a linguist.

This document was returned unopened with the same explanation. Undoubtedly these two messages from the Chinese officials demanded the departure of the British men-of-war from Chinese waters.

At this time Captain Elliot was afraid that the unexplained presence of the British fleet might alarm the Chinese. So he made a trip to Canton on July 25 and had Morrison and Elmslie deliver to the city gate an open paper to the governor-general setting forth an explanation of the innocuous object of the fleet's visit. The paper was returned that evening by the three senior hong merchants for want of the character *pin*. The merchants at the same time repeated the assertion that the governor-general was a peace-loving and understanding man and was willing to go as far as he could to accommodate the British. Elliot should not object to receiving communications addressed through them, they continued, because they were indeed mandarins. This of course did not convince Elliot who, having completed his mission in Canton, returned to Macao.

On December 3, over two hundred catties of opium belonging to James Innes were seized while being landed in front of the factories from a boat. This affair, we shall see in the next chapter, touched off a grave crisis and trade was stopped. The Innes incident and the seriousness of the smuggling situation inside the river compelled Elliot to return to Canton on December 12, 1838, after an absence of more than a year, during which he had continued to press for direct communication whenever opportunities arose, kept a watchful eye on the smuggling, and engineered the Maitland affair. His next step was to re-establish communications with the Chinese government. On the 23rd, he sent the governor-general an address, superscribed with the *pin*, requesting the resumption of intercourse. This document, worded in an unpretentious manner and totally different in tone from his earlier uncompromising messages, bespoke his desperate desire to put an end to the smuggling within the Bogue, which was threatening the lives and property of many innocent men, Chinese and foreign.

The immediate source of the trouble, Elliot told the governor-general, was the extensive opium traffic within the Bogue; and for that reason he had already given orders to all British boats engaged in such operations to leave the river within three days. The fact that these injunctions had not been fulfilled he attributed to his lack of authority. He entreated the governor-general to give his proceedings official sanction, transmitting the reply through the Kwangchow prefect and the commandant rather than the hong merchants, so that all those engaged in the illicit traffic might know that he had received the governor-general's support.

The governor-general, also eager to clear the river of the opium boats, promptly granted Elliot's request, sending his message through the two Chinese officials, as Elliot desired. He made it clear, however, that this procedure was only for an emergency; future communications would still be transmitted through the hong merchants. Moreover, the governor-general actually sent two identical copies of his reply, the first through the merchants in the usual manner and the second through the two officials. In a second address, dated December 28, 1838, Elliot requested that the practice of transmission via the officials be extended to cover all affairs of importance. To this the governor-general replied the next day, in the form of a command to the three senior hong merchants, agreeing that "when hereafter there shall be any really important matter . . . it will of course be fitting to make an arrangement requiring the Prefect and Commandant aforesaid to give him directions." But Teng still insisted that communications concerning ordinary problems go through the medium of the senior merchants.

In reporting to his government, Elliot stated that he did not refuse the governor-general's second communication because he was given the original written document with the governor-general's seal affixed to it, and also because he sincerely felt that the governor-general had conceded as much as could be expected for the present. He also explained that he accepted the *pin* because it was vain to hope that the Chinese government would consent to its abolition unless compelled by extremely urgent circumstances. Lord Palmerston approved of the superintendent's work, but, writing on June 13, 1839, instructed him to look for opportunities to press for the substitution of the *pin* by a less objectionable character.

The question of direct and equal official communication was constantly a major issue, but after a period of twenty months, punctuated by negotiation, maneuvering, and disputes, a compromise was finally reached. Confronting a deep-rooted institution, Captain Elliot was compelled to give up his original demand — the dropping of the superscription *pin*. He rationalized the concession by declaring that native officers of his own rank also addressed the governor-general in this form. By implication, he contended, this meant that British high-ranking officials should claim the same right in communicating with lower Chinese officers.

At the end of the year 1838, conditions in Canton, for the moment at least, took a turn for the better. Satisfied with the arrangement on communications, Elliot hoisted the flag again at eleven o'clock on December 30. On the next day, he reported through the senior hong merchant that all eleven British opium boats had departed from Whampoa. Howqua, meanwhile, announced the resumption of trade.[58]

THE FORWARD PARTY AND THE POLICY OF COERCION

The trade at Canton carried on by private English merchants (as opposed to those of the East India Company) was flourishing long before 1834. In the season 1825–26, of the $21.2 million worth of British goods imported to China, $15.7 million were on private accounts, and of the $21.1 million worth of Chinese exports, $12.6 million were handled by private traders. In 1829 these merchants already equaled in number the servants of the company.[59]

The increase in strength of the free traders was not accompanied, however, by increased unity in their ranks. There was a constant feud going on between the moderates and what we might call the forward faction. This dissension found expression as early as 1834, when, it will be recalled, Lord Napier's hard policy toward China was supported by Jardine, Matheson, Fox, James Innes, Richard Turner, and others, but not by Thomas Dent, Whiteman, or Brightman.[60]

It was the rapid growth of the "hard" group that had made George Robinson uncomfortable. In April 1835, he wrote Palmerston that violent party feelings were rife in Canton. "In no country, in no case, are dissensions so injurious, or unanimity and good will so essential to the public welfare as in China," wrote Robinson, "but I lament to say I have invariably witnessed the evil effects of an opposite state of affairs." He stressed the importance of placing government officers "as much beyond these influences as practicable," and added that the officers' "most strenuous efforts and best exertions must be in vain, if counteracted by a strong undercurrent." [61]

As noted earlier, Captain Elliot had reported privately to the Foreign Office in January 1836 that, among the merchants at Canton, the forward party easily outnumbered the moderates.[62] Thus the termination of the Davis-Robinson policy of quiescence and the appointment of Elliot as the chief superintendent was clearly a victory for the forward party. It marked the beginning of the rise of this group to a dominating position in the formulation of Britain's policy toward China.

Whereas the moderates wanted no radical change lest they lose the privileges they had already acquired, the forward party demanded a firm policy aimed at placing the trade on a more secure and equitable basis. They regarded the civil and military servants of China with profound disdain. Their opinion of the hoppo and the future of the trade can be summed up in an editorial in the *Canton Register*:

The person who is appointed to that situation is usually if not always a slave, a "born thrall" of the Imperial family; and from him is neither expected nor required the political acumen, the historical knowledge, the practised habits, the civil courage, — and, above all, the honesty of intention of a real statesman. — No, let him collect the Imperial duties, and strive to augment them for his own profit by any means however illegal, unjust, oppressive, and extortionate, for his system is even now tottering to its fall; but let him not leave his *Swan-pan* [abacus] to interfere with the great questions of free agency and moral right; and more particularly let him avoid meddling in those cases in which Englishmen are concerned in exercising their privileges either of unrestrained thought, or free action.[63]

With such an attitude, it is no surprise that the *Register* wanted to publish a translation of the hoppo's edict simply "for the *amusement* of our readers," and that Matheson regarded the government's prohibition edicts against the opium trade as "waste paper." The foreign community indeed, as William Hunter reported, "treated their 'chops,' their prohibitions, warnings, and threats, as a rule, very cavalierly." [64]

China during the 1830s was scarcely a nation that could inspire esteem. During the whole Tao-kuang period (1821–1850), inundations, droughts, famine, insurrections, and other calamities occurred continually in one part or another of the empire. Commodities were so highly priced that they were beyond the reach of most people, and as a result thefts and robberies were frequent. Military strength was also at a low point, and, as the foreigners quickly discovered, China was "infinitely inferior to Europe in the art of man-killing." The *Canton Register* expressed the general contempt of the foreigners for the Chinese military forces when it remarked: "The men employed in the army and navy of China must be the most worthless of the nation; and we do not believe we should do the officers, civil and military, any injustice if we applied the same epithet to them."

In this frame of mind British merchants spoke glibly of war with

China, particularly after the failure of the Napier Mission. It was said by many and admitted by all of these men that "embassies and negotiation have utterly failed." They believed that it was "the sacred duty of every government on earth to protect its subjects and maintain its own honor in foreign countries." "Can China wage war with us . . . at sea?" asked the *Register*: "Has it a navy to cope with ours? Can it meet our well-disciplined troops in the field?" Only a person ignorant of Chinese affairs, the journal added, would anticipate a difficult battle in case of hostilities. The worst evil it could foresee from a rupture with the Chinese was a temporary suspension of British trade. "As long as our trade remains in that state of uncertainty in which it now is . . . so long [as] a large British capital and more than three millions of annual revenue" were placed in jeopardy, the *Register* affirmed, "no man will, for a moment, imagine that this could be regarded indifferently and some measures must be taken to bring about a radical change." [65]

Following the death of Lord Napier on November 11, 1834, James Matheson, the first president of the British Chamber of Commerce in Canton, accompanied Lady Napier back to England, both to commission a memorial for Napier and to lobby for stronger action in China. He was disappointed, however, because the Whig cabinet of Earl Grey had fallen and Matheson found the Duke of Wellington, Palmerston's successor as foreign secretary, "a cold-blooded fellow . . . a strenuous advocate of submissiveness and servility."

In December 1835, Matheson petitioned Palmerston, again in charge of the foreign ministry in the second Melbourne cabinet, requesting the frequent visits of British men-of-war to Chinese waters. "And our Indian Squadron . . . might be directed to cruise, as a fleet of observation, along the coast of China, in place of lying at some of the Indian ports, which are usually found very unhealthy to their crews." The harbor of Amoy, with its deep water, easy access, and sheltered position was highly recommended as a secure anchorage for Britain's ships.[66] Matheson made a fuller presentation of his views in *The Present Position and Prospects of the British Trade with China*, published in 1836 in England. In this pamphlet, all possible motives and arguments were enumerated to persuade the British government to adopt coercive measures against the Chinese government. It was suggested that three or four vessels, including a steamer, well armed and manned, would be quite sufficient as a demonstration force to overawe the Chinese — they would quickly change their arrogant tone, remove the restrictions imposed upon foreign traders, and follow a more liberal and equitable line in their conduct of foreign trade at Canton.[67]

The voice of the forward party of the British merchants as represented by Jardine and Matheson could no longer be brushed aside as "crude and ill-digested." For not only did they enjoy a large following in Canton,[68] but, as we shall see, they were quite successful in influencing Palmerston and in dominating Britain's policy behind the scenes. The rise of these aggressive British merchants coincided with the domination in Peking of the party that demanded stronger measures against the opium traffic. The situation was rapidly coming to a breaking point.

THE INTENSIFIED COMBAT
OVER OPIUM

THE rapid growth of the opium trade, the futility of Chinese efforts to stop it, and the economic crisis precipitated by the outflow of silver led many Chinese officials to disagree with the established policy of Peking. As early as 1832, the foreign community of Canton saw a copy of a draft memorial from the governor-general and governor of Canton to the emperor that advocated legalization of the opium trade. The reason for this new approach, as explained in later memorials, was to lessen the outward flow of silver and to "prevent the foreigners from raising the price to an enormous height." [1] The memorial produced no response; in fact, there is no evidence that it was ever brought to the attention of the emperor. In 1834, realizing the danger of the extensive spread of opium to other provinces, Governor-General Lu K'un recommended to the emperor a shift into a more compromising (*chi-mi*) policy, pending a gradual prohibition plan. But he proposed no specific measures, and the emperor's strict policy was not altered.

THE SHORT-LIVED LEGALIZATION MOVEMENT

The difficulties resulting from the imports of opium steadily intensified, and in May 1836 Wang Yueh, a censor of the Hu-Kuang circuit, memorialized that, although soldiers should be strictly forbidden to use opium, other opium smokers, the "vagabonds," could be left alone and allowed to court their own disaster. The nominal purpose of this memorial was to request stricter measures against opium among the troops, but the memorialist's real motive was to suggest a relaxed general policy. [2]

At about the same time, a more straightforward memorial, specifically recommending the legalization of opium, was presented by Hsü Nai-chi, subdirector of the Court of Sacrificial Worship. Hsü admitted the pernicious health effects of opium and pointed out that using it to excess made the breath feeble, the body wasted, the face sallow, and the teeth black. The addicts themselves clearly see its harm, Hsü said, but cannot refrain from it. He did not question the need for severe prohibitions in order to "eradicate so vile a practice," [3] but argued that there were too many evil consequences arising from the prohibitions. Bandits often took advantage of the severe laws and committed robbery by masquerading as public servants sent by the government to search out and prevent the smuggling of opium. Since Hsü had recently served as acting criminal judge in Canton, where a great number of such cases were reported to him, he spoke from experience. He held that in many cases involving blackmail, extortion, and other schemes (such as placing the opium where it could be used to implicate the innocent), countless numbers of law-abiding people were made to suffer.

Hsü argued that the severe laws had not stopped the opium from getting in. Because the lawbreakers coveted profit more than they feared punishment, smokers had increased in number and the practice had spread throughout the empire. Moreover, Hsü insisted that the drainage of silver, seen as the sole cause for the economic crisis, had to be stopped. Since the existing opium policy was a failure, Hsü asked for a restoration of the former system — legalization of the opium trade. A tariff duty would be imposed on the article, which was to be classified as medicine. When cleared with the customs office, the opium would be purchased only by barter and not with silver. Neither sycee nor silver dollars were to be allowed to leave the country.

Civil servants, scholars, and soldiers were not to be allowed to smoke, Hsü added; opium users from other walks of life, since they were idle and frivolous elements, were hardly worthy of consideration. China had enough people, and there was no reason to feel concerned over a decrease in population. But the outward flow of silver must be checked. To supplement his recommendation of a barter system, Hsü asked in a separate memorial for the repeal of laws prohibiting the domestic cultivation of the poppy and the production of opium. He contended that the soil of China was milder and would produce less harmful opium. When cheaper domestic production became plentiful, dealers in the imported drug would eventually go out of business.[4]

This memorial had an electrifying effect on the foreign community. The document was presented to the emperor on May 17, 1836, but no action was taken until June 12, when he referred it to Teng T'ing-chen, governor-general of Canton, for investigation and deliberation. As was the custom, the emperor affixed only a terse rescript and did not express his own opinion.[5] When the memorial reached Canton on July 2, 1836, the foreigners, with the exception of Jardine and possibly a few others, hailed it with great excitement. On July 26, Jardine wrote to John Rees, the most important of his opium ship captains stationed on the east coast: "We have lately had a Chop from the Emperor, ordering the authorities here to report on the propriety of admitting opium as an article of trade, under the name of medicine, on payment of a small duty. The general opinion is in favor of the attempt being made very soon — in two or three months perhaps. I do not think well of the plan as far as our interests are concerned — though it has already enhanced prices." [6] The reason for his objection to the legalization attempt is obvious, for it would quickly obviate the smuggling operations along the coast in which Jardine, Matheson and Company had the lion's share. The *Canton Register*, Jardine's spokesman on most issues, could not with wisdom reflect such private thoughts publicly. It published a complete translation of Hsü's memorial and evaluated it as one of the most important measures that had been brought to the attention of the emperor since the turn of the century. The *Register* urged the foreigners to fan into flame the "glimmer that is breaking through the chaotic darkness of Chinese legislation." [7]

Captain Elliot commented to Palmerston on July 27 that Hsü's memorial was "a public confession that the Chinese cannot do without our opium," and he predicted that the imperial rescript commanding Canton officials to report might be said to signify the emperor's assent. Elliot was of opinion that domestic opium might eventually thrust the British imports out of the market, but it would take a long time. As Elliot predicted, the immediate effect of Hsü's memorial was to stimulate poppy cultivation in India and the exportation of opium to Singapore and directly to China.[8]

During this period, Jardine had a small craft ready to be dispatched for the coast or for India with news of the possible legalization measure.[9] But by the following April he was no longer worried about it and wrote Captain Rees: "All hopes, of the drug being admitted on a duty, have, for the present vanished; and our market is very dull in consequence — particularly for the Bengal drug." [10]

The idea of the legalization of opium traffic had its origin in Canton, among a small group of scholars teaching at the Hsueh-hai t'ang, an academy founded by Juan Yuan in 1820.[11] When Hsü Nai-chi was a taotai in Kwangtung, he was concerned over the opium problem and was convinced that edits could not make it disappear. He discussed the issue with Ho T'ai-ch'ing, a friend who was a retired magistrate from Chapu, and Wu Lan-hsiu, a faculty member of the Hseuh-hai t'ang. Both suggested the policy of legalization. Hsü's memorial to the throne was based entirely on an essay written by Wu Lan-hsiu. At Wu's urging, other faculty members of the academy, Hsiung Ching-hsing and I K'e-chung, also wrote articles in support of his views.

Governor-General Lu K'un and Governor Ch'i Kung were greatly influenced by these men — hence the 1834 memorial recommending a more compromising policy. Lu had spoken less candidly in his memorial only because the time was not yet ripe for proposing a direct shift to legalization.

After Governor-General Teng T'ing-chen assumed office early in 1836, he also came under the influence of this group of Hsueh-hai t'ang scholars. When Hsü's memorial was referred to Canton (received on July 2, 1836), Teng was quite ready to endorse it. A memorial to this effect was prepared for his signature. However, he was dissuaded from taking the action by another scholar, Ch'en Hung-ch'ih, a senior faculty member of a rival institution, the Yueh-hua academy.[12] After hesitating for more than two months, Teng and his colleagues finally sent a memorial on September 7, throwing themselves entirely behind Hsü Nai-chi. In addition to approving Hsü's observations in principle, they outlined a nine-item regulation which would put Hsü's policy into practice.[13]

The legalizationists also had strong backing in Peking. Captain Elliot reported later in April 1839 that the ultimate author of the legalization policy was Juan Yüan, who in 1835 was recalled from his post as governor-general of Yunnan and Kweichow and appointed a grand secretary. It was also reported that the legalization advocates had the blessing of Empress Hsiao-ch'üan, née Niuhuru, who wielded much political influence in this period.[14]

Governor-General Teng was so confident that the new measures would come through that he even instructed the hong merchants to write Jardine and other foreign merchants that he had requested the emperor to rescind the prohibitions. The foreigners were instructed to send all the receiving ships away within three months after the enactment of the new regulations. Indeed, the legalization faction had gained so much strength that Chinese circles in Canton thought that Hsü's memorial was drawn up at the order of the emperor himself. In early October,

Elliot reported from Macao that final orders from Peking for the legalization of opium were expected to arrive soon: "This is undoubtedly the most remarkable measure which has been taken in respect to the Foreign Trade, since the accession of this dynasty. . . . They incline me to believe, that it wants but caution and steadiness to secure, at no very distant date, very important relaxations." [15]

The optimism, however, was short-lived. Before Teng's endorsement of legalization reached Peking, two memorialists, Chu Tsun and Hsü Ch'iu, had strongly attacked Hsü's argument.[16] The first, Chu Tsun, subchancellor of the Grand Secretariat and vice-president of the Board of Ceremonies, argued that the infraction of a law was no justification for its annulment. Where the government enacted a law, Chu contended, there was necessarily an infraction of that law: "prostitution, gaming, treason, robbing are all forbidden by the law, but yet underlings and sharpers extort, even on these accounts, for their profit; and, indeed, by these means they often collect hoards of wealth — but surely, it cannot be said that the laws are, in these cases, a mere pretence and dead letter, and their abrogation, in consequence, should be discussed!" He compared the laws to dikes and held that only the foolish would advise the demolition of a dike because parts of it were imperfect.

Chu Tsun was very doubtful of the feasibility of the barter system recommended by Hsü Nai-chi. He did not believe there would be enough tea to exchange for the opium, and in the end silver would still be surreptitiously used. "If it is possible to prevent the exportation of dollars how can it be an impossible affair to prevent the importation of opium?" he asked. "And if opium could be prohibited, then, indeed, the dollars would not be exported." Solemnly warning the emperor of the bad effects of opium on people's morality and health, Chu said:

Opium is nothing else but a flowing poison; that it leads to extravagant expenditure is a small evil, but as it utterly ruins the minds and morals of the people, it is a dreadful calamity.

The people are the foundations of the empire; and all wealth is produced by their labour; the state of an impoverished people may be changed and improved, but it is not in the power of medicine to save a debilitated people, enervated by luxury and excess.

He cited the case of the troops who were sent to fight the Yao rebels in 1832 and reminded the emperor of the report that stated, "in consequence of smoking opium, of all the effective corps, although they mustered many in numbers, few were fit or strong enough to take the field."

If the supplies of opium were not cut off, Chu argued, it would be difficult to keep it from the troops. Already the soldiers were so much addicted to the drug that, when advancing, they could not fight and, when retreating, could not keep their ranks.

Contrary to the view of the legalizationists, Chu did not believe it would be possible to isolate the opium smokers and prevent civil and military officers, students, and soldiers from being affected, for professionals were not born as such; they were drawn from the masses of the people. Finally, the memorialist cautioned the emperor against possible danger from British encroachments. In recent years, he said, the English have been proud, overbearing, and defiant of the laws. Their ships had traversed the coast of Fukien, Chekiang, Kiangsu, Shantung, Hopeh, and Manchuria with secret intentions. Chu Tsun would not recommend any radical measures, such as the cessation of the British trade or the severance of all connections with the English, but he urged the emperor to consider a means of defense against impending trouble.

Hsü Ch'iu, the other memorialist, supervising censor of the Board of War, also contended that, once prohibitions against opium were rescinded, it would be impossible to prevent the people from consuming it; officers and soldiers, coming from the main body of the populace, could not be kept away from it. He laid the responsibility for the ineffectuality of the opium laws on "traitors" and held that only if the traitorous Chinese who dealt in opium — the hong merchants who arranged the prices, the brokers (yao-k'ou) who made the wholesale purchases, the fast crabs that transported the drug, and the military who were bribed to cooperate — were all subjected to strict surveillance and vigorous punishment could the empire be cleared of the pernicious practice.

Hsü Ch'iu named a host of foreign merchants, including Jardine, Innes, Dent, Framjee, Merwanjee, Dadabhoy, Gordon, Whiteman, and Turner, as the most notorious opium dealers. He suggested that these men be put under arrest until their receiving ships sailed away. Fully aware that his strategy entailed the risk of hostilities, he argued that it was better to face the crisis now than to wait until the wealth of the empire was depleted and the people worn out: "It is better to devise plans to meet the present exigencies, and to support right principles with undaunted resolution; the said foreigners will not then dare to preserve their disdainful opinions [of China], nor to persevere in the execution of their crafty schemes." [17]

The two memorials successfully crushed the nascent legalization movement. The emperor's determination not to relax the prohibition was
clearly expressed in an edict of September 19, which enjoined Governor-
General Teng to make a thorough investigation of the problem and to
devise a long-term plan to remedy it. Moreover, in accordance with
Hsü Ch'iu's memorial, all Chinese who sold the drug, the hong merchants who arranged the transactions, the brokers, the crews of the fast
crabs, and the soldiers and police who accepted bribes were to be
arrested.[18]

The edict reached Teng on October 16 when he was away from Canton; he took action in accordance with the imperial instructions on the
28th. Thus the interval during which the legalization of the trade was
expected lasted from July 2, 1836, when Hsü Nai-chi's memorial reached
Governor-General Teng, to the time when the emperor's sentiments
were made known in Canton — barely four months.[19] But the effect of
the move toward legalization lingered long in the minds of the British.
Even as late as February 1837, Elliot reported that "the legal admission
of the opium may be looked for." The "good folks" of Calcutta, according to reports which reached Canton by the *Kennedy* in late April, were
still "as anxious, beyond measure" about the forthcoming legalization.

On receiving the emperor's edict, Governor-General Teng, the governor, and the hoppo directed the hong merchants to carry out investigations concerning the activities of the nine merchants (all British subjects
except Gordon) named in Hsü Ch'iu's memorial. The Canton authorities wanted to know "in what manner they continue stationary in this
place, and store up and sell their opium; from what year they date the
commencement of their opium transactions; what quantity of the drug
they annually store up and dispose of; and whether they ordinarily insist on payment of the price of it in sycee silver."

The hong merchants replied that the smuggling was done by dealers
outside the river, apparently in an attempt to defend the foreign merchants. Finding this reply unsound, since seizures of opium had been
made within the precincts of Canton, Teng and his associates issued
commands on November 23 requiring the nine merchants to leave the
city within two weeks.[20] The deadline was later postponed, and they were
allowed up to four months to make their preparations. A series of rigorous prohibition measures ensued, and the Chinese efforts against opium
continued apace.

Chu Tsun and Hsü Ch'iu spoke for the majority of the officials in

Peking, and the emperor seemed entirely convinced. Whatever doubt may have remained in his mind was cleared away by a more eloquent memorial from Yuan Yü-lin, a censor of the Kiangnan circuit, presented on November 12. Yuan largely repeated Chu's and Hsü's arguments and enumerated the harms and inconsistencies of the legalization system.[21] This memorial ended the argument, and no one ever again proposed the legal admission of opium.

THE GREAT DEBATE

Because the new measures required some time to be translated into action, the spread of opium remained unchecked. Nor had the silver shortage been alleviated. The grave financial condition of the empire led Huang Chueh-tzu, director of the Court of State Ceremonial, to present his well-known memorial on June 2, 1838, proposing a new course of action. This was the beginning of a vigorous new debate. Huang's main suggestion was to increase the punishment for opium consumers. He observed that previously recommended measures called for strict inspection and an extension of patrols to cover the whole of the coast; stopping foreign trade, whether legal or illegal; or imposing severe punishment on opium dealers and opium-den proprietors. None of these measures, Huang contended, could achieve the purpose, because the bribes were too attractive for the water forces to ignore and the coastline was too long to patrol. Ending foreign trade would not effectively check the imports of opium because traitorous Chinese were always ready to purchase the drug from the foreign receiving ships in the outer waters. Opium dens and dealers were too often offered tacit protection and made immune from legal prosecution because so many officers, police, and other powerful men were smokers themselves. The best course to follow, therefore, would be to bring pressure to bear on the consumers. The smokers were now punished only by flogging and being made to wear the cangue. The pain from such punishment for the inveterate user was far less than that from want of opium. Huang requested that smokers be given capital punishment if they did not renounce opium within one year after promulgation of the law. Once the number of smokers decreased, the demand for the drug would also decrease and eventually its importation could be stopped.[22]

As a result of Huang's memorial, the emperor solicited the opinions of all the governors-general, the military governors in the Manchurian provinces, and other high officials. During the next four months, twenty-seven memorials reached the capital from all over the empire, commenting on Huang's new approach and giving further recommendations. (The twenty-eighth memorial, from Szechwan, was late, arriving on December 2.) Whereas the memorialists unanimously recognized the necessity of stopping the opium traffic, the majority doubted the wisdom of imposing capital punishment on smokers. The consensus of opinion was for the application of pressure at the source of the evil, namely those who supplied, transported, and sold opium. It was contended that smugglers and dealers should receive heavier punishment, for they had perpetrated the more serious crime. It was also argued that the smugglers and dealers, fewer in number, would be easier to control. Only eight of the twenty-eight memorialists upheld Huang Chueh-tzu's recommendation. Lin Tse-hsü was in this minority group.

Many of the memorials were simply perfunctory replies, full of trite phrases and based on high-flown theories rather than on investigation and facts. They revealed the authors' dangerous obliviousness to China's military impotence and administrative inefficiency and their ignorance of foreign affairs. The governor of Honan proposed that all the foreign receiving ships at Lintin be expelled and that their illegal cargoes be confiscated. The director-general of the grain transports advised placing a ban on the export of tea and rhubarb, which were believed to be indispensable to the foreigners. It was recommended that this ban remain in effect until the barbarians begged for their lives and pledged not to bring in any more opium; even after they had pleaded for mercy, several dozen of their leaders as well as a few hundred Chinese collaborators were to be executed before the ban was lifted. Paradoxically enough, the later moderates, notably Ch'i-shan and I-li-pu, wanted to inflict strict punishment on the wholesalers at Canton who had direct contact with foreigners, not realizing that this measure could lead to disputes with the foreign merchants more easily than the measures advocated by the firm party, which included Lin Tse-hsü and Huang Chueh-tzu.[23]

Lin Tse-hsü's presentation was outstanding for its realistic and moderate approach. It betokened careful investigation and a profound grasp of the problem. He did not suggest bringing pressure to bear upon the foreign traders. Instead, he outlined a six-point plan aimed entirely at the Chinese handlers, dealers, and consumers. It included proposed means of helping addicts to abandon the habit and an interesting procedure for a fair trial for violators.

On October 23, the emperor ordered a joint session of the Grand

Secretariat and the Grand Council to deliberate on the recommendations of the nation's top officials. Mu-chang-a, a grand councillor, although observing a period of mourning, was specifically ordered to participate in the conference. The emperor also demoted and dismissed Hsü Nai-chi for expressing an absurd view on the opium question two years before, and he deranked Prince Chuang, Imperial Duke P'u-hsi, and a royal host of others for addiction to opium.

The emperor finally decided to attack the opium evil both at its source and along its path to the consumer. On the last day of 1838, he gave the order dispatching Lin Tse-hsü to Canton as imperial commissioner to suppress the sources of the traffic.[24]

H. B. Morse comments, "If one earnest man could have reformed an unwilling people, Taokwang had done it. His motive was pure and his earnestness unquestioned; but his task was hopeless." Contemporary Englishmen, however, did not appreciate the sincerity of the emperor's efforts.[25] The general opinion of the foreign merchants was probably expressed by an editorial in *Blackwood's Magazine*, which argued that the real purpose of the emperor's stringent policy was to effect a change in the mode of trade, not to prevent the import of an article that would corrupt and destroy his people. "We might have been permitted to quadruple our supply of opium to his subjects, if we would have been content to be paid, *not* in *bullion*, but by taking Chinese goods in exchange."[26] In other words, according to the British traders, the emperor's objection to opium was based on financial rather than moral reasons.

It was argued by contemporary traders and writers that opium smoking was no more deleterious than the drinking of spirits.[27] Forbes, for one, wrote that undoubtedly opium was demoralizing to a certain extent, but its effect on the Chinese people was much less injurious than that of the "vile liquor made of rice."[28] The *Quarterly Review* strongly doubted that the evils of opium were worse than those of gin and whisky.[29] The great majority of the contemporary medical profession, however, were definitely of the opinion that opium was much more harmful, that it produced rapid deterioration in the strongest constitution.[30] It does not, of course, require medical training to detect the adverse effects of the drug on addicts. But one physician put it rather well: The "sallow complexion, stupid visage, and wasted frame of old smokers, and especially the remorseless grip of the craving on every fibre of his nervous system was ample proof of the drug's effect."[31]

It has been argued by later generations that the opium trade, though immoral from the modern point of view, was not generally considered so during the time in question.[32] Nothing could be further from the truth. In 1836, when a measure for making money advances on opium in Calcutta was being contemplated by the Bengal government, the *Bengal Herald* weighed the advantages and disadvantages of the measure. The advantages were numerous: the ease in making remittances to England, the interest derived from the use of the funds advanced and the encouragement such funds would afford to speculators, the fresh stimulus to the trade and an ultimate increase of profit, the circumvention of the need to levy new taxes to pay the dividends, the employment of additional workers, and finally "forcing the Chinese to pay the Hindoos — that is, saving their pockets from further taxation by the Bengal government." The disadvantages were listed as "the immorality of all dealings in opium, and the evil example set by the government to the natives of India; who are, however, covered with so thick a veil of ignorance that it is hoped they may be recipients of the advantages without feeling the evils of the proposed measure." For all the attractions, the writer concluded with his hope that the measure would not be adopted.[33]

When William Jardine chartered the clipper *Sylph* for a voyage to Shanghai and Tientsin to sell opium, he persuaded Charles Gutzlaff to accompany her as interpreter. In his letter to Gutzlaff, Jardine wrote:

Tho' it is our earnest wish that you should not in any way injure the grand object you have in view by appearing interested in what by many is considered an immoral traffic yet such a traffic is absolutely necessary to give any vessel a reasonable chance . . . and the more profitable the expedition the better we shall be able to place at your disposal a sum that may hereafter be usefully employed in furthering the grand object you have in view, and for your success in which we feel deeply interested.[34]

All the edicts of the Chia-ch'ing Emperor prohibiting opium were issued on the grounds that the drug had deleterious effects on morality and health. In the earlier years of the Tao-kuang period, the prohibition edicts were also inspired mainly by moral considerations (*feng-su jen-hsin*). It was in 1830 that the Tao-kuang Emperor for the first time mentioned the money wasted on consumption of opium together with its injurious health effects.[35] It was mainly the economic crisis that roused the Chinese to take action against the import and spread of opium, it is true, but it would be a mistake to assume that the emperor would have been indifferent to the drug's admission in other circumstances. When Prince Su of the Imperial Clan Court presented the emperor with the thirty-nine-article statute on opium prohibition, he reported: "Those who are addicted to opium are entranced and powerless to quit, almost as if seduced by the deadly poison, until they stand like skeletons, their bodily shape totally disfigured and no better than the crippled." The emperor, promulgating the regulations in June 1839, made the statement that opium undermined morality and custom to a great extent; that opium smokers, in the beginning seduced by others, developed a habit and would not give it up even though all their property was squandered and their lives ruined.[36]

On the magistrate level, the officers thought of the problem even more sharply in terms of morality and physical health. Shen Yen-ch'ing, a magistrate and an intimate friend of Hsia Hsieh (author of *Chung-hsi chi-shih*), wrote a *fu* (prose poem) on opium ("Ya-p'ien-yen fu") to caution people against the poisonous effects of the drug. It described opium smokers who boasted of the pleasures of an inebriated world amid high pillows and warm quilts, not realizing that they were hastening down the road to their graves; their talents, supposedly rivaling those of the great Ts'ao Chih, were actually nothing; their great strength, said to be equal to the task of carrying nine caldrons, was really completely exhausted.[37] When Chou Chi-hua, magistrate of T'ai-chou, Kiangsu province, received the new regulations prohibiting opium, he published them with additional admonitions, reminding the people of the harmful effects of the drug. Governor-General Teng's antiopium leaflets, distributed among his people in December 1836, began with the sentence: "The smoke of opium is a deadly poison." While cautioning people that the use of the drug ruined business and dissipated wealth and property, the paper emphasized its poisonous effects and described the horrible physical condition of habitual smokers. They lay asleep like so many corpses, the leaflets said, their skins hanging about them like a sack and their bones as bare as sticks.[38]

Throughout the course of the great debate, though the main topic was the drain of silver, the harmful effects of opium were not overlooked. Pao-hsing, military governor of Feng-t'ien province and Ch'i-shan, governor-general of Chih-li, among others, spoke of the life-destroying nature of the drug. A quotation from Lin Tse-hsü's memorial, "If we continue to pamper it, a few decades from now we shall not only be without soldiers to resist the enemy, but also in want of silver to provide an army," was to be memorized by practically every schoolchild in the following century.[39]

The thirty-nine-article statute against opium was the direct consequence of the great debate. It was drawn up jointly by the Grand Secretariat, the Grand Council, the Imperial Clan Court, and several other divisions of the imperial government in accordance with the views presented in the memorials of Huang Chueh-tzu and other officials. This comprehensive ninety-four-page enactment considerably increased the severity of the punishment to be meted out to anyone connected with the trade, from the farmer who cultivated the poppy to the police who accepted the bribes, from the brokers who bought the drug by the chest, to the retailer who operated an opium den. The statute was promulgated in Peking on June 15, 1839, and on July 6 it reached Canton, where hundreds of chests of opium were already being destroyed at the Bogue. It provided that after a period of eighteen months from the time the new law was made known in a locality, anyone, soldier or civilian, noble or commoner, found to be an opium smoker was to be sentenced to detention for strangling. According to the Ch'ing statutes, all "detention for execution" sentences had to be reconsidered by the "autumn assize" and then referred to Peking for complicated, prolonged reviews and final imperial approval. The former opium punishments, it will be recalled, were flogging and the cangue.

Letters to Lin Tse-hsü from friends in Peking reached Canton on May 8, 1839, informing him that the original decision of the court concerning the punishment of opium criminals was considerably more lenient. It was the emperor who had asked the court to make it harsher.[40] This intervention marked the victory of the minority group led by Huang Chueh-tzu and Lin Tse-hsü.

The punishment for convicted wholesale brokers, according to the new law, was immediate beheading. Those who were convicted of operating opium dens and public servants found to have accepted bribes connected with the traffic would meet their death by immediate strangling. Although the opium smokers were allowed a period of eighteen months to stop the habit, offenders in the other categories were given no such reprieve.

At Commissioner Lin's request, the authorities in Peking enacted a statute particularly dealing with foreign opium traders. It stipulated immediate beheading for the principals and immediate strangling for the accessories. All these "immediate" executions are rather misleading because the sentences had to be reviewed jointly by the Board of Punishment, the Censorate, and the Court of Judicature and Revision, and approved by the emperor. The new law directed at foreign offenders was to take effect eighteen months after it reached Canton, and during this interim period those who voluntarily surrendered their opium would be pardoned. Commissioner Lin received this enactment from the Board of Punishment on July 19, 1839, and it formed the legal basis of his subsequent dealings with the English.[41]

NEW PROHIBITIONS AND THE MAITLAND AFFAIR

As noted earlier, the hopeful expectation of a legalized opium trade lasted in Canton and Peking not more than four months. Having received Chu Tsun's and Hsü Ch'iu's memorials, the emperor dispatched an edict to Canton ordering the investigation of the activities of nine foreign merchants in connection with the opium traffic. After some inquiries conducted by the hong merchants, the governor-general ordered them on November 23, 1836, to "close all their commercial affairs, and within the period of half a month to . . . move off from the provincial city, and to return to their country." They could remain in Macao for a short time before leaving China. The order, however, was not taken seriously by the foreign community. The *Canton Register* asked, "why do they, week after week, issue the most strict and (said to be) unalterable orders to those foreigners whom they affect so much to despise, but who in fact *do* manifest the most utter, profound contempt for these orders?"

The hong merchants found that one merchant, Merwanjee, was no longer in Canton. The other eight all claimed that they had ships coming which would require their attention. Most of them did not promise a definite date of departure. When again pressed for answers, Whiteman and Framjee promised to leave in January and February, respectively. Gordon asked to be allowed to remain until April. Innes promised to leave in January, Dadabhoy in February, Dent and Turner in April, and Jardine in May. By an edict of December 13, 1836, the provincial authorities granted the merchants' requests except in the cases of Jardine, Dent, and Turner, who were ordered to leave Canton in March.[42]

As usual, the foreign merchants paid little heed to orders from the provincial government. Those who actually left Canton stayed away only for a short time. Jardine left China on January 26, 1839, of his own free will.[43] With the possible exception of Whiteman and Gordon, whose records are not readily available, everyone was still in Canton at the time Commissioner Lin arrived.[44]

Meanwhile a vigorous campaign against Chinese opium smugglers was launched. Captures of smuggled opium and silver to the amount of thousands of taels were frequent. In this campaign Governor-General Teng had the assistance of an efficient provincial judge by the name of Wang Ch'ing-lien, who had assumed office in 1835. Wang would stroll about the streets of the suburbs, attended only by his lantern bearer, and investigate the gambling houses, brothels, and opium-smoking shops. It was reported that he also directed many of his servants to spy about the streets. The *Canton Register* reported: "Since the arrival of H. E. Wang, the criminal judge, there has not been a night in which he has not gone about secretly." He visited government buildings, opium dens, and gambling houses alike, and wherever he found opium smoking or gambling he imposed punishments. One night in mid-September 1835, he found a messenger of the Namhoi (Nan-hai) magistrate lying on a bench smoking opium; he immediately had him flogged fifteen strokes with a bamboo switch. Because of his ceaseless efforts, the opium dens in the city were afraid to open their doors.[45]

Governor-General Teng T'ing-chen, the principal actor during this period of gathering war clouds, was a native of Nanking, born on January 26, 1776. After gaining his *chin-shih* in 1801, he started on a political career that was to follow a roller-coaster course, with praise, promotion, dismissal, and punishment.[46] During his early years, his patron was Chiang Yu-hsien (governor-general of Liang-Kuang, 1812–1817), and at the recommendation of Chiang (then governor of Chekiang) he was appointed prefect of Ningpo in 1810. Starting in 1814 he served as prefect in Sian and other localities in northern Shensi for six years. In 1820 he became the provincial judge of Hupeh and in the next year was transferred to the financial commission of Kiangsu. In 1822, he was dismissed because of improper handling of a lawsuit while he was a prefect of Sian. In the following year, thanks to the support of Chiang Yu-hsien, then governor-general of Chihli, Teng was appointed the intendant of the T'ung-Yung circuit. The most peaceful period of his career began in 1826 when he was appointed governor of Hupeh, a post he held for almost a decade; during this time he completed most of his literary works.[47]

Despite the frequent ups and downs of Teng's eventful career, on August 5, 1836, the emperor lavishly praised his integrity and talent (*p'in-hsueh chien-yu*).[48] His views on the opium problem were neatly summed up in two sentences in his memorial to the emperor: "Let the law concentrate and hit hard at the wealthy and powerful; the rank and file will follow suit. Let decrees be strictly enforced on the Chinese soil; the foreign goods [opium] will naturally disappear." Yet Teng's cam-

paign against opium was carried out more as a duty and a gesture to
please the emperor than as a crusade based on high principle — hence his
subscription to Hsü Nai-chi's legalization proposal. Much of his negligence
in disciplining subordinates may be attributed to his distaste for public
affairs, which was connected to his penchant for pure scholarship.[49]
Basically, Teng was a poet and a philologist. His complete works, published in 1919 in twelve *ts'e*, contain six *chüan* of scholarly notes, two
works on archaic phonology, sixteen *chüan* of verse, and two *chüan* of
tz'u. Not a word was said about the Opium War or his political experiences, and the fact that he was involved in the opium crisis is indicated
only by a few poems dedicated to Lin Tse-hsü.[50]

Teng was appointed to the governor-generalship of Kwangtung and
Kwangsi provinces in 1835 and arrived in Canton in February 1836. His
position in regard to the opium situation became a matter of controversy. Many of his Western contemporaries were hostile to him, and in
their judgment his worth could not be lower or his venality surpassed by
any of his predecessors. It was reported in Western circles that under
Teng's administration a Chinese opium dealer had to pay as much as 60
to 80 dollars per chest for the authorities' connivance in the traffic, whereas
before Teng's appointment the rate had usually been 16 to 30 dollars
and never exceeded 40 dollars.[51] Foreign merchants relished a story to the
effect that opium had been found on the person of Teng's son. It was
also said that, in December 1838 and January 1839, on the walls of his
residence were pasted lampoons, one of which read:

> O'er the impoverished but broad eastern land,
> Our venerable Tang [Teng] holds chief command.
> His favour falls on those who seizures make,
> Yet in the daring game he holds a stake.
> For cruizing [*sic*] boats his son and comrades keep
> To scour the waters of the inner deep;
> And in his halls having heaped an untold store
> Of gold, unsatiated still he craves for more;
> While dice and women all his hours employ
> Still the fond father censues [*sic*] not the boy.
> O blind to reason! no distinction seen,
> The good must bow to tyrants and the mean.
> But leogued [*sic*] oppression will resistance cause,
> And men's indigant [*sic*] hearts assert the laws.[52]

Rumors and lampoons like this were rife in Canton. Teng reported them
to Peking in 1839, explaining that they were simply a form of revenge

taken by opium-law violators he had punished in the past three years. The emperor assured him that he and Lin Tse-hsü were his "personal trusted" officials and that they should not let these slanders bother them. He also authorized the governor-general to arrest and punish the authors of the lampoons.[53]

A well-informed author, Liang T'ing-nan, strongly defended the governor-general and pointed out that many of the lower officials accepted bribes and maliciously claimed that the governor-general had a share in them. Liang was particularly angry that the governor-general's third son should also be slandered. He reported that according to the boy's tutor, whom Liang had recommended, the younger Teng was an industrious student who was seldom allowed to go out and was incapable of involvement in any dealings with opium. Moreover, Liang argued, of all the several hundred students with whom Lin Tse-hsü conducted a *kuan-feng-shih*, or custom-finding examination, none had accused the governor-general's son of any participation in the opium trade.[54]

It is almost certain that the accusations concerning Teng's venality were groundless. The alleged increase in the bribery rates during Teng's tenure of office may well have resulted from his strictness in enforcing the opium prohibition. His faithfulness to the pronounced policy of the imperial government was fully reflected in Captain Elliot's reports made throughout Teng's three-year administration. Probably the best evidence of Teng's probity is a letter from Jardine to Captain Rees, dated October 18, 1838, saying that Governor-General Teng was to leave Canton for Kwangsi the next day and that "the Chinese are in hopes that the Trade may improve during his absence." [55]

On February 2, 1837, Captain Elliot wrote to London that, for the last two months, the Canton authorities had been pursuing a system of severe restriction against the opium trade, and it had been largely successful. At the same time, the opium of the first sales of the year in Bengal was to arrive in a few weeks, and Elliot predicted that, if the ban continued to be enforced so strictly, the trade would take on an entirely different nature. "From a traffic prohibited in point of form, but essentially countenanced, and carried on entirely by natives in native boats, it will come to be a complete smuggling trade." In such circumstances, he predicted, British traders would be thrown into direct contact with the inhabitants on the coast, vastly increasing the chances of serious disputes and collisions with government officers.[56]

What Elliot had predicted was already happening. At the end of

January, Jardine reported that the drug trade was at a standstill, but "the article has become so high in the city, that the temptation to smuggle, at all hazard, is becoming very great." Smuggling (by foreigners) through Macao and Hsiang-shan, he said, was going on already.[57] It was against this background that Elliot contemplated requesting British men-of-war from India to visit Chinese waters, and on February 2, 1837, he wrote Palmerston:

> It seems likely that the visits of men-of-war at this crisis, for short periods, and at brief intervals, would have the effect either of relaxing the restrictive spirit of the Provincial Government, or of hastening onwards the legalization measure, and thus, by one mode or the other, of releasing the trade from its actual condition of stagnation.
>
> Your Lordship, I hope, will consider I am justified in respectfully moving these authorities [the governor-general of India and the British naval commanding-in-chief stationed in India] to do what can be done (safely and without inconveniently commiting His [sic] Majesty's Government,) toward the relief of the most important branch of this trade; with the langour [sic] of which the whole British commerce to the empire necessarily sympathises in a very serious degree.[58]

On the same day, Elliot wrote a dispatch to Lord Auckland, governor-general of India,[59] and another one to Rear-Admiral Thomas Bladen Capel, K.C.B., the commander-in-chief (Capel was relieved by Maitland on February 5, 1838), requesting British naval ships. A collection of translated Chinese memorials and edicts concerning the legalization of the opium trade was also forwarded to these authorities. In his dispatch to Governor-General Auckland, Elliot reported his grave concern over the unfortunate commercial situation: the British merchants could not dispose of the only commodity they could sell in quantity to China, and they were now, with respect to the prices of Chinese exports, at the mercy of the hong merchants. Captain Elliot observed that frequent and short visits of British warships to Canton waters and to the neighborhood of the points to which the outside trade had extended would be "movements calculated, either to carry the Provincial Government back to the system which has hitherto prevailed, or to hasten onwards the legalization measure from the Court." He also solicited the participation of one or two of the East India Company's cruisers.

In his letter to Rear-Admiral Capel, Elliot similarly stated the "pressing necessity to use every effort consistent with safety and discretion for the relief of the whole trade, from the embarrassment into which it is thrown by the restrictive spirit of the Provincial Government," and again requested the visits of British vessels to Chinese seas. The attack in the middle of 1835 on the British trading brig *Troughton*, which was plundered by Chinese pirates of seventy thousand dollars almost within sight of the anchorage, would, he said, provide a sufficient pretext for the presence of British men-of-war should the Kwangtung government become alarmed.[60]

On September 20, 1837, Viscount Palmerston transmitted to the Admiralty Lords the queen's directions concerning the protection that British vessels should afford British subjects trading in China. Subsequently Rear-Admiral Maitland, commander-in-chief of British ships in the India seas, was directed that "one or more of the ships under your orders should, as frequently as possible, visit the China station, and should remain there as long as may be consistent with the demands of the service elsewhere within your command; and whenever a frigate can be spared for this service, a ship of that class would be preferable to a smaller one." Maitland was asked to take the earliest opportunity to visit China and make personal contact with Captain Elliot. On November 2, Palmerston informed Elliot of this arrangement.

In Canton, there was no relaxation of the government's severe measures against opium dealers. During the early part of 1837, all the smuggling boats (the fast crabs) were destroyed by their owners. Some new ones were built in the summer, but they were soon burned again by their owners in August and September.[61] At the same time, the provincial government put continuous pressure on the English to stop the opium traffic, but Captain Elliot resorted to evasive tactics.[62] In August two edicts from the governor-general and the governor were issued instructing Elliot to send away the opium vessels from Lintin. On September 18, another edict was issued reminding the opium traders of the goodness of the government in permitting the continuance of trade, in all circumstances, for a space of two hundred years. It deplored the contumacy of the foreigners in supposing that "while they render the Chinese seas a common sewer for the filthy opium the government can fail to put the laws in force against them." [63] Two months later Elliot summed up the year for Palmerston:

It is requisite your Lordship should know, that since my arrival in Canton, in the month of April last, I have frequently been urged by the official merchants (and, as they have always declared, by the special command of the Governor) to dismiss the opium ships from the usual anchorages outside the port. I have invariably replied on these occasions, that my Commission charged me with the superintendence of the trade to Canton; that my Government had no formal knowledge of the existence of any other; and that his Excellency must be sensible I could concern myself only with the duties I had due authority to perform.[64]

In the latter part of 1837, the vigorous measures of the provincial authorities effectively crushed the native smuggling networks at the outside anchorages of Canton and its immediate neighborhood, but there was the side effect of a phenomenal increase in the traffic on the east coast of Kwangtung and the coast of Fukien.[65] Elliot reported on November 19: "Till within the last few months, that branch of the trade on the coast of eastern Kwangtung and Fukien never afforded employment to more than two or three small vessels; but, at the date of this despatch, and for some months past, there have not been less than twenty sail of vessels on the east coasts; and I am sorry to add, that there is every reason to believe blood has been spilt in the interchange of shot which has ever and anon taken place between them and the Mandarin boats." [66]

The price of opium drastically declined: Patna was about $620 per chest, Benares $560, and Malwa $445 at the end of the year. In January, Patna and Benares suffered a further decline of a hundred dollars. In February, Malwa and Benares could be purchased at 400 dollars or lower and new Patna at 450 dollars.[67] Jardine, whose firm held the greater part of Malwa in China, remarked, perhaps with a sigh: "Canton never was in so dull and distressed a state since I have known it. Not a ship loading for England, not a pound of Tea purchased for the Europe, or English markets; and very little for America." [68]

At the end of the year, the governor-general, the governor, and the hoppo in a joint memorial apprised the emperor of their accomplishments in opium prohibition in the past year. From spring through December 1837, they reported, 30 seizures had been made. In these cases, they had arrested 161 offenders and captured 8,661 taels of sycee silver, 3,027 taels of silver in foreign dollars, and 3,842 catties of opium. The criminals were all severely judged; the silver was given as a reward to the captors; and the opium was burned. Those brokerage houses found to be dealing in opium had been closed, while orders were issued for the apprehension of the persons who had frequented them. The memorialists told the emperor that they dared not say their efforts in the past year had produced the full effect desired, but they observed that the price of sycee silver and opium in Canton had dropped drastically. Formerly, traitorous Chinese had been obliged to pay the foreign vessels more than 30 dollars for one opium ball (a chest of Patna contained forty balls), but now the price was only 16 to 18 dollars. The governor-general's report is substantiated by the Bombay Chamber of Commerce returns, which gives the total value of opium exports from Bombay for 1836–37 as 24,249,821 rupees but in the next season, 1837–38, 11,242,325 rupees, a decrease of more than half.[69]

Some twenty-five foreign vessels anchoring at Lintin were the strongest link in the opium-smuggling chain. These vessels, which gave the Canton authorities much difficulty, were, in the emperor's words, "one of the greatest evils under which the province of Canton groans." Since it was not the governor-general's policy to put direct military pressure on foreign ships, he moved to cut off their provisions. The governor-general and his associates observed that these opium-receiving ships were dependent on China for their daily supplies. They also noticed that native *pan-t'ing* (bum-boats), while pretending to go out fishing, were supplying a variety of provisions and other articles to the foreigners at Lintin. "If these supplies were cut off," the Chinese officials maintained, "we might succeed in getting rid of them." At the time of the memorial, four such *pan-t'ing* had been captured with twenty-eight crew members and some cargo.[70]

The memorialists reminded the emperor that, according to the law, whenever foreigners prove refractory the trade ought to be stopped in order to give fair warning. Thus they had prepared to order an embargo if the Lintin ships still refused to leave. They had ordered the hong merchants to inquire how many nations carried on commerce with China, how many of them traded honestly and operated no receiving ships, and how many did possess receiving ships. The Canton authorities only wanted to punish the guilty. Receiving this memorial on February 1, 1838, the emperor fully approved their proceedings and urged them to follow these measures up with thorough strictness (*jen-chen pan-li*).

Under such repeated threats from Peking and Canton, Captain Elliot, who had not yet received a reply to his first request, wrote Palmerston on December 7, 1837, once more demanding "that a small naval force should immediately be stationed somewhere in these seas." Elliot was aware of the fact that the provincial authorities were preparing a memorial formally requesting permission to impose an embargo. But he observed: "Before His Imperial Majesty's commands could arrive, the trade of the season would have been completed." At any rate, Elliot was not so worried about a formal command from Peking as about the grave local situation that might drift into disaster. On February 5, 1838, he reported: "In my judgment, the interruption of the trade is less likely to ensue from the commands of the Court, than from some grave disaster arising out of collision between the Government craft and our own armed boats on the river." Already, in the middle of January, some mandarin runners had visited the boat of a Mr. Just (a British watchmaker residing in Canton) about two miles above the factories, and they found three cases of opium. This was the first time in many years that a European boat had been searched by the Chinese. The case might have been quietly settled, according to Elliot, had Just been willing to offer a large enough bribe. In February, opium was seized aboard another European boat, the *Alpha*.[71]

Fastboats had been burned, native smugglers arrested and scattered, and the opium trade had undergone a total and "very hazardous" change. The drug was now carried in private British-owned passage boats, which made "vast opium deliveries at Whampoa." [72] These boats were but slenderly manned by lascar seamen and armed in a way which, in Elliot's opinion, served more "to provoke or to justify search, accompanied by violence, than to furnish the means of effectual defence." In his report of November 19, 1837, Elliot said that the Canton authorities were well aware of the smuggling by European boats on the river and that their continued connivance could not be counted on much longer. A number of factors, such as intrigue among officials to ensure a greater part of the profits and private reports against one another to Peking, might suddenly change the situation at any time.

That as much as three fifths of the inward trade was carried on in such a precarious manner was a matter of concern to Elliot, and he entreated his home government to take action. "It seems to me that the moment has arrived for such active interposition upon the part of Her Majesty's Government, as can be properly afforded; and that it cannot be deferred without great hazard to the safety of the whole trade, and of the persons engaged in its pursuit." Having received three dispatches of the same tenor, Palmerston replied with a terse statement that the government could not interfere with these proceedings, either by aiding or restraining the pursuits of the smugglers. Conditions deteriorated even more rapidly in 1838. "In the course of the last two months," wrote Captain Elliot on April 20, "the number of English boats employed in the illicit traffic between Lintin and Canton has vastly increased, and the deliveries of opium have frequently been accompanied by conflict of fire-arms between those vessels and the Government preventive craft."

In the early part of April, a Chinese charged with traitorous intercourse with foreigners and the smuggling of opium and sycee silver was strangled immediately outside the walls of Macao. The body was left on display, bearing a sign that informed onlookers of his crime and of the fact that the execution was ordered by the emperor himself. The unusual choice of execution ground and public exhibition of the corpse clearly indicated that this was meant as a warning to foreign smugglers. Captain Elliot did not fail to take notice and he remarked, "with the prisons full of persons charged with similar offences, and with public executions for them, it is not to be supposed that the Provincial Government can venture much longer to permit the delivery of opium out of British armed-boats, almost under the walls of the Governor's palace at Canton: neither is it likely that they will succeed in driving them out without bloodshed."

The naval forces that Elliot had requested on February 2, 1837, arrived in the China seas in July 1838. The *Wellesley*, with Sir Frederick L. Maitland on board, accompanied by the brig *Algerine*, arrived in Tong-koo Bay (T'ung-ku-wan), about seven leagues south of the Bogue, on the 13th. This anchorage was chosen by Elliot because of its safety, its distance from the entrance of the river, and its remoteness "from the anchorage of the ships engaged in the illicit traffic." [73]

Governor-General Teng was informed of the arrival of the British ships on July 15, and the Canton authorities, with the Napier nightmare still fresh in their memories, were immediately thrown into a state of alarm. All forts and fleets were reinforced and ordered to be vigilant in their defenses. All river passages leading to Canton were patrolled day and night by smaller boats. Special forces were secretly dispatched to guard all strategic points on various inland routes leading to Canton. The Tartar general, Te-k'e-chin-pu, the governor-general, and the newly arrived governor, I-liang, considered the problem together and took part in planning precautions. By order of the provincial authorities, the magistrate and territorial regiment commander of Hsiang-shan proceeded to Macao to join the subprefect (*Ao-men t'ung-chih*) in defending that settlement. Meanwhile, a confidential edict was directed to the Portuguese to forestall any possible British efforts to seduce them.[74]

A few days after Maitland's arrival, the subprefect of Macao addressed a communication to Elliot, superscribed with the character *yü* (command), and this was promptly returned unopened with a note dated July 15, objecting to the improper superscription. Another *yü*, this time from the governor-general, soon followed. It was addressed to the three senior hong merchants and forwarded to the superintendent by a linguist. This document Captain Elliot also returned unopened because, as related before, he was fighting for direct official communication with the Chinese provincial government.

The aim of these two communications undoubtedly was to ascertain the purpose of the rear-admiral's visit and to instruct Elliot to send the warships away. The Chinese, until August 5, were entirely ignorant of the nature of Maitland's mission. Admiral Kuan was under the impression that Maitland was to replace Elliot as superintendent.[75] Afraid that such lack of knowledge might induce the alarmed Canton authorities to adopt rash measures against the British, Captain Elliot, who had been living in Macao since December 2, 1837, following the deadlock on the "direct intercourse" issue, went to Canton on July 25; four days later, he had his secretary and interpreter deliver a letter at the city gate to the governor-general explaining the peaceful object of the British commander-in-chief. This letter was returned to Elliot by the hong merchants in the evening for want of the character *pin*. Elliot at once informed the hong merchants that he considered his mission of explaining Sir Frederick's peaceful object accomplished and left Canton on July 31.[76]

At this critical time an unfortunate incident took place at the Bogue. On July 28 a British schooner, the *Bombay* (a passage boat), proceeding from Hong Kong to Canton, was signaled to heave to by two mandarin boats as it approached the Bogue. The signal was disregarded because such flag signs were not usual with the mandarin boats. One of them fired a musket, apparently as a sign to the batteries, which then fired on the *Bombay*. The shots at first fell short, but as the schooner moved nearer the Bogue fort they were better directed; two of them passed between the masts and one within a yard of the bow. The schooner immediately came to and was approached by one of the mandarin boats. An interpreter from the Chinese boat inquired whether "Admiral Maitland, or any of his soldiers, women, or man-of-war's men, were on board." After a negative answer was given, the schooner was allowed to proceed up the Bogue. A passenger asked the mandarin whether he was interested in searching for opium, and the latter said no.[77] A similar questioning took place about an hour later when the *Bombay* approached the Tiger fort. When the officer of the schooner said that neither Maitland nor any persons connected with him were on board, the ship was allowed to pass on. From the Chinese point of view, these inquiries were regarded as the ordinary performance of duty by the officers ordered to stop the naval man, Maitland, from passing through the Bogue. But the British considered them an insult.[78] The only ground for such a complaint was perhaps the language used by the interpreter.[79]

Captain Elliot, still in Canton, protested the incident to the governor-general through the hong merchants, and the latter, speaking on behalf of the governor-general, denied that there was any intention to insult the rear-admiral; whatever rudeness occurred was only a case of misconduct on the part of minor officers. Since Elliot would not accept anything short of a written disavowal, the British fleet, consisting of the *Wellesley*, the *Larne*, the *Algerine*, and the superintendent's cutter, the *Louisa*, proceeded to the Bogue on August 4, largely at the initiation of Elliot, to demand a written disavowal. The next day, at the request of Maitland, Admiral Kuan dispatched Colonel Li Hsien, whose rank was supposed to equal that of the captain of the *Wellesley*, accompanied by an acting second captain, Lu Ta-yueh, to the British flagship. In the presence of the rear-admiral, Elliot, Morrison, and the captains of all the British vessels, Lu Ta-yueh, at the dictation of the senior Chinese officer, wrote the statement disclaiming any intention of insult.[80] "Should any such-like language be used hereafter, the circumstance shall be at once investigated and punished. Their thus offending your Honourable Admiral is one and the same as offending our own Admiral." This action concluded the incident satisfactorily, and some civilities were then exchanged. The fleet returned to the Tongkoo anchorage on the morning of August 6.[81]

While on board the *Wellesley*, the rear-admiral declared that his reason for calling in Chinese waters was to look after British subjects and to see that they were not made to suffer insults. He added that, since the trade in Canton was no longer in the hands of the East India Company, frequent visits of the men-of-war were necessary. He assured the Chinese, however, that such visits would be always with a peaceful purpose. This was the first successful formal notification to the Chinese of the purpose of the Maitland Mission. The monsoon being against his return passage, Sir Frederick announced that he would have to remain in the neighborhood for some weeks more. Li Hsien then entreated him to put a stop to the irregularities committed by British subjects in Canton, but Maitland replied that, since he was a naval commander, merchant vessels were not under his jurisdiction. They were subject to the civil authority, he said, pointing at the superintendent. Upon this, Captain Elliot gave assurance that it was his constant wish to preserve peace and order.[82]

We do not know at what level the Chinese disavowal was suppressed, but it was not reported in the memorial jointly submitted to the emperor by the Tartar general, the governor-general, and the governor. The memorial only reported the visit of Li Hsien and Lu Ta-yueh on board the *Wellesley*, maintaining that their mission was to enjoin the British commander-in-chief to sail away without delay and to reproach him for his impropriety in demanding direct and equal communication with the "celestial authorities." The emperor wrote a long rescript to this memorial on September 15, 1838, upholding the cautious measures of the Canton officials and their refusal to accept any communication from the English not presented in the form of a petition. He ordered the memorialists to keep a watchful eye on the barbarians during the weeks that their ships remained in Canton waters, for the foreigners' dispositions were as unfathomable as those of the goat and dog. If when the northern monsoon returned they were still there, they should be driven away by force and their trade stopped. The emperor's final admonishing words were: "Outwardly manifest calm and inwardly build up defense, in order to suppress the barbarian bandits and pacify the neighborhood." [83]

Maitland and his ships left the China seas on October 5, 1838. The period of his sojourn at the Tongkoo anchorage had been characterized by relative peace and good will. On one occasion Admiral Kuan wrote him a note of condolence over the loss of his niece, and before his departure Maitland presented Kuan with a few bottles of wine. That nothing more serious than the *Bombay* incident occurred was owing to the desire of both sides to avoid hostilities. Maitland had been specifically instructed that, "unless in case of great emergency, when a demonstration or an actual employment of force may be urgently and absolutely necessary for the protection of the lives and property of British subjects, Her Majesty's ships of war are studiously to respect the regulations of the Chinese Government as to the limits beyond which foreign ships of war are not allowed to approach the city of Canton."

But the Maitland Mission did not achieve its original objective. The fleet had been summoned by Captain Elliot to intimidate the Chinese into abandoning their strict measures against opium. It was calculated that frequent visits of British warships would revive and strengthen the legalization movement in Peking, and it was hoped that the presence of Rear-Admiral Maitland in Chinese seas would assist the superintendent in his fight for direct official communication.[84] But the prohibition policy continued unabated; the legalization movement remained a dead letter; and the issue of direct communication continued to be dead-locked. Jardine wrote to Captain Rees in August that Maitland "has alarmed the Chinese not a little," but a year after the Maitland episode Governor-General Teng commented in a memorial that the British war vessels which had visited Canton were not dispatched by the British government; their coming had been privately arranged by Elliot in order to make a show of power without real strength (*hsü-chang sheng-shih*).[85]

THE STORMY WINTER OF 1838–39

In Canton the crusade against opium continued with increasing vigor. By early December 1838, it was estimated that upwards of two thousand opium dealers, brokers, and smokers had been imprisoned. A few executions took place every day.[86] It was not possible to sell a single chest of opium on any terms, since the panic-stricken dealers had all gone into hiding.[87] The traffic on the coast, too, had increasing troubles with the local forces and sales became limited.[88] In early January, the *Canton Press Price Current* could not even quote a price of opium: "There is absolutely nothing doing, and we therefore withdraw our quotations." [89]

Despite the eagerness with which the Canton government was fighting opium, the governor-general received an edict from Peking in early December severely reprimanding him for being too lenient with offenders. There were reports that he was soon to lose his position.[90] This reprimand further intensified Teng's efforts, and in the middle of December Jardine reported that Teng

has been seizing, trying, and strangling the poor devils without mercy — the prisons are full, and three or four are carried off daily by confinement and bad treatment. We hope for some relaxation of these severities ere long; but have no good grounds for doing so. I should think such severity, in your quarter, would produce an open rebellion — they are timid fellows here; and stand a great deal from their oppressive rulers. We have never seen so serious a persecution, or one so general.[91]

Jardine thought the governor-general was determined to see how far the population under his rule would yield to "his harsh, and, in many instances, unjust persecutions of drugsellers, smokers, &c. &c." [92]

On December 3, an official of the hoppo's office seized some supplies of opium immediately in front of the Creek factory, where James Innes lived in the first suite. The two Chinese laborers who had been unloading the boxes were immediately arrested. They confessed, perhaps after torture, that the opium belonged to Innes and had been brought from the ship "Ki-le-wun," a sound resembling the name of an American, Cleveland, master of the *Thomas Perkins*. The governor-general summoned all the hong merchants the next day and announced that Innes and the *Thomas Perkins* had to leave the Canton-Whampoa area within three days. The security merchant for the American ship, who knew nothing of the whole affair, had been forced to wear the cangue. The hong merchants, perhaps at the urging of the provincial government, threatened in a written statement to tear down the building in which Innes lived if he failed to obey the governor-general's injunction. At this the general body of foreign merchants declared their determination to resist such rash measures at all costs. All trade was summarily stopped by order of the governor-general.

The time limit for the departure of the *Thomas Perkins* and Innes was later extended to ten days.[93] Innes eventually agreed to leave on December 16, and before his departure he forwarded a declaration to the governor-general admitting his ownership of the opium and absolving the American ship and the two laborers from any complicity. The laborers were not known to have had any knowledge of the content of the boxes, and the *Thomas Perkins* had become involved only because of confusion arising from the laborers' pronunciation of foreign names.[94] Trade was thus scheduled to resume on January 1.[95]

The excitement caused by the Innes affair had hardly died down when the foreign community at Canton was given still another shock. On December 12, at about eleven o'clock, an officer came to the square and made preparations to strangle a Chinese named Ho Lao-chin (Ho Lao-kin), alleged to be an opium dealer. As soon as the wooden execution cross had been driven into the ground directly under the American flag, seventy or eighty foreigners from the factories gathered to stop the execution. Among them was the crew of an old East India Company ship, the *Orwell*, which had come from Whampoa in the morning. William C. Hunter, a partner in Russell and Company and an eyewitness, wrote, "Suddenly they seized the cross, smashed it in pieces, and began to lay them over the heads and shoulders of the executioners and any Chinamen within reach." They tore down the tent which had been set up for the officer, overturned table and chairs inside, and would have attacked the officer himself if some foreign merchants had not interfered and offered him protection.[96]

At this critical point, a large but "perfectly inoffensive" crowd [97] was gathered in the square, attracted by curiosity. Between one and two o'clock in the afternoon some imprudent foreigners started to push and assail the people with sticks.[98] The crowd, provoked by "this wanton attack," became a furious mob and retaliated by throwing "showers of stones." In a few minutes the foreigners were driven into their factories, where they were besieged by the crowd all afternoon.[99] Some of the foreigners wanted to organize an armed party. If this plan had been carried out, no doubt bloodshed would have resulted. But this was averted by two young Americans, Gideon Nye, Jr., and William Hunter, who slipped out to Howqua for help. They succeeded in eluding the mob by crossing on the roofs from the top of No. 4 Suy-Hong to a shop in Hog Lane, where they descended and reached No. 13 Factory Street, which led them to Howqua's hong. A message was quickly forwarded to the prefect of Canton. By six o'clock in the evening, the sound of the gongs of the mandarins sent to disperse the mob could be heard in the square, and the crowd was instantly thrown into a panic. A number of people fell into the river and drowned; others were whipped by the soldiers; and the rest of them scattered in a few minutes.[100]

Captain Elliot, stationed at Whampoa at the time, received news of the disorder at about four o'clock in the afternoon. He immediately issued a circular to the officers of British ships anchored at Whampoa, directing them to send a force to Canton under the command of Captain Marquis of the *Reliance*, if developments called for it. He then left for Canton. On his way he received more serious reports, which caused him to forward instructions to Marquis to dispatch the emergency force. When Elliot arrived in Canton, however, he found that the crowd had already been dispersed. If the siege had lasted a few moments longer, a clash between Marquis' men and the mob would almost certainly have ensued.

The determination of the Chinese is shown by the fact that they did execute an alleged opium dealer in the public square, eleven weeks later on February 26, 1839. The immediate motive of the December 12 incident was undoubtedly, as Elliot reported, to underscore the seriousness of the governor-general's intention to punish all violators of the opium-prohibition laws.[101] The general purpose, however, was stated in a document in which the governor-general informed the foreign community, shortly after the riot, that the death penalty was the result of the introduction of opium by foreigners; that the selection of the square as the execution ground was meant "to strike observation, to arouse reflection, that the depraved portion of the foreign community might be deterred from pursuing their evil courses; for those foreigners, though born and brought up beyond the pale of civilization, have yet human hearts." [102]

It may be added here that when Palmerston received Elliot's report, he lost no time in expressing his disapproval of the behavior of those who prevented the Chinese from executing a criminal. He wanted to know "upon what alleged ground of right these persons considered themselves entitled to interfere with the arrangements made by the Chinese officers of justice for carrying into effect, in a Chinese town, the orders of their superior authorities."

After James Innes left Canton for Macao, the only serious obstacle to the restoration of normal trade was the illicit opium traffic carried on in small foreign boats within the river. A large number of these boats were stationed at Whampoa, receiving their supplies via similar craft from larger opium ships anchored at Hong Kong or Lintin. Judging from recent developments, Elliot estimated at the beginning of 1839 that "within the space of one year . . . there would have been at least three hundred armed and lawless men carrying on this business in the very heart of our regular commerce." If this traffic persisted within the river and at the factories, Elliot felt that the British government would be "driven into the necessity of very urgent, expensive, and hazardous measures upon the most painful grounds." [103] As soon as Captain Elliot had arrived at the factories at about six o'clock on December 12, 1838, amid the excitement of the riot,[104] the senior hong merchants had come to him and "complained in bitter terms that they should be exposed to the cruel and ruinous consequences which were hourly arising out of the existence of this forced trade, not merely at Whampoa, but at the factories themselves, of which they were the proprietors; and therefore, under heavy responsibility to the Government." They insisted that they would not carry on the regular trade until the river traffic was suppressed.[105]

Aside from the pressure of the hong merchants, Elliot was clearly aware of the gravely detrimental nature of the rapidly growing inner-river smuggling: not only would the legal trade be harmed, but so would the regular opium dealings hitherto carried on outside the Bogue. In order to protect these other pursuits, and to prevent the provincial government from adopting more severe measures, such as cutting off food supplies and withdrawing native servants from the foreign community, Captain Elliot decided that the time had come for interference. Thus he wrote Palmerston: "It had been clear to me, my Lord, from the origin of this peculiar branch of the opium traffic [inner-river smuggling by foreigners], that it must grow to be more and more mischievous to every branch of the trade, and certainly to none more than to that of opium itself." [106]

In this frame of mind, Elliot called a general meeting of the foreign merchants and told them that all British boats engaged in the illicit traffic inside the river, either habitually or occasionally, must withdraw within three days and cease to return for similar pursuits. This announcement was followed on the next day by a written notice of the severe terms that would be applied to violators: "And I, the said Chief Superintendent, do further give notice and warn all British subjects, being owners of such schooners, cutters, or otherwise rigged small craft engaged in the said illicit opium traffic within the Bocca Tigris, that Her Majesty's Government will in no way interpose if the Chinese Government shall think fit to seize and confiscate the same." He also warned them that, if any British subject engaged in such traffic caused the death of a native, he would be liable to capital punishment.

This order was not immediately heeded. The British merchants' defiance of the injunction led the superintendent into temporary cooperation with the Chinese government. On December 23, as we saw in the last chapter, Elliot wrote to the governor-general requesting the latter to sanction his proceedings by a direct and official communication, and he desired that the prefect and commandant of Canton be dispatched to go with him to the place where the boats were stationed in the river to execute the prohibition order. There is no record as to whether or not the officers actually did accompany Elliot, but the governor-general consented to the request that in important matters his commands were to be directed to the prefect and commandant of Canton for transmission to Elliot. Ordinary routine business, however, should be conducted in the traditional manner, through the hong merchants. It is doubtful whether Elliot really needed the governor-general's support; it is on record, however, that he took this opportunity to move a step further in his fight for direct official communication. At any rate, the foreign smuggling boats gradually disappeared from within the river by the end of the year, and the trade was reopened early in 1839.

On the eve of the Opium War, then, the Canton government had done a good job of stamping out the opium traffic. Elliot reported on January

2, 1839, that for some months the prohibition had been carried out with "remarkable vigour, not merely of the local, but of the general government." Opium traffic was virtually cleared from within the river, and outside the river the trade was almost completely stopped. On January 30, 1839, the superintendent reported: "The stagnation of the opium traffic at all points, however, may be said to have been nearly complete for the last four months." On February 8, he again complained: "The stagnation of the opium traffic still continues and the consequent locking up of the circulating medium is already producing great and general embarrassment." [107] Against the Chinese offenders, the policing was more effective. The fast crabs had been destroyed and removed from the smuggling network. Additional water forces and land troops had been sent to guard the river and inland routes. Before Commissioner Lin's arrival, the emperor received a report from Governor-General Teng summing up the accomplishments of his three years' work: 141 brokers, opium dens, and dealers' outfits had been seized; 345 offenders apprehended; and more than 10,000 opium pipes surrendered. [108] Thus the Chinese government, despite its notorious inefficiency and corruption, was still capable of enforcing the opium-prohibition laws when driven by necessity. The corrupt functionaries could be controlled; the obstinate brokers and dealers could be wiped out; and the smuggling machinery could be smashed. The insurmountable difficulties that came later arose basically from foreign sources.

It was admitted by most contemporary writers (such as McCulloch) that the Chinese had the right to forbid the importation of opium. But it was argued that they were not entitled suddenly to seize the article by labeling it contraband after years of connivance and participation in the traffic. It was also contended that the Chinese had promulgated so many unimplemented prohibition edicts that foreign merchants naturally inferred that none of the succeeding laws was meant to be enforced. [109]

This line of thinking was pursued by Palmerston when he wrote his famous letter to the minister of the Chinese emperor and when he drafted instructions to Elliot on war preparations. [110] A fragment of the manuscript found in the Foreign Office files reads:

Therefore H. M. govt. by no means dispute the right of the Government of China to prohibit the importation of opium into China, and to seize and confiscate any opium which, in defiance of prohibition duly made, should be brought by Foreigners or by Chinese subjects into the Territories of the Empire. But these fiscal prohibitions ought to be impartially and steadily enforced; and traps ought not to be laid for Foreigners by at one time letting the prohibition remain . . .

The manuscript abruptly stops here, but W. C. Costin has continued Palmerston's thought by saying that the law against opium in China had been a dead letter for a long time, that the local officials in Canton had connived and derived profit from it, and that suddenly Commissioner Lin had come on the scene and seized the opium by procedures entirely foreign to English legal usage. On this basis Costin comes to the conclusion that "unmistakably . . . the war which was about to be undertaken was not one, as has been sometimes said, to force the Chinese to trade with the British in opium." [111]

In my opinion, there is ample room for dispute about the suddenness of the Chinese government's shift to strict enforcement. It cannot be denied that, before Lin came to Canton, the opium laws had been stringently enforced for more than three years by Governor-General Teng. The memorials written in 1836 by Chu Tsun and Hsü Ch'iu attacking the attempt to legalize the opium trade had been translated and transmitted to the Foreign Office. The memorials submitted during the course of the great debate on the opium problem indicated that every participant was in favor of strict prohibition.

Captain Ellliot himself was fully aware of the change of policy and the genuine determination of Peking and Canton to extirpate the opium evil. As early as February 2, 1837, he reported: "This timid and cautious Government is not prone needlessly to try hazardous experiments upon the patience of its own people or on that of eager foreigners. And it is the very reality of all the actual degree of rigorous prohibition which most convinces me of the certainty of the coming change." [112] It will be recalled that it was the stagnation in the opium trade brought forth by the rigorous prohibition proceedings of the Chinese government that led the superintendent to demand, in February 1837, the visits of the naval forces to the Chinese seas. It was fresh in the foreign community's memory that a Chinese opium dealer had been executed just outside the walls of Macao in April 1838, and another execution had been attempted in December in front of the factories. A third execution took place in the following February in the public square of the foreign community. Moreover, for the first time in the history of the opium trade, the boats of Chinese smugglers had been ousted from the Canton River and replaced by foreign smug boats. If all of this was not a clear indication of the government's genuine determination to put an end to the opium traffic, it is probably fair to say that nothing short of war could convince the British. Elliot wrote to Viscount Palmerston on January 30, 1839:

There seems, my Lord, no longer any room to doubt that the Court has firmly determined to suppress, or, more probably, most extensively to check the opium trade. The immense, and it must be said, most unfortunate increase of the supply during the last four years, the rapid growth of the East coast trade, and the continued drain of the silver, have no doubt greatly alarmed the Government; but the manner of the rash course of traffic within the river, has probably contributed most of all to impress the urgent necessity of arresting the growing audacity of the foreign smugglers, and preventing their associating themselves with the desperate and lawless of their own large cities.[113]

Many foreign firms in Canton fully realized that the Chinese authorities were determined to stop the importation of opium. All opium ships except those belonging to the English were sent away from China before Commissioner Lin's program went into effect. Russell and Company issued a printed circular, dated February 27 (the day after an alleged opium dealer was executed in the square), to all clients informing them that the firm had "resolved to discontinue all connection with the opium trade in China." [114] On March 4, the company issued another letter, enumerating "some of the more prominent" reasons for its action and explaining that the government's measures "must render the opium business dangerous as well as disreputable." The letter informed the clients that the Chinese authorities had changed their course and the trade had taken on increasing odium since the foreign boats had extended the traffic to within the river.[115] Moreover, it was feared that the authorities would embarrass the legal traders by denouncing all agents dealing in the drug.

We have lately witnessed the effects of the trade by an execution directly before our eyes . . . There is at present a total cessation of [opium] business both here and on the coast and no sales are made except a few catties at a time may be got off by the boats outside the river and it had become the interest of every agent here to discontinue its introduction within the Bogue. The question is not now shall we trade in opium or not, but shall we be able to get on quietly with our other business before the Lintin ships are driven away. It is reported that the Imperial Commissioner is incorruptable [sic] and that he will carry out the orders of his master. We have made arrangements to move the fleet to the south side of Lantao [Ta-hsü-shan] which is not considered (we are told) within the Chinese waters.[116]

Thus Russell and Company, for one, had seen the necessity of succumbing to the spirit of the new era. The firm wrote to its agent in London, "if the export of teas is to be kept up, new sources must be opened to procure the means of paying for them." [117] The hope was "that the British government seeing the danger likely to occur to their revenue from tea will discourage the culture of opium and in this way only can the trade be effectively cut off." [118]

Any foreign trading company or foreign government unable to see that the Chinese government was earnestly pursuing a new policy could not with justice criticize the Chinese for failing to give fair warning. Their blindness was more likely due to wishful thinking and to their conviction that the Chinese were too impotent and corrupt to maintain a strict campaign against opium. Hence a small murmur in favor of legalization was taken as an important sign that such a measure would eventually be adopted, while strongly worded pronouncements from the emperor and the governor-general to the contrary were regarded merely as perfunctory gestures.

COMMISSIONER LIN AT CANTON

THE "great debate" was hardly over when the Tao-kuang Emperor decided to strike a still more vigorous blow against opium. In late October of 1838 he summoned Lin Tse-hsü, then governor-general of Hu-Kuang, and assigned him the task of stamping out the opium trade at Canton. The emperor's selection of Lin for this task was not surprising. In the first place, among all the memorials submitted by the nation's leading officials during the debate, Lin's stood out as the most cogent.[1] (The emperor added many small vermilion circles alongside lines that particularly impressed him.) Lin's talent, probity, and loyalty to the government had been recognized by the emperor ever since the early 1820's, and this was not the first time he was employed as a trouble shooter. Furthermore, as governor-general of Hu-Kuang, he had already carried out an antiopium program with remarkable results.[2]

While in Peking, Lin received the special favor of permission to ride horseback in the Forbidden City, and he was admitted to imperial audience nineteen times. It was reported that in discussing the effects of opium on his people, the emperor had wept and said to Lin, "How, alas, can I die and go to the shades of my imperial fathers and ancestors, until these dire evils are removed!" On the last day of 1838, in a very terse edict, he appointed Lin Tse-hsü high commissioner (*ch'in-ch'ai ta-ch'en*) to cope with the opium problem in Canton, giving him command of all the water forces in Kwangtung province. To ensure efficient and smooth proceedings, the emperor three days later dispatched an edict to the governor-general and governor of Canton demanding full support for Lin and clarifying his mission.[3]

The seal of the *ch'in-ch'ai ta-ch'en*, which authorized the bearer to act for the emperor with plenipotentiary powers, was given to an official only on special and urgent occasions. At the very beginning of his Canton assignment, in an edict dated March 18, 1839, Lin warned the foreign community that he was provided with this seal and could therefore act as he saw fit (*pien-i hsing-shih*). Thus he later detained foreigners in the factories and confiscated their opium without imperial sanction.[4] Yet Lin's power was not unlimited. Under the premodern political system of China, a system primarily of men, not of law, power was limited by common sense. With regard to the disposal of the confiscated opium, the use of fire-boat tactics to drive off (or destroy) illicit foreign ships, and other radical measures, the commissioner cautiously requested imperial instructions and approval in advance.[5] Moreover, the powers delegated to the office of the commissioner were made less meaningful by the Ch'ing government's practice of rewarding or punishing an official according to the result of his work, not on the basis of his adherence to or violation of instructions.[6]

LIN THE MAN, THE OFFICIAL, AND THE SCHOLAR

Lin Tse-hsü was a native of Hou-kuan (Foochow) in Fukien province. Although his family had produced many prominent statesmen in the Ming dynasty,[7] his immediate forefathers were not particularly renowned, his father being an obscure teacher. When Lin Tse-hsü was born on August 30, 1785, the popular governor of Fukien, Hsü Shih-lin, and his retinue were passing by the door of the Lin household. Therefore his father named him Tse-hsü, literally, "follow the example of Hsü."

In 1804 Lin Tse-hsü achieved the *chü-jen* degree, and for almost five years he was on the secretarial staff of Chang Shih-ch'eng, governor of Fukien (1806–1814). Since Chang had been a prominent statesman ever since the Ch'ien-lung era and was thoroughly familiar with administrative procedures and government usages, Lin learned a great deal in this period of service. He received good training in law and punishment, military defense, and administrative procedure, and the ground work of his future career as a statesman was firmly laid.[8]

In 1811 Lin became a *chin-shih* and three years later was appointed a compiler at the Hanlin Academy. He made his first trip to Yunnan province as the chief supervisor of the provincial examination in 1819. Early in the next year, he was appointed a censor of the Kiangnan circuit, and during his short term of office he made important suggestions that were accepted by the Chia-ch'ing Emperor. In the same year, he was assigned to the post of intendant of the Hang-Chia-Hu circuit of Chekiang province, where he served until he had to return home in 1821 to look after his ill father. The next year Lin was appointed acting salt controller in Chekiang; in April 1823 he became the judicial commissioner of Kiangsu; and in May of the following year he was transferred to the financial commission of the same province. Although he served for only one year as judicial commissioner, his uprightness so impressed the people that they referred to him as "Lin Ch'ing-t'ien," or "Lin the Clear Sky." [9] No nickname could be more coveted by a Ch'ing official.

In the next several years, Lin's government career was twice more interrupted. When his mother died in the fall of 1824, he had to return home to observe the period of mourning. In 1827 he was appointed judicial commissioner of Shensi and was soon transferred to the same post at Nanking. But in November of that year his father died, and he again retired from government service for almost three years.

In early 1830, Lin again reported to Peking. There he associated with Kung Tzu-chen (1792–1841) and Wei Yuan (1794–1856) and organized the Hsüan-nan poetry club, which consisted of poets, reformers, and men with progressive views. [10] In the summer, he left Peking for Hupeh to assume the post of financial commissioner. Toward the end of the year, he was transferred to the same post in Honan and in the following summer again to the same post in Nanking. In November he was appointed director-general of conservation for the eastern stretches of the Yellow River and the Grand Canal in Shantung and Honan, with his headquarters at Chi-ning in Shantung. [11]

In March 1832 Lin was promoted to the governorship of Kiangsu, and that summer, when he arrived in the provincial capital, thousands of the local inhabitants who were familiar with his good work came to the suburb to greet him. He held the post of governor for five years, being promoted in February 1837 to the governor-generalship of Hu-Kuang (Hupeh and Hunan), where he remained until he was appointed imperial commissioner in late 1838. [12]

As a provincial administrator Lin was known for his industry, his strong desire to improve the government, and his complete devotion to the welfare of the people. In official matters, whether major policies or minute details, it was his practice to investigate problems personally. He regretted that he had not begun his political career as a district magistrate so that he could have learned every aspect of government from the bottom up. Before he set out for the work at Canton, Lin had already gained distinction for his accomplishments in water conservation, flood control, social relief, and management of tax collection.

Lin Tse-hsü's rise in the official hierarchy was remarkably swift. Early in 1837, as governor-general of Hu-Kuang, his rank rivaled that of Governor-General Teng T'ing-chen, ten years his senior, who had gained the *chin-shih* ten years earlier than he. The Tao-kuang Emperor once lavishly praised Teng's ability, but frankly told Teng that his talent was inferior to that of Lin Tse-hsü.[13]

As a scholar, Lin Tse-hsü belonged to the *chin-wen*, or "modern text" school of classical criticism. This school followed the *Kung-yang* commentary of the Spring and Autumn Annals, an important work attributed to Confucius. Through the *Kung-yang* interpretation, they found that Confucius had been in favor of reforms, and they developed the practice of "finding in antiquity the sanction for present-day changes" (*t'o-ku kai-chih*).

The first great scholar of the Ch'ing dynasty to stress the importance of the *Kung-yang* commentary was Chuang Ts'un-yü (1719–1788). Through another exegete, Liu Feng-lu (1776–1829), Chuang's grandson, the *chin-wen* school received new inspiration. Liu's followers applied the doctrine to practical politics and economic problems. It was directly from Chuang and Liu's theory that Lin Tse-hsü and his intellectual associates, mainly Kung Tzu-chen and Wei Yuan, derived their new approach, which was called the *Ching-shih chih-yung chih-hsueh*, or "knowledge for the development of the state and for practical use in the world." [14]

This group of progressive scholars boldly emancipated themselves from the purely classical and traditional discipline and took an increased interest in the more pragmatic fields of political affairs, economy, history, geography, and science. In studying history and geography, Lin Tse-hsü, Li Chao-lo (1769–1841),[15] and Wei Yuan did not limit themselves to the boundaries of the Chinese empire. No doubt in response to the growing challenge from the West, they were anxious to learn about the outside world; in the process they sowed the seeds of modernization for China.[16]

Lin Tse-hsü's political activity cannot be explained as a striving for personal aggrandizement. He was more concerned with effecting reforms than with his own political career. Many of his memorials to the emperor were written primarily to persuade him rather than to please him, and Lin's ideas were often so radical as to incur imperial censure. As early as 1833, he and the governor-general of Kiangsu had recommended that the government mint silver dollars. The emperor reproached them and ridiculed the idea as wholly incompatible with long-established usages (*ta-pien ch'eng-fa, pu-ch'eng shih-t'i*).[17]

Throughout the Tao-kuang period, whenever someone was needed to cope with serious problems in flood control, sea transportation, salt administration, or military affairs, Lin Tse-hsü was a likely candidate for the job. During the 1823 flood of the Sung River, when the stricken people were on the verge of revolt and the governor had already sent for troops, Lin Tse-hsü, as a lieutenant to the governor, stopped the troops and went in one boat to plead with the people. He succeeded in quieting them down, and bloodshed was avoided.[18] In 1825, even though his period of mourning over his mother's death had not yet ended, he was summoned by an emergency imperial decree to repair a broken dike on the Yellow River in Kiangsu. When the Moslems in Yunnan revolted because over ten thousand of their people had been slaughtered in 1846–47, Lin was appointed governor-general of Yunnan and Kweichow; he quickly suppressed the revolt and improved relations between the Moslem and Chinese inhabitants. For this accomplishment he was rewarded with the title of Grand Guardian of the Heir Apparent. Late in his life he had hardly resettled in his home town for a well-earned retirement when the emperor again called him in 1850 to suppress the Taiping rebels. Had he not died in Ch'ao-chou on his way to Kwangsi, he would have been the key figure in the government's battle against the Taipings.[19]

PRELIMINARY INVESTIGATIONS

Commissioner Lin set out for Canton, leaving Peking on January 8, 1839, in a sedan chair carried by twelve bearers [20] and accompanied only by an orderly, six servants, and three cooks. His luggage was carried in three carts. A notice had been passed from station to station ahead of his group, informing all local authorities that, since his men were properly paid and their food provided, they were not allowed to make any demands on the post stations. He added that he was fully aware of the financial burden of the local governments and posts and asked them to prepare for him only ordinary foods (*chia-ch'ang fan-ts'ai*); full-course feasts, especially bird's-nest soup and baked or barbecued dishes, were not to be offered.[21]

Concerning Lin's journey through Hopeh, Shantung, and Anhwei, we only know that it was speedy and without interruption. Passing into Kiangsi by boat on the Kan River, the group observed New Year's Day, February 14, at a place about 170 li north of Nanchang. Shortly after dawn, Lin Tse-hsü kowtowed in the direction of the court to wish the emperor a happy new year. He then honored his ancestors. After covering 110 li, the journey was interrupted by heavy rain in the latter part of the day. The party arrived at the provincial capital on the next day, and Lin was met at T'eng-wang-ko by a large crowd of dignitaries. Among them was the famous progressive scholar Pao Shih-ch'en. Lin paid return calls to those officials and dined with the governor. He spent the whole day on the 16th receiving officials from the provincial government. A fierce storm kept Lin's party from departing for the next two days. On the 19th, anxious to start even though the sky was not yet clear, the commissioner asked the boatmen to embark in the hours of *mao* (5–7 A.M.). An opposing but mild southwest wind prevailed and the boats had to be towed by trackers. The party covered only forty li that day. On the 20th they started early, but, because the river was full of shallows and a fairly swift current was flowing against them, their craft had to be intermittently towed and poled. Thus when the lamps were lit, they had covered only sixty li. In the evening a favorable eastern wind arose, so the commissioner ordered the reluctant crew to re-embark immediately. They arrived at Feng-ch'eng district around midnight, and there was not a soul to be seen. Lin dispatched an orderly to the district magistrate's office to ask that trackers be employed, and it was not until 4 A.M. that the trackers arrived.

From February 21 on, the party traveled day and night whenever possible, to make up for the time lost during the storm. On March 3, Lin arrived at Nan-an, where he was welcomed by the civil and military orderly officers (*wen wu hsün-p'u*) assigned to him by the Canton government. Beyond Nan-an, the Kan River became virtually unnavigable, and on the next day he and his men set out overland and crossed the Mei-ling Pass, covering eighty li for the day. In the evening they transferred to small boats and traveled an additional ninety li. At Shao-chou on March 6, as the river became deeper, they changed back to large boats, and by pushing on day and night they arrived at Canton on March 10.[22] Lin had traveled twelve hundred miles from Peking to Canton in sixty short days, making an average of twenty miles per day.

It was half-past eight in the morning when Commissioner Lin arrived and was met by Governor-General Teng, Governor I-liang, the hoppo Yü-k'un, and a host of other functionaries at the official reception pavilion (chieh-kuan t'ing). Among the large crowd quietly gathered along the banks of the river to witness the event were three Americans on a small schooner lying off the factories. One of them, William C. Hunter, observed that Lin "had a dignified air, rather a harsh or firm expression, was a large corpulent man, with heavy black moustache and long beard, and appeared to be about sixty years of age." Actually Lin was only fifty-four years old (fifty-five *sui*), rather stout, and not tall.[23]

Commissioner Lin took the Yueh-hua Academy as his headquarters and had all the hong merchants move temporarily into neighboring houses so as to facilitate his inquiries. Having paid courtesy calls to all those who had come to meet him at the pavilion, he did not get back to the academy until late at night. On the next day visitors came to the Yueh-hua Academy one after another, and Governor-General Teng, Governor I-liang, the hoppo Yü-k'un, and Admiral Kuan remained for lunch. In the next few days Lin kept in close contact with Teng, I-liang, and other officials.[24]

Lin's basic strategy in carrying out his assignment was to follow a severe and aggressive policy toward all Chinese who were addicted to opium or connected with the trade and an adamant but defensive line toward foreign offenders. It has been pointed out that during the great debate, Lin went along with Huang Chueh-tzu in prescribing capital punishment for smokers as the way to stop the opium imports, and that, unlike many of the other memorialists, he made no suggestions for punishing the foreigners. His position was more clearly expounded just before his departure from Peking for Canton in an exchange of letters with Kung Tzu-chen, a prolific author, co-founder of the Hsüan-nan poetry club, and an assistant secretary of the Board of Ceremonies. These two letters give much insight into Lin Tse-hsü's future proceedings at Canton.

Kung's letter presented Lin with three principles (*chueh-ting-i*), three supplementary rules (*p'ang-i*), three arguments (*ta-nan-i*), and one general maxim (*kuei-hsü-i*). The first principle stated that China could not afford to let any more silver be drained out. The second principle held that opium was an "edible demon" (*shih-yao*), which made people's souls sick and reversed day and night (referring to the smokers nocturnal habits). Civilian smokers should be strangled; military smokers and all sellers and producers of the drug should be beheaded. The third principle stated that the evil traffic could not be stopped at its source for fear the foreigners and the implicated Chinese would rebel. Kung assumed that the commissioner would live in Macao and pleaded that he protect himself with a strong guard.

The first supplementary rule urged Lin to bar the importation not only of opium but also of woolens, for the benefit of the domestic silk and cotton industries; and to bar the importation of clocks, glassware, and bird's-nests because they were simply luxuries. The second advised the commissioner to expel the foreigners from Canton to Macao within a specified time limit. The third maintained that the technique of manufacturing firearms must be carefully studied and improved. Kung entreated Lin to ask the Canton officials to discuss the matter and to recruit talented mechanics to repair the armaments.

The first of Kung's three arguments was his answer to those who might contend that China needed food more urgently than currency. Kung said that this contention would be valid during a period of silver mining, but not at a time when efforts were being exerted to prevent the outflow of silver. Kung also pointed out that the prevention of further loss of silver did not preclude attention to the problem of food; food still had the first priority. In his second argument, aimed at customs officials who might insist that the prohibition of luxury items would decrease the revenue from tariffs, Kung held that the only item in the foreign trade that was beneficial to China was rice. The customs revenue was immaterial to the government, and the revenue quota could, by imperial favor, be lowered. His third argument refuted the ideas that violators of the opium-prohibition laws should be treated with leniency, and that the use of force should be avoided. It was based on a famous quotation from the Duke of Chou, "To rule a chaotic state, severe punishment must be imposed" (*hsing luan-pang, yung chung-tien*). "As for the use of force," Kung went on, "the purpose would be to expel, not to suppress them [violators]; to guard our port and defend our territory, not to fight them in the ocean or on vessels of war. . . . Punishing the reckless and unlawful foreigners and the traitorous natives is not like mobilizing a great army to cause border conflicts." Kung cautioned that there were undoubtedly persons who might try to persuade Lin to adopt lenient views; they could be found among the officials of the Canton government, the secretarial staff, the propagandists (*yu-k'o*), the merchants, and even the gentry. Kung urged him not to be influenced by such men. To this exhortation Lin replied that he was afraid the persuaders were not in Canton but in Peking. Thus it is clear that, from the very beginning, Lin Tse-hsü was aware of the probability of formidable court opposition to his policy in Canton. The final maxim that Kung presented to the commissioner was a warning against spies.[25]

Lin Tse-hsü read this letter in his sedan chair after leaving Peking and replied briefly, expressing approval of Kung's views and complimenting him on his discernment and vision. He said that he had long before sent an appeal to the emperor about the moving of the factories from Canton to Macao, but it had not been approved; and Lin did not dare to venture another request. He told Kung that he had also recently commented to the emperor that the revenue from the tariff collected by the hoppo's office was comparatively unimportant and should not be considered a factor standing in the way of opium prohibition. The commissioner specifically suggested to Kung that he move the third supplementary rule and the third argument to the category of "principles." [26] In other words, Lin agreed with Kung that opium must be eradicated at all cost and that the severest measures should be imposed on the Chinese consumers and smugglers of opium. Harsh proceedings in dealing with foreigners must be avoided — the measures to be taken, though adamant, must be judicious. In enforcing the laws, Commissioner Lin maintained, a strong force with improved firearms would be indispensable, and if conflict with foreigners proved unavoidable China should resort to a firm but defensive strategy.

Commissioner Lin's proceedings at Canton were on the whole consistent with these strategic concepts. On February 24, two weeks before his arrival in Canton, Lin wrote a dispatch to the provincial judge and the financial commissioner of Kwangtung province,[27] stating that the most important aspect of his mission was to suppress traitorous Chinese. He enjoined them to apprehend seventeen alleged yao-k'ou proprietors, opium dealers (ma-chan, transliteration of "merchant"), and chief operators of the fast-crab network. He also directed them to investigate forty-five public servants suspected of dealing in opium; two on the staff of the provincial judge, twelve with the salt controller (yun-ssu), five with the prefect of Canton, six with the magistrate of Namhoi, fourteen with the assistant magistrate of Namhoi, one with the magistrate of Panyü, and five in the military service.

The list, the commissioner stated, was compiled on the basis of investigations and accusations contained in memorials presented to the emperor.[28] Commissioner Lin instructed the provincial judge and the financial commissioner to send reliable men dressed in plain clothes immediately to arrest the alleged opium dealers and to seek evidence of their crimes. He reminded them of the law that excused any official from punishment for negligence if he voluntarily turned over those among his subordinates who were guilty of opium dealings. They were directed to try these suspects and to turn them over to the commissioner on his arrival in Canton. In the latter part of July, after the opium surrendered by the English had been destroyed, Commissioner Lin spent almost ten days personally trying these suspects. Again, for a few days in August, November, and December, he resumed this work, and on some days the trials lasted eight or nine hours, from noon until late in the evening. Records indicate that at least four men were sentenced to death.

Soon after becoming established in Canton, Commissioner Lin issued orders to the several district officers of instruction enjoining them to investigate the civilian and military licentiates under their jurisdiction. Any opium addicts found among students were to be turned over to the local government for punishment. The officers were also asked to organize all the licentiates into five-man groups; the members of each group should mutually guarantee that they were not addicted to opium. Lin issued similar orders to officers of the water forces, claiming that he was aware of the corruption that prevailed in their ranks. Many of the men were accepting bribes from opium smugglers, while others had become addicts themselves. He specifically asked the officers to weed out these wrongdoers and to form the rest into five-man reporting groups.

At the same time, Lin Tse-hsü published a proclamation informing all inhabitants of Kwangtung of the purpose of his office. He told of the harmfulness of opium and of the government's strong determination to put an end to its use, and he ordered all citizens to submit their opium and pipes within a two-month period. Realizing that the existing *pao-chia* system had deteriorated to such an extent that it was a nuisance to the people rather than a useful vehicle of government, Lin began to mobilize and organize the gentry and literati as auxiliaries to his office. They were to disseminate prescriptions for ending opium addiction, transmit government orders, and at the same time investigate and apprehend violators.[29] The effect of this arrangement was remarkable. By May 12, as many as 1,600 violators had been arrested, and 28,845 catties of opium and 42,741 opium pipes had been confiscated. In the next seven weeks 192 Chinese were convicted for violating prohibition laws, and more than 11,000 catties of opium and 27,538 opium pipes were turned over to the government. In sixteen weeks Commissioner Lin put five times as many people in prison and confiscated seven times as many opium pipes as Governor-General Teng had done in three years. On July 17, the commissioner served notice that he was going to hold a custom-finding test (*kuan-feng shih*), a sort of mock provincial examination, on July 25. A total of 645 students from the Yueh-hsiu, Yueh-hua, and Yang-ch'eng academies participated. The roll was called at 5 A.M. and the gate to the examination hall was locked at 8 A.M.; at the hours of *hsü* (7–9 P.M.) the examination ended.[30]

In addition to the regular topics, on which the students were asked to write "eight-legged" essays, there were four special questions. Block cutters and printers had been summoned to the commissioner's office on the previous night to prepare the questions, and these men were not released until the next morning, so that the questions could be kept secret. The four questions concerned the names and locations of the great retail houses and methods of prohibiting the sale and use of opium. The students were not required to write their names on the answer sheets to these special questions. As a result, Lin Tse-hsü learned the names and whereabouts of many opium dealers and officers involved in the traffic.[31]

As mentioned above, Lin had already been familiar with the corruption of the water forces before his arrival in Canton; the names of some members of the water forces were already on the lists he had sent to the provincial judge and the financial commissioner on February 24. He now learned more details from the students. At the trials of these officers, conducted by Commissioner Lin personally during the last week of July, it was found that at least five men had connived with the opium smugglers under the direction of Han Chao-ch'ing, a brigade-general in the water forces: Chiang Ta-piao, a second captain who was at the time in Peking going through the required process for an imperial audience (*yin-chien*) prior to a promotion; Lun Ch'ao-kuang, a second captain; Wang Chen-kao, a first captain by purchase; Hsü Kuang and Liang En-sheng, lance-corporals; and Pao An-t'ai, a demoted lance-corporal.[32] They had been regularly submitting to the government opium and silver provided by the smugglers, claiming that these items had been seized in accordance with the prohibition laws. They had been promoted for their pretended accomplishments, but under their tacit protection the opium smugglers happily pursued their business. At the hand of Commissioner Lin, they now met their punishment.[33]

Shortly before this episode, around the middle of June, Lin Tse-hsü noted that several British ships were still in the waters off Nan-ao, where foreign vessels had never been officially permitted. Infuriated at the water forces' failure to drive them away, he sent a memorial to the emperor advising that the commanders be punished. His memorial, which arrived at Peking on July 8, 1839, recommended the dismissal of Major

Hsieh Kuo-t'ai, acting lieutenant-colonel, who had grown too senile to prevent the approach of opium ships and manage efficiently the defense of the coast. It was also recommended that Shen Chen-pang, the brigade-general, who was still strong and capable, be demoted to the rank of major or first captain as a punishment for being remiss in his duties. Subsequently the emperor issued an edict demoting Shen to the rank of a first captain and appointing a new brigade-general.[34] Commissioner Lin's treatment of any Chinese known to be connected with the opium traffic was drastic, but it was also successful. The difficulties lay in his dealings with foreigners.

THE POLICY OF ADMONISHING THE BARBARIANS

Lin's initial proceedings with respect to the foreign community at Canton were based on several rather unsound convictions. First, he still believed, in the beginning weeks at least, that tea and rhubarb from China were essential to the health and livelihood of the foreigners. In answering an imperial inquiry dated February 22, Lin and Teng confirmed this long-cherished notion. "After careful investigation," they reported, "we conclude that tea and rhubarb are necessities for the foreigners. Moreover, they buy these commodities, sell to other foreigners, and reap great profit. If such exports were really suspended, we would bring about the end of their lives and retrieve the right of making profit." [35] Like many other mandarins who had been in charge of the Canton trade, Lin was to make liberal use of the suspension of trade as a weapon for controlling the foreign traders.

A second conviction that shaped Lin's thinking and strategy was his disparagement of trade with the British and his distrust of the general expansion of China's foreign trade. In a memorial dated May 18, 1839, he argued that formerly, when only thirty or forty foreign ships came to Canton each year, there was no shortage in the customs revenue; but now that over a hundred ships were coming, the result was a rapidly growing influx of opium. Each ship brought at least a hundred foreign merchants and sailors, and the total number of visitors was too large. "It is better to drive away the wicked and keep the good," he contended, "than to assemble a group of evildoers." To those who feared that severe measures would frighten away all foreign merchants, Commissioner Lin replied: "Wherever there is profit, who will not strive to come? If the subjects of one sovereign cease to trade, will traders from another country refrain from coming?" Even if the number of foreign traders decreased in one year, Lin believed it would certainly increase the next year. Convinced that China need never fear any lack of foreign traders, Lin told the emperor that it would be appropriate to impose strict rules on them.[36]

A third conviction behind Lin's actions was his belief that foreign traders could still reap immense profit without bringing opium to China. In his first edict addressed to the foreigners in Canton on March 18, Lin admonished: "Legitimate trade alone would suffice to bring forth profit and riches to you." In his May 18 memorial he maintained that even if the foreigners did not sell opium and engaged purely in honorable commerce, they could easily reap a 300 percent profit.[37] For this reason Lin Tse-hsü saw nothing unfeasible in the eradication of the opium traffic as long as the legal commerce was protected.

Lin was as determined to uphold the legal trade as he was to fight the illicit traffic. But what he did not realize was that stagnation of the opium trade would freeze the entire fund with which the foreigners bought their tea and silk. As stated above, Captain Elliot repeatedly complained about the deadly effect of the opium-prohibition policy of Governor-General Teng on all trade. It was the stagnation of the opium traffic that compelled him to request the visits of British naval forces to Chinese waters. Unless the economy of India and the commercial system linking England, India, and China underwent a drastic revolution, legal trade at Canton could not be carried on without the opium trade. Thus Greenberg was not far away from the truth when he diagnosed: "But the final paralysis of the Old China Trade was brought about by the stopping of its heart, the trade in opium." [38]

Lin's fourth mistaken conviction was his belief that the British government did not stand behind British opium traders in China. In May, Lin memorialized the court saying that the British subjects at Canton were merely traders and were not from influential or official families. The opium was brought in for their own profit, not by order of their sovereign. From the time the East India Company's monopoly of trade in China ceased in 1834, Lin held, the commerce at Canton had nothing to do with the British crown.[39]

This position was elaborated more clearly in a memorial dispatched in mid-June and read by the emperor on July 8. Lin reported that he had recently learned that foreign vessels trading at Canton had to hold licenses secured in their home countries. When they called at foreign ports, these licenses were examined, and a vessel sailing without a license would be confiscated and its master punished. Each ship, before its departure, was given regulations and instructed not to cause trouble in China. Lin told the emperor that those opium vessels, mostly British ships, bypassing Canton and trading at Nan-ao were all unlicensed and illegal. If discovered, they would be punished by the British government according to English laws. How then could China, a land where law and order were strictly preserved, tolerate such an illicit practice? "If Chinese outlaws caused trouble in foreign waters, according to our laws, they should be punished. Should they be put to death by foreigners, it would be the just expiation for their licentious conduct, and the Chinese government certainly would not retaliate on their behalf." By the same token Lin believed that illegal British vessels smuggling opium to China should be punished forthwith and that such actions would cause no repercussions or crisis.

It was with such thoughts in mind that Lin Tse-hsü during his audience with the emperor recommended that an imperial edict be addressed to the sovereign of England seeking cooperation in stopping the shipment of opium to China. The emperor asked him to talk it over with Teng T'ing-chen, to make an investigation at Canton, and then to decide whether such a communication was advisable. If so, Lin was to draft it.

Teng, however, seemed to favor an edict addressed to the foreign merchants from the provincial authorities. In the latter part of February, Teng had already issued such an edict jointly with the governor. In this arrogant and deadly serious document, Teng T'ing-chen and I-liang boasted that the celestial empire did not need to trade with foreign countries, but, they asked, "Could your various countries stand one day without trading with China?" They reprimanded the foreigners for bringing in opium in recent decades. As a result, they charged, traitorous natives had joined in the illicit traffic with the foreigners; common people had become inveterate smokers; and the evil had spread along the entire coast and infiltrated into the provinces. "It is explained by the publicists that your motives are to deplete the Middle Kingdom's wealth and destroy the lives of the Chinese people. There is no need to dwell on the topic that the wealth of the Celestial Empire, where all five metals are produced and precious deposits abound, could not be exhausted by such a mere trifle, but for what enmity do you want to kill the Chinese people?" They told the foreigners that military preparations had been made to cope with opium smugglers on all three routes, and severe measures had been enacted to deal with native offenders. "The smokers have all quit the habit and the dealers have dispersed. There is no more demand for the drug and henceforth no profit can be derived from the traffic." Teng and his associate said that, since many people had perished because of the drug, the Chinese now tossed it away as though it were manure or dirt.

The foreign merchants were then admonished to give up the illicit traffic and to concentrate on legal commerce. They were warned that if they persisted in violating the law, the trade would be totally stopped. "The embargo of tea and rhubarb alone would suffice to cost the lives of the various barbarians. It is found that the kings of your countries have been dutiful and their laws strict. If the supplies of tea and rhubarb were interrupted, they certainly would investigate the cause. Thus even if you could escape the punishment of the Chinese laws it is perhaps difficult for you to dodge the laws of your own countries." When the emperor read this document on March 12, with his vermilion brush he jotted down a four-character remark, "upright and appropriate" (*cheng-ta chou-tao*).[40]

After Lin Tse-hsü arrived in Canton he changed his mind and decided that no communication should be addressed to the British crown by the emperor because of the lack of a dignified mode of conveying it — there were no ambassadors like Macartney and Amherst, who in 1794 and 1817, respectively, had carried letters from the emperor to England. Lin doubted that Elliot would accept a communication containing accusations against himself; and even if he agreed to accept it, Lin was afraid that he would not faithfully transmit it to London. Moreover, Lin's work at Canton in the initial months had progressed smoothly, and he did not think an imperial edict was necessary. The emperor subsequently ruled that the matter should be postponed until the new opium-prohibition statute was promulgated.[41]

Commissioner Lin, however, decided that he himself should address the queen, jointly with the governor-general and the governor. A letter dated the second lunar month (March 15–April 13) was prepared and made public just as Lin was about to go to the Bogue to receive the British opium on April 10. The letter was allowed to circulate among the people, as were many other documents at that time.[42] Many copies of it were distributed among English and other foreign ships, whose officers were asked to deliver it to England. Lin hoped that eventually some of these copies would reach London.[43]

This letter, although written in a pompous and outspoken tone like other documents addressed to foreigners from the "celestials," was nevertheless sincere. It began by asserting that, according to natural law, the injuring of others for one's own advantage could not be sanctioned, and it reminded Her Majesty of the impartial benevolence of the emperor in supplying tea, rhubarb, silk, and such, to the foreigners, without which they would be deprived of the necessities of life. It asked the queen to put a stop to the cultivation of the poppy and the manufacture of opium.

We are of the opinion that this poisonous article is clandestinely manufactured by artful and depraved people of various tribes under the dominion of your honorable nation. Doubtless you, the honorable sovereign of that nation, have not commanded the manufacture and sale of it. . . . And we have heard that in your honorable nation, too, the people are not permitted to smoke the drug, and that offenders in this particular expose themselves to sure punishment. It is clearly from a knowledge of its injurious effects on man, that you have directed severe prohibitions against it. But in order to remove the source of the evil thoroughly would it not be better to prohibit its sale and manufacture rather than merely prohibit its consumption?

Though not making use of it one's self, to venture nevertheless to manufacture and sell it, and with it to seduce the simple folk of this land, is to seek one's own livelihood by exposing others to death, to seek one's own advantage by other men's injury. Such acts are bitterly abhorrent to the nature of man and are utterly opposed to the ways of heaven. . . .

We now wish to find, in cooperation with your honorable sovereignty, some means of bringing to a perpetual end this opium, so hurtful to mankind: we in this land forbidding the use of it, and you, in the nations of your dominion, forbidding its manufacture. . . . Not only then will the people of this land be relieved from its pernicious influence, but the people of your honorable nation too (for since they make it, how do we know they do not also smoke it?) will, when the manufacture is indeed forbidden, be likewise relieved from the danger of its use.[44]

Inasmuch as opium was forever forbidden in China, the letter continued, the manufacturers of the drug would find no market and make no profit. "Is it not far better to turn and seek other occupation than vainly to labor in the pursuit of a losing employment?" It advised that further importation of opium would bid fair to undermine the legal trade of other articles because if opium were found on a ship, it would be destroyed together with the rest of the cargo. The letter concluded: "Let it not be said that early warning of this has not been given."

There is no record of whether or not any ship captains agreed to transmit this letter for Commissioner Lin. On June 17, when Charles W. King, an American merchant, and E. C. Bridgman came to witness the destruction of the opium near the Bogue, Commissioner Lin inquired about the best mode of conveying communications to Queeen Victoria and other European sovereigns in order to seek their cooperation in stopping the opium trade. He also requested Bridgman to convey such a message, but the latter declined.[45]

On July 19, after Lin had supervised the destruction of some Chinese opium and opium pipes, along with Teng and I-liang, he returned to his office, where he received from the Board of Punishment the new statute concerning the penalty for foreigners convicted of smuggling opium. Lin then drew up a memorial in which he reopened the question of how to communicate with European sovereigns in order to make the new law known to the various foreign governments. On August 27 the Tao-kuang Emperor received the memorial in which Lin reported that the Portuguese were almost like natives, having lived at Macao for so long, and that it was easy to communicate with them. The business of the Austrians, Spanish, Prussians, Swedes, and Danes did not amount to enough in recent years to merit a special communication to their sovereigns. Since America had no sovereign, but had as many as twenty-four chiefs (*erh-shih-ssu ch'u t'ou-jen*) governing the people, Lin thought it would be too difficult to contact all of them. Thus the only immediate problem was to communicate with the queen of England. In the same memorial Lin enclosed a draft letter from himself and the provincial authorities to the queen, to which the emperor added a vermilion rescript reading, "appropriate and adequate" (*te-t'i chou-tao*).[46]

The purpose of this letter [47] was to inform the queen of the new statute, which provided capital punishment for foreign merchants found guilty of importing opium to China, and to ask her cooperation in banning the traffic. Lin and his colleagues said they knew that the laws of England were both distinct and severe and that all English ships trading to China were forbidden to carry contraband goods. It was because British ships were too numerous that sufficient care had not been taken to see that the regulations were obeyed. Now that the new statute had been promulgated by the imperial government, they hoped the queen would see to it that her subjects did not violate it.[48]

The letter made an earnest appeal on moral grounds. How could the English have the heart, it asked, to pursue profit by exploiting such an unbridled craving, when the Chinese, on the other hand, provided the English with nothing but indispensable and useful commodities?

Let us suppose that foreigners came from another country, and brought opium into England, and seduced the people of your country to smoke it. Would not you, the sovereign of the said country, look upon such a procedure with anger, and in your just indignation endeavor to get rid of it? Now we have always heard that Your Highness possesses a most kind and benevolent heart. Surely then you are incapable of doing or causing to be done unto another that which you should not wish another to do unto you.[49]

Finally the queen was urged to abolish the cultivation of the poppy in India and to have the land planted with useful crops. "Your Highness ought with determination to have the poppies all plucked up by the very root, have the land hoed afresh, and sow instead the five grains. If any man dare again to plant the poppy and manufacture opium, visit his crime with severe punishment." This, the commissioner went on, would be a most benevolent measure that would promote the beneficial and expunge the pernicious and be assisted by Heaven and blessed by God.[50]

The emperor approved this letter on August 27, and at the same time Yuan Te-hui, the commissioner's senior interpreter, translated it into English. Lin was not entirely sure of Yuan's competence in English; therefore he had William Hunter labor for several hours to translate Yuan's English version back into Chinese to check its accuracy.[51] Apparently Lin was not satisfied with either Yuan's English or Hunter's Chinese, for in November he had Howqua request Peter Parker to translate the letter into English. There is no record of whether Parker did so, but he did read the letter and commented that it contained irrefutable arguments along with "much nonsense and insult." Parker concluded that it would not help Lin's cause.[52]

On December 16, Commissioner Lin interviewed a few survivors of the British bark *Sunda*, wrecked on October 12 near the island of Hainan. He asked them to read an English translation of the letter — obviously Yuan's translation because it was written with "a hair pencil" — and one of the party, a Dr. Hill, wrote an account of the episode:

He then handed us a letter addressed to the queen of England, written in their usual high flowing strain, at which I could scarcely command my gravity, which he observing, immediately asked if it was all proper? We said that it was only a few mistakes at which we smiled, whereupon he requested us to take it into an adjoining room and correct any errors we might find in it, and whither tea and refreshments would we [be] sent us. The letter was a pretty long one, and written in a fair legible hand with a hair pencil. . . . Some parts of it we could make neither head nor tail of.[53]

In January 1840 Commissioner Lin finally found a man who consented to take charge of the message. Captain Warner, of the *Thomas Coutts*, wrote to the commissioner from Canton on January 18, acknowledging the receipt of the letter to the queen and promising to deliver it. On arriving in England, Warner wrote to Lord Palmerston on June 7, requesting an interview for the purpose of giving him Lin's letter to the queen. The Foreign Office replied on the 15th and refused to have any intercourse with Warner.[54]

Lin's reason for having his letter printed and widely circulated was undoubtedly to display his determination in carrying out the antiopium policy. The *Canton Press* commented that he did this "for the edification of his countrymen, who no doubt will think more highly than before of the Imperial Commissioner, seeing him engaged in penning admonitions to foreign potentates." [55] This observation makes little sense, for Lin was already held in the highest esteem by his countrymen, and the Chinese people's knowledge of the outside world was so vague and meager that there was no reason to suppose they would be particularly impressed by any foreign potentate.

The issues involved in all of Lin's public statements during this period, however, are quite clear. The commissioner's strongest argument was that foreigners residing in China were not being persecuted if they were treated on the same basis as the Chinese. He insisted that foreigners be placed under the jurisdiction of the Chinese government and that they abide by Chinese laws. The Chinese government by tradition seems not to have concerned itself with the security of its own overseas subjects. After the massacre of Chinese traders to the Philippines in 1603 by the Spanish, the emperor made it known that, once a Chinese left the empire, he forfeited all claim to the protection of the government. By the same reasoning the Chinese claimed full jurisdiction over foreigners residing on Chinese soil. Thus a number of foreign merchants had served prison terms in China, and others had lost their lives at the hands of Chinese executioners.[56]

However, since China's process of law and her concept of justice were so different from those of the West, the British and other Westerners persistently sought the privilege of extraterritoriality. From 1637, when two merchants of Captain Weddell's fleet became "practically" Chinese prisoners, down to the time of Captain Elliot, who refused to surrender Dent and the suspected murderer of Lin Wei-hsi to the Chinese, conflicts over jurisdiction in criminal cases arose whenever offenses involving Chinese were committed by an Englishman.

Nevertheless, the Chinese stand in the dispute over extraterritorial jurisdiction tended to be less adamant toward the end of the eighteenth century. Frequently jurisdiction was not claimed in cases between foreign parties where no Chinese was involved. In many cases of assault, if no fatal consequences were attendant, Chinese officials did not attempt whole-heartedly to secure the surrender of the culprits. As we have seen, the gunner of the *Lady Hughes*, who accidentally killed two Chinese man-darins in 1784, was the last British subject to be turned over to the Chinese for trial and punishment.[57] When Captain Elliot assumed the office of superintendent, he was as firm as any of his predecessors or the former servants of the East India Company in pressing the Chinese for extra-territorial jurisdiction. Commissioner Lin, on the other hand, clearly saw the need to reassert the right of bringing all wrongdoers under Chinese law. Consequently, the issue of jurisdiction became one of the major obstacles in the negotiations between England and China for a peaceful solution of the opium conflict.

Lin's first edict addressed to foreigners of all nations at Canton, dated March 18, 1839,[58] advised them: "Having come into the territory of the Celestial Court, you should pay obedience to its laws and statutes, equally with the natives of the land." [59] He further expounded this position in an injunction to Captain Elliot on April 8, saying that in China a man moving from one province to another was subject to the authorities of the second province as soon as he crossed the boundary, a principle that applied as well to those who came into the empire from abroad. In England foreigners were required to obey English laws; by the same token, in Kwangtung English merchants should obey Chinese laws. Elliot found Lin Tse-hsü's argument "most luminous" and in his reply he admitted, "It is beyond dispute, then, that those who will come to Canton to trade, must act in obedience to the laws." All he could do was to have British vessels and men depart from Canton.[60] This attitude indicates once more Elliot's firm position on denying Chinese jurisdiction over British sub-jects. He spoke so casually about leaving Canton because he had been confident ever since delivery of the opium that he would soon return at the head of an expeditionary force.

A month later, on May 8, in replying to requests from Elliot and the American and Dutch consuls for permission to leave Canton with their vessels and people, Lin and Teng once more asserted that they must observe Chinese laws, for they had not only eaten the food and trodden the soil of China, but had also reaped great commercial advantage.[61] At the same time, Commissioner Lin presented this view to the court. In a memorial dated May 18, he maintained that in each year the foreigners spent more days in China than in their own countries. Not only did they live in China, but all had amassed wealth.[62] They thus enjoyed more favor than native Chinese. "While affording them happiness and profit," Lin argued, "why should we not regulate them by government and laws?" He pointed out to the emperor that during the reign of Ch'ien-lung, in cases such as that of James Flint, foreigners were often imprisoned for one, two, or three years, and they had not resisted such proceedings.[63] The commissioner also cited other more recent precedents which posited the legal principle that "If individuals from outside the pale of Chinese civilization commit crimes on Chinese soil, they should be punished according to Chinese laws." And since the foreigners had accepted such law enforcement before, they should not and would not resist it now.[64]

These convictions with respect to foreign affairs, together with the emperor's instruction to do a thorough "root and branch" job of weeding out the opium evil, explain Lin's firm actions at Canton. But it would be fallacious to assume that he intended to plunge China into war with Britain. To a certain extent, Lin was aware of the prestige of Great Britain and the might of her armies.[65] It was a maxim for any Ch'ing official not to cause a border conflict, and Lin's desire to avoid war was expressed in his exchange of letters with Kung Tzu-chen, mentioned above. Moreover, he was cautioned by Chang Nan-shan, one of the most respected scholars in the province, that China should not hazard a war with Great Britain. Chang, a native of Kwangtung, was aware of the risk involved in such a conflict.[66]

It was therefore Lin's conviction that, although opium had to be done away with, it could best be managed without military conflict.[67] He repeatedly made this policy clear to Peking. In a memorial of April 12, for example, he explained to the emperor that the principle behind his measures toward the English was to be strict but not obnoxious, and that he had confidentially warned the soldiers guarding the foreign community not to make any rash moves that would lead to trouble.[68]

In March 1840, a year after his arrival in Canton, he elaborated his strategy to the emperor in a memorial that reached Peking on April 8. There were, he said, but two approaches in controlling the barbarians, restraint and leniency; and these two approaches could be applied only through the trade. Thus, like all his predecessors, he considered the suspension and restoration of trade his first and most important weapon in dealing with the British merchants.[69]

THE DETENTION OF THE FOREIGN COMMUNITY

Only when compelled by circumstances and with great reluctance (*wan-pu-te-i*), Lin Tse-hsü memorialized the emperor on September 18, 1839, would he resort to force. To meet such an emergency, Lin told the emperor, he had secretly drawn up plans and would be prepared for war. Even in the following spring, when the situation had deteriorated, Lin presented the same kind of military strategy to the emperor. In a memorial received on April 8, Lin said that it was not worthwhile or wise to fight the barbarian ships amid the rolling billows because, once the water forces were sent out, it would be impossible to call them back within a short time, and this situation could result in danger and embarrassment. He favored a defensive policy of waiting for the enemy's worn-out forces with fresh Chinese troops (*i-shou-wei-chan, i-i-tai-lao*). This line of strategy won the emperor's complete approbation.[70]

Commissioner Lin's preliminary operations were aimed at bringing the foreign traders completely under his jurisdiction and at compelling them to surrender all their opium to the Chinese government for destruction. In order to force the foreigners to comply, he resorted to the old tactic of the boycott in addition to the usual methods of suspending trade — cutting off the foreigners' supplies and depriving them of their Chinese employees — he went as far as to detain the foreign community for forty-seven days. But he was not successful in his attempt to reassert Chinese jurisdiction.

During the first week after Lin's arrival in Canton on Sunday morning, March 10, 1839, nothing occurred to alarm the foreign community or the hong merchants.[71] Lin occupied himself entirely with investigations and official conferences. He dined often with high officials, including the governor-general, the governor, the hoppo, and Admiral Kuan.[72] Thanks mainly to Kuo Kuei-ch'uan and Liang T'ing-nan, Lin was quite well informed from the very beginning. Kuo, a Hanlin bachelor from Kiangsu and an admirer of Lin ever since the latter's service as governor of that province (1832–1837), was at this time a secretary of Yü-k'un, the hoppo. On February 26, two weeks before Lin's arrival, Ch'en Hsi, the messenger dispatched by the hoppo, had met Lin to deliver a letter of greeting from Kuo.[73]

Liang T'ing-nan was president of Yueh-hua Acadamy, where Lin took up residence. He had been commissioned by the hoppo in 1838 to compile the well-known *Yueh-hai-kuan chih* (Gazetteer of the maritime customs of Kwangtung). Since the early 1820s Lin had known Liang's name through his *Nan-Han shu* (History of the Nan-Han kingdom, 917–971 A.D.), a history of one of the Ten Kingdoms in the period of the Five Dynasties. Since Liang had worked in the Hai-fang shu-chü (Maritime Defense Publishing Bureau, which, judging from the nature of its holdings, seems to have been an organ of the governor-general's office) and was in possession of many copies of foreign petitions, prohibition orders, maps of strategic areas on the coast, plans of military zones and forts, and drawings of guns and other weapons, Kuo urged him to select the more important papers pertaining to maritime affairs, for presentation with a detailed explanation to the commissioner. Liang accordingly prepared an enormous amount of material that he then presented to Lin through Kuo. After Lin arrived in Canton, quite contrary to social custom, he paid an immediate visit to Liang and had a lengthy conference with him.[74]

After a week of apparent inactivity, the commissioner made his first move. On March 17 the hong merchants, compradors, and linguists were summoned and interrogated until evening. Lin's inquiries were "close and searching," and "he often surprised them all by the variety and minuteness of his information." [75] In the afternoon of the next day, Lin summoned all the hong merchants to his official residence and conducted a lengthy conference, with the governor-general and the governor also in attendance. Two edicts in the name of the imperial commissioner were handed down to the hong merchants.[76] The first, addressed to the merchants, severely reproached them for being remiss in preventing opium imports — a task that had been specifically assigned to them by an imperial edict of 1816. The commissioner charged that, while the poisonous drug had been pervading the whole empire, they still indiscriminately gave bonds declaring that the foreign ships brought no opium. He maintained that those Chinese in the foreign community who were under their control — the coolies, servants, shopkeepers, shroffs, brokers — all played a part in the illicit traffic.

Lin then severely reprimanded the hong merchants for their perfidious activities. Lacking gratitude to the court for nurturing them, they took traitorous Chinese as their most trustworthy aides. They informed the foreigners in advance of every move contemplated by the Chinese government; but when asked about foreign affairs, they would conceal the facts. In the strongest language, the commissioner reproved them for their untruthful representation of the drain of silver, for being subservient to foreign merchants, and for giving bonds on behalf of Jardine and Innes, both well-known opium traders.[77] He warned them that his first duty in Canton was to punish traitors, and he was uncertain about whether they should be included in this category. His edict then commanded them to transmit his other edict to the foreigners, to explain its tenor to them clearly and with dignity, to require them to submit the tens of thousands of chests of opium in the store-ships to the Chinese government, and to require them to guarantee by bond that they would not again import opium under penalty of confiscation of goods and capital punishment. The hong merchants were given three days to complete this task. Their failure would be taken as adequate evidence of their long-time cooperation with and allegiance to the foreigners. Lin would then request imperial permission to put one or two of the most notorious hong merchants to death and to confiscate their properties.[78]

The second edict, addressed to foreigners of all nations, has been often quoted, but in poor translations. The main ideas were imparted to the foreign community, but, judging from the English versions, the undertones were not fully communicated.[79] The document first reprimanded the foreigners on moral grounds, saying that China had done them a great favor in allowing them to trade, and they, in return, should obey Chinese laws. Enjoying such advantages, they should not harm others: "How can you bring hither opium which you do not use in your own country to defraud others' wealth and undermine others' lives?" The emperor was more determined than ever to enforce the opium-prohibition laws, Lin warned; he himself had vowed not to give up until the evil was extirpated. Inasmuch as no Chinese would dare to collaborate in the illicit traffic and everyone knew that opium was but a "deadly poison" (chen-tu) — the official translation underplays the term as "nauseous poison" — it would be of no use for the foreigners to attempt to sell any more opium.

The commissioner then demanded that the foreigners submit to the Chinese government, within three days, all the opium on board their store-ships; it would be destroyed in order "to stop its harm." They were also required to give bonds pledging that they would refrain from such acts in the future. The bond problem, which soon developed into a deadlock, will be dealt with later at some length; but it should be pointed out here that Commissioner Lin never promised any pecuniary compensation for the surrendered opium. The opium was, to his mind, merely forfeited contraband given up in expiation for serious offenses. All Lin promised was to entreat the emperor to pardon the importers' past crimes. Should the foreign community refuse to conform, Lin warned, he was fully empowered to take effective measures — he had command of the land and naval forces and the support of the people. He could close the port as a temporary measure or shut off all dealings with the foreigners forever, for China was big, rich in all products, and not dependent on foreign goods.[80]

Lin's bringing pressure to bear upon the foreign factories rather than sending a naval force to Lintin to deal with opium ships was a calculated scheme, not an incidental tactic. He explained to the emperor again on April 12 that he was not confident of being able to subdue the foreign ships "amidst the gigantic waves and billows." Moreover, Lin wrote, "Although the opium store-ships are moored out in the sea, the agents who sell opium stay in the Canton factories." Lin felt that it was not necessary to indict them hastily; he wanted to appeal to their reason, and this he attempted to do in the edict.[81]

On the day of Lin's arrival in Canton, Captain Elliot, who was "determined to resist sudden aggression on British life and British property at all hazards, and to all extremity," left for Macao in the belief that the commissioner would direct his measures there. When the hong merchants brought the edict to the factories, the superintendent was not present. At the invitation of the General Chamber of Commerce, Matheson, Dent, Daniell, Dadabhoy Rustomjee, Green, and Wetmore (the first three English, the fourth a Parsee, and the last two American) met the hong merchants at the Consoo House on March 19. After the translation of the commissioner's edict was read, the hong merchants wished to know whether the foreign merchants could agree to Commissioner Lin's demands for the surrender of the opium and the filing of bonds. The foreigners replied that it would take several days of deliberation before they could present an answer. The hong merchants asked them to reach a decision within three days, but they would only promise to answer "as early as possible." The compensation for any surrendered opium was discussed next. The hong merchants supposed that a portion of the current low prices would be happily accepted by the holders. They also informed the foreigners of the full content of the commissioner's first edict.[82]

At this critical moment the Chinese made two more moves that evoked bad feeling and protests. On the 18th the hong merchants called on the principal foreign merchants to inquire what weapons were in their possession. They then went to a committee of the Chamber of Commerce and requested that a circular be issued to all foreign residents asking each to state in writing the number of weapons owned. On the next day, the hong merchants transmitted an edict from the hoppo forbidding the foreigners to leave for Macao pending the commissioner's investigations of both foreign merchants and natives in Canton.[83]

On the morning of March 21, the last day of Lin's announced time limit for surrendering opium, the General Chamber of Commerce convened to decide what answer should be given to the commissioner. As soon as the chairman, W. S. Wetmore, opened the meeting, Fox, the deputy chairman, proposed that an address he and Wetmore had drawn up the previous night be presented as an answer to the commissioner. In their address, Fox and Wetmore told the commissioner that the expectation of a legalized opium trade had caused a boom in opium production in India and an increase in shipments to Canton. They admitted, however, that subsequent events had shown this expectation to be mistaken, and "the question is now set at rest by the lucid proclamation of H. E. the imperial commissioner." They went on to explain that the opium on the store-ships in the outer waters was mainly the property of their constituents in Bengal and Bombay and that the merchants in Canton had no power to deliver it up. All they could do was to pledge that they would not buy or sell opium, or attempt to bring it into China. The address also suggested that the foreign merchants promise the Chinese that "they will also take every measure in their power to induce the vessels in the outer waters to depart immediately to their respective countries, where the opium is produced." The proposal was seconded, but some of the merchants objected and demanded more time for deliberation.[84]

Dent, who had just had a conference with Howqua, told the group that he was sorry to see the meeting convened, because the commissioner might gather that they were in a state of panic. He believed that the hong merchants were merely working on the foreigners' feelings, and doubted that Howqua had actually talked with the commissioner or even with the hoppo. The commissioner's warning that one or two hong merchants would be decapitated should the foreigners fail to surrender their opium was nothing more than an empty threat, and he was "perfectly convinced Howqua never expected it would be enforced." He thus urged his fellow merchants to disregard and resist "such machinations."

Dent suggested postponing any definite answer to the commissioner. He proposed that a committee be appointed to consider the situation and report to the Chamber at the earliest possible time. In the meantime, a deputation should be appointed to tell the hong merchants what had been done and to inform them that "there is an unanimous feeling in the community of the absolute necessity of the foreign residents in Canton having no connection with the opium traffic."

After some discussion, the American merchant King rose to express a different sentiment. He told the meeting that he had recently seen Howqua, who was "crushed to the ground by his terrors," and attested that Howqua's apprehensions were real, not fictitious:

It should be remembered that the property swept away under the present question might easily and in a short time be gathered again; but that blood once shed was like water spilt upon the ground, it was not to be gathered up again . . . the Hong merchants were in instant fear of their lives and properties; it is not my part . . . to defend despotic measures, but when they are once rashly determined it will not be in our power to make either reparation or atonement. The present circumstances are directly destructive to the lives of our fellow-creatures; they are still our friends and neighbours, although we may occasionally have called them hard names; but surely we shall not consent to put the pocket of a constituent in competition with the neck of a neighbour.

When King finished speaking, the meeting voted, and by a majority of eleven votes Dent's proposal was adopted (25 to 14, King abstaining). Two committees were subsequently appointed and a letter to the hong merchants was drafted. The letter, signed by Wetmore on behalf of the foreign residents, stated that the question was of such vital importance and involved such complicated interests that a reply was possible only after careful deliberation in committee. It informed the hong merchants that a deputation from the meeting was authorized to tell them "that there is an almost unanimous feeling in the community" — a qualification of Dent's original phrase — against the opium traffic. Wetmore added that the committee would report in time to enable the Chamber to give a reply on or before Wednesday, March 27.[85]

The hong merchants went to the city in the afternoon with this answer and were summarily dismissed by the commissioner.[86] He warned them that, unless the opium were surrendered before the next morning, he would come to the Consoo House to sit in judgment and order the decapitation of two of them.[87] An extraordinary meeting of the Chamber of Commerce was then convened at 10 P.M. At Dent's suggestion, Fox and Green were sent to learn from the hong merchants whether they had seen the commissioner in person. Fox reported that the hong merchants had solemnly declared that they had seen the commissioner himself and that the threats were real. Dent then moved that the hong merchants be called to the meeting for further inquiries.[88] This was done, and, upon their arrival a short time later, the following exchange took place:

Question — What took place during your interview with the high commissioner today?

Answer — We took the words of your letter to him and he gave them to the Kwangchowfoo [Canton prefect] to examine. On hearing them read, he said, you are trifling with the hong merchants, but you should not do so with him, he declared *that if opium was not delivered up, he should be at the Consoo hall tomorrow at 10 o'clock, and then he would show what he would do.*

Question — How many chests do you require?

Answer — About one thousand.

Question — What security can you give that he will be satisfied with that quantity?

Answer — None; but we think if the opium is given up, he will be satisfied that his order has been obeyed; but whether more will be required, or not, we cannot answer. . . .

Question — Is it intended to carry out the edict word for word[?]

Answer — As H. E. says, so will he act.

Question — Seriously and solemnly are you in fear of your lives?

Answered by the hong merchants, separately and individually questioned, in the affirmative.[89]

The hong merchants were then ushered into an adjoining room and a heated argument ensued. Dent, Bell, and Braine objected to altering the resolution made in the morning, while Green, speaking for the majority, contended that they should give up the opium to save the lives of the hong merchants. As a result, 1,036 chests were to be given up under solemn protest by the community. When the meeting was adjourned, it was already past one o'clock in the morning.[90]

On the next day the hong merchants again went to the city and begged the governor-general to communicate the result of the meeting to the commissioner in the hope that he would modify his demand. The governor-general, however, was of the opinion that the surrender of the 1,036 chests would be of no use, knowing Lin's determination to confiscate *all* of the opium in Canton, and indeed the commissioner made no response to the gesture. Yet he did not come to the Consoo House to punish the hong merchants.[91]

From Lin's point of view, a token surrender of opium represented no success in his first major move against the foreign community. The frustrated commissioner now turned his attention to Lancelot Dent, whose name was on the list of offenders given to him by the court. It was alleged that Dent handled more than half of the opium imports and silver exports. He was accused of making frequent contacts with natives, teaching them English and learning Chinese himself, purchasing and reading the Peking gazettes, and inquiring about Chinese government affairs. An earlier attempt to arrest him had been prevented by the prefect of Canton and the magistrates of Namhoi and Panyü, who had convinced the commissioner that further investigation was advisable. The prefect and magistrates now reported to Lin that Dent was the main hindrance to his proceedings and that many American traders were willing to submit their holdings of opium but were prevented by Dent, who possessed the largest share of the drug.[92] On March 22, the commissioner issued an order for Dent's arrest to the prefect of Canton and the two magistrates. Dent at first consented to appear in the city on the next day; but afterwards he refused to go at all unless provided with a passport under the commissioner's seal assuring his safe return.

On the next day, between 10 A.M. and 5 P.M., some of the most dramatic events took place. In the morning, a group of hong merchants, all deprived of the buttons usually worn on their caps to signify their official rank, came to Dent's house to urge him to appear in the city. The two leading hong merchants, Howqua and the elder Mowqua, each wore small, loose, iron chains round their necks. By this time, Howqua's son and the younger Mowqua and Gowqua had been cast into jail. The Chinese said that unless Dent complied with the commissioner's order, Howqua and the elder Mowqua would lose their heads before night. Dent remained adamant. It was then suggested that a general meeting be convened immediately in the hall of the British consulate. But A. R. Johnston, the deputy superintendent, would not admit Howqua and Mowqua, "in their present degraded and felonious condition," into the hall. A meeting was finally called in the Chamber of Commerce after Howqua pleaded desperately, pointing at his buttonless cap and the chain around his neck and saying that he would surely be put to death if Dent did not go into the city.[93]

At the meeting, Howqua explained that Commissioner Lin had demanded to see Dent for the purpose of making some inquiries and asked whether it was reasonable for Dent to refuse to comply with such an order. Leslie, Dent's partner, told the hong merchants again and again that Dent would not go unless the commissioner would permit him to return within twenty-four hours. The meeting was then "adjourned or rather went to Dent's own house," where both sides of the argument were anxiously gone over many times.[94]

After considerable delay, a group of foreigners, including Inglis, Ibar, and Morrison, accompanied by linguists, went to the Consoo House, where Lin's functionaries were impatiently waiting. Thus direct negotiations between the mandarins and the foreigners commenced. At the prefect's request, a *wei-yuan* (deputy) from Lin's suite, another from the hoppo's office, and the magistrate of Namhoi followed the foreign deputation back to the factory and officially delivered the commissioner's command to Dent and, in the presence of other foreigners, admonished him to obey it. Meanwhile, Morrison was detained at the Consoo House for about one hour, and it was believed that he was being held as a hostage until Dent complied with the summons. However, the deputy superintendent soon secured his release.[95]

The commissioner's summons having been officially served to Dent, the community's opinion was again solicited, and the whole body of foreign residents present stood almost to a man behind Dent.[96] They insisted on a written guarantee from the commissioner that Dent would be treated with respect and allowed to return safely. But neither the hong merchants nor the mandarins dared to request the commissioner's guarantee. The mandarins could only call Heaven to witness their promise that "they would safely conduct and bring back Dent." Without guarantee of safe conduct, Dent declared, he would not go to the city unless taken out of his house by force, and in that case he would not resist. He then left the room.

Following a brief conference among the officials, they again asked to see Dent. The *wei-yuan* of the commissioner spoke at some length, "giving his assurance in every way, and pledging his own word, for the safety of Mr. Dent's return." Considering the past irresponsibility of the mandarins, the foreigners remained firm. The *wei-yuan* then said he would spend the night in Dent's house and would not leave except with Dent. He was told that should he persist in this intention, a bed and meals would be provided for him.[97] Once he asserted that force would be used to compel Dent to go. Waiting for about half an hour in vain, the officials finally proposed that Inglis, the second partner of Dent's firm, go to the Consoo House to inform the prefect of Canton of

Dent's conditions. The foreigners agreed, and Inglis left accompanied by Gray, Thom, Fearon, and Slade. At the Consoo House, the prefect asked them to accompany him to the city.

The group was interviewed at the temple of the Queen of Heaven (T'ien-hou-kung) by the financial, judicial, salt, and grain commissioners, and they were again urged to advise Dent to appear in the city. Owing to the poor ability of the linguist, much confusion and misunderstanding resulted. The Chinese authorities wanted them to plead with the other foreigners to surrender the opium, but there is no evidence that this intention was ever communicated. After a stay of three hours, during which they were "treated with courtesy, but were questioned separately," the party was excused, each member being given two rolls of red silk and two jars of yellow wine.[98]

The legal background of the Dent affair has been greatly misunderstood. Contemporary foreigners in Canton and many Western scholars in later times thought that Commissioner Lin intended merely to make Dent a hostage for the delivery of the drug.[99] Thus Captain Elliot's condition of compliance was "to let Dent go into the city *with me*, and upon the distinct written stipulation, (sealed with the High Commissioner's signet,) that he was never to be removed for one moment out of my sight."[100] Apparently, under pressure from Lin, the hong merchants, the prefect of Canton, and the other mandarins were compelled by desperation to entice Dent with fair words and irresponsible guarantees for his safe and prompt return. In this manner they failed to convey the true strength of Lin's warrant of arrest. It is beyond doubt that, if Commissioner Lin had been successful in arresting Dent, the latter would have been tried and convicted according to Chinese law and might not have been set free even after all the opium had been surrendered. Lin might not have arrested Dent if his other demands had been met, but, once the warrant had been served, the legal machinery was in motion.

When English translations of Commissioner Lin's edicts reached Macao, Captain Elliot immediately dispatched copies of them to London on March 22. He assured Lord Palmerston that he would take "the most prompt measures for meeting the unjust and menacing disposition of the High Commissioner." A firm tone and attitude, he said, would check the "rash spirit" of the Chinese.[101]

On March 23, Elliot left Macao for the Canton factories at great risk to his own safety. He passed through the Bogue the next afternoon and reached Whampoa at four o'clock. Disregarding the pleas of the

Chinese officer there, who tried to dissuade him from going further, Elliot pressed on. Two hours later, just as the Chinese boats were closing in to intercept him, Elliot managed to land and rejoin his countrymen.[102] Inasmuch as Captain Elliot had ignored the official's entreaties at Whampoa, his detention could well be regarded by the Chinese authorities as a voluntary one. Had he stopped at the Bogue and carried on his communications from that point, as he had originally intended,[103] he would have enjoyed freedom throughout the stormy days ahead. He seemed to think that the presence of a person of his rank would protect British life and property, but his arrival did not cause the Chinese to change their plans.

After hoisting the colors and calling a meeting of all the foreigners in Canton, Captain Elliot hastened to Dent's factory with a group of Englishmen and personally escorted Dent to the Company Hall, passing through a crowd of excited Chinese onlookers and a detachment of coolies stationed in the square to prevent Dent's escape.[104] He informed the Chinese through the hong merchants that Dent would be ready to go into the city only with him and upon the high commissioner's written stipulation that Dent was always to remain in his sight.[105] This position was in keeping with his policy of firmness in rejecting Chinese jurisdiction over British subjects, Less than three months earlier, on January 2, he had assured Palmerston that he held it his duty "to resist to the last the seizure and punishment of a British subject by the Chinese law, be his crime what it might." [106]

No sooner had Dent left his factory when the Chinese guards and officers began to suspect that he was planning an escape with Elliot's assistance. (Indeed the commissioner, the governor-general, and the hoppo later sent a memorial to the emperor, implying that Dent had actually attempted to escape but had been intercepted by the Chinese.) Lin now — it was March 24 — ordered the hoppo to stop all trade; all the Chinese compradors and servants, whom he accused of transmitting messages for the foreigners, were instructed to withdraw from the factories; and finally he reinforced the guards and set up a blockade around the community.[107] Thus some 350 foreigners [108] were to be confined in the 80,000-square-yard hong area along the river for 47 days.

The order to leave was received by the Chinese servants, cooks, coolies, and compradors at about 8 P.M., and within a short time an estimated eight hundred Chinese, carrying their beds, trunks, and boxes, left the hongs "as if they were running from a plague." By half past eight, there

The Canton Factories at the Time of the Detention of 1839

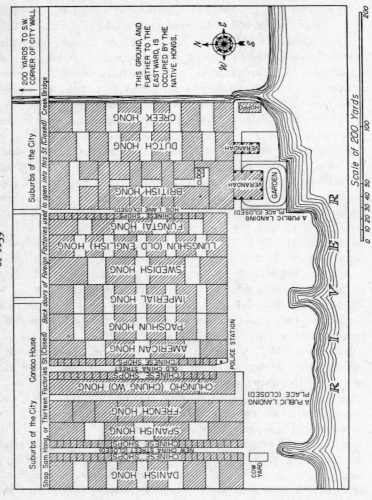

Suburbs of the City

Consoo House

Suburbs of the City

Shop Sam Hong, or Thirteen Factories used to open into this St (Closed)

Back doors of Foreign Factories used to open into this St (Closed)

← 200 YARDS TO S.W. CORNER OF CITY WALL

Creek Bridge

THIS GROUND, AND FURTHER TO THE EASTWARD, IS OCCUPIED BY THE NATIVE HONGS.

CREEK HONG

DUTCH HONG

BRITISH HONG

FUNGTAI HONG

LUNGSHUN (OLD ENGLISH) HONG

SWEDISH HONG

IMPERIAL HONG

PAOSHUN HONG

AMERICAN HONG

CHUNGHO (CHUNG WO) HONG

FRENCH HONG

SPANISH HONG

DANISH HONG

CHINESE SHOPS (CLOSED)
HOG LANE (CLOSED)

CLOU

VERANDAH

VERANDAH

GARDEN

HOPPO

A PUBLIC LANDING PLACE (CLOSED)

CHINESE SHOPS

OLD CHINA STREET

CHINESE SHOPS

POLICE STATION

A PUBLIC LANDING PLACE (CLOSED)

CHINESE SHOPS
NEW CHINA STREET (CLOSED)
CHINESE SHOPS

COW YARD

R   I   V   E   R

Scale of 200 Yards

0 10 20 30 40 50   100   200

was not a single Chinese left. The empty factories, wrote Hunter, resembled "places of the dead." The scene at the square presented a sharp contrast; under a clear, bright sky and a nearly full moon, the innumerable lanterns of the different hongs formed one blaze of light, while three or four hundred coolies noisily gathered to prevent the foreigners from leaving Canton.

In the rear of the hongs, the Chinese built bridges across the street to the roofs of the factories in order to have a better view. New China Street was blockaded with wooden bars and guarded by police. All other avenues open to the city except Old China Street were bricked up; beginning on March 29, a guard of fifty men was stationed at Old China Street and foreigners were denied access to it. Under the arch of the old East India Company factory, the hong merchants took turns keeping watch. At night they slept in large chairs. The linguists stood their watch at the square between the factories and the water in a large temporary shed constructed of mats.

Every night the factories were guarded by five hundred men — servants and coolies drawn from the several hongs and armed with pikes, spears, and long heavy staves. They were deployed from the creek across the entrance of the factories in one line. Beneath the arches and in the passageways, they were posted on both sides. The grounds in front of the factories and Old China Street were patrolled all night long by parties of these guards, beating gongs and blowing horns. The nightly noisemaking continued until the latter part of the confinement. The guards presented a fine appearance in their special uniforms, and, being acquainted with all the foreigners, they treated their captives with great civility and propriety. At times they gathered around some of the foreigners and talked about the day's news. On one occasion six of them were hired by men of Russell and Company to wash out the hong, at the rate of twenty-five cents a person.[109]

Behind the factories, infantrymen equipped with matchlocks and cartouche boxes lined up on both sides of the street. The Consoo House was used as officers' quarters. On the waterfront, a large number of boats formed three concentric arcs along the whole area of the factories, and over three hundred soldiers, with matchlocks, bows and arrows, and flags, were distributed among these boats. The first two lines, separated by a space of about one hundred feet, consisted of large tea boats, and the third line was chopboats. At night the soldiers continuously blew their conch shells and beat gongs.[110] Foreign boats of all descriptions, including the *Larne*'s gig on which Captain Elliot had arrived at the factories, were hauled up on land into the already crowded square. As an additional precaution, two rafts were stationed in the river about halfway between Canton and Whampoa to guard the passage. The total strength of the guards was estimated at between 1,000 and 1,200 men.[111]

During the confinement, foreigners could move across the square into other hongs under the watch of the guards, but they were not allowed to go beyond the square.[112] The anxiety and hardships they suffered during the detention have been exaggerated. By mustering 500 coolies who had formerly served in the factories in menial capacities to guard the foreigners, the Chinese were not trying to demean the foreigners, as one confinee commented; they were trying to minimize irritability. The coolie-guards, meanwhile, conversed freely with their captives, did work for them, and even smuggled in food.[113] The only fear that cast a shadow over the foreign community in the early days of the detention was the possibility that the 800 to 1,000 men from the foreign boats at Whampoa might try to force their way in to rescue the detained group, thereby provoking the Chinese to retaliate against the factories. Many foreign traders were, of course, worried about the final outcome of the affair, but other chief sources of discomfort were the monotony of the restricted life and the hot, muggy weather.[114]

The life in the factories, however, also had a lighter side. Amusement was provided for the foreigners and the Chinese guards alike by thirty English, American, Malay, and Bengali sailors who happened to be in the factories at the start of the detention. They passed the time by playing games; every afternoon many guards as well as captives met in the square to participate in or watch games of cricket, leapfrog, and the like. On April 14, one of the sailors impressed the crowd of spectators by climbing up to the top of the hundred-foot American flagstaff.

The infantrymen assigned to watch the foreigners were also friendly. Their officers occasionally joined the foreigners for beer and conversation. On April 20, an episode took place that furnished a bit of fun and illustrates one interesting aspect of the relations between the Chinese and the English on the unofficial level. On that day several Chinese officers came to the Consoo House on horseback. Their horses were taken to the square, where one of the grooms in jest offered an Englishman a ride, not dreaming that the offer would be accepted. The Englishman immediately jumped on and charged ahead at full gallop. The groom was so badly frightened that he could not move. The scene — the Englishman with his white jacket, cap, and stick, on the high saddle with big basket stirrups, racing to and fro in the square — amused the spectators no end.[115]

The most difficult role in the drama was perhaps that assigned to the hong merchants and the linguists, for they had to watch the foreigners without really being able to control them. To them this was a period of anxiety, humiliation, and fear. Time and again they were threatened with death if they failed in securing the foreigners' compliance to Commissioner Lin's demands. Those hong merchants who were not constantly on the move had to sit under the company's veranda day and night to prevent Dent's escape. What with so much walking and standing, old Howqua's feet and legs became noticeably swollen.[116]

It was the small group of linguists — Old Tom, Young Tom, Ahtone, Alanci, and Ahin — who kept an eye on the foreigners and at the same time looked after their needs. Stationed on a large boat alongside the small hoppo house opposite the factories, these men had to satisfy the wants and listen to the complaints of every foreigner. William Hunter used to spend a few hours every day on the linguists' boat to watch the daily transactions between them and the foreigners. On April 14, he wrote in his journal:

They [the foreigners] come to them, on all and every Business — One wants his Clothes sent to wash, another, his trousers or Coat procured from the Tailor — in comes another, who blows them up sky high — because he has not had his daily supply of Spring Water. One comes & says, His cows are starving, as the Cow Man sent to look after them has run Away. Mr. B — appears and in great distress begs them to send a few Coolies, to wash out his Hong — it being unwashed for 10 days. Mr. K. wants a basket of oranges, and Mr. F. comes to complain, of some of the Guard having been insolent, with threats of his being about to go and annihilate them, with his stick, at which the Linguists say, ["]Hae Yaw. How can do? Mandarin Angry to muchee[.]" Then Mr. C. comes in with a bundle in his hand, which proves to be a ragged Jacket or two, which he insists upon it, must be mended instanter — Others come to hoax the poor fellow, with threats of forcing their way up China Street, which alarms them, & brings out, the usual, ["]Hae Yaw, how can do ? no good talkee so."

Others come to complain that rats, hungry dogs, cows, and calves were wandering in or about their hongs and threatened to fire at them if the guards did not keep them away. In short, the linguists received constant complaints, demands, and threats from the foreigners on every kind of problem. Besides the headman, each linguist had between six and eight clerks and eight or ten coolies who, from dawn until late at night, were steadily on the move to meet the needs of the imprisoned foreigners. In Hunter's opinion, the linguists and their assistants were "the best natur'd set of fellows living." "They laugh at us," Hunter wrote, "they cannot help it, our situation is so entirely that of a closely confined prisoner — and making known our wants excite [sic] their fun. But they do everything they can to relieve us, and go on all manner of Errands, with great good will."

Considerable inconvenience was brought on the foreigners by the departure of their cooks, porters, and servants. At least in the initial days of the period, the foreigners had to milk their own cows, carry water, and do their own cooking. Many of the foreigners formed groups in which each took a turn at cooking for the whole group. While such domestic work was a chore to some, it did not produce discontent and impatience among the majority of prisoners. "Not at all," wrote Hunter, "we in the Suy-Hong — and it was the same with our fellow-prisoners in the other Factories, with few exceptions — made light of it, and laughed rather than groaned over the efforts to roast a capon, to boil an egg or potatoe." [117]

The sailors and lascars stranded in Canton by the embargo were distributed among the hongs to help with the cooking. Toward the end of the confinement, Matheson wrote to Jardine: "By the kindness of Heerjeebhoy in lending us his Indian servants, with the assistance of some sailors who happened to be up, we have not only lived comfortably all along, but have entertained the remaining inmates of the Hong including Slade and his Printers." The chore of preparing food was lightened by the hong merchants and linguists. For instance, on the morning of March 26, less than forty hours after all the cooks and servants had departed, a purser from the linguist Ahtone's establishment brought a Chinese to Hunter's hong to act as cook and left them six loaves of bread that the purser had carried secretly in his sleeves. The next day, the linguists took Hunter aboard their boat for supper, and when he came back he found stationed as guards at the gate two of Howqua's coolies, who, by order of their master, managed to slip him a small bag containing two boiled capons, a boiled ham, three loaves of bread, and some crackers. From April 5 on, breakfast and dinner were prepared for Hunter and his colleagues at Old Tom's house and brought to them in covered boxes.[118]

According to the terms stipulated by Commissioner Lin for the surrender of the opium, the compradors, cooks, and servants were to return when the foreigners had delivered one fourth of the opium; the passage boats that took foreigners to and from Whampoa and Macao would be allowed to run again when they had surrendered half; the guards would be removed when three quarters of the total amount had been surrendered; and the trade would be placed on a normal footing as soon as the total quantity had been given up.[119] On the morning of April 12, when only fifty chests of opium were in Lin's hands, he sent a communication to Captain Elliot from the Bogue saying that the compradors and cooks had been ordered to return. This order perhaps was not generally disseminated until around April 15, when 4,515 chests and bags of opium had been delivered. When further complications developed over the question of the passage boats, Lin frequently reminded Elliot that he had done better than keep his word and had restored the compradors and servants to the foreign community even before he had received one fourth of the opium. On April 17, Elliot was able to report to Palmerston that "the servants are coming back gradually." However, it is interesting to note that from March 29 on, a cook and coolie of Russell and Company came in over the roof of the rear factory every day for quite some time. Two more of the company's coolies reported for duty as early as April 14. Their comprador was somewhat reluctant to come back, but on April 17 he promised that in a couple of days he would return for good, bringing cooks and coolies with him. On April 20 he and his crew did come; however, they left again the next day because of difficulties that had developed over the bond problem, which will be taken up in detail later.[120]

The shortage of food, water, and other supplies during the period of detention has also been exaggerated. At the commencement of the blockade, Captain Elliot sent a dispatch to his home government reporting that supplies were cut off. The written edict imposing the blockade did not explicitly order that the supplies to the foreign community be cut off. It specified that the trade be stopped, that all foreign passage boats be prohibited from sailing close to foreign ships, that all Chinese employed by the foreign factories be withdrawn, that no Chinese houses or boats be rented or hired by the foreigners and no Chinese laborers of any kind be employed by them, and that if any Chinese should enter into a transaction with foreigners or rent houses or boats to the factories, they would be punished according to law as if they were in treasonable collusion with another state. Whatever hardship the foreigners suffered from lack of provisions was due to the interpretation given by the lower officers to the terse and vague language of this last item. Nevertheless, no one suffered for want of important provisions. In the first few days of the confinement, sufficient supplies were brought in with the help of the hong merchants and linguists. Just after the embargo was declared, the coolies of one foreign house managed to bring in "about 60 fowls, 15 tubs of water, a tub of sugar, some oil, a bag of biscuits, and a few other things." [121]

After Captain Elliot agreed on March 27 to turn over the opium, the commissioner and his colleagues gave the factories two hundred and fifty animals for meat. Among these, the American residents were allotted on March 29 two sheep, four pigs, sixteen hams, ten fowls, sixteen geese, and six bags of rice. On April 2 Elliot reported to Palmerston that the factories were now permitted to purchase food. [122]

The Parsees seemed to have enjoyed special privileges. Their servants, as natives of India, had access to the food market at the top of China Street and could bring back capons and chickens. Friends from other countries could then come to enjoy curried chicken for "variety's sake." Ample records are available to attest to the fact that, throughout the whole period of confinement, bread, eggs, mutton, potatoes, spring water, grass for the cows, and other items were brought in.

Communication between the factories and the outside was cut off only nominally. Commissioner Lin's surveillance did not stop scraps of intelligence from being smuggled to and from Whampoa and Macao by Chinese bringing messages concealed in cigars or hidden in other ingenious ways. During the first week of detention Captain Blake received two messages from a Mr. Maclean, an English merchant on board the *Reliance* at Whampoa, written on small slips of paper tucked in the thick part of the soles of the messenger's shoes. These messages from Captain Elliot assured Blake that "all is quiet, do nothing, there is no apprehension or fear of any personal violence." Hunter repeatedly mentions in his journal that messages and reports were exchanged with Whampoa and Macao. [123]

On May 2, when the commissioner and his colleagues were convinced that all the opium would be delivered in due time, edicts were issued to restore the passage boats and to remove the blockade of the factories. With the exception of sixteen alleged habitual opium traders, including Dent, all foreigners were set free. This edict was promulgated by the Canton prefect on May 4, and the next morning all the guards were ordered to withdraw. The hong merchants and most of the coolie-guards also dispersed, leaving only seventy men in the middle of the square to prevent the escape of the detained sixteen. On the next day, the first passage boat left for Macao with about fifty passengers on board. [124]

Forty-seven days had passed since March 19, when the hoppo had notified the foreigners that they would not be allowed to leave until the opium question was settled, and six weeks had elapsed since March 24, when the blockade was imposed. During this period, the foreigners suffered from humiliation, monotony, and uncertainty rather than from actual physical hardship. In these circumstances the confinees did not lose their courage and cheerfulness. One foreigner called the blockaded factory a "comfortable prison," and another claimed that "not a night has passed that I have not enjoyed undisturbed repose." [125] While the foreign residents at Canton were confined in the factories, the shipping at Whampoa was similarly detained. As at Canton, the crews did not suffer from want of daily supplies. Plenty of wholesome food was supplied every day by the Chinese, and the general needs of the foreigners were attended to by the compradors.[126]

Officials of the Ch'ing government were accustomed to carry out their duties according to precedent. In reporting the situation to Peking, Lin and Teng frequently cited earlier cases to justify their tactics. But in 1839, Lin faced a unique situation. Never before in Anglo-Chinese relations had a Chinese official been asked to do such an impossible job. The age-old modes of regulating the Canton trade were no longer adequate, and some innovation in strategy was necessary. Lin's daring policy of imprisonment — and its boldness is emphasized if we remember that it was instituted only two weeks after Lin first arrived in Canton — was resorted to primarily because the Chinese water forces were incapable of enforcing his orders. Only by holding the foreigners as hostages could the Chinese secure delivery of the opium.[127]

On the other hand, imbued as he was with the ancient tributary-system ideology, Commissioner Lin did not realize the seriousness of his actions. He was altogether sincere when he called Captain Elliot's complaint at being imprisoned a ridiculous one. In replying to Elliot's protest, Lin pointed out that he had only withdrawn the Chinese employees from the factories because he had suspected them of preparing to help Dent escape and he had restricted Elliot's movements because of his lack of good faith. When Elliot had reported the quantity of opium to be surrendered, Lin had immediately sent a present of food. Was this, the commissioner asked, the way prisoners were usually treated?

But the Chinese government, in Elliot's view, had incurred "heavy responsibilities" that called for immediate retaliation. When the confinement was about to end, Matheson wrote Jardine and commented on Lin and Elliot's tactics:

Their still keeping us in durance ever since 22d [the blockade was actually imposed on the 24th] is even fortunate as adding to the account for which we have to claim redress, and as proving to our own Government how inveterately bent the Chinese are in following up their declared purposes . . . as Lord Napier was blamed by Lord Palmerston for having provoked the severity of the Chinese, it would appear as if Elliot had determined to steer clear of such an accusation by doing their will in all things. . . . To a close observer it would seem as if the whole of Elliot's career were expressly designed to lead on the Chinese to commit themselves, and produce a collision.[128]

To Lin, the detention of the foreign merchants at Canton was the enforcement of Chinese law, the rightful punishment of a group of degraded opium smugglers and a fitting conclusion to the shameful period of the opium trade. But, to Elliot, the Chinese government had committed a serious piratical act against British life, liberty, and property and against the dignity of the British crown. His aim was not only to avenge these wrongs, but to revolutionize China's foreign-trade system and to begin a new and honorable era in Britain's relations with China.

OPIUM SMOKE AND WAR CLOUDS

WHILE the foreign community was under confinement, Commissioner Lin was successful in confiscating all the opium in British hands. But the victory was only illusory. As we look at it now, the confiscation did not benefit the Chinese; but it did provide the British authorities with a justification for their later revenge. Since the opium trade in the 1830s had fallen into such a depression and since the British needed a pretext for their larger military operation in 1840, the surrender of the drug, as we shall see, was more of a voluntary action than it was a move made under duress.

CAPTAIN ELLIOT'S PREPARATIONS FOR EMERGENCY

Elliot's policy in early 1839 was both firm and flexible. At the end of February, he went to Macao to confer with P. J. Blake, commander of the sloop *Larne*, which had just arrived in the Macao Roads. In view of the increasingly strict opium prohibition, he requested Captain Blake to remain in Chinese waters to enable him to communicate with the commander-in-chief of British naval forces and the governor-general of India in case of emergency.[1]

On February 28, Elliot was informed of the execution of a Chinese opium dealer two days earlier in front of the factories, and two hours after receiving the news he boarded the cutter and sailed to Canton, arriving on March 2. Two days later, he submitted a strongly worded protest to Governor-General Teng against the execution and posted a copy of it at the factory. Elliot returned to Macao on the 10th to continue his conference with Captain Blake. He had chosen to remain in Macao because he believed Commissioner Lin's efforts would be directed there, and he also wanted to keep in contact with the *Larne*. The blockade of the foreign factories, however, changed his whole plan.

First, Captain Elliot took precautions to meet every emergency. On March 22, he issued public notices requiring all British ships at the outer anchorages to proceed immediately to Hong Kong and, under the command of Blake, to prepare to resist every act of aggression of the Chinese government. Meanwhile he dispatched an address to the governor-general asking whether it was the intention of the Chinese government to make war upon the British. The execution of a Chinese in the public square of the factories, the unusual assemblage of troops and vessels of war, and Lin's rash proceedings had led him to consider that, if these did not amount to an act of declared war, they constituted "at least its immediate and inevitable preliminary." He enjoined all British subjects, by a notice dated March 23, to prepare immediately to move their property on board the *Reliance, Orwell, George the Fourth*, or other British vessels at Whampoa. On the same day he also addressed a secret letter telling Captain Blake of his intention to go to Canton and asked him to adopt immediate and suitable measures for the relief of the detained British community if no further message was received from him within six days.[2]

Having made these arrangements, Elliot set out for Canton on March 23 and arrived at the factories at about 6 P.M.[3] He had already assured Viscount Palmerston that he would "take the most prompt measures for meeting the unjust and menacing dispositions of the High Commissioner and the Provincial Authorities," believing that firmness toward the Chinese would be the best policy.[4] In this frame of mind, Elliot did not wait for daybreak to serve the Chinese a severe protest, which reached the governor-general shortly after midnight.[5] His note demanded passports for all the British subjects and ships at Canton within three days so that they might leave during the next ten days. "And if Elliot shall not hear that the passports are granted within the space of three days from the date that this application reaches your Excellency's hands, he will be reluctantly driven to the conclusion, that the men and ships of his country are forcibly detained, and act accordingly. . . . And in the name of the Sovereign of his nation, he declares himself free from the responsibility of all the consequences that may arise."[6]

Governor-General Teng referred this address to Commissioner Lin in the early hours of *ch'ou* (1–3 A.M.), with a letter accusing Elliot of ignoring the order to surrender the opium and the summons calling Dent to appear for questioning. "It is most requisite," Teng wrote, "that, in obedience to the commands of you, the High Imperial Commissioner, the opium laid up on board the store-ships should at once be delivered up to the Government, when of course immediate permission will be accorded to apply for permits for the men and vessels of the said nation to come and go; and assuredly there shall be no causeless obstruction and delay." Lin sent the prefect and the commandant of Canton to the factories without delay and, in the name of these two highest officials in Canton, issued an edict in reply to the superintendent. The edict largely quoted Teng's letter to the commissioner.

As Hunter wrote in his journal on April 2, the greatest fear among the foreigners detained in the factories was the possibility that the foreigners at Whampoa might attempt to force their way to Canton to rescue them, and in that case "the Chinese would probably fall upon and massacre us." [7] Captain Elliot, on second thought, may have realized this danger, for he dispatched another address to the governor-general in the early afternoon (the hours of *wei*, 1–3 P.M.). This one was written in a much more diplomatic tone, and Elliot withdrew his previous violent protest by asking the governor-general to return the earlier address. He assured Teng that he was anxious to obey the wishes of the emperor as far as it was in his power to do so and requested the governor-general to depute an officer to visit him during the day.[8] The most enigmatic development is that when the prefect of Canton, the subprefect of Fo-kang, and the magistrates of Namhoi and Panyü repeatedly called on Elliot (while the provincial judge and the financial commissioner were directed to wait nearby for the results), the superintendent simply avoided contact with them. On the same day, a voluntary pledge "not to deal in opium, not to attempt to introduce it into the Chinese Empire," was drawn up and signed by most of the foreign merchants in Canton; but this paper was not delivered to the commissioner until the 27th.[9]

Commissioner Lin, however, insisted that the opium be delivered immediately. On March 26, the prefect of Canton and the magistrates of Panyü and Namhoi delivered two more edicts transmitting Lin's commands in reply to Elliot and reiterated the order for the surrender of the opium.[10] Lin accused Elliot of not making a single reference in his communications to the prevention of the traffic.

To the second edict Lin attached an interesting admonition.[11] First, he exhorted the foreigners to deliver up the opium quickly in accordance with the principles of Heaven. It was argued that the foreigners in the past few decades had amassed great wealth at the expense and injury of the natives by means of the opium trade, which was a sinful pursuit and could not escape the inevitable retribution of Providence (*T'ien-tao*).[12]

"If, however, you will now repent and deliver up your opium, by a well timed repentance, you may yet avert judgment and calamities; if not, then your wickedness being greater, the consequences of that wickedness will fall more fearfully upon you!" If Commissioner Lin had stopped here, his argument would have seemed plausible enough, but he went on to cite the names of a few foreigners who had died in China, such as Lord Napier and Dr. Morrison, as instances of divine retribution.

Next, Lin pleaded with the foreigners to surrender the opium for legal reasons. He warned them that Chinese laws punished dealers more severely than consumers. Depriving even one individual of his life was a crime punishable by death. Lin declared that anyone who sold opium was guilty of swindling people out of their money and depriving them of their lives. He asked them to ponder carefully whether this crime should be punishable by death. As a third argument Lin appealed to the foreigners in terms of human feeling and wisdom. He pointed out that they could still make an immense profit trading solely in other articles. Such profit, he argued, would be made legally and would not earn them harsh heavenly retribution. On the other hand, if they insisted on engaging in the opium traffic, all trade would be stopped.

Finally, the commissioner pointed out that the force of circumstances indicated that the opium should be surrendered immediately. Coming to trade from afar, the foreigners depended entirely on peaceful relations with other people and lawful proceedings to make profit and avoid harm. "But by your traffic in opium you imperil the very existence of our people, and men of correct and virtuous principles are exceedingly grieved at heart and annoyed at your course. . . . The common people, too, have become indignant at your conduct." The commissioner warned them that the wrath of a mob was difficult to oppose. "Sincerity and righteousness are the sole assets that men far away from home can depend on. Now the various Chinese officials have shown sincerity and righteousness to you but you have not returned the same. Can you be at ease in your hearts? Is this in harmony with the circumstances?" Since opium was not consumed in foreign countries and was at the time absolutely prohibited in China, Lin could not see why foreign merchants should have any difficulty in deciding to deliver it up.[13]

As S. Wells Williams puts it, "For once in the history of foreign intercourse with China, these commands were obeyed."[14] At six o'clock the next morning, the superintendent put out a public notice requiring all British subjects to surrender their opium to him before 6 P.M. for deliverance to the Chinese government; he stated the responsibility of himself and of the British government for the value of the drug surrendered.[15]

In the hours of *ssu* (9–11 A.M.) on the 27th, Elliot notified Commissioner Lin that the opium would be delivered, and on the next day Elliot wrote Lin again pledging to deliver up 20,283 chests of British-owned opium.[16] This was a complete change of strategy. A week before, on March 21, the hong merchants had difficulty in persuading the foreign merchants to surrender even one thousand chests.[17] When Captain Elliot had first arrived, he planned to withdraw all British men and goods to Macao, and he talked freely about the use of force; [18] he certainly did not have the idea then of readily surrendering such a large amount of property. There was perhaps not a single foreign merchant detained in the factories who was really afraid for his life. Elliot himself sent a message on the 28th, the day after he consented to surrender the opium, to Captain Marquis, senior commander among the British ships at Whampoa, saying that he was "without apprehension as to the safety of life and property." [19] It would be naive to assume that Elliot and the foreign merchants were intimidated into this new line of action. This was seen by the *Quarterly Review*, among others: "We certainly shall not easily believe that the mere duress of two days, with a vague intimation that offenders of the laws were liable to punishment, could have frightened Captain Elliot into his grand step!" [20]

THE MOTIVE FOR THE OPIUM DELIVERY

Captain Elliot no doubt decided to deliver up the opium because it was a step favorable to the interests of the foreign merchants. Owing to the severe prohibition measures, the opium trade was at this time entirely at a standstill. It will be recalled that, on January 10, Elliot reported the stagnation of the traffic at all points over the previous four months, and on February 8 he wrote Palmerston that the dullness continued.[21] Russell and Company had already charged their clients one dollar per month on each chest of opium stored at Lintin because the only sales being made were transactions involving a few catties at a time, which were unloaded outside the river.[22] On March 22, when the General Chamber of Commerce convened to deliberate on a reply to Commissioner Lin's edict of March 18, Matheson insisted that "it should be noted in the address, as an important fact, *that not a chest of opium had been sold in Canton for the last five months.*" [23]

To make matters worse, according to Elliot's estimate, an unsurpassed amount of opium — 50,000 chests — was ready for the Chinese market, where the annual consumption had never exceeded 24,000 chests; there were 20,000 chests on the coast of China, more than 20,000 in Bengal, and almost 12,000 ready to be shipped from Bombay. Later, in January 1842, when the problem of compensating the opium claimants was being deliberated by the government, Elliot wrote that "Commissioner Lin's measure was one of great relief, and I have a conviction, that the actual deliveries on the 27th of March, 1839, will recover as good a price for that opium, as they could have done under any other circumstances." [24] There is little wonder that many opium holders "submitted" more than they actually had on hand, for the whole amount offered up was not at the time in Chinese waters. Forbes wrote, "Some delay occurred in the delivery of the opium, by reason of anxious holders giving in schedules not only of what they had in hand, but of what was on the way, it being very desirable, in the existing state of the market, to deliver as much as possible to the Queen's order." He also wrote that some of the holders, unable to make up their quota, resorted to all sorts of expedients to meet the requirements. Some of them repacked their opium and expanded one hundred chests into one hundred fifty; others managed to send fast clippers to India to buy more. Hunter wrote in his journal that it was his intention to leave Canton as soon as ten thousand chests were delivered because there were doubts that the entire quantity was on hand to deliver, but the commissioner had promised that, when half of the amount was turned in, the passage boats would be allowed to run again.[25]

Matheson wrote to Jardine on May 1 that he was glad he had not sent the opium ships away, and he lauded Elliot's move as "a large and statesmanlike measure, more especially as the Chinese have fallen into the snare of rendering themselves directly liable to the British Crown. Had the Chinese declined receiving it . . . our position would have been far less favourable." [26] Through Captain Elliot's intervention, the problem had undergone a total change. It was no longer the commissioner punishing the opium traders and confiscating their contraband; it was now a larger issue, involving the two governments. Regardless of the motives behind Elliot's decisive measure, the protection of the interests of the British merchants — with whom he had long identified himself under stress of isolation from his home government and the lack of clear instruction from Palmerston — was certainly one of the most important considerations. The *Quarterly Review* was perhaps not far from the truth when it commented, "it seems to be clear that he, almost from the beginning of his superintendency, got into relations of private intercourse with some of the chief parties engaged in the illicit traffic. This appears to have been the *origo mali*." [27]

After Elliot consented to surrender the opium, the negotiations concentrated on the details of its delivery. On March 28, Commissioner Lin requested that the twenty-two store-ships come to anchor near the Shachiao (Sandy Head) offing between March 31 and April 2 so that the Chinese officers could receive the opium. Captain Elliot, however, notified the commissioner on March 30 that he had instructed Johnston, the deputy superintendent, to proceed outside the river as soon as possible for the purpose of making the delivery. In the same communication he requested a boat to convey Johnston to Macao where he would be able to make use of Elliot's cutter. [28] Lin could not see why Johnston should be dispatched to surrender the opium; on April 1 he issued an edict commanding that each foreign merchant should submit his own bill of delivery to the Chinese government, which the Chinese would exchange for opium at the store-ships. "I, the High Commissioner, have given repeated official replies, requiring of all the foreigners to write orders themselves, on the ground that, in the ordinary manner of selling opium, they have always thus unloaded the goods, without committing an error once in a hundred times. Why, then, is not the opium surrendered in this comparatively simple, convenient, and easy way?"

Captain Elliot immediately replied: "Elliot . . . desires to send Mr. Johnston to deliver up the opium, for no other object than that of clear and orderly arrangement; it being requisite that a person should be sent on board the vessels, to take note of each delivery, and so prevent error or confusion." He explained that the opium had been surrendered to him as a representative of his country; therefore, turning it over to the Chinese was not similar to an ordinary sale of a small amount. Five days later, Elliot explained his position to Palmerston in less subtle terms: "His [Lin's] purposes were plain; and it was my clear duty to let them reach me, and not the merchants acting principally for absent men, and therefore wholly incapable of taking consentaneous courses, or any other than those [courses] which would lead to separate and ruinous surrenders of all this immense mass of property."

Unaware of the legal intricacies involved in receiving the opium from an agent of the British crown, Lin did not insist that his procedure be followed. What mattered was the surrender of all the opium. On April 2 he wrote Elliot and outlined the rules under which the opium was to be delivered. He stipulated that a group of Chinese officers would take John-ston in a chopboat outside the river so that he might direct the store-ships to repair to Lung-hsueh (Lankeet) just south of Ch'uan-pi (Chuen-pee) outside the Bogue. It will be recalled that the commissioner had promised that when a fourth of the opium had been delivered, he would see to it that the compradors and servants were immediately restored; when half had been delivered, the passage boats would be allowed to apply for passes and to run again; when three fourths had been delivered, the trade embargo would be removed; and when the whole surrender was completed, normal conditions would be restored. At the same time, punish-ments such as the cutting off of food and water supplies were prescribed for any delay in the delivery.[29] Elliot agreed to these arrangements.

On April 3, the commissioner sent two officers, Liu K'ai-yü and Li Tun-yeh, to take Johnston outside the port to arrange the delivery. At half past five in the afternoon, Johnston, Thom, the linguist Alantsae, and three servants left the point in front of the Creek hong in Howqua's boat, which took them to a larger chopboat anchored opposite the factories, where they were to be joined by two hong merchants and the Chinese officers.[30] On the same day, Lin drew up a seven-point regulation that he distributed the next day to the Chinese personnel who were to oversee the receiving of the opium. It outlined every detail. Twenty teams, each consisting of one civil and one military official, would actually supervise the job, a single team handling no more than one hundred chests. Two store-ships would be unloaded at a time. The manner of marking the chests and sealing the loose opium was all carefully specified. Precautions were to be taken to prevent cheating. If crewmen were caught overturn-ing a boat in order to retrieve the opium at a later time, they would be severely punished. At the end of the document, Lin solicited further sug-gestions from those who would be doing the work.[31] This was character-istic of Lin, for, unlike other high officials of his time, he never hesitated to ask for advice from persons under him in rank.

A number of large chopboats left Canton on the 5th for Lung-hsueh to participate in the receiving work. Since each store-ship required dozens of chopboats to take over its cargo, a great many boats were now needed. On the evening of the 9th, Lin received a letter from Admiral Kuan in-forming him that some opium ships had already arrived, so Lin left Can-ton at noon the next day with the governor-general and the hoppo. The party arrived at the Bogue on the 11th and spent two hours talking with the admiral before the receiving work commenced. On the first day, it was slow, only fifty chests being taken over. On the second day, six hundred chests were received, and from the third day on the number increased. Despite the small amount received in the beginning and the slowdown caused by a storm on the 19th when only 314 chests were delivered, the amount turned over to the Chinese during the first ten days averaged over 1,100 chests per day. This rate dropped considerably afterward because many opium ships had not yet arrived; they had to come a long way from the coast. Three of the ships had come from Nan-ao, Lin reported to the emperor, and three all the way from the Fukien coast.[32]

In order to supervise the work more closely, Commissioner Lin moved onto a boat on April 14 and virtually lived on it for twenty-four days. The surrendered opium was handled with great care; all the good chests were left intact, and the loose opium was placed in bags sealed with the commissioner's signet. Every store-ship was meticulously inspected to make sure that no opium was left.[33]

The opium-receiving work proceeded smoothly until April 22, when it was halted for three days by a dispute between the deputy superintendent and the commissioner. By the 19th, 9,256 chests had been delivered; of these 1,194 were bags. On the 20th, the halfway mark would be passed and the passage boats would presumably start to run again, as the commissioner had promised. Long before the 20th, Lin had prepared an edict directing the prefect of Canton to restore the service of the passage boats but to prevent the departure of the fifteen foreign merchants (one name was added later) who were considered the most notorious opium traders; the latter were to be released only when the total amount was in hand.[34] Just before this edict was to be dispatched, however, a report reached the commissioner alleging that Johnston had written Elliot that he intended to halt delivery when the halfway mark was reached, until he saw the passage boats conveying some foreign merchants out. Commissioner Lin did not like this highhanded attitude, so he withheld his edict.[35]

On the 20th, Johnston wrote Lin requesting the restoration of the passage boats. He said that ten store-ships were anchored in the Sha-chiao offing.[36] Some of them had already been unloaded, and when all were cleared over half the opium would have been delivered. Commissioner Lin immediately wrote a long rescript to this communication rejecting Johnston's request and assailing him for want of good faith. Not only had the unloading of the ten ships not yet been completed, Lin charged, there had also been submitted along with the regular opium stock some smaller chests, loose bags, broken pieces, and even some ersatz "opium." [37]

Lin said that orders had been given some time ago requiring all twenty-two store-ships to proceed to the Sha-chiao offing, but only ten had done so by April 18. Among these ten ships only two or three were full; six or seven were only partially loaded; and some of them contained only a few hundred chests or even less than a hundred. On investigation, Lin found that all these ships bore higher watermarks, and he suspected that some of them had illicitly unloaded some of the opium before reporting to the Chinese officers. Lin had also received reports from Chinese officers stationed at Macao and from the patrolling water forces to the effect that, though four store-ships had sailed from the Macao roads to Lintin on April 13 and 15, they had not yet arrived at Sha-chiao.[38]

Commissioner Lin came to the conclusion that Johnston had decided not to cooperate with the opium-receiving program. He pointed out that the opium was to be surrendered in expiation of past crimes and warned Johnston that there would be no difficulty in enforcing the law against the foreigners. Lin promised that, as soon as all the store-ships arrived at Sha-chiao, the passage boats would again be allowed to run. And since many chopboats were already waiting, it would take only two or three days to complete the delivery, once all the store-ships arrived. At the end of the rescript, he reprimanded Johnston for sending a communication directly to him instead of transmitting it through the hong merchants: "[The messenger] should be detained and punished by a beating with the club (*kun-tse*). Considering that this was his first offense, the punishment was waived, but if such violation of proper usage should be repeated, it would not again be forgiven."

On the same day (the 20th) Lin wrote Elliot to explain why the passage boats had not been restored, but before the note reached Canton, Elliot had already addressed one to the commissioner, asking their restoration. Receiving this request on the 21st, Lin replied that, as soon as all the store-ships had arrived at Sha-chiao, the passage boats would be allowed to run. He denied that this was a breach of faith and reminded Elliot that earlier, before one fourth of the opium had been delivered, he had ordered the compradors and servants to return to the factories.[39] On the 22nd, Johnston again submitted an address to the commissioner; the document was apparently composed by Thom in Chinese and it was barely intelligible.[40] Its general purpose was to deny that Johnston had prevented the store-ships from coming and to insist that the passage boats be permitted to resume service. Lin's reply — only two lines — reprimanded Johnston for having stopped the delivery on the 22nd and announced that he had decided to stop the receiving. The commissioner thus returned to the Bogue and anchored his boat at Chen-k'ou.[41]

On April 23 Lin received another address from Elliot requesting the restoration of the passage boats and enclosing a copy of an order from him directing Johnston to speed up delivery of the opium. Johnston also wrote Lin to inform him of Elliot's order. This short letter, again unclear in meaning, apparently was intended to pledge his cooperation. The delivery of opium was subsequently resumed on the 26th.[42] Since everything seemed to go well, on May 2, when 14,873 chests had been delivered, Commissioner Lin gave an order to restore the passage boats, remove the blockade of the factories, and reopen the trade.[43] Two days later, the prefect of Canton received Lin's order and carried out his instructions. With the exception of sixteen foreign merchants, including Dent, the three Mathesons (James, Alexander, Donald), and Dadabhoy, who were to be detained until the whole quantity of opium was delivered, the confinement of the foreign community in Canton ended.[44] On May 18, the opium delivery was completed.

The total amount of opium that passed into Chinese hands is difficult to determine. One Chinese author has listed five figures given by different writers, ranging from 19,179 to 20,283 chests.[45] The amount pledged by Elliot on March 27 was 20,283 chests, and on May 18, at the end of the delivery, the prefect of Canton gave a receipt for the same amount.[46] To this figure was added eight more chests of Innes' opium, which was captured at Macao by the Portuguese governor who shipped it to Sha-chiao on May 5. The total amount of opium surrendered on paper was thus increased to 20,291 chests.[47]

The amount actually received by the Chinese was greater than this. Lin Tse-hsü memorialized the emperor on May 18 that he had received altogether 19,187 chests and 2,119 bags of opium. He maintained that this was over a thousand chests more than the amount Elliot had pledged.[48] Since the amount of opium in a bag was the same as that in a chest,[49] the total quantity received was 21,306 chests. However, some of the holders had cheated, and undoubtedly not every chest was full. At any rate, it is on record that, with the exception of eight chests saved as samples, Lin ultimately destroyed a total of 2,376,254 catties (2,613,879 pounds) of opium. He reported that the normal weight of the opium in each chest was 120 catties; some dried out and weighed less, but the contents of no chest weighed under 100 catties.[50]

Lin Tse-hsü could congratulate himself now, since all of the opium in

China was in his hands. As soon as the delivery was completed, he memorialized the emperor and boasted, "Millions [of dollars] of the barbarian's capital is now laid waste, and probably they would not dare to repeat the same [crime]" [51] He did not realize what complicated and serious repercussions were to follow.

THE DISPOSAL OF THE SURRENDERED OPIUM

The question now was what Lin would do with the immense amount of opium, which cost the foreign merchants nearly eleven million dollars originally and, even at the current low market price, was still valued at nine million dollars.[52] Would he really destroy it, as he had previously announced? Long before the delivery was completed, Captain Elliot reported the care with which the commissioner was superintending the grading and repackaging of the drug and predicted that the Chinese would legalize the trade as a government monopoly. The profits from the sale of such a vast amount would make it easy for the Chinese authorities to set up a fund to compensate the original owners. Elliot was certain, at this stage, that the Chinese government intended "to pay something by some means." [53] Later developments proved Elliot's prediction wrong. Although Lin Tse-hsü had offered five catties of tea for each chest of opium he received, this was to be a reward for the foreigners' compliance with his orders, not an indemnity for the opium surrendered.[54] The Chinese government has been often accused, not without justification, of being corrupt, backward, and erratic but, with regard to opium prohibition in the late 1830s, it was unwavering. It did not expect to pay merely to have its laws obeyed.

On April 12, the day after the opium receiving had begun, Lin Tse-hsü memorialized the emperor suggesting that all the opium be shipped to Peking for examination before it was destroyed. The emperor consented forthwith on May 2. But six days later he received a memorial from Teng Ying, a censor of the Chekiang circuit, pointing out the infeasibility of such an undertaking.[55] The censor estimated that in Kwangtung, Kiangsi, and Anhwei, it would take at least forty thousand bearers to carry the opium overland, and more than a hundred large boats with crews totaling one or two thousand men to transport it by water. North of Anhwei, over a thousand carts with the same number of laborers and five or six thousand horses and mules would be required; and even if the opium were transferred from the river in Kiangsi through the Yangtze to the Grand Canal, it would require several times the number of boats used in the regular shipment of copper and lead. He could not see the point of spending money on the transportation of such a useless article. Moreover, he warned, there was the possibility of irregularities and mishaps during the journey; some of the opium might be stolen or replaced by a cheaper domestic product. He concluded by citing an imperial order of the previous year which turned down a suggestion to transfer to Peking opium seized in the various provinces from native holders.[56] The emperor overruled his former order and instructed Lin to destroy the opium on the spot.[57]

On May 25 at the Bogue, Lin had a discussion with Admiral Kuan and Yü Pao-ch'un, his main lieutenant, about the ways and means of transporting the opium to Peking, and three days later he memorialized the emperor recommending a new measure — shipping the opium north by sea. He received the new imperial order, however, on the 30th. As if in expectation of the emperor's order to destroy the opium at Canton, around May 13 Lin had ordered several trenches to be dug. On the 19th, the day after the last chest of opium had been surrendered, Lin composed a prayer to the God of the Sea (*Chi Hai-shen wen*) that all aquatic animals might take refuge when the decomposed opium was thrown into the ocean. The idea of this literary composition, written in the most elaborate parallel-prose style, seems amusing from today's point of view; however, it does give some evidence of the gentleness of Lin's nature. On June 1, having offered a sacrifice in the morning, Lin again addressed the God of the Sea that within a few days the destruction would begin.

The destruction work commenced in the hours of *wei* (1–3 P.M.) on June 3 and lasted until nightfall. The governor, the financial commissioner, the hoppo, and Ying-lung, brigade-general of the right wing of the Banner force, had all come to witness the event. On that day 170 chests were disposed of. In the next two weeks all the important officials, including the Tartar general, the brigade-general of the Banner left wing, the governor-general, and the salt controller came in turn from the provincial capital to supervise the work.[58]

The method of destroying the opium was determined after extensive inquiry. Lin and his associates decided to disintegrate it by mixing it with salt and lime. They had three trenches dug at the village of Chen-k'ou, each about one hundred fifty feet long, seventy-five feet wide, and seven feet deep, and lined with flagstones on the bottom and heavy timber on the sides.[59] The opium balls were first broken into pieces and then thrown into a trench, which was filled with two feet of fresh water. Salt and lime were scattered profusely over it. Laborers with hoes and shovels stirred and turned the mixture while the opium slowly dissolved. When the drug was completely decomposed, the liquid was made to flow through screens (to prevent the escape of any large lumps of opium) to the nearby creek which carried it to the ocean.

The work was performed by about five hundred laborers under the strict surveillance of more than sixty civil and military officers. Large crowds were attracted to the scene, but no unauthorized persons were allowed to enter the palisade. Any workman leaving the site was subjected to a careful search. The opium was stored in small enclosures within the compound and before any chest or bag was disposed of, it was checked to make sure that it bore the markings made on it when taken from the British store-ships. Altogether, more than ten Chinese made attempts to steal some of the drug, but none succeeded. On June 19, several thieves were caught, and the strong police force was further reinforced.[60] One man caught trying to carry off a small portion of opium was executed immediately. E. C. Bridgman, who witnessed the destruction, wrote that "the degree of care and fidelity, with which the whole work was conducted, far exceeded our expectations; and I cannot conceive how any business could be more faithfully executed."[61]

When the job was about half done, Lin memorialized the emperor on June 13, informing him of the method and progress of the destruction, and the emperor wrote back his approval.[62] On July 5, Lin and his colleagues dispatched a memorial to the emperor reporting that a total of 2,376,254 catties of opium received from the British had been destroyed by June 25.[63] Apart from these, eight chests, two of each kind (Patna, Malwa, Turkey, and small Patna), were withheld for possible shipment to Peking as samples. If the emperor did not want them, they could be destroyed later, together with opium captured from native holders. The emperor refused the offer, saying that it was too much trouble, but he was greatly pleased by the completion of the destruction and wrote: "This is one thing that is greatly delightful to the hearts of mankind."[64]

The memorialists also stated that among the many spectators were a few Americans, Mr. and Mrs. King, Reverend Bridgman, and Captain Benson, who, when watching the opium balls being cut into quarters, stamped into pieces, and spread with salt and lime, frequently nodded their heads and covered their noses to ward off the fetid odor.[65] Bridgman subsequently wrote an interesting account for the June number of the *Chinese Repository*. King wrote to a friend in Singapore giving detailed accounts of the process, and extracts from his letters were included in the *Singapore Free Press* (July 25, 1839).

No matter how faithfully Commissioner Lin carried out his task, nothing could quiet the inveterate skeptics. Charles Gutzlaff insisted until his death that the opium was only nominally destroyed.[66] It was charged by the *Quarterly Review* that no Chinese boatmen were allowed to approach the scene and that the editor of the *Canton Register* had applied for permission to watch the destruction but was refused.[67] These statements, made in London by one who had never been on the spot, are contradicted by the eyewitness account of Bridgman. Moreover, the Chinese officials were ordered by imperial edict to urge and welcome spectators, foreign or native, to see the destruction with their own eyes and thereby be awakened to the fact that the government was adamant in its prohibition of opium. According to Lin, many people came from near and far.[68]

A pamphleteer pointed out that a letter was received from the agent of Lloyd's, dated Macao, June 25, saying: "The last of the opium is to be destroyed this day." Thus he maintained that the Chinese had completed in twenty days a job originally planned to require seventy.[69] On this basis the *Quarterly Review* calculated that not more than 6,600 chests, or less than a third of the British opium surrendered, was actually destroyed (at the rate of three hundred chests per day). It was asked, "Has Lin, too, become a smuggler of opium?"[70] The fact is that from June 3 to June 21, with the exception of the first day, when the process was still under experiment, and June 15, a holiday, the smallest quantity destroyed in any one day was 830 chests (on June 4). After June 21, there remained only 196 chests to be disposed of in the remaining four days.[71]

Lin's accomplishment won applause from people not connected with the opium trade. King was impressed "that while Christian Governments were growing and farming this deleterious drug, this Pagan monarch should nobly disdain to enrich his treasury with a sale which could not fall short of $20,000,000."[72] A printed circular letter from the China mission of the American Board of Commissioners for Foreign Missions, addressed to "Christian Brethren and Friends," concluded:

For tens of years past, those who ought to have introduced the gospel, with all its happy accompaniments, have instead been bringing in a flood of desolation.

This tide is now checked, but not yet entirely stopped. The destruction by the Chinese government, of twenty thousand chests of opium, which if sold would have brought into its treasury ten or fifteen millions of dollars, will long be referred to as an act, illustrative of the combined power of conscience and correct principle, operating even in pagan hearts. The novel plan by which the article fell into the the [*sic*] hands of the Chinese may have been wrong, but when once in their possession, it seemed incredible that it should be destroyed. Yet so it was — entirely destroyed.[73]

Commissioner Lin's methods were indeed rash and novel. It has been pointed out that, whether or not the opium had been justly forfeited, Lin should have gone out and taken the opium instead of seizing the consignees and depriving them of food and water.[74] But in the final analysis the matter was, as pointed out by the *Dublin Magazine*, "a question of Chinese usage; and is not to be either condemned or justified by those rules of action which are applicable to contraband trade in other nations." [75] Lin acted under the theory that commercial intercourse with foreigners was but a manifestation of the emperor's condescension and his exercise of despotic power was fully sanctioned by Chinese tradition. At any rate, it is beyond doubt that Lin could not have successfully suppressed the opium traffic by less severe tactics or by ordinary government measures.[76] Whatever his degree of enlightenment, Lin was at least morally and politically consistent. He did what he believed was desirable for the people, foreign and native. He punished offending Chinese merchants more strictly than he attempted to punish foreign smugglers. He obeyed his superiors and expected the same from his subordinates.

Lin's counterparts, however, were not so consistent in their actions. The foreign opium traders, while demanding the protection and freedom prescribed by international law and usage, did not themselves abide by any such law. They despised the mandates of the Chinese empire, disregarded the officials' warnings, and persistently supplied the Chinese with an article that was known to be detrimental to probity and health.[77] In defiance of the injunctions, their vessels obstinately hovered about the Chinese coast to engage in the contraband trade and frequently fired on government boats that were trying to perform their prescribed duty. It was argued that the Chinese government was corrupt and inept and that a number of its officials connived in the illicit traffic. But government corruption does not repeal the law; police inefficiency does not justify a crime; and official connivance does not make a disreputable practice less so. One fact that has often been conveniently overlooked by the spokesmen of the traders was that, for three years prior to Commissioner Lin's arrival in Canton, the provincial authorities (with the exception of a few officers in the water forces) were no longer cooperating in the opium trade; vigorous prohibition proceedings never ceased and repeated warnings were given.

Captain Elliot did not morally approve of the opium traffic; he considered it "a trade, which every friend to humanity must deplore." Nevertheless, he pledged his full protection to English as well as other foreign opium traders.[78] At the end of January 1839, he admitted to Palmerston: "Whilst such a traffic existed, indeed, in the heart of our regular commerce, I had all along felt that Chinese Government had a just ground for harsh measures towards the lawful trade, upon the plea that there was no distinguishing between the right and the wrong." [79] Still, when Elliot was informed in Macao of Commissioner Lin's proceedings at Canton, without awaiting further details or investigation, he immediately ordered the English ships to assemble in Hong Kong and "be prepared to resist every act of aggression" of the Chinese government.[80]

Regarding the traffic outside the Bogue, Elliot pursued a policy of noninterference. But when the Chinese government adopted measures that were effective against the opium trade, he quickly came to the aid of the traders. Palmerston himself was the coauthor of the noninterference policy. On June 15, 1838, he directed Elliot: "With respect to the smuggling trade in opium . . . I have to state, that Her Majesty's Government cannot interfere for the purpose of enabling British subjects to violate the laws of the country to which they trade. Any loss, therefore, which such persons may suffer in consequence of the more effectual execution of the Chinese laws on this subject, must be borne by the parties who have brought that loss on themselves by their own acts." [81] Elliot was frequently urged by the Chinese to order the departure of the opium ships outside the Bogue, but he always replied that, since he was only charged with the superintendence of the trade within the port of Canton, his government had no formal knowledge of the existence of the opium ships.

When the Maitland fleet arrived in the Canton waters in July 1838, Elliot chose Tongkoo Bay as their anchorage partly because of its remoteness from the anchorage of the ships engaged in the illicit traffic. On March 23, just before his departure from Macao for Canton, he wrote to Captain Blake, commander of the Larne, the only British vessel of war in Canton at the time: "Cordially assenting with me in the propriety of avoiding any unnecessary or ostensible intercourse with the British shipping at the outside anchorages (many of which have no doubt been engaged in the illicit traffic), it is at the same time most satisfactory to me to reflect, that in the event of any well-sustained evidence of aggressive attempts, British life and property will have the benefit of all the protection and countenance which you can afford."

It should be noted that on March 22, 1839, when Elliot addressed a communication to the governor-general asking whether it was the intention of the Chinese government to make war against British subjects and vessels, he ended the paper with these terms: "He [Elliot] claims immediate and calming assurances upon this subject; and he has at the same time to declare his readiness to meet the officers of the Provincial Government, and to use his sincere efforts to fulfill the pleasure of the great Emperor, as soon as it is made known to him." On the same day Elliot wrote Palmerston recommending a "firm tone and attitude" in dealing with the Chinese. He informed Palmerston of his note to Governor-General Teng offering his "best efforts for fulfilling the reasonable purposes of this Government, whenever they are authentically made known" to him.[82] On April 2, Elliot again wrote Palmerston maintaining that his note to Teng made it clear that Commissioner Lin's proceedings amounted to an unprovoked aggression:

This is the first time, in our intercourse with this Empire, that its Government has taken the unprovoked initiative in aggressive measures against British life, liberty, and property, and against the dignity of the British Crown. I say *unprovoked*, advisedly, because your Lordship will observe, in my address to the Keun-Min-Foo, dated at Macao, on 22nd ultimo, that I offered to adjust all things peacefully, by the fulfilment of the Emperor's will, as soon as it was made known to me.[83]

This statement was about as meaningful as Elliot's assertion that his government had no formal knowledge of the opium traffic that was going on immediately outside the port of Canton. He had fully three years to do something about the relations between the two countries before it was too late. The emperor's will had been made known to him repeatedly by numerous edicts, injunctions, and official acts. It was to stop the opium trade. Elliot could not plead ignorance of the Chinese government's purpose, and he could not accuse it of being vague and unreasonable. But he could, as he did, technically deny the existence of the opium trade. In his report to Palmerston, dated Canton, April 6, 1839, Elliot wrote: "Before the arrival of the High Commissioner, I had steadily considered the expediency of formally requiring all the British ships engaged in the opium trade to sail away from the coasts of China. But the objections to that measure were very strong, and the result has proved that I took a sound view in refraining from it." At one time he had strong misgivings about the sincerity of the prohibition measure and how long it would last. At another time he was convinced of the seriousness of the measures adopted by the Chinese, but was skeptical of the government's ability to enforce them. In the document referred to above, he explained, "although I had certainly come to the conclusion, for some months since, that the determination of the Court to put down the trade was firmly adopted, I had neither then nor now formed such a judgment of its power effectually to accomplish that object." [84]

These facts and statements no doubt serve to defend Lin's moral position. But the dispute, of course, cannot be appraised on straight moral grounds — it is much more complicated than to say that Elliot's motives were less pure than Lin's. As the world's leading colonial power, Britain in the nineteenth century could no longer "afford" morality, or rather felt that she could not. Her political and commercial policies were predicated on this notion; even the most honest and upright colonial servants were imbued with it. In defending British interests and property, Elliot could not really see that the Chinese demand was something to be taken seriously. The danger of the situation lay in the lack of viable alternatives for both Lin and Elliot. On strict orders from Peking, Lin had to eliminate opium and maintain the status quo, and Elliot could not act against the climate in Canton, as his two unsuccessful predecessors had done, by following a soft policy toward China.

The destruction of the immense amount of opium was the climax of Lin Tse-hsü's mission in Canton. Considering his job largely done, the commissioner now directed his attention to ways of bringing the situation back to normal. Captain Elliot, for his part, was determined to abandon his rather vacillating strategy toward the Chinese government. He would now seek to launch a campaign for the punishment of China and to open a new era in the China trade.

THE BOND PROBLEM AND THE AFTERMATH

Lin Tse-hsü's mission as specified by Peking was not merely to stop the opium trade, but also to prevent its recurrence. Three days after Lin's appointment as imperial commissioner, the emperor issued an instruction (on January 3, 1839), to Lin, Teng, and I-liang, to root out the practice forever. On April 12, the day after Lin's arrival at the Bogue to receive the opium, the three officials pledged the emperor that they would seek to prevent the return of the trade.[85] Accordingly, they wanted each foreign merchant to sign a bond promising never again to participate in the opium trade.

In his March 18 edicts addressed to the foreign and hong merchants, Commissioner Lin ordered each foreign merchant to file a bond with the government, both in his own language and in Chinese, declaring that thereafter foreign ships would never again bring opium and that, if they were found guilty of violating this pledge, they would be willing to suffer the consequences: confiscation of all cargoes and immediate execution of the individuals concerned.[86] The terse phrase *jen chi cheng-fa* (the persons will receive capital punishment) gave rise to great misunderstanding. Lin's intention was to impose capital punishment only upon those who actually brought in the opium. The foreign community, however, interpreted the phrase to include the entire ship's crew.

The form of the bond was first proposed by the Chinese on April 4. The document was translated by Morrison and a portion of it reads as follows:

From the commencement of autumn in this present year, any merchant vessel coming to Kwangtung, that may be found to bring opium, shall be immediately and entirely confiscated, both vessel and cargo, to the use of Government; no trade shall be allowed to it; and the parties shall be left to suffer death at the hands of the Celestial Court; such punishment they will readily submit to.

As regards such vessels as may arrive here in the two quarters of spring and summer, now current, they will have left their countries while yet ignorant of the existing investigations and severe enforcement of prohibitions; such of them as, in this state of ignorance, bring any opium, shall surrender it as they arrive, not daring in the smallest degree to conceal or secrete it.[87]

Unfortunately I could not obtain the Chinese version for comparison. At any rate, it was understood by all foreigners in Canton that the capital punishment prescribed in the draft of the bond would involve innocent men. Everyone violently objected to it. Russell and Company interpreted the penalties described in the commissioner's March 18 edict as "confiscation of the ship, and the capital punishment of capt., crew, and consignees." Gutzlaff wrote that the bonds required each captain to pledge himself "to undergo capital punishment with his crew, and to have his whole ship and cargo confiscated, if any opium were found in his possession on board." A memorial to Palmerston, signed by most of the British subjects in Canton and dated May 23, accused the Chinese government of attempting "to force foreigners to sign bonds, rendering not only themselves, but all others coming to China, over whom they have no control, liable to the same penalty, and on the refusal on the part of foreigners to sign such bonds, in the promulgation of an edict by the High Commissioner, declaratory of the determination of the Government to enforce such penalty." [88]

On October 14, Warner, the master of the English ship *Thomas Coutts*, signed a bond that has survived in both English and Chinese versions. The language used in this bond, filed after the new opium laws were promulgated, was more severe and definite than that in the first one proposed to the English in April. The English version of Warner's bond, done by a Chinese in bizarre style, reads as follows.[89]

A truly and willing bond.

The foreigner ———— commander of ship belong to ———— under ———— consignment, present this to His Excellency the Great Government of Heavenly Dynesty, and certificate that the said ship carry ———— goods come and trade in Canton; I, with my officer, and the whole crew are all dreadfully obey the new laws of the Chinese Majesty, that they dare not bring any opium; if one little bit of opium was found out in any part of my ship by examination, I am willingly deliver up the transgressor, and he shall be punish to death according to the correctness law of the Government of Heavenly Dynesty; both my ship and goods are to be confiscate to Chinese Officer; but if there found no opium on my ship by examination, then I beg Your Excellency's favor permit my ship enter to Whampoa and trade as usual; so if there are distinguish between good and bad, then I am willingly submit to Your Excellency: and I now give this bond as a true certificate of the same,

Heavenly Dynesty, Taou-Kwang
year ———— moon ———— day,
Name of Captain ———— " " Ship ———— " " Officer ————
" " Crew ————

Commissioner Lin's intention to punish by death only the "transgressors," not those who took no part in the opium trade, is shown in this document, and it was repeatedly pointed out to Elliot by edicts and the hong mechants' explanations.[90]

The Chinese labored persistently to obtain a bond that would be acceptable to both sides; it became the sole topic of negotiation during the week prior to Lin's departure for the Bogue on April 10. On the 5th, Howqua and Mowqua called on Elliot in the morning to present a draft of the bond, but Elliot refused it. It was then submitted in the afternoon to the General Committee of the Chamber of Commerce. The committee, however, adjourned until the following Monday, April 8. On the evening of the 5th, Elliot received an edict from the prefect of Canton transmitting Lin's command that all the foreigners in the factories give bonds. Elliot made no reply.

On the afternoon of the 6th, Elliot received a direct edict from the commissioner urging him to make haste on the bond. With the usual celestial references, Lin praised him for surrendering the opium but insisted that demanding bonds from the foreign merchants should be a much easier task for Elliot than demanding the surrender of the opium was. If the bonds could not be speedily obtained, the commissioner would no longer rate his competence so high. Elliot replied to Lin on the 8th that the foreign merchants at Canton had already pledged to discontinue the trade in opium. He was referring to the pledge voluntarily given by forty-two firms and individual merchants on March 25, 1839. He assured the commissioner that this document could be depended upon, since the foreigners would place honor far above disgraceful profit. The opium could be surrendered, Elliot explained, because it was actually in the foreigners' possession. "But the bonds," he said, "have relation to the future; and would involve terrible responsibilities in any possible case of disobedience to the prohibitions. They would involve, too, not alone parties themselves but others also." Moreover, he concluded, it was against English law for him to compel the merchants to give such bonds.[91]

After Elliot's reply, Lin responded with an edict that was the most outspoken of all his utterances concerning the bond issue. It argued that foreigners coming to trade in Kwangtung province were required to abide by the laws of the province, just as were any Chinese coming from other provinces to trade. Lin refuted Elliot's contention that signing the bond violated English law: "You represent that your nation has its laws. These will serve only so long as you do not come to the inner land [China]. But since you will come to Kwangtung to trade, even your Sovereign then must command you to keep obediently the laws and statutes of the Celestial Empire. How can you bring the laws of your nation with you to the Celestial Empire."

As long as the foreigners had already pledged themselves not to continue in the opium trade, Lin continued, it would do them no harm to give the bond. If they refused, he said, "it will be clearly seen that you wish to preserve to yourselves room for the introduction of opium." He emphatically assured them that the bond would not incriminate inno-

cent men and insisted that it was the minimum requirement for the resumption of the legal trade on a permanent and secure basis.

Be it said that the foreign slaves and seamen may, it is to be feared, smuggle
it — it is requisite that the owners of the goods and masters of the ships should
maintain a faithful restraint. If amid the vast amount there be a single petty
illegality, of course the heaviness or lightness of the punishment must be
regulated in such cases by the amount brought and the party concerned shall
alone be punished; how can punishment be carelessly inflicted without dis-
crimination being made? or how, as represented in your address, can other
parties be involved? The officers of Kwangtung of every grade, have hitherto
always treated you with an excess of indulgence, and never with the excess of
severity. How is your mind so void of clear perception?

At this time, when opium has so extensively pervaded the land with its
poisonous influence, and when I, the High Commissioner, have received the
Great Emperor's special commands to extirpate this thing, how can I fail to
require of you the execution of an agreement to put a stop to it? So soon as
these bonds shall be executed, I shall assuredly report to the Great Emperor,
that your foreign merchants of all nations are all ready to observe their duty,
and fear the laws; that they may be allowed still to continue a permanent
trade. And from thenceforth they will be trusted; nor will depravity and
deceit on their part be any longer apprehended. Thus all the foreigners will
stand in an honourable position, and still more so will you, Elliot. Be careful,
then, not to damage yourself by obstinacy.[92]

On the same day (the 8th), the General Committee of the Chamber
of Commerce convened at the residence of its chairman, W. S. Wetmore.
It was moved by Delano and carried unanimously that, as a commercial
body, the committee should not get involved in problems of a political
and personal nature. Furthermore, since all foreigners were prisoners in
their own factories, the committee should cease its function until the
blockade was removed. The resolution was subsequently transmitted to
the hong merchants by Wetmore. In the evening, the prefect of Canton,
the magistrates of Panyü and Namhoi, and a *wei-yuan* of the commissioner invited the leading merchants for a conference. The Englishmen
declined to come on the grounds that they had entrusted the issue to their
superintendent. Senn van Basel (the Dutch consul), Snow (the American
consul), Wetmore, Fearon (interpreter of the Chamber of Commerce),
King, and Forbes met the officers at the Consoo House at 9 P.M., with
Howqua, Mowqua, Samqua, and the linguists also present. During the
meeting, the prefect repeatedly assured the merchants that the bond
would affect only the offenders or the prospective owners of the smuggled opium. The officers insisted that they had to have the bond by 5 P.M.

on the next day, since the commissioner was leaving for the Bogue in two or three days. The meeting continued late into the night, and the Chinese simply persisted in their urging, at one time threatening to detain the party of foreigners if they did not comply with the order. The foreigners, with equal determination, refused. Because little reasoning either for or against the bond was presented and the time was entirely spent in repeated proddings and refusals, this meeting was referred to by some as a "childish piece of Chinese diplomacy." [93]

The foreign merchants' sentiment was reflected by some contemporary records. William Hunter wrote in his journal on the 7th: "It is needless to say, that nothing can compel us to sign such a bond as this." Three days later he explained that the refusal was "for the best of reasons, that it might be made use of hereafter, and acted upon, if mere suspicion was attached to any person besides endangering the lives of the entire Foreign Community in Canton." [94] A letter of Russell and Company dated the 10th stated: "During the last three days efforts have been made to obtain from all foreigners, through their Supt or Consuls by promises, by threats, and by fraud, the bonds required by the Comr in his first edict — The foreigners have firmly united . . . and distinctly intimated their determination not to sign them under any circumstances unless forced to do so, in which case a regard to their own safety would render it necessary for them to leave the country as soon as permission could be obtained and for which they would forthwith apply." [95]

On the 9th, Lin again dispatched a *wei-yuan* to the factories and waited for the foreigners' answers in the Consoo House. Van Basel and Snow sent in written replies refusing to give the bond. The former promised only to inform his sovereign by the first ship available of the new opium laws and apprise his countrymen that all who carried opium must face the penalties. Snow's communication stated that, if the bond were insisted upon, the American traders would ask for permission to leave the country. [96]

Captain Elliot did not reply to the April 8 edict until the 10th. In this address he admitted the reasonableness of Lin's demand that foreigners conform to Chinese law, but repeated that such bonds would be in violation of British law and, if the Chinese insisted, he would leave the country: "It is beyond dispute, then, that those who will come to Canton to trade, must act in obedience to the laws. But the new regulation regarding these bonds is incompatible with the laws of England. If, therefore, its observance be imperatively insisted upon, and these bonds be absolutely required, there will remain no alternative but for the English men and vessels to depart." [97]

Commissioner Lin never believed that the British really wanted to leave China; so he pressed hard despite Elliot's threat. The issue over the bond turned into a vicious circle. The more difficult it was to obtain, the more Lin wanted it. In an October memorial, he explained to the emperor: "The barbarians take their promises very seriously; they never break an agreement or even fail to keep an appointment. A bond, as they look at it, is a very serious matter and is rarely given. It is not as in China where bonds were so liberally used that their effect has become doubtful. The more reluctant they are to give the bonds, the more sure we are of the dependability of their bonds, and the more we should strive to acquire them." [98]

On April 19 Lin, writing from the Bogue, replied to the communications of the superintendent and the consuls that he had received at the time of his departure from Canton. Although Elliot refused to sign the bond, in his communication of April 10 to Lin he had asked that the effective date of the new regulation be postponed. He had requested moratoria of five and ten months from the opening of the trade for merchants of India and England, respectively, so that he could inform them of the new rules. The request had been accompanied by a promise that English ships bringing in opium within this period would be sent away.[99] The commissioner now ruled that the requested postponement was too long — he was willing to give four months to Indian ships and eight months to ships coming directly from England. The English bringing in opium within this period would be dealt with by the existing laws; their opium would be confiscated, but the offenders would not be punished or their lawful cargoes seized.[100]

The prefect of Canton and the magistrates of Panyü and Namhoi brought this edict to the Consoo House on April 20, and, when old Howqua presented the document, Elliot immediately tore it up into a "thousand pieces and threw it into the Fire place." He asked the hong merchants to tell the officers "that they might take my life as soon as they saw fit; but that it was a vain thing to trouble themselves or me any further upon the subject of the bond." He reminded the Chinese that there had been men with swords stationed about his doors for over four weeks, presumably with orders to kill any foreigner who attempted to escape, and that there was no precedent for such a bond of consent. On the same day he replied to the edict, reiterating his position as presented on the

10th and formally asking permission to leave Canton with all English ships and men.[101]

The struggle over the bond was clearly an issue of extraterritoriality. Commissioner Lin's persistent efforts to assume jurisdiction over the foreigners trading in China were resisted with equal vigor by the British (and other Western merchants), who, although acknowledging Chinese legal sovereignty, wanted to have the benefit of Western legal protection. The bond, however, was not the sole obstacle in the way of restoring the trade. Elliot, for one, was not willing to go back to the old Canton system; he intended to take the offensive in putting British trade in China on a new footing. On April 6, while still confined by the commissioner, he wrote Palmerston that "the more practical and fit reply" to Commissioner Lin's demand for the bond would be the removal of all British subjects from the sway of the Chinese government. "Trade with China at any point remote from the station of our ships . . . is no longer a possible state of circumstances." On the 22nd, he again wrote Palmerston: "It was competent for the Emperor of China to make laws he saw good, incurring the risks of their execution, risks which it was not to be denied were very considerable, and about which they should hear more, when I could find a suitable occasion to treat so grave a subject."

While Lin was busily engaged in receiving and destroying opium, Elliot was glimpsing larger possibilities. On April 13, he managed to send a note to the Portuguese governor of Macao, Don Adriao Accacio da Silveira Pinto, from the blockaded factories, to make arrangements for the withdrawal of all British subjects to Macao under Portuguese protection. He offered the Portuguese "immediate facilities on the British Treasury" — as much as would be required by the Portuguese governor. A public notice to British subjects was enclosed ordering any Englishman to whom the notice might be presented to place himself under the command of the governor of Macao "for the defence of the rights of Her Most Faithful Majesty, and the general protection of the lives, liberty, and property of all the subjects of Christian Governments now or hereafter resorting to that settlement." [102]

The governor of Macao politely refused the offer. Only if there was "evidence of the imminent peril which the Superintendent seems to fear, as being about to happen" would the governor accept such an arrangement. Otherwise, he stated, a strict neutrality prevented him from taking advantage of Elliot's recommendations. The governor, however, repeated his promise to protect the lives and properties of English subjects in Macao, with the exception of persons engaged in the opium trade.[103]

On May 6, Elliot gave Palmerston a résumé of the military strength and financial condition of the Portuguese at Macao and revealed his designs on that settlement: "This may not be an inconvenient occasion to press upon your Lordship's attention the strong necessity of concluding some immediate arrangement with the Government of Her Most Faithful Majesty, either for the cession of the Portuguese rights at Macao, or for the effectual defense of the place; and its appropriation to British uses, by means of a subsidiary Convention. A garrison of 1,000 good troops, principally artillery, and a few sail of gun-boats, would place Macao in a situation to cover the whole trade with this part of the empire."

With this scheme in mind, Elliot had his secretary issue a public notice on May 4, when the blockade of the factories was lifted, referring British subjects to his public notice dated from Macao, March 23, which had instructed the British to make immediate preparations for transferring their property to Macao. Fully convinced that there would be no insuperable difficulty in making some sort of arrangement to carry on the trade from Macao, Elliot on May 11 peremptorily ordered all British subjects to leave Canton. The motive advanced for this radical move was the unreasonableness of Chinese laws and the injudicious way in which they were executed. The superintendent would consider those who chose to remain in Canton as assenting to the reasonableness of China's laws.[104] Lin and his colleagues made no protest. On May 8, they issued an edict giving the foreigners permission to leave, but warned: "After you have thus returned, you will not be allowed to come again." [105]

The word that the last chest of British opium had been delivered to the Chinese reached Elliot on the morning of May 21, and his obligation to the commissioner was thus fulfilled. On the next day Governor-General Teng issued an edict requiring the remainder of the sixteen foreign merchants still detained in the factories to give bonds that they would not come back again. On Elliot's recommendation, they signed the bonds. On the 24th, Elliot gave notice to the governor-general that he was leaving Canton for reasons of health, and at 5 P.M. he embarked for Macao with all the British subjects recently detained in Canton.[106]

Teng naively wrote Elliot that it was desirable for him to recover his health quickly, for, although the opium was all delivered, the commissioner and he still had many matters for Elliot to look after. "The said Superintendent having a respectful sense of duty, and being able in action, must hasten to recover his health speedily. . . . Let him also, on his arrival at Macao, faithfully and truly examine, and if the foreigners of every nation residing at Macao are guilty of secreting any opium, he must instantly command them, one and all, to deliver up the entire quantity." [107]

Elliot indeed had matters to look after, but not those that the Chinese would have wished. As soon as he heard that the Chinese had opened Whampoa for trade, he informed British subjects by a brief notice on May 4 not to bring any ship to the port of Canton until he had declared it safe for British life, liberty, and property. This was an extract from a longer notice that Elliot had prepared in April but had not published until May 23 (the day before he left Canton), lest the blunt language irritate the Chinese into prolonging the detainment or taking even more rash measures.

In this May 23 document, Elliot attacked the Chinese government for imprisoning the foreigners and despoiling British property. He reiterated his lack of confidence in the justice and moderation of both the provincial government and the commissioner and asserted that "it became highly necessary to vest and leave the right of exacting effectual security, and full indemnity for every loss, directly in the Queen." He solemnly warned that anyone making shipments to the Canton River after this notice would do so entirely at his own personal risk, and that the British government would disregard all future claims of those British subjects who remained in or came to Canton. Arriving in Macao, Elliot was able to report on May 27 that, within the week, all British ships and most British subjects would have left the river.[108]

Commissioner Lin, of course, could not allow the British to trade at Macao. It was incompatible with the ancient foreign-trade system at Canton; it would be difficult for the hoppo to control the trade; and, most important, it would be more difficult to prevent the opium traffic.[109] It was clearer than ever that the differences between the two sides could not be solved by peaceful means.

THE COMING OF THE WAR AND
THE FALL OF LIN

THE destruction of the confiscated opium and the detention of the foreign community blocked every avenue to a diplomatic conclusion of the dispute at Canton. Almost every Englishman who had an interest in the China trade, from the superintendent in Canton to the financiers and manufacturers in London and Manchester, entreated the government to intervene. It was not difficult for Lord Palmerston to reach a decision: an entirely new policy toward China could no longer be postponed.

THE BRITISH DECISION FOR WAR

During his detention, the young and ambitious Elliot had time to expound his line of thought to Palmerston and to recommend his program for a new system of trade with China. On April 6, 1839, he wrote that the chief mischief of Commissioner Lin's recent proceedings in Canton was the excessive feeling of revenge aroused in the opium traders. "Every species of retaliation," Elliot observed, would be justified "in the consciences of such persons." He maintained that the only way to save the Chinese coasts from warfare and rebellion would be the "very prompt and powerful intervention" of the British government for "the just vindication of all wrongs, and the effectual prevention of crime and wretchedness by permanent settlement." In fact, he thought it was the obligation of Britain to both the Chinese government and her own interests to make such an effort. "There can be neither safety nor honour for either Government," he concluded, "till Her Majesty's flag flies on these coasts in a secure position."

Although the Chinese had shelved the papers on legalization of the opium trade three years earlier, Captain Elliot was still contemplating the possibility of the measure. He informed Palmerston on April 13 that he thought the real author of the legalization policy to be the "great minister Yuen Yuen [Juan Yuan], a man of singular moderation and wisdom, and probably more versed in affairs of foreign trade and intercourse, than any statesman in the empire." He believed that the anti-legalization sentiment would become even more entrenched if the present actions of Lin and the Canton authorities were treated lightly: "Immediate and vigorous measures on the part of Her Majesty's Government will as suddenly and completely restore the wise and liberal party [the legalization party] to the ascendant in the Emperor's Councils, as it was lately cast out." The time had come, Elliot wrote, when the British government must choose either to promote the "rapid growth of relaxations" or to consent to the restrictionist policy currently followed by China. In other words, if Britain did not actively advance the legalization cause, she would be in fact endorsing the prohibition program. In Elliot's opinion, although the "more sinister" of the two policies was in operation, the government was too weak to follow it through: "The Chinese Government is utterly without the spring of power to jerk back . . . to the accomplishment of the present reactive purposes." He predicted that the unavoidable result of Lin's recent work in Canton would be his own overthrow by "Her Majesty's prompt, powerful, and measured intervention" or by rebellious outlaws on the coast.

On April 16 Captain Elliot wrote Lord Auckland, governor-general of India, requesting warships:

The general measures to be taken, must no doubt require the sanction of Her Majesty's Government; but immediate countenance and protection are necessary for the safety of life and property; and I am sensible your Lordship will not require any importunities on my part to do whatever may be in your Lordship's power in that respect.

As many ships of war as can be detached, and armed vessels, to be employed under the command of the naval officers, (the whole to be instructed to conform to my requisitions,) seem to be the most suitable means of protection available at this moment.[1]

On April 22, Elliot again wrote Palmerston to urge that "the necessary reply to all this violation of truth and right is a blow, and that is consistent neither with my power nor authority to inflict." He assured Palmerston that "the immense extension of our peaceful trade and intercourse" with China could be attained only by "immediate vigorous measures, founded upon the most moderate ulterior purposes," and he maintained that there had never been a "more just, necessary, or favourable conjuncture for action." To waste such an opportunity would be tantamount to sacrificing the trade with China, which Her Majesty's government would not for a moment consider. Moreover, he believed that a just indemnity for every British subject could be recovered from the Chinese government.[2]

In May, after the blockade of the factories ended, Elliot talked more freely about war with China. On the 18th, he suggested in a dispatch to Palmerston that a short manifesto be issued under the queen's name, to be translated into Chinese at Canton, instructing all officers in the proposed expeditionary force and all British subjects in China to refrain from molesting the natives or their property and from violating local customs. The same manifesto was also to set forth "that the general objects of the expedition were to make known to the Emperor the falsehood, violence, and venality of the Mandarins, and to establish peace and honourable trade on a permanent footing."[3] After he arrived in Macao, Elliot wrote a private letter to Backhouse, the undersecretary, admitting that "it has not been an easy task to refrain from letting this Government understand that its hour of reckoning was at hand." Acknowledging that it was up to the government to treat such "most serious affairs," Elliot nevertheless recommended "prompt and vigorous proceedings."[4]

At the same time, the opium traders were exerting their best efforts to induce the British government to recognize Captain Elliot's promise of reimbursement, made when he requested the surrender of their opium.[5] A few days before their release, all of the merchants who had surrendered opium declared their support for a plan to nominate a deputation consisting of Jardine, Alexander Matheson (James Matheson's nephew), H. H. Lindsay, Robert Inglis, and a member each from Magniac Smith and Company and Dent and Company for the purpose of promoting the recovery of the opium claims. The sum of $20,000 was to be raised from the claimants, with contributions assessed at a dollar per chest of opium surrendered; this was to be placed at the disposal of Jardine to cover the expenses of the campaign. "You will not, however, be limited to this outlay," wrote James Matheson to Jardine, who left Canton on January 26 to influence the government on its China policy, "as the magnitude of the object can well bear any amount of expense that may be considered necessary or desirable and it is even contemplated that you may find it expedient to secure, at a high price, the services of some leading newspaper to advocate the cause. The best legal advice will of course be engaged at the outset to make the most of the strong points of our case; and we are told there are literary men whom it is usual to employ for drawing up the requisite memorials in the most concise and clear shape." [6]

As soon as the British traders left Canton, a petition, signed by most of the British firms and merchants residing in China, was presented to Palmerston. It asked his mediation to obtain the earliest possible fulfilment of the guarantee given by Elliot on behalf of the British government, and urged Britain's intervention to put the trade with China on a permanent and secure basis.

Shortly after the surrender of the opium was pledged, Captain Elliot begged Palmerston to declare the government's intentions in order to uphold confidence. On April 22, when half of the opium had been delivered to the commissioner, Elliot again urged Palmerston to clarify the government's attitude. A declaration of its intention to exact a full indemnity for all the losses incurred by British subjects would stimulate the Chinese authorities' willingness to come to a reasonable agreement. [7] In India, the Bombay Chamber of Commerce sent a letter to the various China and East India associations in Great Britain. The letter, dated June 3, asked these associations to "join in most strongly representing to the government to avail of this opportunity, and to take the proper means of now and for ever establishing our commercial intercourse with China, on the firm and honorable position its importance to both countries demands." [8]

In London, numerous pamphlets and articles appeared in late 1839 and early 1840 to tell the public that the British flag had been insulted and that Her Majesty's officer and the group of British merchants were being imprisoned, deprived of food and water, and even threatened with death. The Chinese, it was said, wanted to stop the importation of opium for selfish reasons. Lin Tse-hsü and others were accused of having "some thousands of acres laid down as poppy-plantations," and to protect the home growth it was essential to exclude foreign imports. One pamphleteer even drew up a few treaty provisions: "You take my opium; I take your island in return, we are therefore quits; and henceforth, if you please, let us live in friendly communion and good fellowship." [9]

When news about the confinement reached England, almost three hundred firms in Manchester, London, Leeds, Liverpool, Blackburn, and Bristol, which were connected with the cotton industry and had considerable amounts of cotton goods in Canton with their agents, asked Palmerston to intervene. Thirty-nine Manchester firms wrote Palmerston on September 30 that £685,000 worth of plain, printed, and dyed cottons and cotton yarn were shipped to Canton via Liverpool in 1838. From the beginning of 1839, they maintained, £462,000 worth of such goods were shipped to Canton. They were interested not only as manufacturers cut off from a market, but also as exporters of goods from other parts of England to India. The interruption of the opium trade, the source of funds on which their Indian customers depended, was causing them "most serious inconvenience" and might, they feared, involve heavy losses. In early October, ninety-six houses of London (nearly all the merchants of the city connected with the China trade) and fifty-two firms of Liverpool petitioned Palmerston strongly advocating an early decision with regard to the China trade and soliciting an interview for their representatives, one of whom was the powerful John Abel Smith. Similarly, petitioners of Leeds and Bristol urged Palmerston to protect British shipping, property, and lives in Canton and to adopt measures to ensure the continuance of the China trade.[10]

Even before his return to England, Jardine's influence on the Foreign Office had been exerted through his London agent, John Abel Smith, for Palmerston depended almost exclusively on Smith for intelligence from Canton.[11] In late September Jardine saw Palmerston, and on October 26 he presented his views in writing, suggesting the blockade of the principal ports along the coast of China for the purpose of enforcing four demands: (1) an ample apology for the insult incurred by the British in Canton, (2) the payment for the opium surrendered to Commissioner Lin, (3) the conclusion of an equitable commercial treaty to prevent the repetition of such proceedings, and (4) the opening of additional ports to foreign trade, say Foochow, Ningpo, Shanghai, and Keeson-chow (Kiaochow). Temporary occupation of certain islands, such as the Chusan, Amoy, and Quemoy, might be required to obtain these demands. Should it be necessary to take possession of an island or harbor near Canton, Jardine suggested Hong Kong, which commanded a safe and extensive anchorage.[12]

This letter was followed by a memorandum on the next day in which Jardine offered his services and outlined the forces needed to enforce his demands. "One ship of the largest class of First Rates, — not that a vessel of this capacity is likely to be required, but that the appearance of such a concentrated force may tend to convince the Chinese of our strength and their own weakness. From such a vessel, when at anchor in a safe harbour, many of the small opium vessels might be equipped and placed under the command of Lieutenants of Her Majesty's navy — their masters, officers and crew (who are generally well acquainted with the coast and Islands) acting under them." About twelve additional men-of-war of various descriptions and transports sufficient to carry two thousand tons, as well as six or seven thousand marines, were also suggested.[13] On November 2, several influential merchants headed by John Abel Smith wrote Palmerston and elaborated the ideas put forth by Jardine. Nothing concerning the proposed expedition was left uncovered.[14]

Palmerston had long been contemplating some ventures in China. It will be recalled that on September 20, 1837, he had instructed Rear-Admiral Maitland to visit the China waters personally to confer with Captain Elliot. Palmerston believed that an interchange of information between the two men "would in many possible future contingencies, be highly advantageous to British interests in that quarter." Shortly after his interview with Jardine, Palmerston sent Elliot a secret dispatch on October 18, 1839, informing him that the government had decided to place Britain's relations with China on a proper footing. An expeditionary force to blockade Canton and the Pei-ho was to arrive in Chinese waters by the following March.[15]

On November 4, two days after Smith's group presented its letter, Palmerston sent a communication to the Admiralty informing the Lords that the government had decided to send a naval and military force to China to demand satisfaction and reparation for the injuries suffered by British subjects. The communication outlined a plan of the expedition that contained all the points recommended by the Smith-Jardine group; Palmerston assured the Admiralty that it was worked out by "persons possessed of much local knowledge."[16] Later, when the war was over and the treaty concluded, Palmerston gratefully wrote John Abel Smith: "To the assistance and information which you and Mr. Jardine so handsomely afforded us it was mainly owing that we were able to give our affairs naval, military and diplomatic, in China those detailed instructions which have led to these satisfactory results. . . . There is no doubt that this event, which will form an epoch in the progress of the civilization of the human races, must be attended with the most important advantages to the commercial interests of England."[17]

Within the framework of the British constitution, Parliament has very little voice in foreign-policy decisions. The decision to wage war against China in 1839 was made by Palmerston alone, under the strong influence of Smith, Jardine, Elliot, and a few others. The people of Great

Britain did not know the facts of the case; nor had Parliament learned of Palmerston's intention before the crucial decision was made.[18]

THE CHIEN-SHA-TSUI AFFRAY AND EXTRATERRITORIALITY

In China, the period between the retirement of the British merchants to Macao in late May 1839 and the arrival of the British expeditionary forces a year later was punctuated by futile negotiations, crises, and some actual fighting. In the month of June, Commissioner Lin concentrated his efforts on directing the British ships to Whampoa in order to resume the regular trade. On June 9, he issued an edict ordering all ships genuinely interested in trade to proceed to Whampoa: "If they are not willing to trade, then they ought to return home as speedily as possible, there is no use in their remaining hankering about here." On the 14th, the prefect of Canton and the subprefect of Macao reiterated Lin's order that lawful traders should enter the port. They quoted the commissioner's reprimand of Elliot for not allowing the traders to resume their normal pursuits. It was pointed out that Elliot had deluded the English traders with "the extravagant notion" that trade could be carried on at Macao, and Lin's prohibition of trade in the outside anchorages was repeated. The proclamation was distributed among the British ships anchored in Hong Kong Bay and placarded in the streets of Macao.

But Lin's wish to reopen the trade and resume the old order of things was now even more remote. On the 21st, Captain Elliot recapitulated Lin's actions, which, he maintained, had caused him to order the British retreat from Canton. He criticized the Chinese for trying to incite the British merchants to disobey his injunctions.[19] Thus, in the beginning of June, as Peter Parker reported, only about six Englishmen, fifteen or twenty Americans, and no Parsees were left in Canton, and by July 4 all the British had departed.[20] A letter written in June by an Englishman not connected with the trade well summarizes the uncertainty of this period:

You will, of course, be acquainted long ere this can reach you with the desperate state of our affairs in China. I can scarce find words to describe the pass to which matters have been brought. The opium trade is the cause; but it does not end with the opium trade. It had also embarrassed seriously our legal trade, which is in such a position that I can see no medium course to re-open it, except by means of a successful war, or the most cringing and humiliating concessions. The former I deprecate, as we have a bad, a notoriously unjust, cause to build upon; and if circumstances compel us to the second, why then the sooner the better, and let us put the best face upon matters that we can.[21]

Commissioner Lin came back from the Bogue on June 26, and he had hardly rested from the excitement of the opium destruction when he encountered another difficult issue. On July 12, he was informed of a clash at Chien-sha-tsui (on the Kowloon side of the Hong Kong anchorage) between some English seamen (perhaps also Americans, as Elliot insisted) and the villagers, which resulted in the death of a certain Lin Wei-hsi. The next morning Lin and Teng called on Governor I-liang, and the three top officials discussed the case over the breakfast table. The incident was subsequently investigated by the magistrate of Hsin-an, who reported that on July 7 the victim had been beaten to death by drunken English seamen. The body bore wounds inflicted by wooden clubs on the head and chest.[22] S. Wells Williams' report reads:

In the early part of July, a party of sailors were on shore from the shipping lying at Hongkong, and became ungovernable from the liquor they had taken, and in the excitement of the moment, they set upon the Chinese around them, and killed a man besides nearly demolishing a small temple. This outrage upon the unoffending people on shore was wholly unprovoked, and a partial reparation to the family of the deceased, a sum of money was paid by the shipping. . . .

As Elliot was unwilling to single out any one man, Lin threatened the 150 English residents of Macao and brought such pressure on the Portuguese that their governor, unable to resist the Chinese, told the English to depart.[23]

When Elliot learned of the incident, he hurried to the scene, arriving on the morning of July 10. He found, as he reported to Palmerston, that several seamen of the *Carnatic* and the *Mangalore* had been "most improperly allowed to go on shore at Hong Kong, and thus became engaged in a riot" that resulted in the death of the villager.[24] A reward of two hundred dollars was offered by Elliot for anyone who produced evidence leading to the conviction of the murderer and one hundred dollars to anyone who produced evidence leading to the conviction of the instigators of the riot. Meanwhile, at his "private account and risk," Elliot advanced fifteen hundred dollars to the family of the victim as compensation for the loss, four hundred dollars to protect them from the extortion that the larger sum might induce the lower officers to demand, and one hundred dollars to be distributed among the villagers as a means of soothing the ill feeling caused by the riot. The money was later charged to Jardine, Matheson and Dent and Company, agents for the two ships whose men were engaged in the affray.[25]

Capital punishment for murder was a fundamental principle in Chinese criminal law. The Chinese repeatedly demanded the murderer of Lin Wei-hsi, but it was the established English practice, since the *Lady Hughes* affair of 1784, that no British criminal, regardless of his crime, should be delivered to the Chinese for trial. Elliot insisted on this policy to such an extent that he later refused to receive any document whatever from the commissioner or any other Chinese authorities. On August 27, he wrote Palmerston: "I should inform your Lordship that since the walls of Macao have been covered with false and insulting proclamations respecting myself, and the servants and supplies taken away, I have refused to receive any official papers from the government. By this means, I have been enabled to reject any direct application to myself for the delivery of the man." [26]

In order to placate the persistent demands of the Chinese government, Elliot held a trial of six suspects on August 12 and 13 aboard the *Fort William*. The Chinese were invited but did not attend the trial. A bill of indictment for murder against one seaman, boatswain of the *Mangalore*, was ignored by the grand jury; [27] two were convicted of rioting and sentenced to three months' confinement with hard labor in any jail or house of correction in England, in addition to fines of fifteen pounds sterling each; three were found guilty of both riot and assault and were sentenced to six months' imprisonment plus fines of twenty-five pounds each.[28]

When the seamen were sent home, they were set free by the government on the grounds that Captain Elliot had no authority to exercise such control over the persons and liberty of British subjects. Elliot's authority to handle criminal cases was very uncertain, and he himself admitted that the trial of the six seamen was conducted "to the very utmost verge of my powers (and probably exceeded them)." [29] The case of Lin Wei-hsi was clearly an issue of extraterritoriality, and it became the most difficult topic of negotiation over the following months. It is important to examine Elliot's policy and authority concerning the issue of criminal jurisdiction, for this was to a great extent responsible for the crisis in the latter part of 1839.

On September 20, 1837, a similar but less serious case had taken place on the north shore of the Canton River, about two miles below the factories. A Chinese was stabbed several times by two lascars belonging to an English passage boat. The Chinese police arrested the two men, together with two others who seemed not to have taken part in the affair. The four were confined at the Consoo House, and on the next morning the magistrate in whose district the incident had occurred sent the lascars to Elliot for examination, but refused to turn them over. Elliot insisted that, if they were not surrendered to him before 10 P.M. on the same day, he would leave Canton. He cautioned the Chinese that "as soon as it were known I had left the Factories, it was too probable some eight hundred or a thousand men might come up to Canton from Whampoa, to carry a petition to the city gates for the restoration of the people." Upon such repeated threats, the four lascars were delivered to Elliot. Elliot had assured Palmerston: "I will never give them up to any other form of trial than that to which I have pledged myself — namely, a trial according to the forms of British law." He took this occasion to request that adequate judicial and police institutions for the government of British subjects in China be set up without delay, adding that, except in cases of homicide, the Chinese seemed to make no effort to settle quarrels between Chinese and foreigners.

Not long after this incident, at the end of September 1837, a minor mutiny broke out aboard the *Abercromby Robertson*. After suppressing the disturbance, Elliot formulated and promulgated a set of regulations for the more effective preservation of peace on the British ships at Whampoa, where "most serious disturbances" had been frequent. Upon receiving Elliot's report, Palmerston referred the matter in December 1838 to legal experts. On March 23, 1839, he informed Elliot, that according to the law officers, he had promulgated his regulations without sufficient authority. "With respect to the territorial rights of China, the Law Officers are of the opinion that the regulations, amounting in fact to the establishment of a system of police at Whampoa, within the dominions of the Emperor of China, would be an interference with the absolute right of sovereignty enjoyed by independent states, which can only be justified by positive treaty, or implied permission from usage." [30] At the time of the trial of the six seamen on August 12–13, this instruction apparently had not yet reached Canton.

The Chinese did not find the trial satisfactory and peremptorily demanded the murderer of Lin Wei-hsi to be turned over to the Chinese authorities. Commissioner Lin posted a lengthy proclamation in Macao on August 2, saying that he would have ordered the immediate execution of a Chinese who had struck and killed a foreigner and mentioning the severe punishment he had inflicted on some Chinese soldiers who had wounded a foreigner at Macao shortly before. The commissioner also cited an earlier homicide case of the Ch'ien-lung period, which involved a Frenchman and an Englishman, asserting Chinese jurisdiction even over criminal cases in which no Chinese was a party. He insisted: "He who kills a man must pay the penalty of life; whether he be a native or a foreigner, the statute is in this respect quite the same." [31]

Meanwhile Lin suspected that Elliot might have some design on Macao. So he followed the precedent of 1808, when Captain Drury's force had intruded into Macao, by stopping the supplies of food and fuel to the English and ordering all Chinese servants and compradors to stay away. To supervise the execution of these orders and to intimidate the English, on August 15 Lin and Teng left Canton for Hsiang-shan, forty miles north of Macao, with two thousand troops.

It was hoped by the governor of Macao and the merchants as a group that Elliot's departure from the settlement might relax the tension. Thus Elliott moved to the *Fort William* on August 24, his wife and child having already left. This gesture, however, did not produce the desired effect. In the morning of August 25 the governor of Macao showed J. H. Astell, head of a committee appointed to look after the safety of English subjects in Macao after Elliot's departure, an edict from the Chinese ordering the Portuguese to send the English away immediately. At 6 P.M. Astell again saw the governor of Macao, who had just received a more strongly worded edict from the Chinese warning that they would send troops to surround the British houses in Macao that night. Astell was asked to present the English position on the homicide at Chien-sha-tsui, but he refused for lack of authority. "There is even a threat of an attempt to surround British houses tonight," Matheson wrote Elliot on August 25, "but the Governor has declared his determination to resist this; and it is not likely that, if really intended, they would have given notice of it. I think, however, none of our countrymen at Macao will venture to go to sleep to-night." The Portuguese governor, however, had notified the British that he could not be responsible for their safety after noon the next day.[32]

At this point a British subject by the name of Mark Moss and a lascar seaman, Hassan Tindal, arrived at Macao in the early morning. They were the only two survivors from Moss's schooner, the *Black Joke*, which had been plundered at Lantao on the previous evening. Their deposition revealed a frightening tale of atrocity. They said that at about 10 P.M., five or six boats filled with Chinese pirates masquerading as soldiers had approached and boarded the schooner. Seven lascar crewmen were killed and Moss was savagely wounded, his left ear being cut off and put into his mouth. Tindal escaped death by jumping overboard and hanging on to the rudder for about half an hour.

Alarmed by this incident and compelled by Chinese and Portuguese pressure, Astell's committee recommended the departure of all the British from Macao. The embarkation took place on the 26th, attended by Portuguese troops under the supervision of the governor.[33] Lin Tse-hsü was able to report to the emperor on September 1 that, within the ten days prior to August 27, the occupants of fifty-seven English houses had left Macao. In this memorial Lin was naively optimistic, thinking that by driving the English out of Macao and stopping supplies to their ships, he was putting them under control. He pledged that he would not permit their servants and compradors to return or allow them to go back to the Canton factories until: (1) the murderer of Lin Wei-hsi was delivered up, (2) all opium was surrendered, (3) the merchant ships consented to enter the river and be inspected at Whampoa, (4) all empty store-ships left China, and (5) everything was carried out according to law. He and Teng decided to take up residence at Hsiang-shan and the Bogue alternately, sometimes together, sometimes separately.[34]

On September 2, Lin and Teng left Hsiang-shan at the hour of *mao* (5–7 A.M.) for an inspection tour of Macao. They traveled overland for 108 li and stopped overnight at Ch'ien-shan-chai, where the subprefect of Macao was stationed. On the next day the party started at the same early hour, traveling 10 li to arrive at Macao. Lin wrote in his diary:

As soon as I entered the wall of Macao, a hundred barbarian soldiers dressed in barbarian military uniform, led by the barbarian headman, greeted me. They marched in front of my sedan playing barbarian music and led me into the city. When we passed Wang-hsia, there was a temple, named the Hsin-miao (new temple), of the God of War. Having burned incense to the God, I held an audience with the headman. I presented the barbarian officers with colored silk, folding fans, tea, and rock candy and the soldiers with cows, sheep, wines, noodles, and four hundred foreign silver dollars.

Having entered the San-pa Gate, we proceeded from north to south and when we arrived at the Niang-ma-ko Temple I burned incense for the Goddess of Heaven. After a little rest, we proceeded through Nan-huan Street, from south to north. Thus we looked at most of the barbarian edifices. The barbarians are fond of architecture. Some of their buildings are as high as three stories; the fancy doors and green windows looked like gold and jade.

On this day, everyone, man and woman, came out on the street or leaned from the window to take a look. Unfortunately the barbarian costume was too absurd. The men, their bodies wrapped tightly in short coats and long "legs," resembled in shape foxes and rabbits as impersonated in the plays. . . . Their hair, full of curls, was cut off and only several inches was saved. Their beards, with abundant whiskers, were half shaved off and only a piece was kept. Looking at them all of a sudden was frightening. That the Cantonese referred to them as "devils" was indeed not vicious disparagement.

Moreover, there were some devil-slaves . . . who were in the menial service of the barbarians. Their black color, naturally born, exceeded even that of lacquer.

The hair of their women was parted into two or three locks with no high hair-do. As to their costume, on the top their bosom was exposed and at the bottom they wore multi-layered skirts. Spouses were freely chosen by the boys and girls themselves; even individuals of the same surname may be married. What a barbarian custom!

Lin's party left Macao in the hours of *ssu* (9–11 A.M.) and returned to Ch'ien-shan-chai for lunch. After the meal they followed the same route to the north, but were soon interrupted by a severe rainstorm. They took refuge in a clan temple of the Cheng family, about forty li from Ch'ien-shan-chai. Since the heavy rain made the mountain path impassable, Lin and Teng stayed overnight at the temple. By coincidence, the hoppo, coming from Canton, also arrived there. Thus the three officials dined together and, after the second drum (9–11 P.M.), the hoppo left to pass the night in another clan temple.[35]

Lin and Teng's joint memorial reporting this inspection tour of Macao reached Peking on October 11. They told the emperor that they had enjoined the Portuguese governor to obey the laws, not to store any contraband goods, and not to give any protection to opium-smuggling foreigners. They found that the houses which had been occupied by the English were all closed. When they passed the forts at San-pa, Ma-ko, and Nan-wan, each fort fired nineteen shots. Upon inquiring at Macao, Lin and Teng learned that this was the Portuguese great salute, performed only on unusual occasions. The tour was very satisfactory to them, and they recommended that such tours be repeated every year alternately by the governor-general, the governor, the provincial judge, and the financial commissioner. The emperor approved completely of what Lin and Teng had done in Macao, but did not think it worth the trouble for high officials to make annual inspection tours.[36]

At the end of August, the H.M.S. *Volage* arrived bearing a dispatch dated July 8 from the authorities in India. They fully supported Elliot's demand and promised everything that would be needed to defend Macao. This prompted Elliot to write the governor of Macao reiterating his former offer and stating that a force of eight hundred or a thousand men could be placed at his disposal. Elliot requested the governor's permission to move all the British subjects back to Macao, since the presence of the *Volage* and the forthcoming vessels from India would put him in a better position to defend the settlement. The Portuguese governor, however, once again turned down the request, on the grounds that he was obliged to preserve strict neutrality.[37]

THE KOWLOON CLASH AND THE CHUENPEE ENGAGEMENT

The British had now fifty vessels and several thousand men concentrated at Hong Kong. Some of these trading ships were armed with the twenty-two eighteen-pounders that had been bought by Captain Douglas of the *Cambridge* in Singapore. Up to about July 18, there was no difficulty in purchasing supplies from the Chinese.[38] When Elliot refused to deliver up the murderer of Lin Wei-hsi and Commissioner Lin ordered that their provisions be cut off, it was no longer possible to get rice or water from shore for this large fleet. The springs all along the coast were poisoned, and notices were put up to warn the Chinese not to touch the water. Captain Elliot decided to protest to the mandarins, and on August 25 he sent four armed boats with over eighty men aboard to the bay of Kowloon. At 2 P.M. they encountered two Chinese government junks and succeeded in delivering a document to the mandarins, fortunately with no bloodshed.

On September 4, Captain Elliot led a small fleet back to Kowloon again to demand provisions. This led to a major clash between the English and the Chinese, the first shots of the Opium War. At 9 A.M. Elliot and Captain Smith of the *Volage* boarded the cutter *Louisa* and, accompanied by the schooner *Pearl* and the *Volage*'s pinnace, proceeded to Kowloon. At noon the fleet arrived off the town of Kowloon where there were three large war junks and a strong battery.

Two letters were presented to the Chinese by Gutzlaff, who had approached with two other unarmed men in a small boat. One letter threatened grave consequences if the Chinese continued to deprive the several thousand Englishmen of regular supplies. If this state of things persisted, it was warned, there would be frequent conflicts. The other letter was addressed to the Chinese people and urged them not to poison the water. The Chinese refused the letters, claiming they lacked the authority to receive them.[39] On board the *Louisa* was a young sailor named A. W. Elmslie, brother of Elliot's secretary, who wrote a letter to another brother, in London, relating in close and vivid detail the subsequent events:

After a long interview with the mandarins, the Cutter "Louisa," "Pearl," and the "Volage's" pinnace anchored a short distance from the Junks. At 2 P.M. Capt. Elliot sent a message to the mandarins and told them that if they did not get provisions in half an hour, they would sink the Junks, — The half hour expired, and no provisions arrived. — Capt. Smith ordered his Pinnace to fire, which was immediately done . . . the Junks then triced up their Boarding nettings, and came into action with us at half pistol shot; our guns were well served with Grape and round shot; the first shot we gave them they opened a tremendous and well directed fire upon us, from all their Guns (each Junk had 10 Guns, and they brought all these over on the side which we engaged them on.) . . . The Junks' fire, Thank God! was not enough depressed, or if otherwise, none would have lived to tell the Story. — 19 of their Guns we received in mainsail, — the first Broadside I can assure you was not pleasant, all of us had to work the Guns. . . . The battery opened fire upon the English at 3:45 P.M. and their fire was steady and well directed which concentrated on the cutter as she had up a Pendant. At 4:30, having fired 104 rounds, the cutter had to haul off as she was out of cartridges. The junks immediately made sail after the *Louisa* and at 4:45 they came up with the English vessels. We hove the vessel in stays on their starboard Beam, and the "Pearl" on the larboard Bow of the van Junk, and gave them three such Broadsides that it made every Rope in the vessel grin again. — We loaded with Grape the fourth time, and gave them Gun for Gun. — The shrieking on board was dreadful, but it did not frighten me; this is the first day I ever shed human blood, and I hope will be the last.[40]

During the action, Commissioner Lin and his associates reported, two Chinese soldiers were killed, two seriously wounded, and four slightly wounded. On the English side, Captain Douglas of the *Cambridge* suffered a flesh wound on the arm; two other crewmen of the same ship were injured more seriously. However, the Chinese memorial to the emperor, dated September 18, claimed that at least seventeen British men lost their lives and one British ship was sunk.[41]

In the middle of September, Elliot made overtures to the Chinese through the Portuguese to resume negotiations. On September 14, he went back to Macao and, accompanied by the Portuguese governor, met the Chinese subprefect stationed there. Elliot was willing to let British traders give bonds, but they were not to be worded as Lin had instructed. Since the

Chinese position on the deliverance of the murderer of Lin Wei-hsi had not altered and since the difference between the two sides over the issue of the bond was still great, there was no longer any chance that the British trade would be resumed.[42]

The immediate incident leading to the break-off of negotiations in October was the action of two defiant British ships. One ship, the *Thomas Coutts*, under Captain Warner, arrived in China from Singapore in the latter part of October. Warner proceeded directly toward the Bogue and, as we have seen, signed the bond in the form that the Chinese authorities demanded; having thus defied Elliot's injunctions, he entered the port.[43] This conduct effectively upset Elliot's plans to resume trade without yielding to the Chinese on the bond issue.

It was reported by Elliot's secretary, Elmslie, that an agreement was reached in October whereby the British trade could be carried on outside the Bogue between Anunghoy and Ch'uan-pi (Chuenpee) without the need to sign a bond, on the condition that the ships be subjected to examination.[44] The alleged agreement was soon abrogated. On October 26, Elliot wrote Smith, Captain of the *Volage* and British naval officer in command in China, blaming the entrance of the *Thomas Coutts* for the change in the Chinese position. Elliot asked Smith to keep all British shipping outside the Bogue. On the next day, Smith issued a public warning to this effect to all captains, officers, and crews of British ships.[45]

Commissioner Lin was now growing more impatient over the issue of Lin Wei-hsi. On October 26, he addressed an edict through the sub-prefect of Macao to Captain Elliot once more demanding the murderer and threatening to arrest the suspects in Elliot's custody by force. The edict reads in part:

Regarding the murderer in the case of homicide, Elliot must still, as in my former reply, be required to send up for trial the five men detained by him. If he continues to oppose and delay, I must call upon the naval commander-in-chief to proceed at the head of his war vessels and fire-ships, as also of the land soldiery encamped at all the various points of ingress, that they may aid in seizing the murderous foreigner, making it imperative on them to bring him up for trial and punishment; and at the same time to search for and apprehend all the traitorous Chinese in shelter and concealment on board the various ships.[46]

It was reported to Elliot that Admiral Kuan's forces at the Bogue had been considerably reinforced and that the admiral intended to send his force to Hong Kong to seize the murderer of Lin Wei-hsi. In Macao, edicts were circulated forbidding any intercourse between the Chinese and the English; native servants were forced to leave; all Englishmen were required to abandon the settlement; their supplies were cut off; and military forces, were deployed — some four or five hundred men pitched their tents just outside the barrier of Macao. In such circumstances, the British ships at Hong Kong moved to T'ung-ku Bay, a more secure anchorage.

On October 27, Elliot suggested to Captain Smith that the ships move to the Bogue and that Smith present a moderate but firm address directly to the commissioner to prevent any rash movement on the part of the Chinese. On November 2, Elliot and Smith arrived at a place about one mile below the Ch'uan-pi battery, and in the evening Smith's address to the commissioner was delivered to Admiral Kuan. It was received with civility and a reply was promised for the next morning.[47]

On the next day, another English ship, the *Royal Saxon*, which had also signed the bond against Elliot's and Smith's orders, approached the Bogue to enter. The *Volage*, attempting to stop her, fired a shot across her bow. The Chinese water forces tried to protect the *Royal Saxon*, and the ensuing engagement was described by Elliot as "the most serious collision which has ever taken place between Her Majesty's forces and those of this Empire, during our whole intercourse with this country." The signal to engage was given by Captain Smith at about noon, and a formidable barrage was aimed at the Chinese squadron of twenty-nine junks. One was immediately blown up, three were sunk, and several more were seriously damaged. According to official reports to Peking, fifteen Chinese soldiers were killed and many more were wounded. The damage done to the British was greatly exaggerated, as usual.

Lin and Teng's memorial reported that this engagement was touched off by the British attempt to prevent the *Royal Saxon* from entering the port. In Elliot's dispatch to Palmerston, however, he made no mention of the fact that the first British shot in the Ch'uan-pi engagement was aimed at the *Royal Saxon*; nor did he give any reason why the Chinese squadron suddenly "broke ground and stood out towards Her Majesty's ships." The dispatch only explained that the British ships could not retire before an approaching flotilla, if the honor of the flag was to be upheld. But Captain Smith's letter of November 3, addressed to the commanders of the Chinese ships, revealed his rather more aggressive attitude. It reads:

"Smith commanding the English naval force, hereby sends information to the various commanders. He has peremptorily to request that all their vessels instantly return to the anchorage north of Shakok [Sha-chiao]. It will be well to do so." [48] Admiral Kuan could not take this kind of insult lightly.

After the battle of Ch'uan-pi, the Chinese abandoned any attempt to bring the British ships into Whampoa to trade. It was proclaimed that, beginning on December 6, trade with Britain would be stopped forever. The emperor approved Lin's measures and stated that all British ships must be driven away. [49] Still, the foreign trade at Canton was not interrupted by the political storms; it simply took on a new form. The British trade now passed into the hands of the Americans. Between October 1, 1839, and June 18, 1840, as much as 24,826,599 pounds of tea were shipped to England, not counting the one and a half million pounds sent to Singapore for transshipment to England. It was estimated in May 1840 that the tea exported to the United States and the continent would exceed the usual supply. [50]

The transshipping trade by the American houses was a singular and interesting phase in the course of developments at Canton. Before the British left the city, Elliot had personally "begged" Russell and Company to go with them: "If your house goes, all will go, and we shall soon bring these rascally Chinese to terms." Robert Forbes's reply, as he reported it, was that "*I had not come to China for health or pleasure, and that I should remain at my post as long as I could sell a yard of goods or buy a pound of tea . . . we Yankees had no Queen to guarantee our losses.*" Elliot asked whether Forbes would do business with a chain on his neck and threatened to make Canton "too hot" for the Americans. To this Forbes replied that the chain was "imaginary" while the duty to his clients and the commission account was real; if Canton were made "too warm," he would go to Whampoa "retreating step by step, but buying and selling just as long as I found parties to operate with." [51] From home, his younger brother, John M. Forbes, wrote to him:

I note Elliot's warlike aspect and only hope *you* will keep the peace[.] You're so chivalrous that I have had hard work to make up my mouth to tell folks how *quiet* you will keep and let Jn Bull fight his own battles and that your only idea is money, — that (and this I hope is true) that you will neither be wheedled nor frightened out of Canton —

I don't fear hostile measures until a fleet from England get out and then even I guess they will move slowly and to let Damaresq get in and out — If there should be a long blockade how delightful it would be to see the Acbar [the *Akbar*, built by J. M. Forbes in 1839] arrive 1st Oct next with a full cargo — largely for a/c of her junior owner! eh? [52]

The Americans had retreated quite a way from their original position on the issue of the bond. Warren Delano, the vice-consul, convened a meeting of the American merchants and shipmasters on July 2, 1839, at the consulate, and it was resolved that they would not sign any paper written in Chinese, a language they did not understand. When a committee presented the resolution to Howqua, he protested, insisting that Forbes had already promised him that the Americans would sign the bond written in Chinese, and this fact had already been reported to the government. A technical device was subsequently worked out whereby the bond was written in both languages on the same sheet of paper, the Chinese on top and the English below, and the merchants put their signatures in between the two versions. When the commander of a ship signed the bond before the vice-consul, it was declared that he was signing only what he understood and that he did not know Chinese. The bond, in the English version at least, mentioned no capital punishment. It merely stated that the signer had received commands from the celestial dynasty rigidly prohibiting opium and had been informed that certain new regulations had been established to that effect; the foreigner would not dare to violate them.[53] John C. Green signed the bond on behalf of Russell and Company, contemplating an early retirement from the house, and he departed for America shortly afterward.[54]

So immense an amount of British business had passed into the hands of the Americans that the latter began to "talk with contempt of the sort of business done formerly, for now a ship can make 18000 drs. freight from Lintin to Whampoa." [55] (British goods were carried at thirty to forty dollars per ton; Indian cotton at seven dollars per bale.) To get tea and silk out through the ninety-mile passage, a ship was paid more than it would get for the voyage from Canton to the United States under normal conditions.[56] Thus an American trader wrote: "Nye does for Dent & Co., [James] Ryan of Philadelphia for Jardine — ; Delano for Macvicar; R [Russell] & Co. for Grey; Wetmore for some others. We are all in doubt what is to happen for the Admiral is expected in a month . . . in this case we should be idle together." [57] The English houses, however, were not entirely idle. Some of the greater firms, such as Jardine and Dent, held out for a while, but when they saw that others would "get all the cream," then they too sent their agents, tea tasters, and so on, to Canton under cover of the American flag.

Although the British merchants complained about the fantastic freight charges for the transshipment, Captain Elliot was no longer opposed to the Americans' remaining in Canton. When he met Forbes later in Macao, he received him cordially, saying: "My dear Forbes, the Queen owes you many thanks for not taking my advice as to leaving Canton. We have got in all our goods, and got out a full supply of teas and silk. If the American houses had not remained at their post, the English would have gone in. I had no power to prevent them from going. Now the trade of the season is over, and a large force at hand, we can bring the Chinese to terms." [58]

This anomalous commercial phenomenon lasted for nearly a year. In March 1840, because of the impending hostilities, there were already indications that at least some American residents in Canton intended to move to Macao. One firm had issued a circular saying that it had to stop accepting further consignments of English property or commissions of any description. In June, all the Americans, thirty-five in number, left Canton for Macao. [59]

While the lawful trade was carried on through the Americans at Canton, the illicit traffic was resumed on the coasts of eastern Kwangtung and Fukien. Elliot reported in mid-July 1839 that, in several places along the Fukien coast, formidable organizations of native smugglers had become active and "a most vigorous trade" was carried on at places about two hundred miles east of Canton. He predicted that the high opium price in China would "soon bring on the immense stocks in India." Elliot's prediction, however, proved wrong. From the winter of 1839 through the summer of 1840, the provincial governments of Kwangtung and Fukien carried out zealous campaigns of suppression, and, as a result, opium prices fell drastically. In June 1840 it was reported that, for 1,400 chests of opium arriving in Singapore, buyers had offered only $295 for Patna and $268 for Benares. [60]

The first six months of 1840 passed with little excitement. While Commissioner Lin quietly made military preparations, the merchants were busily engaged in trade, shipping all the tea and silk they could get out before hostilities erupted. In Canton, no foreign flag flew over the factories. Some twelve or fifteen foreign ships waited at Whampoa, and fifty or sixty British vessels were anchored at T'ung-ku under the protection of the *Volage* and the *Hyacinth*. [61]

TINGHAI AND THE DISGRACE OF LIN

The first vessel of the British expeditionary forces to arrive was the *Alligator*, which reached the Canton waters on June 9, 1840. Other ships soon followed, and a blockade of Canton was declared.[62] Thus the Opium War formally began.

A fleet consisting of the *Wellesley, Conway, Alligator*, the troopship *Rattlesnake*, and two transports under the command of Brigadier-General George Burrell sailed to the north and arrived at the anchorage of Chusan Harbor on July 4. In the evening Brigade-General Chang Ch'ao-fa, accompanied by two Chinese officials and the British officers who had served the summons to him, came on board the flagship *Wellesley*. Gutzlaff pointed out to them the large guns and explained how formidable the broadside of a man-of-war was. Chang was asked to surrender before dawn. The Chinese brigade-general, whom Gutzlaff thought a dull and stupid man, admitted the military superiority of the English and agreed that there was no point in resisting, but said: "Still I *must* fight."

On the following morning, as the British troops were ready to land, the *Wellesley* fired a shot calling the Chinese to surrender. But Chang Ch'ao-fa returned fire from his junks and from a few wretched guns installed on shore. The *Wellesley, Conway*, and *Alligator* immediately returned fire and methodically bombarded a tower on shore. In a minute, all the Chinese troops deployed on the hill and the shore of the island disappeared. The British troops landed with no opposition and took the outer city, which was less than a mile from the beach. The officers immediately began to destroy a large supply of wine they had come upon, in order to prevent the soldiers and sailors from getting drunk. The island apparently had a brewing industry, and the outer city of Tinghai seemed to be the depot for their product. Although several thousand large jars of wine were broken and the liquor "flowed through the streets in sounding torrents," there was still plenty left to intoxicate the sailors. All the shops were broken into and looted by the sailors and Chinese boatmen, who took advantage of the general confusion.

On the morning of July 6, the British troops advanced to storm the city of Tinghai but found that it had been virtually deserted during the previous night. "All the houses were shut up," reported Robert Thom, who followed the expedition forces as interpreter, "and the silence of death reigned through all the streets!"[63] Chang Ch'ao-fa was severely wounded in the thigh and had retreated to Chen-hai. The magistrate of

Tinghai drowned himself and the district police master and jail warden (*tien-shih*) committed suicide. The *Times* of London happily reported: "The British flag waves over a portion of the Chinese empire for the first time! Chusan fell into the hands of the English on Sunday, the 5th of July, and one more settlement in the Far East was added to the British Crown." [64]

In the initial period of the occupation of Tinghai, people were allowed to come and go freely. As a result, almost every respectable individual left, and thieves came in from the country and carried off an enormous amount of plunder. The civil administration of the city was entrusted to Gutzlaff, who with Thom took the district magistrate's yamen as quarters. Gutzlaff managed to enroll for his assistance a few Nanking men, whom he called "fine fellows" and "most intelligent men." "I have often thought — could one of the Hong merchants have seen Gutzlaff seated on the Chehëen's [the magistrate's] chair and waited upon by his blackguard Nankingmen," Thom commented, "they wd certainly have muttered something about *hu-chia hu-wei*, the Fox borrowing the dignity of the Tiger — or as we might quote from scripture — 'my house — ye have made it a den of thieves.' Civil government I look upon *in the meantime* as a perfect farce — until our authority is firmly established we ought to have military law — and military law *only*." [65]

On August 9, 1840, Admiral George Elliot arrived at the Pei-ho, accompanied by Captain Elliot. They presented Palmerston's letter addressed to the Chinese premier on the 15th, and negotiations followed. Since the first two thirds of Palmerston's letter consisted of nothing but complaints against Commissioner Lin's injudicious proceedings at Canton, the emperor took the complaints as being directed against Lin Tse-hsü personally.[66] The phrase "to demand from the Emperor satisfaction and redress" was translated as *ch'iu-t'ao huang-ti chao-hsueh shen-yuan* (to beg the emperor to settle and redress a grievance), which added a distinct flavor of accusation against Lin. Thus the emperor naively felt that all the trouble with the British could be solved if he agreed to punish the one man. It was reported by one of the five Englishmen who participated in the negotiation at the Pei-ho that the Chinese offered to surrender Lin to the British to be dealt with as they saw fit.[67]

It has been pointed out by Tsiang T'ing-fu that Lin's acts in Canton had been previously planned at Peking even before his departure for Canton.[68] This may be overstated, but it is on record that every measure Lin took in Canton before August 1840 had not only won the emperor's complete approval but his lavish praise. In fact, up to August 1840 the emperor had always taken a stronger position than Lin Tse-hsü in dealing with the British. It will be recalled that the emperor had repeatedly and emphatically instructed Lin and Teng to do a thorough job in rooting out the opium. He referred to Lin's destruction of the opium in June 1838 as an act which greatly pleased the human heart (*ta-k'uai jen-hsin*). On September 24, while cautioning Lin against rash measures, he nevertheless instructed him not to show any weakness toward the British.

Lin Tse-hsü memorialized the emperor on September 18, 1839, reporting the Kowloon clash and concluding that, if the British could now obey the Chinese laws, he would certainly extend the imperial benevolence and forgive past faults; but if compelled to use force again, he assured the emperor that he was well prepared to do so. Next to these comments, the emperor wrote two lines in vermilion, dated October 11: "Since such action [in Kowloon] had taken place already, weakness should not be shown. It is not our worry that you might be reckless, but we want to warn you not to be timid." The emperor was so pleased to learn of the "victory" in the Kowloon clash and of the alleged sinking of a British ship that he immediately promoted two officers who had taken part in the action.

On January 6, 1840, the emperor once more instructed Lin to extirpate opium once and for all. At the end of January, when he learned that Lin had refused Elliot's overtures, he approved the action and warned that, if Lin could not thoroughly clear away the opium evil, he would be held responsible. Four months later, the emperor consented readily to the commissioner's request to build more forts at Chien-sha-tsui. In June 1840, when Teng T'ing-chen had already been transferred to Fukien, the emperor instructed him that, if the barbarians were not submissive, he should immediately fire at them with guns.

The emperor gave his complete approval in mid-July to Lin's plan for burning British ships by means of fire rafts. He did not blame Lin's policy at Canton for the British landing at Chusan; instead he severely reprimanded the governor-general of Fukien and Chekiang for being negligent in defense work. As late as August 8, 1840, the emperor instructed the officers in Chekiang province to repel the invading British forces without mercy. The next day, however, the emperor suddenly faltered and began to wonder what policy would be best for dealing with the British. He directed Ch'i-shan to accept any communication, whether written in a foreign language or in Chinese, which the British might present. Four days later, when he received a joint memorial from the top officials in Fukien recommending a measure for acquiring more guns and armaments, he refused the request. On the 15th, he directed Yü-ch'ien, the acting governor-general of Liang Kiang, to be cautious with regard to any barbarians who might appear along the coast of his territory and to make sure whether they came to present petitions or to attack. Only if they came to cause trouble was Yü-ch'ien allowed to fight. The emperor's attitude toward the British was thus completely and strangely reversed. On August 21, 1840, he harshly accused Lin Tse-hsü: "Externally you wanted to stop the [opium] trade, but it has not been stopped; internally you wanted to wipe out the outlaws [opium smugglers and smokers], but they are not cleared away. You are just making excuses with empty words. Nothing has been accomplished but many troubles have been created. Thinking of these things, I cannot contain my rage. What do you have to say now?" On September 28, Lin Tse-hsü and Teng T'ing-chen were referred to the Board of Punishment for judgment, and Lin was replaced as imperial commissioner by Ch'i-shan.

In the fall and winter of 1840, by order of the court, Lin remained in Canton to offer assistance to Ch'i-shan. The views of the two men, however, were diametrically opposed, and Lin was never consulted. On April 15, 1841, the court partially restored Lin's official rank by conferring upon him the fourth-grade title, and he was sent to Chekiang to help in the defense work of the province. During the summer of 1841, however, the court was lulled into a state of euphoria under the influence of exaggerated and false reports from Canton alleging that Chinese victories had cleared the way for peace. A gesture of appeasement now seemed politic. So on June 28, 1841, Lin Tse-hsü, again deprived of his rank, and Teng T'ing-chen were exiled to Ili.

In August, the Yellow River broke through its dikes at Kaifeng, and Lin was diverted from his original destination to work at flood control. Early the next year, the dikes having been repaired, Lin had to resume his trip to Ili, despite numerous officials' appeals to the court that he be spared this punishment because of his meritorious service at Kaifeng.

In Ili, Lin engaged in irrigation work. By 1844, he had reclaimed over 3,700,000 *mou* of land. It was not until late in 1845 that the court recalled Lin and appointed him acting governor-general of Shensi and Kansu provinces. In the spring of the following year, he became governor of Shensi. In these capacities, Lin contributed greatly to the suppression of various rebellions by minority groups. He introduced new and larger guns based on the Western models he had seen in Canton. On April 30, 1847, Lin was appointed governor-general of the Yunnan and Kweichow area, a position he held until the summer of 1849 when, after repeated requests, he was permitted to retire on account of poor health. In this last position he distinguished himself by settling the Mohammedan rebellion that had plagued Yunnan province for decades.

Lin had hardly begun to enjoy a much needed rest when the court again recalled him. On October 17, 1850, he was appointed imperial commissioner to suppress the Taipings in Kwangsi. Lin, though still a sick man, set out the day after receiving the emperor's edict, but he never reached Kwangsi. He died in mid-journey on November 22, at the age of sixty-seven.[69] Had he survived a few more years, the Taiping rebellion might well have taken a different course.

LIN'S ROLE IN CHINESE HISTORY

The sudden change of the emperor's attitude in 1840 from fanatical antiforeignism to abject appeasement has long been a topic of discussion. Hsiao I-shan maintained that his shift in policy was due to the fall of Tinghai, but this view was refuted by Hsia Nai because, after the emperor first learned about Tinghai, he still favored a strict policy for a brief period.[70] It is generally agreed that the emperor was influenced by Mu-chang-a, grand councilor and a favorite of the emperor since childhood. The interests of the Ch'ing dynasty, from the Manchu court's point of view, evidently transcended those of the Chinese state. (In Lin's Confucian mind, however, the two were not really separable. It might be said that Lin did his work too well; the weak Ch'ing dynasty was in no position to accept the consequences.) The emperor, taking the easy way out, became convinced that all the British wanted was Lin's punishment and that this would be enough to solve the problems.[71]

It is difficult to make an objective judgment of Lin's work at Canton because the moral-legal issue of opium can hardly be separated from the rest of the dispute. However, a comparison of Lin's and Elliot's motives, their methods, and the causes of their success or failure can be made on the basis of available evidence without the risk of supporting or denouncing either party.

The major issues that confronted Commissioner Lin were the suppression of the opium traffic, the preservation of Chinese control, and the restoration of the lawful trade at Canton. His persistent demand for the murderer of Lin Wei-hsi and the recurring requests for the bonds were motivated by the desire to assert Chinese jurisdiction over foreigners trading on Chinese territory. He had no other aim or design on the British.

For Elliot, the questions were how his government could establish diplomatic relations with the Chinese on an equal basis, how much longer British merchants should trade under the obsolete Canton system, and how British legal protection could be extended to Englishmen in China. While Commissioner Lin was striving to preserve the status quo, Elliot was striving to effect a fundamental change in the trading system and to reform the relations between the two countries. Thus he suggested the establishment of permanent bases on the coast of China, which would eventually lead to larger possibilities. This line of reasoning fit perfectly into the Victorian, colonialist pattern of thinking in Britain.[72]

The problem of equal and honorable communications between the two governments was not in itself sufficient ground for waging a war, but the opium trade and extraterritorial rights were of vital and immediate concern to the governments and people of both countries. The records indicate that the most violent and recurring disputes arose from these two issues. Without neglecting other factors, it is justifiable to say that the direct origins of the clash in 1840 lay in the opium traffic and England's insistence on extraterritoriality in China.

One major cause of Lin's failure at Canton was his premodern concept of foreign relations, which he shared with every Chinese statesman of the time. In accord with the tributary system, he came to Canton to dictate, not to negotiate. Had he been willing, or rather permitted by China's political tradition, to face the reality that England was not a vassal state but a great power, it would have been possible for him to sit down at a conference table with Elliot and iron out the differences. Instead he depended on a group of hong merchants and ignorant officers to gather information and to carry out his policies. It was unfortunate for both sides that problems as serious as those confronting Lin and Elliot should have been handled mainly by such a group of incompetents. There was much truth in Elliot's statement that, "In ninety-nine cases out of a hundred, connected with foreigners, which are submitted to high Chinese authorities, their determination must be taken upon the report of low and corrupt officers; and the higher functionaries are not in a situation to detect error, or to repair it when made." [73]

Despite the unrealistic instructions from Peking and the strait jacket of an obsolete political system, it cannot be denied that Lin followed an inflexible and uncompromising approach. He relied too much on Confucian righteousness and morality in advancing his cause. Against China's palpable military inferiority he pitted her uncertain potential strength; a less loyal servant of the emperor or a more shrewd politician of the regime would have attempted to avoid hostilities at all costs. He knew that, owing to the strict prevention measures along the Kwangtung and Fukien coasts, the opium traders were already having difficulty in disposing of their cargoes.[74] Had he continued the vigilant program toward the Chinese outlaws without resorting to drastic measures against the British, the trade might have gradually dwindled to a harmless state and war might have been averted, at least during Lin's tenure of office in Canton. On the other hand, the British could not tolerate a serious and chronic stagnation of the opium traffic, since Britain's legal trade with China and her economy in India depended and thrived on it. The Opium War could only have been avoided by the legalization of the opium trade and by China's relinquishment of her legal jurisdiction over foreigners, a stand which neither Peking nor Lin Tse-hsü could accept.

The real contribution of Lin to his country was his timely warning of the pernicious effect of opium on the health of the people and the economy of the nation. Many historians have done injustice to Commissioner Lin in criticizing his general policy as one built on backwardness. But stronger armed forces and superior weapons have not always predetermined the outcome of wars — history abounds with examples of the small and the weak emerging as ultimate victors. Militarily, Lin Tse-hsü did not foresee an easy and quick task. In a letter to two of his former teachers, written on his journey of exile to Ili, Lin revealed a strategic concept very similar to that practiced by the Chinese Nationalist and Communist forces in the 1930's and 1940s in their war against the Japanese. In this letter Lin envisaged a protracted struggle against the British, and he wanted the Chinese to fight to the end, using the interior provinces of Hupeh, Shensi, and Szechwan as bases.[75]

Many thoughtful Britons were concerned with the danger involved in Britain's expedition if China were to follow such a strategy. The *Quarterly Review* stressed the hazardous difficulties of inland operations. It cautioned that in China the population was abundant and soldiers, though not in the best state of training and discipline, were many in number; everywhere they would be found to swarm and sting like hives of bees. Wrote *Blackwood's Edinburgh Magazine*: "Indeed, it is a more hopeful concern to make war upon the winds and the waters; for both are known to suffer great changes during some time after the continued cannonading of a great sea-fight; whereas China is, like Russia, defensible, without effort of her men, by her own immeasurable extent, combined with the fact of having no vulnerable organs — no local concentrations of the national power in which a mortal wound can be planted. There lay the mistake of Napoleon in his desperate anabasis to Moscow." [76]

But a protracted war can be waged and won only by a determined, spirited people, indoctrinated in an unwavering ideology and led by a popular, incorruptible, and able government. Neither the deteriorating Manchu regime, with its volatile and vacillating emperor, nor the fanatic but spineless court nobles shared any of the fortitude or wisdom of Lin Tse-hsü: he was a faithful statesman serving the wrong master and an idealist born a century too early. The emperor pushed him into the course of rash actions but soon withdrew his support. Thus even the best efforts of Lin Tse-hsü, a man of undoubted talent, probity, and vision, were doomed to utter futility from the outset.

Benefiting from hindsight and access to Chinese and British documents, we may now criticize Lin for his obstinacy and lack of finesse in handling foreign affairs. But, given the hopeless circumstances, was there a better man available for the task? Was there any other strategy that could have successfully stopped the opium trade and still averted the conflict? Could China have reasserted her authority within her boundaries without adhering to an obsolete isolationist policy? The records available to us now seem to give negative answers to these questions and tend to confirm the views of many Chinese historians who have long since vindicated Commissioner Lin. As more and more documents are discovered and studied, Western historians will also have to re-evaluate Lin's role in modern Chinese history.

Reading Lin's diaries and letters, we cannot help but sense his distrust of the emperor and his contempt for many of his reactionary colleagues. But he was too much ingrained in Confucian culturism (as opposed to modern nationalism) to be a Hung Hsiu-ch'üan or a Mao Tse-tung; there was no question of his challenging the wisdom and authority of the throne, whether occupied by a Manchu or a Chinese. He was at once a traditionalist and a nonconformist.

Of all the nineteenth-century Chinese statesmen, Lin outshines the others in stature and influence. The Opium War has had a far-reaching impact on domestic developments and foreign relations. Two or three generations before Tseng Kuo-fan and Li Hung-chang, Lin Tse-hsü preached and launched a program of self-strengthening by learning from the barbarians. Indeed, he was more profound a thinker than Tseng and much less shrewd a politician than Li. If the later men excelled in the art of doing what was possible, Lin surpassed them in the science of fore-seeing what was inevitable. It is ironic that Lin should have been blamed and punished for touching off the Opium War, for war was ineluctable. The longer the conflict was delayed, the greater the price the Chinese would have to pay. At that moment in history, when an upsurging Western imperialism was about to clash headlong with the disintegrating Manchu-Chinese political and cultural system, a man could probably do no more than to warn and prepare his people for the oncoming collision.

Lin's mission, then, was not confined to the technical opium question. He may or may not have been completely aware of it, but he went to Canton to formulate a new foreign policy, to lay the foundation for the transformation of the Canton system into a more modern institution, and, most important of all, to make preparations for an unavoidable increasing contact with the West. In this broad sense, Lin did not really fail in his mission. The roaring guns of the Opium War awakened the empire from centuries of lethargy. This ushered in a new era in Chinese history, and the people were started on the path toward modernization which, owing to China's unwieldy traditions and years of complacence, was bound to be long, winding, and anguished. In a way, are not the Chinese today still treading this path as a response to the continued challenge from the West?

APPENDIX A

PRINCIPAL OPIUM EDICTS, 1729–1839

1729   A law was enacted that made opium dealers punishable by the cangue for one month and compulsory military service at a frontier post. Proprietors of opium dens were to be punished by strangulation.

1780   An imperial edict prohibited the consumption of opium and reiterated the prohibition of its sale.

1796   An imperial edict prohibited the importation of opium.

1799   The governor-general issued a strong edict prohibiting the opium trade. [Note: all governors-general and governors mentioned in this appendix, unless otherwise specified, are those stationed in Canton.]

1800   An imperial edict prohibited the domestic cultivation of the poppy and repeated the prohibition against importing opium.

1806   (January) The hoppo issued an edict against the importation of opium.

1807   The new hoppo issued an edict against the importation of opium. Later in the year the emperor reiterated the old prohibition order.

1809   (June 4) The governor-general issued an edict against the opium trade.

1809   (August 17) The governor-general reiterated the order prohibiting opium imports and sales.

1810   An imperial edict repeated the order prohibiting the smoking of opium and instructed provincial officials to stop the opium smuggling.

1811   (April) An imperial edict was issued to urge the several superintendents of customs offices and the gubernatorial authorities to step up the enforcement of the prohibition laws.

1813   (July) The emperor discovered opium addicts among his bodyguard. At his command, the Board of Punishment enacted laws which provided that guards found to be addicted to the drug were punishable by a flogging of a hundred strokes and two months of wearing the cangue. Ordinary military and civilian addicts would be flogged a hundred strokes and made to wear the cangue for one month. The emperor also authorized the several governors-general to cashier any supervisors of customs offices who were found conniving in the importation of opium.

1814   (June 21) The emperor issued edicts to remind the several superintendents of the customs offices of the opium-prohibition laws.

1815   (May 2) The emperor issued an edict approving the governor-general's proposal to inspect Portuguese ships at Macao for opium.

1815   (June 7) An edict issued by the subprefect of Macao called the attention of the foreign community to the opium-prohibition laws.

1817   An imperial edict reiterated the prohibition of opium traffic and smuggling.

1820   (April 13) The governor-general and the hoppo issued an edict requiring the hong merchants to search all foreign ships for opium and bear full responsibility for any ships they passed.

1820   (July 1) The governor-general and the hoppo reiterated the above order.

1821   (November) The emperor endorsed the governor-general's and the hoppo's proposal to reduce Howqua's official rank as a punishment for not preventing the import of opium.

1821 (November 17) An edict issued by the district magistrates of Panyü and Namhoi ordered the departure of the opium ships from the Canton River.

1821 (December 2) The governor-general issued an edict reiterating the orders given by the magistrates.

1822 (March 8) The emperor issued an edict to the governor-general confidentially instructing him to report whether the hoppo had connived in the opium trade.

1822 (March) The governor-general issued an edict against the opium trade.

1823 (January 19) An imperial edict was issued to the governor-general and the hoppo urging them to be more vigorous in stopping the opium imports. This edict was in response to a censor's accusations against corrupt functionaries.

1823 (March) An edict issued by the governor-general reiterated the opium prohibition.

1823 (September) The emperor approved a regulation proposed by the Board of Civil Office and the Board of War for punishing negligent officials. It repeated an old rule that any official who was found accepting bribes for conniving in opium growing or importing would be dismissed from office. It added an article providing for the punishment of officials who, owing to ignorance, failed to confiscate or suppress imported or domestically produced opium. If the amount involved was more than a hundred catties, the official in charge of the territory where the opium was found would be fined one year's salary; if more than a thousand catties, he would be demoted one grade.

1828 English ships were found on the coast of Fukien, Kiangsu, and Chekiang. The emperor ordered the provincial authorities to expel them.

1829 The emperor approved a regulation drafted by the governor-general forbidding the export of silver and the import of opium.

1831 (March) The emperor issued an edict to the several governors-general and governors asking them to report annually assuring him that there was no opium in their respective territories. The taotai and prefects were required to file bonds with the governor-general at the end of each year guaranteeing that there was no cultivation of the poppy or sale of opium in their area.

1831 (May 9) The hoppo issued an edict forbidding the opium traffic.

1831 (June) Imperial rescripts approved the proposals that: (a) The punishment for opium smoking be increased from one month of wearing the cangue to two months, and the offender was to receive a flogging of a hundred strokes. (b) The several governors-general, governors, prefects, and magistrates were required to file annual bonds to the effect that there was no one smoking opium in their jurisdictions. (c) Anyone found making smoking extract from crude opium was to be punished as if he had been manufacturing gambling devices.

1831 (July 24) The emperor issued an edict repeating opium prohibition.

1831 (August) The emperor issued an edict directing all governors-general and governors to have all their subordinates down to the *pao-chia* level search for areas of poppy culture. It was decreed that all lands so used were to be confiscated and the offenders punished as if they had been selling opium.

1831 (November 5) The governor-general issued an edict prohibiting the opium trade.

1832 (February 9) Another edict of the governor-general repeated the opium prohibition.

1832 (April 13) An edict from the hoppo repeated the prohibition against opium.

1832 (July) English ships were found on the Shantung coast; the emperor asked the coastal provinces to prevent the ships from repeating such visits.

1834 In response to an imperial edict ordering an investigation of the causes of the phenomenal growth of opium importation, Governor-General Lu K'un, Governor Ch'i Kung, and P'eng-nien, the hoppo, memorialized that some local people were in favor of legalizing opium importation and rescinding the order against poppy cultivation. The memorialists held that such views were not entirely unsound, but the emperor did not accept their recommendations. Instead he ordered them to enforce the prohibition laws strictly and to drive the opium-receiving ships away by force if they had not gone by the end of each trading season.

1835 (August) English ships were found on the coast of the Shantung peninsula. The emperor issued orders to the governors-general of all the maritime provinces to be prepared to expel these ships.

1836 (November 23) The governor-general, the governor, and the hoppo issued an edict commanding the hong merchants to expel nine foreign merchants alleged to have been engaged in the opium trade.

1837 (August 4, August 17, and September 18) Three edicts were issued by the governor-general and the governor enjoining Captain Elliot to send away the opium-receiving ships anchored outside Canton.

1837 (November 20) An edict from the prefect and the commandant of Canton demanded the departure of the opium-receiving ships.

1838 (February 1) An imperial rescript approved the governor-general's proposal that, if the opium-receiving ships did not sail away from Lintin, regular trade would be stopped.

1838 (May) An imperial rescript ordered all military governors, governors-general, governors, and other top officials of the empire to present their views concerning Huang Chüeh-tzu's memorial recommending the death penalty for opium smokers. This nationwide discussion of the problem was referred to as the "great debate."

1838 (December 26) The governor-general issued an edict to the prefect and commandant of Canton sanctioning Elliot's proposal to drive foreign smuggling boats out of the Canton River.

1839 (June) As a result of the great debate, a thirty-nine-article statute was promulgated, stricter than all previous opium laws. Anyone convicted of opium smoking eighteen months after the law was published would be strangled on Peking's final approval. An additional article was subsequently added at Lin Tse-hsü's request, that foreigners who imported and sold opium were punishable by execution.

APPENDIX B

OPIUM EXPORTED from BENGAL and BOMBAY and
IMPORTED to CANTON on BRITISH ACCOUNTS, 1816–1840

Opium tables often differ from one another. The discrepancy usually arises from different statistical bases. Theoretically a complete table should contain all opium supplied to China, not only that produced in British India, but also that produced in Portuguese India and Turkey; not only that imported by the British, but also that brought in by other nationals; not only that delivered at Canton, Lintin, and Macao, but also what was smuggled in on the eastern and northern coast. Owing to the surreptitious nature of the trade, such a complete table cannot be compiled.

The export column in this appendix contains only opium produced in British India from which the East India Company (EIC) derived a profit. Since it does not include Turkish and Portuguese products, the amount in some cases is below that of the imports in the corresponding seasons. The import column in this appendix contains only opium delivered at the port of Canton (including Lintin) by British traders; therefore the figures are considerably lower than what was exported from British India in the 1830s. The smuggling on the coast east of Canton began to be of importance in the 1832–33 season and, to quote McCulloch, it "bids fair to exceed that carried on at the Lintin station."

The export figures here are taken from a table entitled "Tabular View of the Quantity of Opium Exported from Bengal and Bombay, with the Profits Derived therefrom by the East India Company," inclosure 4 in dispatch No. 26 from Sir J. Bowring to the Earl of Clarendon, dated Hong Kong, Jan. 8, 1856, printed in *Parliamentary Papers: Papers relative to the Opium Trade in China, 1842–1856*, p. 50. The import figures are based mainly on: (1) statistical statements submitted to the Committee of the House of Commons on the East India Company's Affairs by Charles Marjoribanks in 1830, printed in *Parliamentary Papers: Opium Trade*, p. 33; (2) statements of the British trade at Canton published by order of the superintendent (Appendix C); (3) J. R. McCulloch, *A Dictionary, Practical, Theoretical, and Historical, of Commerce and Commercial Navigation* (London, 1854), II, 939.

| | Bengal (Patna & Benares) | | Malwa | | Total | | EXPORTS FROM BENGAL AND BOMBAY | |
| | IMPORTS TO CANTON | | | | | | | |
Years	Chests	Value $	Chests	Value $	Chests	Value $	Chests	Profits by EIC (rupees)
1816–17	2,610	3,132,000	600	525,000	3,210	3,657,000	4,618	–
1817–18	2,530	3,200,450	1,150	703,800	3,680	3,904,250	3,692	–
1818–19	3,050	3,050,000	1,530	1,109,250	4,580	4,159,250	3,552	–
1819–20	2,970	3,667,950	1,630	1,915,250	4,600	5,583,200	4,006	–
1820–21	3,050	5,795,000	1,720	2,605,800	4,770	8,400,800	4,244	–
1821–22	2,910	6,038,250	1,718	2,276,350	4,628	8,314,600	5,576	–
1822–23	1,822	2,828,930	4,000	5,160,000	5,822	7,988,930	7,773	–
1823–24	2,910	4,656,000	4,172	3,859,100	7,082	8,515,100	8,895	–
1824–25	2,655	3,119,625	6,000	4,500,000	8,655	7,619,625	12,023	–
1825–26	3,442	3,141,755	6,179	4,466,450	9,621	7,608,205	9,373	–
1826–27	3,661	3,668,565	6,308	5,941,520	9,969	9,610,085	12,175	–
1827–28	5,114	5,105,073	4,361	5,251,760	9,475	10,356,833	11,154	–
1828–29	5,960	5,604,235	7,171	6,928,880	13,131	12,533,115	15,418	–
1829–30	7,143	6,149,577	6,857	5,907,580	14,000	12,057,157	16,877	–
1830–31	6,660	5,789,794	12,100	7,110,237	18,760	12,900,031	17,456	11,012,826
1831–32	5,672	5,484,340	7,831	5,447,355	13,503	10,931,695	22,138	13,269,945
1832–33	8,167	6,551,059	15,403	8,781,700	23,570	15,332,759	19,483	9,742,886
1833–34	8,672	6,545,845	11,114	7,510,695	19,786	14,056,540	23,902	11,110,385
1834–35	7,767	4,431,845	8,749	5,223,125	16,516	9,654,970	21,011	7,768,605
1835–36	11,992	8,838,000	14,208	8,550,622	26,200	17,388,622	30,202	14,920,068
1836–37	8,078	5,848,236	13,430	8,439,694	21,508	14,287,930	34,033	15,349,678
1837–38	6,165	3,903,129	13,875	6,980,028	20,040	10,883,157	34,373	15,864,440
1838–39	–	–	–	–	–	–	40,200	9,531,308
1839–40	–	–	–	–	–	–	20,619	3,377,775
1840–41	–	–	–	–	–	–	34,631	8,742,776

APPENDIX C

STATEMENTS of the BRITISH TRADE at CANTON, 1834–1836

Statement of the British Trade at the Port of Canton, 1 April 1834 to 31 March 1835

	IMPORTS (*in Spanish dollars*)			
Item	*Quantity*	*Average price*	*Per*	*Total value*
Broadcloth	22,028	31.54	Piece	694,829
Cotton yarn	3,850	40.44	Picul	145,609
Scarlet cuttings	541	77.43	”	41,890
Cotton, Bengal	136,415	16.70	”	2,278,992
Cotton, Bombay	291,770	16.41	”	4,789,355
Cotton, Madras	16,889	16.33	”	275,900
Sandalwood	3,025	14.85	”	44,926
Pepper	1,972	7.34	”	14,476
Rattans	18,508	2.55	”	46,434
Rice	288,580	2.19	”	623,135
Betel nut	11,601	2.92	”	33,963
Putchuck	3,224	8.27	”	26,666
Olibanum	2,593	3.11	”	7,985
Ivory and elephant teeth	132	52.65	”	6,950
Saltpeter	3,095	7.74	”	23,971
Oil	30	6.00	”	180
Bichodemar	156	12.69	”	1,981
Lead	3,713	4.68	”	17,379
Iron	4,473	1.95	”	28,346
Tin	2,715	11.79	”	32,031
Steel	390	3.84	”	1,500
Spelter	725	4.00	”	2,900
Smalts	296	58.00	”	17,168
Copper	171	32.11	”	5,472
Quicksilver	1,107	67.27	”	74,470
Flints	5,431	1.18	”	8,436
Tortoise shell	74	60.00	”	4,440
Cochineal	18	277.77	”	5,000
Ebony	42	3.00	”	126
Gambier	97	3.00	”	291
Coral fragment	150	40.00	”	6,000
Fish maws	2,482	49.88	”	123,833
Shark's fins	3,280	20.74	”	68,037
Mother o'pearl shells	635	12.16	”	7,924
Cotton piece goods	11,000	8.95	Piece	98,460
Long ells	66,180	9.19	”	608,250
Camlets	103	30.82	”	3,175
Chintzes	2,631	5.60	”	14,748
Cow bezoar	327	23.00	Catty	7,521

Statement of the British Trade at the Port of Canton, 1 April 1834 to 31 March 1835
(*continued*)

IMPORTS (*in Spanish dollars*)				
Item	Quantity	Average price	Per	Total value
Amber	6	11.00	Catty	66
Woollens, various kinds	–	–	–	12,238
Pearls and cornelians	–	–	–	297,707
Watches and clocks	–	–	–	11,660
Glass ware	–	–	–	515
Dollars	–	–	–	60,000
Sundries	–	–	–	157,917
Opium, Patna	6,245	576.75	Chest	3,602,045
Opium, Benares	1,522	545.20	"	829,800
Opium, Malwa	8,749	596.99	"	5,223,125
				20,387,822

For East India Company's advances on remittances at rate of 4s. 7d.
per dollar

2,231,831
$22,619,653

EXPORTS (*in Spanish dollars*)				
Black tea	287,287	29.15	Picul	8,374,435
Green tea	70,841	39.17	"	2,775,239
Raw silk, Nanking	4,756	349.94	"	1,664,326
Raw silk, Canton	2,579	241.70	"	623,355
Sugar candy	17,569	10.73	"	188,645
Soft sugar	31,870	6.00	"	191,220
Cassia lignea	12,864	9.17	"	117,986
Tortoise shell	35	57.14	"	2,000
Mother o'pearl shells	715	16.00	"	11,440
Camphor	1,248	28.88	"	36,052
Alum	15,995	2.20	"	35,312
Rhubarb	449	46.32	"	20,799
Dragon's blood	319	87.00	"	27,753
Aniseed star	65	11.76	"	765
Colored paper, various sorts	339	16.71	"	5,667
Cochineal	209	224.79	"	46,983
Quicksilver	98	65.40	"	6,410
Arsenic	150	17.00	"	2,550
Copper	3,753	18.29	"	68,560
Iron	500	1.95	"	975
Tin	112	16.00	"	1,792
Cubebs	212	22.00	"	4,664
Indigo	60	40.00	"	2,400
Glass beads	672	25.50	Picul	17,140
Nanking cloth, all sorts	48,003	1.36	Piece	65,331

Statement of the British Trade at the Port of Canton, 1 April 1834 to 31 March 1835
(continued)

EXPORTS *(in Spanish dollars)*

Item	Quantity	Average price	Per	Total value
Vermilion	1,300	50.00	Box	65,000
Brass leaf	290	48.53	"	14,095
Tobacco	300	17.66	Case	5,300
Cigars	189	4.94	"	935
Silk piece goods	—	—	—	197,684
Gold jewels	—	—	—	3,858
Pearls	—	—	—	11,700
Chinaroot, galangal, musk	—	—	—	10,784
China ware	—	—	—	13,165
Paper kittisols, lacquer ware	—	—	—	60,704
Dollars	—	—	—	1,036,923
Sundries	—	—	—	158,150
Sycee silver	—	—	—	2,368,511
Marble slabs	4,335	317.18	1000	1,375
Bamboos, whangees	1,560,380	9.40	"	14,575
Gold (taels weight)	—	—	—	554,019
				18,808,577
Disbursements on 75 vessels at Whampoa		$8,000 each		600,000
" " 26 rice vessels at Whampoa		1,500 "		39,000
" " 46 vessels at Lintin		1,500 "		69,000
				19,516,577
Balance				3,103,076
				$22,619,653

Source. Canton Register, 8.44:176 (Nov. 3, 1835). Signed: "By order of the Super-intendents of the Trade of British Subjects in China, Edward Elmslie, Acting Secretary & Treasurer."

An Abridged Statement of the British Trade at the Port of Canton,
1 April 1835 to 31 March 1836

IMPORTS *(in Spanish dollars)*

Item	Quantity	Average price	Per	Total value
Cotton	494,666	16.89	Picul	8,357,394
Sandalwood	3,982	19.98	"	79,584
Pepper	9,896	8.76	"	86,705
Rattans	16,414	3.15	"	51,843
Rice	372,929	2.08	"	776,492
Betel nut	29,948	3.00	"	89,845

An Abridged Statement of the British Trade at the Port of Canton,
1 April 1835 to 31 March 1836
(*continued*)

	IMPORTS (*in Spanish dollars*)			
Item	*Quantity*	*Average price*	*Per*	*Total value*
Fish maws	4,458	29.10	"	129,740
Lead	19,385	6.22	"	120,632
Iron	28,011	3.78	"	105,930
Tin	32,510	17.17	"	558,437
Cotton yarn	12,336	39.95	"	492,867
Cotton piece goods, all sorts	164,699	4.70	Piece	775,466
Camlets	7,581	30.13	"	228,416
Long ells	21,805	13.53	"	295,026
Woollens, all sorts	—	—	—	963,224
Broadcloth	25,491	27.50	Piece	701,097
Tin plates	3,512	9.65	Box	33,921
Pearls and cornelians	—	—	—	184,723
Watches and clocks	—	—	—	60,193
Dollars	—	—	—	71,211
Sundries	—	—	—	359,629
Opium, Patna	9,692	744.82	Chest	7,218,800
Opium, Benares	2,300	704.00	"	1,619,200
Opium, Malwa	14,208	601.81	"	8,550,622
Opium, Turkey	911	566.00	Picul	515,626
				$32,426,623

	EXPORTS (*in Spanish dollars*)			
Black tea	312,481	31.79	Picul	9,936,835
Green tea	71,508	48.60	"	3,475,408
Raw silk, Nanking	7,920	412.91	"	3,270,291
Raw silk, Canton	1,948	253.50	"	493,824
Sugar candy	17,194	9.93	"	170,843
Soft sugar	33,933	5.42	"	184,177
Cassia lignea	14,699	9.87	"	145,113
Camphor	1,420	31.22	"	44,340
Alum	19,230	2.12	"	40,828
Aniseed star	2,923	11.25	"	32,911
Copper	4,277	16.95	"	72,503
Musk	1,106	49.18	Catty	54,400
Vermilion	12,010	58.70	Box	705,000
Silk piece goods	—	—	—	314,021
Dollars	—	—	—	1,589,742
Sycee silver	—	—	—	2,384,606
Gold	21,251	23.24	Tael	494,063
Sundries	—	—	—	443,994
				$23,852,899

An Abridged Statement of the British Trade at the Port of Canton,
1 April 1835 to 31 March 1836

(*continued*)

EXPORTS (*in Spanish dollars*)		
Disbursements on 93 vessels at Whampoa	$8,500 each	790,500
" " 79 rice vessels at Whampoa	2,200 "	154,000
" " 67 vessels at Lintin	1,200 "	80,400
		24,877,799
Balance		7,548,824
		$32,426,623

Source. *Canton Register*, 9.43:177 (Oct. 25, 1836). Signed: "By order of the Super-intendents of the Trade of British Subjects in China, Edward Elmslie, Secretary & Treasurer."

APPENDIX D

The INCARCERATED BRITISH in CHINA

[This is an account of the 1839 confinement of the foreign shipping at Whampoa, by the surgeon of a detained ship, taken from *The Times* (London), August 19, 1840, p. 3.]

Mr. Paterson, late surgeon to the George IV, Indiaman, and who was one of the "incarcerated," has just published the following letter: —

"Glasgow, Aug. 10

"Sir, — From the desultory discussion regarding the expedition now on its way to China which lately took place in the House of Commons, I observe that in one or two very important circumstances connected with the late unfortunate transactions in that country great ignorance and misconception appear to prevail amongst many of the members of the house, not excepting even Her Majesty's Ministers. Having been one of the 'incarcerated' during the embargo or duress referred to in the debate, and being also entirely unconnected with the opium or any other kind of traffic (one of those, in short, whom Commissioner Lin in his edicts uniformly designated in the most marked and considerate manner, the [']good foreigners'), perhaps you will regard the testimony I now beg to submit to you, in reference to my own condition and treatment, while under incarceration in China, as calculated to disabuse the public mind of the prejudices attempted to be excited against the Chinese by a misrepresentation of facts, and therefore deserving a place in the columns of your journal.

"Mr. Gladstone, during the late discussion, very properly refused to admit that Captain Elliot, or any of his countrymen, was at all maltreated by the Government of China during the few weeks of their imprisonment. While I was under detention, the treatment I experienced was altogether unexceptionable, as you will observe from the following statement of facts: — The meals daily served up on board the George IV. Indiaman (the ship with which I was connected), while lying under embargo in Whampoa Reach, were regularly supplied by a Chinaman named 'A'Quhan,' the 'compradore' of the ship, and in that capacity acting under the immediate superintendence and holding the commission of the Government of China. It is true the Chinese would not permit to be brought alongside the ship a large boat nearly the size of a small river steam-boat, and commonly called the 'compradore's boat,' containing, besides about a score of the compradore's servants, dependents, and clerks, a large supply of fruits, articles of clothing, &c., for the ship's company. A smaller boat, however, called a 'sampan,' came regularly alongside the ship every morning, bringing abundance of supplies for the cuddy, and whatever else had been ordered during the previous day. The 'sampan' did not leave the ship till the evening. A round of dinner parties, I may mention, was given by the principal commanders of the fleet, at which I had the honour of being present, and I am bold to say that the whole of these parties were distinguished by an abundance of joyous hilarity and capital cheer, that would have gratified the most fastidious *bon vivant*. Who furnished, pray, the turkeys, mutton, capon, &c., as well as the rich selection of fresh vegetables which graced the tables? The barbaric and inhospitable Chinese Government. So far from the British in Whampoa entertaining any apprehension of their personal security, as has been alleged in Parliament and in other high quarters, I distinctly and most confidently declare, that no such idea could ever have entered the head of any individual but the veriest poltroon. The favourite amusement of the incarcerated (for we were allowed to enjoy as much fun of any description as we chose) consisted in playing quoits on a beautiful green knoll on the banks of the river tigris, which was generally wound up by a rather riotous game at leapfrog. An excursion to the English burying-ground, a little way up the river, was also permitted, and frequently undertaken. So much for the treatment of myself and other foreigners by the heads of the Celestial Empire.

"In addition to the preceding facts, I may state, that early on the morning the embargo was placed, the yawl of the George IV. had proceeded to Canton on some important business, with a crew of nine men, under the command of our second officer and a midshipman. The officers and boat's crew were of course detained by the Chinese, and not permitted to return to their ship until the delivery of the confiscated opium had been completed. On their return, I do not recollect having ever observed so remarkable a change for the better in the appearance of both officers and men. I interrogated each of them very particularly regarding the treatment which he received while detained in Canton, and they all assured me that they were never better fed or more comfortably situated. Our second officer informed me, that the gentlemen under duress in Canton, like those in Whampoa, were treated in the kindest and most indulgent manner, and allowed freely to enjoy themselves at cricket and other games in the square opposite the English factories.

"A day or two after the embargo was raised I visited Canton, and from the top of the Dutch Hong a British merchant pointed out to me a spot, about a hundred yards distant, where a large stock of pigs, of the finest Chinese breed, as well as abundance of poultry of every despection, were kept, and which had been offered during the embargo to Captain Elliot as a present from Commissioner Lin, but refused by Her Majesty's representative, from an apprehension that their acceptance might compromise his peculiar position.

"But I must bring this hasty communication to a close; and, after perusing the above statement of facts, I feel assured that you, as well as every other true friend of justice and humanity, will concur with me, that I cannot do this more appropriately than by expressing an earnest hope that the rude and barbaric conduct of the Chinese towards the incarcerated may always be imitated by the proud and overbearing nations under the sway of European civilization.

"I have the honour to be, Sir,
"Your most obedient servant,
"Charles Paterson,
late Surgeon to the George IV., Indiaman."

NOTES

BIBLIOGRAPHY

GLOSSARY

INDEX

ABBREVIATIONS

CR	*Chinese Repository.*
CHCK	*Ch'ing-hua chou-k'an.*
CHHP	*Ch'ing-hua hsueh-pao.*
PP: China Corr.	*Parliamentary Papers, Correspondence relating to China (1840).*
CSK	*Ch'ing-shih kao.*
CSL	*Ta-Ch'ing li-ch'ao shih-lu.*
FEQ	*The Far Eastern Quarterly.*
FO 17	Foreign Office, General Correspondence, China. Filed in the Public Record Office, London.
HJAS	*Harvard Journal of Asiatic Studies.*
JM	Jardine Matheson Archives, MSS deposited in the University Library, Cambridge, England. Unless otherwise specified, JM denotes local letters of unbound correspondence in the Correspondence Section of the Archives.
IWSM	*Ch'ou-pan i-wu shih-mo.*
KYLT	"K'uei-yung liu-tu."
Lin, *CS*	Lin Tse-hsü, *Lin Wen-chung-kung cheng-shu.*
Lin, "JC"	Lin Tse-hsü, *Lin Tse-hsü jih-chi.*
Lin, *HCL*	Lin Tse-hsü, *Hsin-chi lu.*
THL	*Tung-hua ch'üan-lu.*
TKP	*Ta-kung pao.*
YHKC	*Yueh hai-kuan chih.*
YJSS	*The Yenching Journal of Social Studies.*
YPCC	*Ya-p'ien chan-cheng.*

NOTES

Chapter I. Sino-British Contact under the Old Order

1. H. B. Morse, *The Chronicles of the East India Company Trading to China,
1635–1834* (Oxford, 1926), I, 66.
2. *Ibid.*, pp. 1–6; John K. Fairbank, *Trade and Diplomacy on the China Coast:
The Opening of the Treaty Ports, 1842–1854* (Cambridge, Mass., 1953), 1, 58.
3. John Phipps, *A Practical Treatise on the China and Eastern Trade . . .* (Calcutta, 1835), p. 1.
4. Morse, *Chronicles*, I, 6.
5. Chang Te-ch'ang, "Ch'ing-tai ya-p'ien chan-cheng ch'ien chih Chung-Hsi yen-
hai t'ung-shang" (Maritime trade between China and the West before the Opium
War in the Ch'ing dynasty), *CHHP*, 10.1:97–138 (1935); Earl H. Pritchard, "The
Crucial Years of Early Anglo-Chinese Relations, 1750–1800," *Research Studies of
the State College of Washington*, 4.3–4:114 (September and December, 1936).
6. For an illuminating discussion of the theory and practice of the tribute system,
see Fairbank, *Trade and Diplomacy*, I, ch. 2.
7. Phipps, *China and Eastern Trade*, pp. 6–7; Pritchard, "Crucial Years," pp. 113–
114; Chang Te-ch'ang, pp. 97–138.
8. Earl H. Pritchard, "Anglo-Chinese Relations during the Seventeenth and Eighteenth Centuries," *University of Illinois Studies in Social Sciences*, 17.1–2:186–188
(March–June 1929).
9. Chiang T'ing-fu, "Chung-kuo yü chin-tai shih-chieh ti ta-pien-chü" (China
and the great changes of the modern world), *CHHP*, 9.4:804 (October 1934);
Morse, *Chronicles*, I, 67.
10. Pritchard, "Crucial Years," p. 128.
11. H. B. Morse, *The Gilds of China* (New York, 1909), p. 67.
12. H. B. Morse, *The International Relations of the Chinese Empire: The Period
of Conflict, 1834–1860* (Shanghai, 1910), p. 53.
13. Morse, *Chronicles*, pp. viii-ix.
14. Fairbank, *Trade and Diplomacy*, I, 59.
15. Morse, *Chronicles*, I, 68, 76.
16. Fairbank, *Trade and Diplomacy*, I, 59–60.
17. Morse, *Conflict*, p. 66.
18. The exact origin of the hong merchants in Canton still eludes us. Liang
Chia-pin, who made a thorough study of the history of the hong merchant
system, maintained that it had already been in existence in 1685 when the hoppo's
office was first established in Canton. Wu Han thought that the system commenced
between 1682 and 1685. A recent study by P'eng Tse-i, however, fixes the time of
its emergence as the late spring of 1686. P'eng's evidence was Governor Li Shih-
chen's proclamation initiating the Yang-huo hang (foreign goods guild) in 1686, a
year after the installment of the Canton customs office. The Yang-huo hang, according to P'eng, marked the beginning of the hong merchant system; he rejected
the theory that the thirteen hong merchants were derived from the Ya-hang (the
brokerage firms or the commission merchants) of the Ming dynasty.

P'eng Tse-i's study is very convincing but not definitive. A ballad of Ch'ü Ta-
chün depicting the city of Canton included a line which, translated, reads "silver
piled up in the thirteen hongs." It was found recently that this ballad was com-

posed in the spring of 1684, casting doubt on P'eng's theory that the thirteen hongs emerged in 1686; further research on this point is required. See Liang Chia-pin, *Kuang-tung shih-san-hang k'ao* (A study of the thirteen hongs at Canton; Shanghai, 1937), pp. 37–38, 43–44, 58; P'eng Tse-i, "Ch'ing-tai Kuang-tung yang-hang chih-tu ti ch'i-yuan" (The origin of the *hang* system at Canton in the Ch'ing dynasty), *Li-shih yen-chiu* (Historical studies), 1:3, 19, 24 (1957); Wang Shu-an, "Shih-san-hang yü Ch'ü Ta-chün Kuang-chou chu-chih-tz'u" (The thirteen hongs and Ch'ü Ta-chün's ballad of Canton), *Li-shih yen-chiu*, 6:22 (1957).

19. Morse, *Conflict*, pp. 65–67.

20. Fairbank, *Trade and Diplomacy*, I, 51.

21. The hong merchants are commonly referred to as the "thirteen hongs," but P'eng Tse-i maintained that the number thirteen was simply an ordinal number meaning the thirteenth category of the licensed firms, not a cardinal one giving the total number in their ranks. To prove it, he made an investigation of the number of hong merchants in forty-one years between 1720 and 1839 and found that only in two of these years, 1813 and 1837, were they actually thirteen in number. In other years the hong merchants ranged from four to twenty. See P'eng Tse-i, p. 21.

22. Morse, *Conflict*, p. 86.

23. There is so far no satisfactory explanation as to the origin of "hoppo." Some theories are given in Fairbank, *Trade and Diplomacy*, II, 4, n. 15.

24. Fairbank, *Trade and Diplomacy*, I, 48–49; II, 4, n. 16.

25. William C. Hunter, *The "Fan-Kwae" at Canton before Treaty Days, 1825–1844* (London, 1882), pp. 17, 52, 54, 85, 94; Morse, *Chronicles*, p. ix.

26. The pilots, usually numbering fourteen, were licensed by the subprefect of Ch'ien-shan (Casa Branca), near Macao, on the payment of an amount between $800 and $1,000. See E. C. Bridgman, *A Chinese Chrestomathy in the Canton Dialect* (Macao, 1841), p. 219.

27. For a detailed breakdown of the *cumsha* and other charges, see John Robert Morrison, *A Chinese Commercial Guide Consisting of a Collection of Details Respecting Foreign Trade in China,* 2nd ed. (Canton, 1834), pp. 108ff.

28. Hunter, *Fan-kwae*, p. 53.

29. Dept. of Oriental Printed Books and Manuscripts, British Museum, Add. 15730B.

30. This translation is partly adapted from *Description of the City of Canton . . .* 2nd. ed. (Canton, 1839), pp. 113–114.

31. Morse, *Conflict*, p. 71. There is still an original lease dated the third lunar month of 1832 in a box of miscellaneous Chinese papers in the Jardine Matheson Archives. The paper reveals that Jardine leased his hong from Howqua for a rent of $6,500 per annum. The company later sublet five factories in the Danish hong to John Slade, editor of the *Canton Register*, for an annual rent of $2,000. See JM, Canton 475, Alexander Matheson to John Slade, July 16, 1836.

32. The shroff was the silver expert employed as teller of the firm and held responsible for the quality of the silver, whether ingots or dollars, passing through his hands. The silver dollars used in the China trade were of a large variety and required expert handling. Pillar dollars, ryals of eight, and pieces of eight minted at the Royal Mint of Seville in southwest Spain were the most common ones. The Chinese accepted them by weight in taels modified by the touch, never by count. It is interesting to examine a manual prepared for the shroffs in 1864, a copy of which is now preserved in the British Museum, Dept. of Oriental Printed Books and Manuscripts (15299.a.3). See Morse, *Conflict*, pp. 73–74; Morse, *Chronicles*, I, 68.

33. Lin Tse-hsü's memorial, *IWSM*, 9:21b–22; *Description of Canton*, pp. 116–117.

34. Hunter, *Fan-kwae*, pp. 20–21; Morse, *Conflict*, p. 71.

35. *Description of Canton*, pp. 116–117. For a full discussion of these regulations and other grievances, see Pritchard, "Crucial Years," pp. 133–134, and *Canton Register*, 8.8:31 (Feb. 25, 1835).

36. For an account of the stir caused by Harriet Low and her aunt's visit to Canton in November 1830, see Elma Loines, ed., *The China Trade Post-Bag of the Seth Low Family of Salem and New York, 1829–1873* (Manchester, Maine, 1953), pp. 131–135.

37. William C. Hunter, *Bits of Old China* (Shanghai, 1911), pp. 266–267. George Chinnery (fl. 1766–1846) produced numerous portraits of figures connected with the old China trade and etchings of the Bay of Macao. His art has so benefited those who have since studied the history of this period that he deserves at least a note in passing. It appears that he lived in London from the 1760s through the 1780s. In 1766 he exhibited some crayon portraits at the Free Society and in 1791 some miniature portraits at the Royal Academy. Late in the eighteenth century he resided in Dublin for a short period and moved back to London probably in 1802. Sometime thereafter he moved to Macao where he painted and taught until his death in about 1850. In 1830, he sent from Canton two portraits, "Dr. Morrison engaged in translating the Bible into the Chinese language" and "The Portrait of a Hong Merchant," to the Royal Academy. His own portrait was in the Royal Academy in 1846. One of Chinnery's students was a Chinese by the name of Lamqua. It was in commenting on Lamqua's works that the *Canton Register* (Dec. 8, 1835) thought that Chinnery "should be *ordered* home by the ladies of the land in the U.K. for we can assure them, now that they have lost Sir Thomas Lawrence, that they will never *again* look so beautiful unless under the *vivida vis* of the sparkling and magic touch of Chinnery. The knighthood would then follow as a matter of course, as having been mostly deservedly earned and richly merited." A self-portrait of Chinnery is found in Maurice Collis, *Foreign Mud: Being an Account of the Opium Imbroglio at Canton in the 1830's and the Anglo-Chinese War that Followed* (New York, 1947), facing p. 244. See Leslie Stephen, ed., *Dictionary of National Biography* (London, 1887), X, 258–259.

38. Morse, *Conflict*, pp. 69–71.

39. *Description of Canton*, p. 106.

40. *YHKC*, 24:34–40b, has a record of the number of foreign ships calling at Canton for 91 year-periods beginning with Feb. 2, 1750. For this statistical purpose, each successive year-period invariably consists of 354 days regardless of the intercalary months. Thus the nominal year-period of *keng-tzu* (roughly 1840) actually began with May 29, 1837, and ended with May 17, 1838.

41. Bridgman, *Chrestomathy*, p. 223; Morrison, *Commercial Guide*, pp. 13–14. For a more detailed description of the practice under the Canton system, see Morrison, *Commercial Guide*, pp. 108ff; Bridgman, *Chrestomathy*, pp. 219–223; *Description of Canton*, pp. 108, 112–113.

42. Hunter, *Fan-kwae*, p. 26.

43. Morse, *Conflict*, p. 85.

44. *Ibid.*; Hunter, *Fan-kwae*, pp. 42–44, 56, 107.

45. Morse, *Conflict*, pp. 34–35.

46. Lu K'un, Ch'en Hung-ch'ih et al., comps., *Kuang-tung hai-fang hui-lan* (Maritime defense in Kwangtung; n.d.), 36:23a-b.

47. Morse, *Chronicles*, I, 67. Pidgin English is a singular admixture of corrupted

Portuguese, English, Hindustani, and other foreign words spoken largely in a Chinese syntax. The word "pidgin" itself is a corruption of the English word "business." Words of Portuguese origin include such jargon as "mandarin," from *mandarim*, derived from the Malay word *mantri* (minister of state); "comprador," from *compra* (to buy); "grand," from *grande* (the chief); "junk," from *junco* which has a Javanese origin. "Shroff" (money dealer) and "coolie" (laborer) are examples of words borrowed from Arabic and Hindustani respectively. Cf. Hunter, *Fan-kwae*, pp. 61–62. For examples of dialogues in pidgin English and points of its grammar, see Fairbank, *Trade and Diplomacy*, I, 13–14; II, 2, n. 16.

48. There is preserved in the Jardine Matheson Archives a letter from James Innes to James Matheson, dated Oct. 30, 1832, requesting the renewal of Morrison's service and praising his ability. JM, Canton 357.

49. Bridgman, *Chrestomathy*, ch. 6, "Commercial Affairs." After the Opium War, Robert Thom became Her Majesty's Consul at Ningpo and published a forty-page pamphlet entitled *Hua-Ying t'ung-yung tsa-hua* (Chinese and English vocabulary, part first; Canton, 1843), which was lavishly praised by the *Hongkong Gazette* (Oct. 26, 1843).

50. The fables were entitled *I-shih mi-chuan*. See the bibliography (under Lo Po-tan) and *Supplement to the Canton Register*, June 23, 1840.

51. Robert Thom to William Jardine, Dec. 8, 1838, JM, Canton 544.

52. FO 17/37, John Backhouse to Captain Elliot, Nov. 4, 1840.

53. FO 17/32, Captain Elliot to John Backhouse, June 30, 1839.

54. See Fairbank, *Trade and Diplomacy*, I, 43.

55. Pritchard, "Crucial Years," p. 307. For details of the Macartney Mission see *ibid.*, pp. 272–384; Herbert J. Wood, "Prologue to War: Anglo-Chinese Conflict, 1800–1834," unpubl. diss. (University of Wisconsin, 1938), p. 319. For details of the Amherst Mission, see *ibid.*, pp. 306–432.

56. See, e.g., their organ, *Canton Register*, 7.14:53 (Apr. 8, 1834).

57. William A. Pew, *China's Struggle for Nationhood* (Salem, Mass., 1927), p. 6.

58. Robert Philip, *The Life and Opinions of the Rev. William Milne, D.D., Missionary to China* (London, 1840), pp. 248–249.

59. For a detailed account, see *Canton Register*, 7.1:2–3 (January 1834); Pritchard, "Crucial Years," pp. 226–230.

60. Morse, *Conflict*, p. 244.

61. Pritchard, "Crucial Years," p. 307.

62. Fairbank, *Trade and Diplomacy*, I, 58–59.

63. *Ibid.*, I, 60; Michael Greenberg, *British Trade and the Opening of China, 1840–42* (Cambridge, Eng., 1951), p. 144.

64. Greenberg, p. 148.

65. Fairbank, *Trade and Diplomacy*, I, 60–61.

66. Greenberg, p. 147.

67. Fairbank, *Trade and Diplomacy*, I, 63.

68. The Ch'ien-lung Emperor's letter to George III, Sept. 11, 1816. For a translation, see Eliza Morrison, *Memoirs of the Life and Labours of Robert Morrison, D.D.* (London, 1839), I, 461–462.

69. *Canton Register*, 8.8:31 (Feb. 25, 1835).

70. Greenberg, p. 153; Morse, *Conflict*, p. 69.

71. Morse, *Conflict*, p. 85. The amount due British merchants alone, in the season of 1837–38, was $2,770,762, well over 11 percent of their total imports to Canton.

FO 17/36, General Chamber of Commerce at Canton, "Statement of Trade in British Vessels at Canton, July 1, 1837 to June 30, 1838."

72. In 1837, the liability of the bankrupt Hing-tae (Hsing-t'ai) hong was $2,261,438, of which $2,179,386 was due to British creditors. It was finally agreed that the debt would be paid by installment in eight and a half years beginning Nov. 30, 1837. Kingqua was in difficulty in 1838 but not officially declared insolvent. The Cohong agreed to pay his foreign creditors $125,000 annually beginning July 1, 1838, for ten years plus interest. Elliot to John Backhouse, Macao, April 30, 1838, *PP: China Corr.*, p. 264; memorial to Palmerston from Dent and Co. et al., Canton, Nov. 26, 1838, *ibid.*, pp. 321-322. Also see Morse, *Conflict*, pp. 67, 164.

73. Greenberg, p. 150.

Chapter II. The Rise of the Opium Trade

1. Wu Wen-tsao, *The Chinese Opium Question in British Opinion and Action* (New York, 1928), p. 7.

2. Hsü K'uan-hou, "Ya-p'ien huo-hua ch'u-shih" (The early history of the opium evil in China), "Shih-ti chou-k'an" (Historical and geographical weekly), No. 124, in *TKP* (Feb. 19, 1937), p. 3; H. B. Morse, *The Trade and Administration of the Chinese Empire* (London and New York, 1908), p. 324.

3. Hsü K'uan-hou, p. 3; Morse, *Conflict*, p. 173; J. G. Kerr, "Opium and the Smoking Extract," *The China Review*, 12.1:41-47 (July–August 1883); Fairbank, *Trade and Diplomacy*, I, 63; Jen Tsung-chi, "Tao-kuang ch'ao chin-yen chih ching-chi pei-ching" (The economic background of the opium prohibition during the Tao-kuang period), "Ching-chi chou-k'an" (Economic weekly), No. 127, in *TKP* (Aug. 21, 1935), p. 3.

4. Hsü K'uan-hou, p. 3.

5. Andrew Ljungstedt, "History of Macao . . . " MS in the British Museum (preface dated Macao, November 1822), pp. 140-141.

6. "War with China, and the Opium Question," *Blackwood's Edinburgh Magazine*, 47.293:370 (March 1840). The East India Company acquired in 1761 the exclusive right to produce and sell Bengal opium in India, and the monopoly was greatly strengthened after 1765. However, with the exception of the *Nonsuch* adventure, and a few instances when junior officers of the company acted as agents for private firms in India, the company did not distribute opium outside India. In 1781 the Indian government went through a serious economic crisis. There was a shortage of specie as a result of the wars with the Spanish, French, Dutch, Hyder Ali, and the Marathas, and a two-year stock of Bengal opium lay unsold. Meanwhile, there was also a shortage of treasure at the Canton factory. Thus by order of Warren Hastings, the *Nonsuch*, laden with 1601 chests of Patna opium, sailed for China and arrived at the Macao Roads in July 1782. The adventure proved a failure since Sinqua was the only serious bidder, finally buying the cargo at the low price of 210 head dollars per chest. (Each of the newly coined Spanish head dollars contained only 90 percent fine silver as compared with 92 percent in Mexican dollars; therefore the former were discounted 2 percent at Canton.) The company lost more than 18 percent on the transaction. Thereafter, opium was never again shipped to China on the company's account; the trade was left in the hands of country traders and non-British ships. But because of the company's great stake in the opium industry of Bengal and the large amount of specie that the opium trade supplied the Canton factory, the company remained vitally concerned over every stage of the

traffic. Thus David Owen concludes that the company "did not hesitate to provide goods for smuggling and to encourage private merchants to transport these goods to China." (For the company's monopoly, see I. Durga, *Some Aspects of Indian Foreign Trade, 1757–1893* [London, 1932], p. 70, and David Edward Owen, *British Opium Policy in China and India* [New Haven, 1934], p. 53; for the *Nonsuch* affair and the company's interest in the opium trade, see Owen, pp. 53, 56–58, and 65.)

With the company's assistance in advance payments, the poppy was cultivated and the drug manufactured. When the product was ready for sale at the Calcutta exchange, the auction was executed under very lenient terms. As a rule, the company required a down payment of one rupee on each lot of five chests to bind the bargain and a deposit of 30 percent in cash or the company's paper to be made within ten days after the purchase. The ten-day period could be extended by permission of the Opium Board. The purchaser had three months to pay the rest. The three-month limit was not always observed; when market conditions at Canton were unfavorable, the company would issue bills to the traders to enable them to wait for a higher price. See Owen, pp. 26–27; Amales Tripathi, *Trade and Finance in the Bengal Presidency, 1793–1833* (Bombay, 1956), p. 156; Wood, p. 164; Phipps, p. 232.

7. See the testimony of H. Magniac in the Committee of the House of Lords relative to the affairs of the East India Company in 1830. Magniac testified that the trade he carried on when he resided in Canton, aside from his activity as an agent, "was principally in opium, almost entirely indeed," and he thought that it was out of the Chinese government's power to prevent the smuggling of opium, which was so much an article of necessity for those who had contracted a habit of using it. *PP: Opium Trade* (1832), pp. 22, 25.

8. Morse, *Chronicles*, IV, 16; Wood, pp. 163–165; A. J. Sargent, *Anglo-Chinese Commerce and Diplomacy*. (Oxford, 1907), p. 45.

9. John Ouchterlony, *The Chinese War: An Account of All the Operations of the British Forces from the Commencement to the Treaty of Nanking*, 2nd ed. (London, 1844), p. 5.

10. Greenberg, pp. 112, 114; Ljungstedt, p. 141; Wood, pp. 162, 166.

11. Greenberg, p. 116; Wood, p. 166.

12. *YHKC*, 18:11, 12–13b, 16; Wood, pp. 170, 180–183.

13. *YHKC*, 18:14; JM, Correspondence Section, Letter Books, Y. & Co., 17.5, cited in Greenberg, p. 121.

14. *YHKC*, 18:17–18; Greenberg, pp. 121, 124.

15. For prices per chest, see John R. McCulloch, *A Dictionary, Practical, Theoretical, and Historical, of Commerce and Commercial Navigation*, new ed. (London, 1854), II, 939. But the price of Malwa in 1823–24 was erroneously given as $425. It should be $925.

16. Greenberg, pp. 129–130.

17. See Appendix B. The figures are exclusive of fractions.

18. Greenberg, pp. 113, 130–131.

19. See Appendix C. The conventional units of Turkey opium were piculs. A case of opium and a chest of opium are roughly the same for statistics of Turkey opium. Each held approximately a picul. See Charles C. Stelle, "American Trade in Opium to China, 1821–39," *Pacific Historical Review*, 10:66, n. 35 (March 1941), and *PP: Opium Trade*, p. 33.

20. *PP: Opium Trade*, p. 25: Greenberg, p. 138; McCulloch, II, 939.

21. Fairbank, *Trade and Diplomacy*, I, 134; JM, Canton 360, Jardine, Matheson

and Co. to James Innes, dated Canton, Nov. 24, 1832; JM, Chinchew 1, Innes to Jardine, Matheson and Co., dated Chinchew, Jan. 5, 1833.

22. Jardine wrote to Captain Rees from Canton on April 24, 1833: "You managed matters admirably well and completely to our satisfaction." See JM, Canton 365.

23. JM, Chinchew 2, Captain McKay to Jardine, Matheson and Co., August 6, 1833.

24. JM, Chinchew 3, Captain McKay to Jardine, Matheson and Co., August 31, 1833.

25. JM, Chinchew 4, Captain McKay to Captain Rees, dated *John Biggar*, Sept. 5, 1833.

26. JM, Canton 450, Jardine to Rees, March 19, 1835; Canton 456, Jardine to Rees, July 16, 1835.

27. The voyages and duties of these vessels were of course not fixed; there was a good deal of flexibility, and schedules were often rearranged. See JM, Canton 457, Jardine to Rees, July 30, 1835; Canton 497, Jardine to Rees, April 5, 1837; Coast 29, E. W. Brightman to Jardine, Matheson and Co., Feb. 10, 1833.

28. JM, Canton 390, Jardine, Matheson and Co. to Captain Rees, Dec. 14, 1833.

29. JM, Canton 390, Jardine, Matheson and Co. (in Jardine's own hand), Dec. 14, 1833.

30. Arthur Waley, *The Opium War Through Chinese Eyes* (London, 1958), p. 223. For a sketch of Gutzlaff's life, see *ibid.*, pp. 223–224, 228–235 and *CR*, 20:511–512 (1851).

31. Apparently penned by Gutzlaff himself, a series of editorials, written in an awkward style, exhorted the reader to keep away from opium and argued that the eradication of the opium traffic was the only way through which the teachings of Christ could be spread. See *Tung-Hsi yang k'ao mei-yüeh t'ung-chi chuan* (Examiner of the East and the West, a monthly magazine), July 1837, p. 14b; May 1837, p. 14.

32. Captain McKay of the *Fairy* complained that Gutzlaff gave ten handkerchiefs for the dollar whereas the captain was authorized only to sell at two and a half dollars per dozen. See JM, Coast 64, McKay to Jardine, Matheson and Co., July 26, 1834.

33. JM, Canton 398, Jardine to Rees, Jan. 13, 1834; Canton 417, Jardine to Rees, July 3, 1834.

34. Jardine was very much concerned with safeguarding his monopoly and cautioned Rees of the "advantage of secrecy in everything connected with these operations." See JM, Canton 379, Jardine to Rees, Oct. 5, 1833; JM, Canton 428, Jardine to Rees, Dec. 1, 1834.

35. JM, Canton 448, Jardine to Rees, March 9, 1835.

36. JM, Canton 450, Jardine to Rees, March 19, 1835; Canton 458* (distinguish from Canton 458), Jardine to Rees, Oct. 16, 1835; Canton 461, Jardine to Rees, Dec. 9, 1835.

37. JM, Canton 472, Jardine to Rees, April 12, 1836; Canton 471, Jardine to Rees, April 1, 1836.

38. Jardine was dubious at first about the usefulness of this agreement which, as he commented, required good faith on all sides. When later he proposed to Rees that he lower the price, even in a bay that was not used by a competitor's ship, he cautioned the captain that he must first reach an understanding with the captain of the *Amherst* and that he must not break the agreement. See JM, Canton 473, Jardine to Rees, June 4, 1836, and Canton 492, Jardine to Rees, Jan. 27, 1837.

39. JM, Canton 473. Jardine pointed out to Rees, on March 19, 1835, that the

suspension of the drug trade was so complete at Canton that "not a chest can be sold or delivered, on any terms." On Nov. 3, 1836, he reported a similar crisis. On both occasions he was of the opinion that the crises in Canton would prove favorable to the operations on the coast. On other occasions he had stressed the increasing importance of the coast operation brought about by the decline of trade in Canton. See JM, Canton 450, Jardine to Rees, March 19, 1835, and Canton 487, Jardine to Rees, Nov. 3, 1836.

40. JM, Canton 417, Jardine to Rees, July 3, 1834; Canton 472, April 12, 1836; Canton 508, Jardine to Rees, Jan. 24, 1838; Canton 509, Jardine to Rees, Feb. 13, 1838.

41. JM, Canton 517, Jardine to Rees, June 5, 1838; Canton 521, Jardine to Rees, July 13, 1838; Canton 527, Jardine to Rees, Sept. 5, 1838.

42. JM, Canton 473, Jardine to Rees, June 4, 1836. On July 26, 1836, Jardine wrote to Rees and expressed his hope that the *Fairy* would have "a profitable trading trip to the northward." See JM, Canton 476.

43. It was not found out whether a group of mutinous crew members or some Manila men committed the crime. The governor of Manila issued orders to all officials, residents, and commanders of cruisers to take possession of the *Fairy* wherever they might fall in with her and secure her crew. At the same time, the Manila police were in pursuit of the murderers. It appeared from the evidence obtained at Manila that the Chinese servant and some of the Lascars were aware of the intended crime. See JM, Canton 490, Jardine to Rees, Nov. 20, 1836; Canton 495, Jardine to Rees, Feb. 17, 1837; Canton 499, Jardine to Rees, June 3, 1837.

44. JM, Canton 493, Jardine to Rees, Jan. 27, 1837.

45. JM, Canton 483, Jardine to Rees, Oct. 16, 1836; Canton 490, Jardine to Rees, Nov. 20, 1836; FO 17/34, Sir John Barrow (Admiralty) to W. Fox Strangways (Foreign Office), Jan. 16, 1839; FO 17/34, W. Fox Strangways to Sir John Barrow, Jan. 24, 1839.

46. Read his letter to Jardine, Matheson and Co. dated July 26, 1834. JM, Coast 64.

47. JM, Canton 492, Jardine to Rees, Jan. 27, 1837; Canton 496, Jardine to Rees, March 11, 1837.

48. JM, Canton 461, Jardine to Rees, Dec. 9, 1835; Canton 500, Jardine to Rees, July 17, 1837; Canton 501, Jardine to Rees, August 19, 1837; Canton 507, Jardine to Rees, Jan. 2, 1838; Canton 514, Jardine to Rees, May 3, 1838.

49. "Commerce of China," *Hunt's Merchants' Magazine*, 3.6:471 (December 1840); Greenberg, p. 104; "Narrative of a Voyage Round the World, during the years 1835, 36, and 37, including a Narrative of an Embassy to the Sultan of Muscat, and the King of Siam, by W. S. W. Ruschenberger," *Edinburgh Review*, 68:73 (1838–39).

50. "Chinese Affairs," *Quarterly Review*, 65.130:548 (March 1840).

51. George H. Danton, *The Culture Contacts of the United States and China, the Earliest Sino-American Culture Contacts, 1784–1844* (New York, 1931), p. 25; Stelle, "American Trade in Opium to China, 1821–39," p. 73; PP: *Opium Trade*, p. 27.

52. [Charles W. King,] *Opium Crisis: A Letter Addressed to Charles Elliott, Esq., Chief Superintendent of the British Trade With China* (London, 1839), p. 24; Fairbank, *Trade and Diplomacy*, I, 137, 141; Greenberg, p. 209.

53. Morrison, *Memoirs*, II, 87, 458.

54. *CR*, 8:3 (1939).

55. Hsü Chi-yü, the author of the celebrated *Ying-huan chih-lueh* (A brief description of the world), estimated that in Fukien and Kwangtung there were no less

than several hundred thousand men engaged in the opium trade. See Hsü Chi-yü, *T'ui-mi-chai wen-chi* (The collected works of Hsü Chi-yü), in *YPCC*, I, 512.

56. Hsü K'uan-hou, p. 3; Hunter, *Fan-Kwae*, p. 64.

57. Lewis J. Shuck, *Portfolio Chinensis: or a Collection of Authentic Chinese State Papers Illustrative of the History of the Present Position of Affairs in China with a Translation, Notes and Instruction* (Macao, 1840), p. 183; Hunter, *Fan-Kwae*, pp. 64–65; Yü En-te, *Chung-kuo chin-yen fa-ling pien-ch'ien shih* (History of the changes in Chinese antiopium laws; Shanghai, 1934), p. 54.

58. Greenberg, p. 116; Hsü K'uan-hou, p. 3.

59. The price of opium in Chinchew was $5–6 per tael (*liang*); when shipped to Chien-ning in western Fukien not more than 200 miles away, it became $16–17. On those engaged in the trade, see Chiang Hsiang-nan, "Yü Huang Shu-chai hung-lu lun ya-p'ien-yen shu" (A letter to Huang Chueh-tzu discussing the opium problem), in *Ch'i-ching-lou wen-ch'ao* (Collected works of Chiang Hsiang-nan; 1920), 4:34b; Hsü K'uan-hou.

60. KYLT, 1:[1b–2]; 1:[1b–2, 60].

61. Pao Shih-ch'en, *An-wu ssu-chung* (Collected works of Pao Shih-ch'en; 1846); 26:5; this passage was reprinted in *Shih-huo* (Journal of Chinese economic history), 2:101. The total population of the Soochow prefecture in 1820 is given as 5,908,435 in Feng Kuei-fen, comp., *Su-chou fu-chih* (The gazetteer of Su-chou prefecture; 1881), 18:9a–b. But the figure for the city in that time is not available. The total population of the city of Soochow was estimated as 260,000 in 1931, although some estimated it as 500,000. See *Webster's Geographical Dictionary*, rev. ed. (Springfield, Mass., 1960), p. 1727.

62. Thelwall, *Iniquities of Opium Trade*, p. 123; "Chinese Affairs," p. 567; Ouchterlony, *The Chinese War*, p. 5.

63. KYLT, 1:[26]; Lin, *CS*, in *YPCC*, II, 141; Pao Shih-ch'en, 26:5.

64. A quantity of crude opium bought from the market yielded two thirds as much smoking extract of a deep brown color. J. G. Kerr, a physician, made a personal investigation of the process through which opium extract was prepared and reported it in *The China Review*, 12.1:45 (July–August 1883).

65. C. Toogood Downing, *The Stranger in China: or, the Fan-Qui's Visit to the Celestial Empire in 1836–7* (London, 1838), II, 157. Cited in Fairbank, *Trade and Diplomacy*, II, 5, n. 17.

66. *The Rupture with China, and Its Causes: Including the Opium Question, and Other Important Details: in a Letter to Lord Viscount Palmerston*, by a Resident in China (London, 1840), pp. 5–6. On the basis of this statement, it was estimated that the cost to each smoker "would be something less than a penny a day." See "Chinese Affairs," p. 568. The editor overlooked the fact that the consumers had to pay many times more for an ounce of opium than the brokers paid the English at Canton.

67. China, Imperial Maritime Customs, II, Special Series, no. 4, *Opium* (Shanghai, 1881), cited in Fairbank, *Trade and Diplomacy*, II, 5, n. 17. Hart's estimate seems to be conservative. It should be borne in mind that the same smoking extract was smoked over and over as many as six times by the poor. See Chun Ch'iu, "Mo-fan-sheng ti ya-p'ien" (Opium in the model province [Shansi]), in T'ao K'ang-te, ed., *Ya-p'ien chih chin-hsi* (Opium, its present and past; Shanghai, 1937), pp. 47–48. Chun Ch'iu lived in a small three-hundred family village in Shansi, in which one third of the inhabitants had become opium addicts; his own mother and grandmother were among them. Another third was on the verge of developing a habitual craving for the drug. The young males included a higher percentage of

smokers than did other classes of the population. Many of these smokers were compelled to steal or commit other crimes in order to obtain money for opium. See *ibid.*, pp. 46–47. Another author, Kuo Ch'ueh, in his article "Ssu-ch'uan ti chin-yen" (The opium prohibition in Szechwan), *ibid.*, p. 79, recorded his "conservative" estimate that among the 16,000 rickshaw pullers, 12,000 were opium smokers.

68. Downing, *The Fan Qui in China in 1836–7*, III, 182.

69. Chiang Hsiang-nan, 4:34; KYLT 1:[26b].

70. *IWSM*, 3.5; John F. Davis, *China: A General Description of that Empire and Its Inhabitants*, rev. ed. (London, 1857), I, 287; Yü En-te, p. 49. Opium smoking by the troops, however, has continued down to modern times. It was recorded that the army of Li Hung-chang was addicted to opium and the troops under his command were so ferocious toward innocent tradesmen and cowardly on the battlefield that foreigners satirically called them "Li's lambs." In more recent times, troops of Yen Hsi-shan and a host of other warlords, particularly those situated in the southwest and northwest, were not free from the practice. It was commonly held that Yen's army was defeated by Chiang Kai-shek's troops in 1930 because, among other reasons, the rainy season prevented Yen's soldiers from lighting their lamps to have a few whiffs of opium in the trenches and foxholes. See Herbert A. Giles, *A Glossary of Reference on Subjects Connected With the Far East* (Hongkong, Shanghai, and London, 1886), p. 135; Chun Ch'iu, "Mo-fan-sheng ti ya-p'ien," in T'ao K'ang-te, p. 49.

71. McCulloch, 2:939; *Hsüan-tsung sheng-hsün* (Sacred instructions of the Tao-kuang Emperor), 8:16, quoted in full in Yü En-te, p. 47.

72. Lin, *CS*, in *YPCC*, II, 140–141.

73. Ch'en Ch'i-t'ien (Gideon Chen), *Shan-hsi p'iao-chuang k'ao-lueh* (A brief historical study of the Shansi banks; Shanghai, 1937), pp. i–ii, 27, 30–31. Wei Chü-hsien maintained that the Jih Sheng Ch'ang dye store set up a *p'iao-chuang* in 1824. This apparently is the year when remitting became so important that an independent branch had to be established to administer it exclusively. See Wei Chü-hsien, *Shan-hsi p'iao-hao shih* (A history of the Shansi banks; Chungking, 1944), p. 36.

74. Ch'en Ch'i-t'ien, pp. 30, 157. The three stores were Wei Sheng Ch'ang, Wei T'ai Hou, and Hsin T'ai Hou. See Wei Chü-hsien, *P'iao-hao shih*, pp. 36–38.

75. Kao, an economist, was on the staff of the Shansi government. His article was well documented and drew heavily on Japanese source materials. See Kao Shu-k'ang, "Shan-hsi p'iao-hao ti ch'i-yuan chi ch'i ch'eng-li ti nien-tai" (The origin and date of establishment of the Shansi banks), *Shih-huo*, 6.1:31, 35 (July 1, 1937).

76. See Ch'en Ch'i-t'ien, pp. 20, 22, 27, 30, 31, 35, 165, 166; also the Editorial Committee's reply to Wang Yü-ch'üan's review of Ch'en's book in *YJSS*, 1.2: 325 (January 1939).

77. Ch'en Ch'i-t'ien, p. 152. For an account of the "milking" nature of the office of the hoppo and the payments made to him for his connivance in the opium trade, see Morse, *Trade and Administration*, pp. 99, 331.

78. Ch'en Ch'i-t'ien's observation was based on Srinivas R. Wagel, *Chinese Currency and Banking* (Shanghai, 1915), p. 161. Wagel's book was written mainly on the basis of personal investigation in China, and his scholarly technique could have been much improved. However, despite numerous unreliable passages and sweeping statements, the book offers valuable information on China's monetary and banking problems. Ch'en was able to use Wagel's book discriminatingly.

79. Wagel, p. 180. Upwards of 27 million dollars worth of opium was brought in at Canton by all foreign merchants during the two annual seasons ending March 31,

1832, the period when the Shansi banks began to operate formally and actively. This amount constituted about 52 percent of the total imports. After the end of the company's monopoly, in the four seasons ending March 31, 1838, British merchants imported through Canton over sixty million dollars worth of opium, which was well over 52 percent of their total imports during this period. See Jen Tsung-chi, *Canton Register*, 8.44:176 (Nov. 3, 1835) and 9.43:177 (Oct. 25, 1836); P. C. Kuo, p. 34; and McCulloch, II, 939.

80. Ch'en Ch'i-t'ien, p. 107. The banking operation was handled by stores of other kinds, such as dye, cloth, tea, and paper stores. It was only after 1830 that these houses engaged solely in banking activities. See *ibid.*, pp. 69–73.

81. *THL: TK*, 8:3; *YHKC*, 18:20b; Yü En-te, pp. 114–115. It is interesting to note that in his well-known realistic novel, *Lao-ts'an yu-chi*, written at the turn of the century and printed in book form for the first time in 1906, Liu E (1857–1909) took great pains to explain the term *T'ai-ku teng*, or opium lamp made in T'ai-ku. He maintains that Shansi was full of wealthy people and that they were all addicted to opium. Hence the best kind of apparatus for opium smoking was produced in T'ai-ku. See Liu E, *Lao-ts'an yu-chi* (Adventures of Lao-ts'an; Shanghai: Ya-tung t'u-shu-kuan, 1925), chap. 12, pp. 12–13; also Harold Shadick, tr., *The Travels of Lao Ts'an* (Ithaca, N.Y., 1952), p. 136.

82. Fairbank, *Trade and Diplomacy*, I, 76.

83. John W. Hall, "Notes on the Early Ch'ing Copper Trade with Japan," *HJAS*, 12.3 & 4:452, 454, 458 (December 1949); Morse, *Trade and Administration*, pp. 124–125; P'eng Hsin-wei, *Chung-kuo huo-pi shih* (A history of Chinese currency; Shanghai, 1954), II, 527.

84. This table is based mainly on P'eng Hsin-wei, II, 529–530, 538–539; some dates have been drawn from the account books and ledgers of the shop owned by the family of historian Jung Meng-yuan; see Wan Ssu-nien, "Ya-p'ien chan-cheng shih-tai Hua-pei ching-chi shih-liao ti hsin-fa-chien" (Newly discovered materials on the economic history of North China during the period of the Opium War), *T'u-shu chi-k'an* (Quarterly bulletin of Chinese bibliography, Chinese edition), 2.3:154 (1935).

85. *YHKC*, 17: 17b-18b.

86. See Huang Chueh-tzu's memorial in *IWSM*, 2:5b. Generally government spending and taxation were, by statute, supposed to be carried out in both silver and copper cash in the proportion of seven parts of the former and three parts of the latter. For certain purposes, and presumably at different times and localities, this ratio varied somewhat. For instance, in Yunnan, virtually the only copper mining area in the country, the legal exchange ratio between silver and copper was uniquely fixed at 1 to 1200, and in 1831 the Board of Revenue ruled that the soldiers were to be paid monthly in six parts of silver and four parts copper, if the market price of silver rose above the legal ratio. In the same year, the board ruled that in Shansi, Chekiang, and Shensi allowances to prisoners for salt and vegetables were to be charged not in cash but in silver. The board's regulations also provided that in Chekiang, when the rice tribute was levied in money on small proprietors, four parts were to be paid in cash at the ratio of 1400 cash to a tael of silver and six parts in silver. Thus Fairbank concludes that "the populace, who used copper day by day, were obliged to convert it into silver very extensively when making tax payments. If silver became more valuable in terms of copper, they would suffer." Fairbank, *Trade and Diplomacy*, I, 75. See also J. Edkins, *Chinese Currency* (Shanghai, 1901), pp. 58–59.

87. *YHCK*, 17:17b–19b; T'ang Hsiang-lung, "Tao-kuang ch'ao yin-kuei went-t'i"

(Outflow of silver in the Tao-kuang period, *She-hui k'o-hsueh tsa-chih* (Quarterly Review of Social Sciences), 1.3:9, 16 (September 1930). Their alarm is entirely justified. The seriousness of the problem of silver supply and its close connection with the opium trade is attested by Nye, an American merchant long resident in Canton, who observed: "Until the taste for this pernicious drug had spread insidiously over the empire, and the traffic in it had largely increased, China was the recipient of the precious metals from the West nations . . . but since the expiration of the East India Company's charter, the consumption of it has so largely augmented that, although the exports of Chinese produce have also greatly increased, yet the export of the precious metals, in adjustment of the balance adverse to China, has reached the annual sum of about $10,000,000; thus inflicting upon China a two-fold injury, in the demoralization of her people, and the undermining of the most grave moment, as threatening the very integrity of the empire." See Gideon Nye, Jr., *Tea: and the Tea Trade*, 3rd ed. (New York, 1850), pp. 17, 36; *IWSM*, 2:5b; T'ai-p'ing Shan-jen, "Tao-kuang ch'ao yin-huang wen-t'i" (The problem of the silver shortage in Tao-kuang's reign), *Chung-ho yueh-k'an* (Chung-ho monthly), 1.8:64 (August 1940); Lin, *CS*, in *YPCC*, II, 141.

88. Greenberg, p. 7. For an example of the "country traders," we may cite Magniac. When asked about his course of trade by the House of Lords in 1830, Magniac replied: "The trade we carried on, independently of acting as agents, was principally in opium, almost entirely indeed; and the simple proceeding in that was, to remit funds from China to India, for the purchase of the opium, which was then transmitted to the house in China, and the funds returned again to India for a repetition of the proceeding the ensuing season." See *PP: Opium Trade*, pp. 22–23.

89. P'eng Hsin-wei, II, 564–565.

90. Very early in this period, the best mode of getting large supplies of sycee "quickly to England on moderate terms" was of concern to Jardine and Matheson. In July 1832, Jardine devised a plan whereby treasures were first landed at St. Helena where a Mr. Robinson was willing to carry the batch to the island on the *Spartan* at a half percent freight, only a half of the rate they had paid at an earlier occasion. See JM, Canton 352, Jardine to Matheson, July 23, 1832.

91. See Appendix C; Ch'ien Chia-chü, "I-ko li-shih shih-shih ti hsin-k'an-fa" (The Opium War seen from a new angle), *Chung-shan wen-hua chiao-yü-kuan chi-k'an* (Quarterly review of the Sun Yat-sen Institute for Advancement of Culture and Education), 2.3:795 (1935).

92. FO 17/36, Memorial from John Abel Smith et al. to Palmerston, Nov. 2, 1839, and General Chamber of Commerce at Canton, "Statement of Trade in British Vessels at Canton, July 1, 1837 to June 30, 1838."

93. Charles F. Remer, *The Foreign Trade of China* (Shanghai, 1926), pp. 24, 25; Greenberg, p. 162.

94. *YHKC*, 17:15b–16, 21a–b, 22b, 25b–26; Greenberg, pp. 158–159; John Slade, *Narrative of the Late Proceedings and Events in China* (Macao, 1840), pp. 142–144.

95. Greenberg, p. 142; Wood, pp. 181–182.

96. Fairbank, *Trade and Diplomacy*, I, 77; Wang Ming-lun, "Ya-p'ien chan-cheng ch'ien Yün-nan t'ung-k'uang-yeh chung ti tzu-pen-chu-i meng-ya" (The early growth of capitalism in the Yunnan copper-mining industry before the Opium War), *Li-shih yen-chiu* (Historical Studies), 3:40, 45–46 (1956). From 1754 to 1772, the average annual production of copper in Yunnan was 6,000 tons; from 1773 to 1822, between 6,000 and 7,800 tons; in the period 1823–58, only 4,800 to 6,000 tons were produced annually. See also Fairbank, *Trade and Diplomacy*, I, 77.

97. Morse, *Trade and Administration*, pp. 124, 126; see also Chiang T'ing-fu, "Chung-kuo yü chin-tai shih-chieh ti ta-pien-chü," p. 814.

For a table showing the continued process of debasement of copper coins, see T'ang Hsiang-lung, pp. 29–30.

98. Eduard Kann, *The Currencies of China; an Investigation of Silver and Gold Transactions Affecting China* (Shanghai, 1927), pp. 209, 211, 220.

99. A. W. Pinnick, *Silver and China; An Investigation of the Monetary Principles Governing China's Trade and Prosperity* (Shanghai, 1930), p. 2.

100. Fairbank, *Trade and Diplomacy*, I, 75.

101. Pao Cheng-ku, *Ya-p'ien chan-cheng* (The Opium War; Shanghai, 1954), p. 56; Pao Shih-ch'en, 26:2.

102. P'eng Hsin-wei, II, 528–529. For the annual number of copper cash coined during the first hundred years of the Ch'ing dynasty, see tables in *ibid.*, II, 533–534, 538; Kann, *The Currencies of China*, p. 441.

103. When Jardine asked Captain Rees to send him $5,000 worth of copper coins if Rees could procure them on the coast at the rate of one thousand or more per dollar, he cautioned: "The small ones are 'Japan cash.'" See JM, Canton 474, Jardine to Rees, June 30, 1836; J. H. Stewart Lockhart, *The Currency of the Farther East, from the Earliest Times up to 1895* (Hong Kong, 1907), I, 127; Neil Gordon Munro, *Coins of Japan* (London, 1905), pp. 111–112.

104. P'eng Hsin-wei, II, 525, 538; Lockhart, I, 111, 114, 120–121; Edkins, *Chinese Currency*, pp. 38–39. The Spanish dollars, unacceptable to the government, took an inferior place in the monetary system. Nevertheless they were widely circulated south of the Yellow River. The fact that 58,000 Spanish dollars were found among the confiscated properties of Ho-shen indicates the wide range of their circulation. See P'eng Hsin-wei, II, 504–505.

105. W. H. Steiner and Eli Shapiro, *Money and Banking*, 3rd ed. (New York, 1956), p. 55.

106. Among many of the memorials and writings, see Pao Shih-ch'en, 26:1–7; *IWSM*, 2:4ff; Liang Chia-pin, p. 168.

107. Hummel, I, 290.

108. Lo Erh-kang, "Ya-p'ien chan-cheng ch'ien-hou Chung-kuo ti li-chih ho chün-pei" (Government and defense in China during the era of the Opium War), "Shih-ti chou-k'an," No. 25, in *TKP* (Mar. 8, 1935), p. 11.

109. "On the China and the Opium Question," *Blackwood's Edinburgh Magazine*, 47.296:848 (June 1840); J. W. Edmonds, *Origin and Progress of the War between England and China, a Lecture delivered before the Newburgh Lyceum, December 11, 1841* (New York, 1841), p. 9. Lin, *CS*, in *YPCC*, II, 141; Pao Shih-ch'en, 26:2.

110. *Canton Register*, 8.15:59 (Apr. 14, 1835). The *Canton Register*, as an organ of Jardine Matheson, would naturally dramatize the corrupt aspect of the Chinese government regarding its opium policy. The accusation seems to be too caustic. The Canton authorities did enforce the law with good faith during Governor-General Teng's administration, and prior to 1836 there was no want of sporadic proceedings in Canton to stop the trade, as related in letters in the Jardine Matheson Archives.

111. *YHKC*, 18:16a–b; Chiang Hsiang-nan, 4:33b; Sa Shih-wu, "Pu-ch'ung Lin Wen-chung-kung nien-p'u ti liang-chung shih-liao" (Two collections of source materials supplementing *Lin Wen-chung-kung nien-p'u*), "Shih-ti chou-k'an," No. 127, in *TKP* (Mar. 12, 1937), p. 3; Liang Chia-pin, pp. 197–198.

112. Liang T'ing-nan, *I-fen wen-chi* (An account of the barbarian invasion),

YPCC, VI, 12–13. To the best of my knowledge, there is no evidence to show that Governor-General Teng knowingly tolerated Han's misconduct in office.

113. See Fan Wen-lan, *Chung-kuo t'ung-shih chien-pien* (A general survey of Chinese history; Shanghai, 1947), I, 716ff.

114. *Canton Register*, 9.9:33 (Mar. 1, 1836); F. S. Turner, *British Opium Policy and its Results to India and China* (London, 1876), p. 53.

115. Most opium consumed in China was Indian-produced. The Chinese used less than a thousand chests a year of the Turkish product. Similarly, most opium produced in India was shipped to China. The way the opium was prepared and packed marked out its destination, since opium intended for home use was not packed in balls. See Turner, p. 54; McCulloch, II, 939; *Canton Register*, 9.9:36 (Mar. 1, 1836); "Commerce of China," p. 471; "War with China," p. 380.

116. Wood, p. 173, 174; "War with China," p. 370; Fairbank, *Trade and Diplomacy*, I, 64; *PP: Opium Trade* (1832), p. 113; *PP: China Corr.*, p. 418.

117. Wood, p. 15.

118. "War with China," pp. 380, 381.

119. *PP: China Corr.*, pp. 156, 190. In the late 1830s, disinterested parties had expressed their grave concern over the nature of the opium trade. The *Westminster Review* commented: "We were smuggling a prohibited drug, with the connivance of the viceroy, it is true, but still in defiance of repeated procl. nations from the Imperial government." The *Chinese Repository* remarked: "The slumbering of Chinese officers over the approaching crisis, seems ascribable rather to their love of quiet and their dread of foreigners resenting any interference, than to their hopes of receiving bribes." See "China: Its Early History, Literature, and Language; Mis-translation of Chinese Official Documents; Causes of the Present War," *Westminster Review*, American ed., 34.67:141 (September 1840); *CR*, 8.1:5 (1839).

120. "On the China and the Opium Question," p. 848.

121. "War with China," p. 380.

Chapter III. The Diplomatic Crisis

1. For an interesting account of the campaign for free trade, see Greenberg, pp. 175–184; *Canton Register*, 7.9:33 (March 4, 1834).

2. *Shih-liao hsün-k'an* (Historical materials published thrice monthly; Peking, 1930–1931), 21:767; Wang Chih-ch'un, *Ko-kuo t'ung-shang shih-mo chi* (A complete account of the foreign trade with the various countries; 1895), 8:4; Hsia Hsieh (pseud. Chiang-shang-chien-sou), *Chung-Hsi chi-shih* (A record of Sino-Western affairs; 1865), 3:10.

3. *PP: China Corr.*, pp. 1, 4, 7, 9; W. C. Costin, *Great Britain and China, 1833–1860* (London, 1937), p. 21.

4. *YHKC*, 29:106, 111, 119–120.

5. *PP: China Corr.*, pp. 8, 20.

6. *A Sketch of Lord Napier's Negociations with the Authorities at Canton* (London, 1837), p. 7.

7. *PP: China Corr.*, pp. 9, 31; Kuo T'ing-i, *Chin-tai Chung-kuo shih* (Modern Chinese history), 2nd ed. (Shanghai, 1947), II, 6. For an interesting narrative of this conference, see Morse, *Conflict*, pp. 132–134.

8. *Canton Register*, 7.31:121–122 (Aug. 5, 1834) and 7.33:131 (Aug. 19, 1834).

9. *PP: China Corr.*, p. 29; *Canton Register*, 7.35:139 (Sept. 2, 1834).

10. *PP: China Corr.*, 13.

11. Morse, *Conflict*, p. 134.

12. *PP: China Corr.*, pp. 32, 71.

13. *Canton Register*, 7.36:143 (Sept. 9, 1834); Hunter, *Fan-kwae*, p. 128; *PP: China Corr.*, p. 4.

14. Liang Chia-pin, p. 185.

15. Hugh Murray, John Crawford, et al., *An Historical and Descriptive Account of China* (Edinburgh, 1836), II, 411.

16. *CR*, 3:285 (1834–1835).

17. *Kuang-chou fu-chih* (A gazetteer of Canton; Canton, 1880), 81:31; Murray and Crawford, *Account of China*, II, 412.

18. Sir John Francis Davis, *China: A General Description of that Empire and its Inhabitants* (London, 1857), 1:117; *Shih-liao hsün-k'an*, 23:844; 25:916.

19. J. Daniel, T. C. Smith, and J. Jackson, the agents of the East India Company in China, sent a report to the Court of Directors in London dated Sept. 29, 1834, stating in effect that there was no particular necessity for this protection and that the arrival of the frigates in Whampoa had not produced the expected effect on the Chinese government. See *PP: China Corr.*, p. 42; *Canton Register*, 7.29:114 (July 22, 1834). Several other well-informed Englishmen also stated that the protection which the two frigates were asked to offer was unnecessary since the Chinese troops were not likely to attack the Europeans. See [Mr. Gordon,] *Address to the People of Great Britain Explanatory of Our Commercial Relations with the Empire of China, and of the Course of Policy by which it may be Rendered an almost Unbounded Field for British Commerce* (London, 1836), p. 107, and Sir George Thomas Staunton, *Remarks on the British Relations with China, and the Proposed Plans for Improving them* (London, 1836), pp. 23–24.

20. *Canton Register*, 7.33:130 (Aug. 19, 1834).

21. *PP: China Corr.*, pp. 3, 6, 26–28, 46; Davis, *China*, I, 117; Greenberg, p. 192.

22. *A Sketch of Lord Napier's Negociations*, p. 14; *PP: China Corr.*, p. 27.

23. *CSK*, 373:5b; Li Huan, ed., *Kuo-ch'ao ch'i-hsien lei-cheng ch'u-pien* (Ch'ing biographies systematically arranged; Siangyin, Hunan, 1884–1890), 198:9; Li Yuan-tu, ed., *Kuo-ch'ao hsien-cheng shih-lueh* (Biographies of leading personages of the Ch'ing dynasty; 1866), 24:15b–16; Hsiao I-shan, *Ch'ing-tai t'ung-shih* (General history of the Ch'ing period; Shanghai, 1928), II, 850–851.

24. Miao Ch'üan-sun, ed., *Hsü pei-chuan-chi* (Ch'ing biographies from the Tao-kuang period through the Kuang-hsü period; Soochow, 1910), 24:1ff; *CSK*, 377:3b; Li Yuan-tu, 24:16.

25. Ch'ien I-chi, ed., *Kuo-ch'ao pei-chuan-chi* (Ch'ing biographies through the Chia-ch'ing period), 198:15b; *CSK*, 375:10; Wang Chih-ch'un, *Kuo-ch'ao jou-yuan chi* (Record of the ruling dynasty's graciousness to strangers; 1891), 8:8.

26. *Shih-liao hsün-k'an*, 23:843b, 21:766b; Liang Shao-hsien, ed., *Nan-hai hsien-chih* (Gazetteer of Nan-hai district; 1872), 26:5; *PP: China Corr.*, p. 42.

27. Yü Hung-kan, *Yen-hai hsien-yao t'u-shuo* (The strategic places of the Chinese coast, with maps; Shanghai, 1903), 13:7b; Yü Ch'ang-hui, *Fang-hai chi-yao* (Essentials of maritime defense; 1842), preface, p. 2; Lin Tse-hsü, "Hua-shih i-yen" (Foreigners speak of Chinese affairs), in Wang Hsi-ch'i, comp., *Hsiao-fang-hu-chai yü-ti ts'ung-ch'ao* (Collection of geographical works from the Hsiao-fang-hu studio; 1877–1897), ts'e 79:3; *Shih-liao hsün-k'an*, 21:768b–769, 23:842b–843, 844b; *A Sketch of Lord Napier's Negociations*, pp. 12–13.

28. Hsü Shih-ch'ang, *Ta-Ch'ing chi-fu hsien-che chuan* (Biographies of eminent statesmen of the Ch'ing dynasty; Tientsin, n.d.), 5:28b; Lu K'un et al., 37:32; *Shih-liao hsün-k'an*, 23:843, 844b–845. The river blockade, according to the testimony of Jardine in Parliament in May 1840, was effective in preventing the British

vessels from proceeding further to Canton. See *PP: Report from the Select Committee on the Trade with China* (1840), p. 93.

29. *Shih-liao hsün-k'an*, 21:767; *CR*, 3:326 (1834–35). For a comparison, see John K. Fairbank and S. Y. Teng, "On the Transmission of Ch'ing Documents," *HJAS*, 4:43; *Shih-ch'ao sheng-hsün* (Sacred instructions of ten reigns; last preface Jan. 6, 1880), 120:3b.

30. *CR*, 3:335–336 (1834–35); *Shih-liao hsün-k'an*, 23:844; Fairbank and Teng, p. 45.

31. *THL*, 30:4b–5; *CSL*, 256:7b–8.

32. *Canton Register*, 7.36:144–145 (Sept. 9, 1834); 7.41:161 (Oct. 14, 1834).

33. *PP: China Corr.*, p. 51; *Canton Register*, 7.31:121–122 (Aug. 5, 1834).

34. Kuan T'ien-p'ei lost his life on February 26, 1841, in the Opium War. See Kuo T'ing-i, *Chin-tai Chung-kuo shih-shih jih-chih* (Modern China chronology; Taipei, 1963), I, 103; Hsü Shih-ch'ang, 5:28b–29.

35. *Hai-fang hui-lan*, 37:34b–39.

36. *Canton Register*, 7.42:165 (Oct. 21, 1834); Morse, *Conflict*, pp. 145–146; Morse, *Chronicles*, 3:91, 209. Another Chinese novel, *Hao-ch'iu-chuan* (The fortunate union), was translated by Davis and published in two volumes in 1829.

37. Morse, *Chronicles*, 3:259; 4:110; 4:144, 252, 324.

38. Hunter, *Fan-kwae*, p. 109. It is interesting to note that a more complete quotation of Charles Grant was printed on the head of the first page in every issue of the *Canton Register*.

39. *Canton Register*, 7.43:170–171 (Oct. 28, 1834).

40. *Ibid.*, 7.52:208–209 (Dec. 30, 1834), 8.3:9 (Jan. 20, 1835); *PP: China Corr.*, pp. 80–81.

41. Morse, *Conflict*, p. 150; "Chinese Affairs," *Quarterly Review*, 65.130:552 (March 1840).

42. Morse, *Chronicles*, 4:345. In January 1836, he claimed that he had been in China for sixteen years. This establishes that he came to China early in 1820. See *PP: China Corr.*, p. 12.

43. *PP: China Corr.*, pp. 165, 166, 120.

44. *Canton Register*, 7.45:179 (Nov. 11, 1834); see also Morse, *Conflict*, pp. 146–147.

45. *PP: China Corr.*, pp. 100, 101, 104–105, 106, 108–110, 112, 120, 131, 132; see also Turner, *British Opium Policy*, pp. 74, 82–86, 110, 131.

46. Too much significance can be attached to the publication of a supplement, since the *Canton Register* frequently did this. The editorial commented: "For although the hire of a *fastboat* is, by the customs of the port, illegal, or at least interdicted, still the detention of a foreigner and the exaction of a fine is equally contrary to the laws. We are glad we say to exhibit and condemn such grossly shameful, such open, undisguised acts of contemptuous oppression, because we feel our grounds of complaints are firm, our right of redress unquestionable, and our power to obtain it invincible. We are now speaking in behalf of all foreigners; and we would ask them very seriously to recollect their own dignity; and to reflect how powerfully their great wealth, their united talents, their high respectability and moral courage, their national determination and perseverance, their individual character and personal influence could avail them as opposed to the ignorant and timorous hong-merchants, to the rapacious and cowardly officers of government? How much longer shall the glorious flags of Europe and America be lowered to the many coloured frippery-drapery of China? . . . in a word, how much longer

shall the world lay supine at the feet of the Tartar emperor of China?" See Supplement to the *Canton Register*, Dec. 11, 1835.

47. *PP: China Corr.*, pp. 109–110, 118. On Oct. 10, 1836, Robinson wrote Palmerston, "and I confidently await the proper period, when, being in possession of your Lordship's despatches, we shall see our course clearly, and ultimately succeed in carrying into effect the very spirit of those instructions with which we may be furnished." Less than a month later, he wrote again, "I shall carefully abstain from any measures . . . until in possession of further information and definite instructions." *Ibid.*, p. 101.

48. Costin, pp. 31–34.

49. *PP: China Corr.*, pp. 113–114, 119, 130, 136.

50. Gideon Nye, Jr., *The Opium Question and the Northern Campaigns* (Canton, 1875), appendix. William R. O'Byrne, *A Naval Biographical Dictionary* (London, 1849), p. 332.

51. Davis to Foreign Office, Dec. 9, 1834, quoted in Costin, p. 31; also see p. 32.

52. *PP: China Corr.*, p. 130ff; Hummel, II, 716.

53. *PP: China Corr.*, pp. 139–140.

54. Costin, pp. 35, 36; *PP: China Corr.*, pp. 123, 144–145, 193, 197–201, 203–206; YHKC, 27:35a–b.

55. *PP: China Corr.*, pp. 123, 192, 207–209, 214, 234–240, 246–248.

56. Elliot wrote on December 4: "In my mind, my Lord, the peaceful establishment of direct official intercourse is no longer of questionable or difficult accomplishment. The principle that officers were not to reside in the Empire, has been formally renounced by the Emperor himself, and that was the main obstacle; the clearest admission of my right to direct sealed communications with the Governor upon the ground of my official character, has been conceded; an official mistake in an edict describing me to be a merchant, has been publicly acknowledged and corrected; facilities (especially upon the plea that I was an officer, and involving a direct official intercourse with the Mandarin here) have been accorded; striking proofs of the disposition to devolve upon me in my official capacity the adjustment of all disputes, even between Chinese and my own countrymen, have been afforded. On one occasion the Provincial Government has already communicated with me in a direct official shape; and upon my late departure from Canton, it was easy to perceive that the Governor was prepared to fall entirely into that course, upon the condition that I should waive the proposed change in the superscription of my addresses." *Ibid.*, pp. 248–249, 258.

57. *Ibid.*, pp. 299, 300. The prefect's grade was 4b; the commandant's, however, was 3b; see William Frederick Mayers, *The Chinese Government* (Shanghai, 1897), pp. 37, 62.

58. *PP: China Corr.*, pp. 299–301, 308–310, 313–314, 319, 325, 327–329, 334–337; Morse, *Conflict*, pp. 196–197.

59. Greenberg, p. 175; Morse, *Chronicles*, 4:186–187.

60. *Canton Register*, 7.36:144 (Sept. 9, 1834). The latter group was not among the 86 men who petitioned the king-in-council for a stronger policy against China. See *ibid.*, 7.52:208–209 (Dec. 30, 1834). The stands of the two Houses were neatly summarized by the editor of the *Canton Register* as follows, "among the British and foreign merchants in Canton, there are two parties . . . the one in favour of prosecuting the objects of commerce on such terms only as consist with peace, while the other insist on enforcing such terms on the Chinese, as they have heretofore been indisposed to adopt." *Ibid.*, 9.44:181 (Nov. 1, 1836).

61. *PP: China Corr.*, pp. 94–95. Robinson frequently complained of the discordance of the British community at Canton. See *ibid.*, pp. 105, 106, 131.

62. Costin, p. 32.

63. *Canton Register*, 7.1:2 (Jan. 7, 1834).

64. *Ibid.*; Greenberg, p. 201; Hunter, *Fan-kwae*, p. 77.

65. *Canton Register*, 7.13:49 (April 1, 1834); 7.15:57 (April 15, 1834); 8.15:59 (April 14, 1835); 8.8:30–31 (Feb. 25, 1835).

66. Among the merchants, Matheson and Jardine, each contributing $100, were the two largest contributors to the fund for a monument to be erected to the memory of Lord Napier. There were four others in Macao who made equal donations, but they were officers of Napier's mission, not merchants. *Ibid.*, 8.8:30 (Feb. 25, 1835), 9.26:104 (June 28, 1836); Greenberg, p. 193.

67. Reviews of this pamphlet are in the *Canton Register*, 9.33:133–135 (Aug. 16, 1836) and 9.44:181 (Nov. 1, 1836).

68. Jardine's popularity among his fellow traders at Canton was demonstrated by a dinner party in his honor, which took place in the company's dining hall in November 1838, shortly before his departure for England to lobby for a stronger policy toward China. The entire foreign community entertained him, and the event was much talked about afterwards among the residents. Hunter, *Fan-kwae*, pp. 134–135; Costin, p. 28.

Chapter IV. The Intensified Combat over Opium

1. *PP: China Corr.*, p. 153.

2. *YHKC*, 18:26; Kuo T'ing-i, *Chin-tai Chung-kuo shih*, II, 81–82.

3. Hsü Nai-chi, memorial in *YPCC*, I, 471; *PP: China Corr.*, p. 156.

4. Hsü Nai-chi, *YPCC*, I, 472–474.

5. *IWSM*, 1:5a–b.

6. JM, Canton 476, Jardine to Rees, July 26, 1836.

7. *Canton Register*, 9.28:112 (July 12, 1836).

8. *PP: China Corr.*, pp. 137–138; "Chinese Affairs," *Quarterly Review*, 65.130:544 (March 1840).

9. JM, Canton 495, Jardine to Rees, Feb. 17, 1837.

10. JM, Canton 498, Jardine to Rees, April 26, 1837.

11. For the founding of the academy, see Hummel, I, 401.

12. Liang T'ing-nan, *I-fen wen-chi*, in *YPCC*, VI, 6–7.

13. *IWSM*, 1:5b–12. It was reported in Canton "from good authority" that Teng, "fearful of committing himself on the opium question, sent a private despatch to his friends in Peking begging them to ascertain correctly whether the emperor was determined to bring the drug in or not. In the interim he prepared his report and laid it aside. On receiving answers to the letters addressed to his Peking friends, assuring him the emperor was in earnest on the subject, he revised his report and forwarded it on the 6th Ulto." See *Canton Register*, 9.40:164 (Oct. 4, 1836).

14. *PP: China Corr.*, p. 389; for Juan's Peking appointment, see Hummel, I, 401. On the occasion of the empress' death on Feb. 13, 1840, *The Times* (London) published an article which in part says that the empress "during the years 1835 and '36 exercised great power over her husband. . . . During the Zenith of her glory, she sent many of her creatures into the provinces, where they held the highest offices. . . . It was generally believed that she was at the head of the party which we might style Whigs, though they are very stanch [*sic*] Conservatives in their own way. Heu-nae-tsze [Hsü Nai-chi] and others belonged to her coterie. This race has

passed by, and there are now in the cabinet a set of gray headed Torries that would surprise even the good people of Queen Ann's time, and leave nothing to blame for the *Quarterly*." See the *Times*, July 4, 1840, p. 5.

15. The letter was dated Aug. 6, 1836. *Canton Register*, 9.32:126–127 (Aug. 9, 1836); *PP: China Corr.*, p. 138.

16. *CSL*, in *YPCC*, I, 377. Although an English translation of these two important memorials was widely circulated, the Chinese version was not included in any of the collections of Chinese state papers. Kuo T'ing-i and Ch'i Ssu-ho both are of the opinion that they are no longer extant. But early in the summer of 1959, the British Museum acquired an enormous amount of *Peking Gazettes*, and the two documents are found in a volume dated the 10th month of the 19th year of Tao-kuang (Nov. 6–Dec. 5, 1839). For the English translation, see *CR*, 6:398–404 (1837), or John Slade, *Narrative of the Late Proceedings and Events in China* (Macao, 1840), appendix, pp. 18–26. For Kuo T'ing-i and Ch'i Ssu-ho's comments on these memorials, see Kuo T'ing-i, *Chin-tai Chung-kuo shih*, II, 91, and *YPCC*, I, 475.

17. *Canton Register*, 9.45:186, 190, 192 (Nov. 8, 1836); *ibid.*, 9.49:202 (Dec. 6, 1836); Slade, appendix, pp. 20, 31–32.

18. *CSL*, in *YPCC*, I, 377; Slade, appendix, p. 34.

19. *Canton Register*, 9.50:209 (Dec. 13, 1836); King, *Opium Crisis*, p. 4.

20. JM, Canton 498, Jardine to Rees, April 26, 1837; *PP: China Corr.*, pp. 153, 183–185.

21. Li Kuei, *Ya-p'ien shih-lueh* (A brief account of the opium question), in *YPCC*, VI, 208; *IWSM*, 1:12–17b.

22. Huang Chueh-tzu, "Huang-shao-ssu-k'ou tsou-kao" (Memorials of Huang Chueh-tzu), in *YPCC*, I, 485–487.

23. Gussie Esther Gaskill, "A Chinese Official's Experiences during the First Opium War," *American Historical Review*, 39.1:82–83 (October 1933); *IWSM*, 2:14a–b, 15b, 20b–26, 28–31b; 3:4b, 7b–9, 12b, 13, 15, 16ff., 21, 27b; 4:1ff., 10b, 14b, 22a–b; 5:10b–12; T. F. Tsiang (Chiang T'ing-fu), "China and European Expansion," *Politica*, 2.5:7 (March 1936); Chiang T'ing-fu, "Tao-kuang ch'ao *Ch'ou-pan i-wu shih-mo* chih shih-liao ti chia-chih" (The value of the *Ch'ou-pan i-wu shih-mo* of the Tao-kuang reign), *CHCK*, 37.9:7 (1936).

24. *IWSM*, 2:20b–26; 5:8b, 9, 16b; Li Kuei, *YPCC*, VI, 209; Tsiang, "China and European Expansion," p. 7.

25. Morse, *Conflict*, p. 214. The *Dublin Magazine*, as might be expected, took a different view: "There is one thing for which the Emperor of China has not got the credit which we believe he deserves; and that is, his sincerity in desiring to exclude opium from his dominions, because of its depraving and contaminating effect upon his people." See "China," *Dublin University Magazine*, 40.89:593 (May 1840).

26. "Great Britain at the Commencement of the Year 1843," *Blackwood's Edinburgh Magazine*, 53.327:20 (January 1843).

27. *The Rupture with China, and its Causes, in a Letter to Lord Viscount Palmerston*, by a Resident in China (London, 1840), p. 4.

28. Robert B. Forbes, *Personal Reminiscences*, 3rd ed. rev. (Boston, 1892), p. 144.

29. "Chinese Affairs," *Quarterly Review*, p. 569.

30. Downing, *The Fan-Qui in China in 1836–7*, III, 177.

31. Kerr, "Opium and the Smoking Extract," pp. 41, 46.

32. David Owen, a modern author, also states such a view; see his *British Opium Policy*, p. 25.

33. *Canton Register*, 9.10:37 (March 8, 1836).

34. Quoted in Greenberg, pp. 139–140.

35. *YHKC*, 18:11, 13, 14, 17b, 18b; Yü En-te, p. 47.

36. *IWSM*, 7:1b; *YHKC*, 7:3b; 19:8b, 58b.

37. Shen Yen-ch'ing, *Huai-ch'ing i-kao* (Collected works of Shen Yen-ch'ing; 1862), 1:7.

38. Chou Chi-hua, "Ts'ung-cheng-lu (Hai-ling)" (Records during term of office as magistrate of T'ai-chou, Kiangsu), in *Chia-yin-t'ang hui-ts'un* (Collected works of Chou Chi-hua; 1958 ed.), 2:106–111; *Canton Register*, 9.50:209 (Dec. 13, 1836).

39. *IWSM*, 2:11b, 28b; Lin, *CS*, in *YPCC*, II, 142.

40. Lin, "JC," *YPCC*, II, 15, 21 *et passim*; *YHKC*, 19:28.

41. *YHKC*, 19:10b, 12b-13, 23, 60b–61; Lin, *CS*, in *YPCC*, II, 149; Lin, "JC," p. 23.

42. *Canton Register*, 9.48:196, 197 (Nov. 29, 1836); 9.51:209, 210 (Dec. 20, 1836).

43. JM, Correspondence Section, Letter Books, William Jardine, 7:156. Jardine, Matheson and Co. to Captain Rees, Jan. 29, 1839.

44. Their names kept appearing in memorials to Palmerston, addresses to Lin, and minutes of conferences held early in 1839. See *PP: China Corr.*, pp. 262, 322, 298; Slade, pp. 37, 42, 57. Dadabhoy, Dent, and Framjee were included in the list, issued by Lin on May 2, 1839, of sixteen merchants to be detained in the factories after the general body of foreign merchants were freed from confinement. See Lin, *HCL*, in *YPCC*, II, 280; *PP: China Corr.*, p. 260; and Slade, p. 87.

45. *Canton Register*, 9.51:209 (Dec. 20, 1836); *YPCC*, VI, 375. The provincial judge's name was mentioned in one of Teng's memorials that reached Peking on Oct. 6, 1837. It was bound by mistake into an earlier volume of the newly acquired *Peking Gazettes* in the British Museum (see note 16 above). This volume contains some imperial edicts (*shang-yü*) issued in the period from the first month of the 12th year of Tao-kuang to the first month of the following year. See also *Canton Register*, 8.36:141 (Sept. 8, 1835); 8.38:149 (Sept. 22, 1835).

46. Mei Tseng-liang, *Po-chien-shan-fang wen-chi* (Essays of Mei Tseng-liang; 1856), 14:18b.

47. A sketch of Teng's life, reprinted from *Ch'ing-shih lieh-chuan*, is in *YPCC*, VI, 374–379; see also Hummel, II, 716–717.

48. *CSL*, in *YPCC*, I, 377. The emperor's encomium was shared by impartial foreigners. *The Description of Canton* warmly commented: "The present governor . . . is of a different character, active, intelligent, ambitious, but often hasty, and not very discreet or prudent" (p. 37).

49. Mei Tseng-liang, *Po-chien-shan-fang wen-chi*, 14:17b–18b.

50. See Teng T'ing-chen, *Shuang-yen-chai ch'üan-chi* (The complete works of Teng T'ing-chen; 1919); the poems dedicated to Lin Tse-hsü are in *YPCC*, II, 573–582.

51. "War with China, and the Opium Question," *Blackwood's Edinburgh Magazine*, 47.293:379 (March 1840).

52. Slade, p. iv. On March 21, 1839, C. W. King, partner of D. W. C. Olyphant's firm at Canton, which had the honor of being the only foreign house in China not engaged in the opium trade, spoke in the General Chamber of Commerce, "it is well known that but few years have elapsed since all the high officers of this provinces [*sic*] were engaged in the traffic." Since Governor-General Teng did not assume office until February 1836, King's remark serves to vindicate Teng from any illicit dealings in the traffic. See Slade, p. 37. For King's noninvolvement in the opium trade, see Morrison, *Memoirs*, II, 187.

53. *YPCC*, VI, 377; *PP: China Corr.*, pp. 257–258.

54. Liang T'ing-nan, *I-fen wen-chi*, in *YPCC*, VI, 12–13. For a biographical sketch of the tutor Lin Po-t'ung, eminent Cantonese scholar, see Hummel, I, 510–511.

55. JM, Canton 532, Jardine to Rees, October 18, 1838.

56. *PP: China Corr.*, p. 155.

57. JM, Canton 492, Jardine to Rees, Jan. 27, 1837.

58. *PP: China Corr.*, pp. 155–156.

59. Since Elliot did not have a previous understanding with Palmerston, he may seem to have been somewhat impetuous in addressing these letters to the Indian authorities. But a look at his family relations perhaps makes it understandable. Elliot's father, the governor of Madras, was a brother of the first Lady Auckland and of the first Earl of Minto. See Nye, *The Opium Question*, appendix.

60. *PP: China Corr.*, pp. 188, 189.

61. *Ibid.*, pp. 192, 193*(distinguish from p. 193), JM, Canton 499, Jardine to Rees, June 3, 1837; *ibid.*, Canton 501, Jardine to Rees, Aug. 19, 1837; *ibid.*, Canton 502, Jardine to Rees, Sept. 28, 1837.

62. Ting Ming-nan et al., "Ti-i-tz'u ya-p'ien chan-cheng — wai-kuo tzu-pen-chu-i ch'in-lueh Chung-kuo ti k'ai-tuan" (The first Opium War — The beginning of foreign capitalist aggression against China), in *Chung-kuo k'o-hsueh-yuan li-shih yen-chiu-so ti-san-so chi-k'an* (Monograph series of the Third Branch, Institute of Historical Studies, Chinese Academy of Science), Vol. I (Peking, 1955), p. 130; *IWSM*, 2:2a–b.

63. *PP: China Corr.*, p. 235.

64. *Ibid.*, p. 233. For Captain Elliot's replies to the governor-general of Canton on Sept. 25, Nov. 17, and Nov. 21, 1837, see *ibid.*, pp. 236, 240, and 252.

65. Jardine saw no prospect of the government's relaxing its severity at Canton. He reported that many vessels had left for Namoa and that vicinity. See JM, Canton 504, Jardine to Rees, Oct. 18, 1837.

66. Elliot to Palmerston (received May 15, 1838), *PP: China Corr.*, p. 241. Captain Elliot underestimated the number of vessels engaged in the coast operation prior to its sudden and phenomenal increase in the latter part of 1837.

67. JM, Canton 507, Jardine to Rees, Jan. 2, 1838; Canton 509, Jardine to Rees, Jan. 24, 1838; Canton 512, Jardine to Rees, Feb. 27, 1838.

68. JM, Canton 504, Jardine to Rees, Oct. 18, 1837. On Nov. 10, Jardine again reported to Captain Rees that "everything extremely dull, not a ship loading for England; and only two for America." See JM, Canton 505. Without the opium trade, the legal trade could not thrive. Cf. Elliot's report: "The stagnation of the opium traffic still continues, and the consequent locking up of the circulating medium is already producing great and general embarrassment." FO 17/30, Elliot to Palmerston, dated Canton, Feb. 8, 1839.

69. *IWSM*, 2:3b–4; *PP: China Corr.*, p. 257; Wang Yen-wei, "Yang-wu shih-mo ta-lueh" (An account of China's foreign affairs), *Chung-kuo hsueh-pao* (Chinese studies), 1:26 (1912); "War with China," *Blackwood's Edinburgh Magazine*, p. 370.

70. *PP: China Corr.*, p. 254, 257; *IWSM*, 2:3a–b.

71. *IWSM*, 2:2b, 3, 4; *PP: China Corr.*, pp. 245, 250, 253, 256; P. C. Kuo, p. 76.

72. *PP: China Corr.*, pp. 241, 247. The price of opium delivered at Whampoa was considerably higher than that delivered at Lintin. A chest of old Benares at Whampoa sold for $490 at the end of March 1838, but at Lintin it sold only for $395. The average difference in price of all descriptions of opium between Whampoa and Lintin was $71. If delivered at the Dutch Folly or abreast of the factories, the price would be $30 higher than the Whampoa price. When the smuggling in the river by foreign boats increased, the profit dropped accordingly. In August, the Whampoa price was between $30 and $50 higher than the Lintin price. See JM,

Canton 513, Jardine to Rees, March 31, 1838; Canton 525, Jardine to Rees, Aug. 14, 1838.

73. *PP: China Corr.*, pp. 241, 242, 247, 258, 299, 300, 309; P. C. Kuo, p. 76.

74. *IWSM*, 4:16, 17b–18.

75. *PP: China Corr.*, pp. 309–315.

76. *IWSM*, 4:16b, 17; *PP: China Corr.*, p. 310.

77. *PP: China Corr.*, p. 314.

78. Maitland reported to the Admiralty that "forbearance in a case of this kind, would only give encouragement to a repetition of similar offensive conduct." He therefore decided to proceed to the Bogue to demand disavowal of "any intention to insult the British flag." See FO 17/34, Maitland to Charles Wood, dated the *Wellesley* in Toongkoo Bay, Aug. 11, 1838; also see *PP: China Corr.*, pp. 315, 316.

79. The written disavowal stated: "It was not done in consequence of any official orders: the wrong language was that of the natives aforesaid themselves." See FO 17/34, Maitland to Charles Wood, Aug. 11, 1838, encl. D.

80. Li and Lu were both from the Ta-p'eng battalion; the former was in his early fifties and the latter in his middle twenties. See "A List of Officers in the Kwang-tung Water Forces, 1841" (no Chinese title), MS in the British Museum (Add. 14271), pp. 23, 27; 4:18b; *PP: China Corr.*, pp. 310–311.

81. *PP: China Corr.*, pp. 311, 316; *IWSM*, 4:18b.

82. For the minutes of the conference on board the *Wellesley* between Maitland and the Chinese officers on Aug. 5, 1838, see FO 17/34, Maitland to Charles Wood, Aug. 11, 1838, encl. E.

83. *IWSM*, 4:18b, 19b–20.

84. *PP: China Corr.*, pp. 193* (distinguish from p. 193), 308, 319, 320.

85. JM, Canton 525, Jardine to Rees, Aug. 14, 1838; KYLT, 2:15a–b.

86. JM, Canton 545, Jardine to Rees, Dec. 10, 1838.

87. Jardine repeatedly complained to Captain Rees of the desertion of all the brokers and the complete stagnation of the opium trade. See JM, Canton 526, Sept. 4, 1838; Canton 530, Oct. 4, 1838; Canton 542, Nov. 18, 1838; Canton 543, Nov. 27, 1838; Canton 545, Dec. 10, 1838; Canton 547, Jan. 11, 1839.

88. JM, Canton 530, Jardine to Rees, Oct. 4, 1838; Canton 543, Jardine to Rees, Nov. 27, 1838. Jardine was so anxious to "run off" the huge amount of Malwa held by his firm that he instructed Rees to sell it at the best terms he could get without giving him any limit as to price. See JM, Canton 545, Dec. 10, 1838.

89. *Canton Press Price Current*, 4.18 (Jan. 5, 1839).

90. JM, Canton 545, Jardine to Rees, Dec. 10, 1838.

91. JM, Canton 546, Jardine to Rees, Dec. 16, 1838.

92. JM, Canton 547, Jardine to Rees, Jan. 11, 1839.

93. *PP: China Corr.*, pp. 323, 324.

94. Innes apparently did attempt, without success, to get out of his dilemma at the expense of others. He prepared some documents to be submitted to the local government and, through Jardine, asked Robert Thom to translate them into Chinese. Thom refused Jardine's request at the risk of being discharged from Jardine, Matheson's employ and becoming "pennyless on the wide world." He wrote: "I cannot reconcile the task either with my feelings or my conscience . . . I have now no prospects before me of ever making a fortune and returning home. My simple object in being here — is to endeavour to promote a *good feeling* between this country and my own — by means of placing my native country before the Chinese in the most amiable and honourable light wherever I can find opportunity: — and whether be it be by means of translations from our words — or by acting

under the guidance of Reason and Justice — to convey to them an idea of the high moral tone of Europe. To this object I intend dedicating my slender ability — my humble fortune — and my life.

"Now my dear Mr. Jardine with views of this kind before me — can you wonder at my refusal to put a document into Chinese — which I look upon as conveying down to future ages the dishonour of my country? or how should I like in after life to be thus taunted — 'While two poor coolies have had their limbs racked by cruel torture for merely carrying the opium from one place to another — while an innocent Hong merchant at this moment wears the cangue for another's crime — while an equally innocent American merchant has his trade stopped for the same reason — while all the other Hong merchants quite as innocent as the former — are exposed to all the fines and penalties which an arbitrary government can inflict — in steps the guilty foreigner and turns the whole to capital account — making some $50,000 or more by the cruel position into which he by his violation of the laws, had forced the said innocent parties! and you Sir (this to myself) were the dastardly foreigner — who so [abused*] your knowledge of the Chinese as to translate a document which hands down the disgrace of your country to future ages!'

"I confess my dear Mr. Jardine that a taunt of this kind would stab me to the heart — and the more keenly — as — were I to render the paper into Chinese — I shd too well deserve it. I have not closed my eyes all night revolving the subject in my mind — and I cannot if my life depended upon it — see it in any other point of view." See JM, Canton 544, Robert Thom to William Jardine, Dec. 8, 1838. [*One word illegible.]

95. *PP: China Corr.*, p. 326; Ouchterlony, *The Chinese War*, pp. 6–7.

96. Hunter, *Fan-kwae*, pp. 74, 75. See also Mary G. Mason, *Western Concepts of China and the Chinese*, 1840–1876 (New York, 1939), p. 100; *IWSM*, 5:27; *CR*, 7:445 (1838–1839).

97. Forbes estimated it at ten thousand (*Personal Reminiscences*, p. 348). Elliot reported that it was at least six thousand (*PP: China Corr.*, p. 324).

98. Letter of J. L. Shuck, Macao, Jan. 10, 1839. *The Baptist Archives*, Library of the University of Richmond, quoted in Cranston, p. 41; *PP: China Corr.*, p. 324.

99. *PP: China Corr.*, p. 324.

100. Hunter, *Fan-kwae*, pp. 74–76. Although Hunter gave a most remarkable narrative of this exciting incident, he was mistaken about the date. He confused it with another execution that took place in the square on Feb. 26, 1839, and was successfully completed. His error is revealed by a careful comparison of his narratives of the two incidents on pp. 27, 73, and 135–136. Although most of Hunter's writings are invaluable as historical materials, they are not free from errors. For a discussion on his inaccuracy in regard to dates, see P. de Vargas, "William C. Hunter's Books on the Old Canton Factories," *YJSS*, 1.2:91–117 (July 1939), and Arthur W. Hummel, "Correspondence Regarding William C. Hunter," *YJSS*, 2.2:294–295 (February 1940).

101. *PP: China Corr.*, p, 324; Forbes, p. 348; Hunter, *Fan-kwae*, pp. 135–136.

102. "Chinese Affairs," *Quarterly Review*, p. 547.

103. *PP: China Corr.*, pp. 325, 326, 328.

104. As it will be recalled, Elliot first established himself in Canton as the Chief Superintendent of British Trade on April 12, 1837. His vigorous but futile struggle for direct official communication with the provincial government was launched immediately and carried on throughout the rest of the year. Chagrined by his failure, he left Canton in protest on December 2, 1837, and took up residence at

Macao. With the exception of a few days at the end of July 1838, when the Maitland fleet came to the Canton waters, he did not return until December 12, 1838.

105. FO 17/30, Elliot to Palmerston, Jan. 2, 1839; *PP: China Corr.*, p. 326.

106. *PP: China Corr.*, pp. 326–327.

107. *Ibid.*, pp. 327, 328, 332–336, 343, 345.

108. "Ya-p'ien tsou-an," in *YPCC*, II, 91; *IWSM*, 5:18.

109. McCulloch, *Dictionary of Commerce*, II, 941.

110. Palmerston's letter also accused the Chinese government of applying the opium laws to foreigners but not to the natives. See FO 17/37, Palmerston to the minister of the Emperor of China, February 20, 1840.

111. FO 17/37, Palmerston to Elliot, Nov. 4, 1839, quoted in Costin, *Great Britain and China*, p. 60.

112. *PP: China Corr.*, p. 155.

113. *Ibid.*, p. 343.

114. Letter from Russell and Company to Baring Brothers and Company, dated Canton, April 10, 1839, and circular letter from Russell and Company to John M. Forbes, dated Canton, Feb. 27, 1839, Forbes Collection (MSS in Baker Library, Harvard University), case 1.

115. It is difficult to give a clear-cut date for the commencement of foreign smuggling within the river; it developed gradually after Governor-General Teng started his strict policy in late 1836. Such activities had already assumed remarkably large proportions by Nov. 19, 1837, when Elliot reported that the native boats had been burned, the Chinese smugglers scattered, and both replaced by foreigners in foreign-owned boats. See *PP: China Corr.*, p. 241.

116. Letter from Russell and Company to John M. Forbes, dated Canton, March 4, 1839, Forbes Collection, case 1.

117. Letter from Russell and Company to Baring Brothers and Company, dated Canton, April 10, 1839, Forbes Collection, case 1.

118. Letter from Russell and Company to John M. Forbes, dated Canton, March 4, 1839, Forbes Collection, case 1.

Chapter V. Commissioner Lin at Canton

1. [Wei Yuan], "I-sou ju-k'ou chi" (Account of the invasion by barbarian vessels), in *YPCC*, VI, 105.

2. *YPCC*, VI, 322 (reprinted from *Ch'ing-shih lieh-chuan*). Tsiang, "China and European Expansion," p. 7; Ting Ming-nan et al., p. 126; Hummel, I, 511; Wu Chia-pin, *Ch'iu-tzu-te-chih-shih wen-ch'ao* (Collected works of Wu Chia-pin; 1866), 10:1b.

3. *YPCC*, VI, 322 (reprinted from *Ch'ing-shih lieh-chuan*). S. Wells Williams, *The Middle Kingdom* (New York, 1883), II, 498; Chen Ching-Jen (Ch'en Ch'in-jen), "Opium and Anglo-Chinese Relations," *Chinese Social and Political Science Review*, 19.3:399 (1935–1936). *IWSM*, 5:16b–17b.

4. According to Williams, Ch'ang-ling (1758–1838) was the only Ch'ing official before Lin Tse-hsü to receive such full powers. He was vested with such powers when sent to Turkestan to quell the insurrection. See Williams, I, 457–458. Chinese sources corroborating or refuting this point are not readily available to me; see Lin, *HCL*, in *YPCC*, II, 243. Lin reported the confiscation proceedings to the emperor on April 12, when the surrender of the opium had already commenced and fifty chests had been taken over on the previous day. This memorial was not

received until May 2. See Lin, "JC," p. 12; "Ya-p'ien tsou-an," pp. 91–94; *IWSM*, 6:11–16.

5. Lin, *CS*, in *YPCC*, II, 153, 158–159.

6. See pp. 210–213.

7. During the Ming dynasty, the Lin household produced five ministers in three generations, and they were all known for their probity. See Chin An-ch'ing, "Lin Wen-chung-kung chuan" (Biography of Lin Tse-hsü), reprinted from Miao Ch'üan-sun, in *YPCC*, VI, 319.

8. Hummel, I, 511; Chin An-ch'ing, in *YPCC*, VI, 319.

9. Hummel, I, 511.

10. Chang Hsi-t'ung, "The Earliest Phase of the Introduction of Western Political Science into China," *YJSS*, 5.1:21 (July 1950); Hummel, I, 432.

11. *YPCC*, VI, 311–312 (reprinted from *Ch'ing-shih lieh-chuan*).

12. Chin An-ch'ing, in *YPCC*, VI, 321; *YPCC*, VI, 313, 315 (reprinted from *Ch'ing-shih lieh-chuan*).

13. Ch'en k'ang-ch'i, *Lang-ch'ien chi-wen* (Memoirs of a retired gentleman; 1844 ed.), 8:3; Hummel, I, 511, and II, 716; *YPCC*, VI, 312, 314 *et passim* (reprinted from *Ch'ing-shih lieh-chuan*); Teng T'ing-chen, *Shuang-yen-chai shih-ch'ao* (Collected poems of Teng T'ing-chen), in *YPCC*, II, 581. Liang Chang-chü, a fellow Fukienese, ten years Lin's senior, gained his *chin-shih* nine years earlier than Lin did and became Lin's subordinate as the governor of Kwangsi when Lin was the governor-general of Liang-Kuang in 1840. See Hummel, I, 500.

14. Hummel, I, 207, 432, 519–520; *ibid.*, II, 851; Chang Hsi-t'ung, p. 1.

15. Li's sojourn in Canton in 1820–21 aroused his interest in foreign lands. In the early 1820s he produced two accounts of foreign countries. In 1833 he had a coppersmith build a few astronomical instruments for him. In the late 1830s he produced several works on Chinese geography that have not been entirely superseded by modern works. See Hummel, I, 449–450.

16. Chang Hsi-t'ung, p. 2.

17. *YHKC*, 17:22a–b.

18. Chin An-ch'ing, in *YPCC*, VI, 320, 327.

19. Hummel, I, 511; Chin An-ch'ing, in *YPCC*, VI, 325–326; *YPCC*, VI, 318 (reprinted from *Ch'ing-shih lieh-chuan*).

20. A private individual was permitted to have only two sedan bearers, an ordinary magistrate four, a governor-general eight; the emperor alone had sixteen bearers for his sedan. See John Francis Davis, *China: A General Description of that Empire and Its Inhabitants* (London, 1857), I, 408–409.

21. Lin, *HCL*, in *YPCC*, II, 229.

22. "Ya-p'ien tsou-an," p. 89. See Hummel, II, 610–611 and I, 432 for a description of Pao Shih-ch'en's life. The account of his trip is based on Lin, "JC," pp. 1–8.

23. Lin, "JC," p. 8; Hunter, *Fan-kwae*, pp. 136–137; Chin An-ch'ing, in *YPCC*, VI, 327; *CR*, 8:77 (1839–1840).

24. Liang T'ing-nan, *I-fen wen-chi*, *YPCC*, VI, 25; Lin, "JC," pp. 8–9.

25. Hummel, I, 432; Kung Tzu-chen, *Ting-an ch'üan-chi* (Complete works of Kung Tzu-chen; Shanghai, 1933), *pu-pien* (supplement), 4:2b–3, 3–4. Letter of Lin replying to Kung Tzu-chen, in *YPCC*, II, 593.

26. Letter of Lin replying to Kung, in *YPCC*, II, 592–593.

27. These officials were all civil servants of Kwangtung. Lin did not bring his own lieutenants. Even his adjutant and assistants were all provided by the Canton government. See Lin, *HCL*, in *YPCC*, II, 229, 230; Lin, "JC," pp. 5, 8, 9.

28. On February 22 Commissioner Lin wrote in his diary that a messenger of

the governor-general and a messenger of the governor brought dispatches from officers of various levels of the Canton government. It is highly possible that some of the suspects on the list were provided by these dispatches. Two days later Lin issued the command to the provincial judge and the financial commissioner to arrest them. Lin, "JC," p. 2.

29. Lin, *HCL*, in *YPCC*, II, 231–234. See Lin, "JC" under July 21–30, August 25, November 3, 7, and 8, December 9, 1839 (pp. 23, 24, 27, 36, 39); Lin, *HCL*, in *YPCC*, II, 235, 236–238, 239, 240.

30. Lin, *CS*, in *YPCC*, II, 162–163; in the three years prior to the commissioner's arrival in Canton, Teng T'ing-chen arrested 345 men and confiscated 10,158 opium pipes. *IWSM*, 5:18; Lin, "JC," pp. 22, 23.

31. Liang T'ing-nan, *I-fen wen-chi*, *YPCC*, VI, 12–13.

32. The days on which he held these trials were July 23–24, 26–28, and 30; Lin, "JC," pp. 23–24; Lin, *HCL*, in *YPCC*, II, 232–234.

33. Lin, *CS*, in *YPCC*, II, 173–174; Liang T'ing-nan, *I-fen wen-chi*, *YPCC*, VI, 12–13.

34. Lin, *CS*, in *YPCC*, II, 155–157; *IWSM*, 10:8.

35. Lin, *CS*, in *YPCC*, II, 144, 148; "Ya-p'ien tsou-an," p. 97.

36. Lin, *CS*, in *YPCC*, II, 148–149.

37. Lin, *HCL*, in *YPCC*, II, 243; Lin, *CS*, in *YPCC*, II, 148. The "300 percent profit," of course, is figurative speech.

38. *CR*, 8:2 (1839–1840); Greenberg, p. 198.

39. Lin, *CS*, in *YPCC*, II, 149.

40. *IWSM*, 7:9–11; 5:22–25b, 26b–28.

41. Liang T'ing-nan, *I-fen wen-chi*, *YPCC*, VI, 13–14; *IWSM*, 7.29b–30.

42. The letter was included in *I-fen wen-chi*, *YPCC*, VI, 14. It is also in Li Kuei, reprinted in T'ao K'ang-te, pp. 140–142. Both versions are included in Kuo T'ing-i, *Chin-tai Chung-kuo shih*, II, 165–167, and minor variations are pointed out. Many errors were corrected by collating these versions with an English translation of the letter in *CR*, 8:9–12 (1839–1840).

43. Liang T'ing-nan, *I-fen wen-chi*, *YPCC*, VI, 14.

44. Kuo T'ing-i, *Chin-tai Chung-kuo shih*, II, 165–166; *CR*, 8:10–11 (1839–1840).

45. *CR*, 8:11–12, 76 (1839–1840); Gideon Nye, Jr., *Peking the Goal, the Sole Hope of Peace* (Canton, 1873), p. 37.

46. Lin, "JC," p. 23; *IWSM*, 7:30b–31, 36b.

47. This letter was more widely circulated than the first one. See *IWSM*, 7:33–36b. It is also printed in Lin, *CS*, in *YPCC*, II, 169–171; Kuo T'ing-i, *Chin-tai Chung-kuo shih*, II, 162–164. An English translation of the letter can be found in *CR* 8:497–503 (1839–1840); *The Canton Press*, January 11, 1840; Teng and Fairbank, *China's Response to the West*, pp. 24–27. There is a Chinese version as well as an English translation in Shuck, *Portfolio Chinensis*, pp. 128–149.

48. Lin, *CS*, in *YPCC*, II, 170; *CR*, 8:500 (1839–1840); Shuck, p. 140.

49. Lin, *CS*, in *YPCC*, II, 170; *CR*, 8:500 (1839–1840). Compare this statement with a passage in the *Analects of Confucius*: "Tzu Kung asked, saying 'Is there one word which may serve as a rule of practice for all one's life?' The Master said, 'Is not reciprocity such a word? What you do not want done to yourself, do not do to others' (chap. xxiii, bk. xv)."

50. Lin, *CS*, in *YPCC*, II, 170; *CR*, 8:501 (1839–1840); Shuck, p. 142.

51. Yuan Te-hui arrived at Malacca in the fall of 1825 and studied at the Anglo-Chinese college, where he and Hunter were schoolmates for sixteen months. Hunter

left Malacca for Canton at the end of 1826, and Yuan visited him there in the fall of 1827. See Hunter, *Fan-kwae*, p. 261. For further discussion of Yuan's competence in English, and that of Lin's other interpreters, see below.

52. Letter of Peter Parker, dated Canton, Nov. 29, 1839, American Board of Commissioners for Foreign Missions, South China, 1838–1844, Letters and Papers of the Board (MSS in Houghton Library, Harvard University), vol. 130, item 123.

53. *CR*, 8:485 (January 1840). Hill's account of the interview was reprinted in J. E. Bingham, *Narrative of the Expedition to China, from the Commencement of the War to the Present Period* (London 1842), I, 358–365.

54. FO 17/37, Leveson to Elliot, July 2, 1840; Lin, *HCL*, in *YPCC*, II, 361–362.

55. *The Canton Press*, March 21, 1840, quoted in *The Times* (London), July 4, 1840, p. 5.

56. G. W. Keeton, *The Development of Extraterritoriality in China* (London, 1928), I, 4. For a résumé of the principal criminal cases involving both foreigners and Chinese, see *ibid.*, pp. 27–46.

57. *Ibid.*, p. 37; Wesley R. Fishel, *The End of Extraterritoriality in China* (Berkeley, 1952), p. 7; Keeton, I, 43, 143, 147.

58. According to J. Lewis Shuck, first Baptist missionary to China, this proclamation was the first exception to the long-established and much-protested custom of communication through the hong merchants. See Shuck, p. 99.

59. Lin, *HCL*, in *YPCC*, II, 243. The passage quoted was translated by J. Robert Morrison, Chinese secretary and interpreter to Captain Elliot; see *PP: China Corr.*, p. 350. A slightly different English version was printed and circulated at the time. It rendered this quotation as "and ye foreigners who come to our central land to reside ought . . . to submit to our statutes as do the natives of China themselves." See American Board of Commissioners for Foreign Missions, Letters and Papers, vol. 130, item 29.

60. *PP: China Corr.*, pp. 395, 397.

61. *CR*, 8:19 (1839–1840).

62. *Shih-mao chien-t'u*, "to eat the food [lit., herbage] and tread the soil" was an allusion to the *Tso-chuan*, used by Lin Tse-hsü on many similar occasions. Under the seventh year of the reign of Duke Chao in the *Tso-chuan*, there appear two rhetorical questions: "Within the borders, which is not the emperor's land? Among those who feed on the herbage [meaning the grains, vegetables, etc., of the soil], who are not the subjects of the emperor?"

63. In late 1759 Flint was imprisoned at Macao for three years for having presented memorials through the Chinese officials at Ningpo and Tientsin. See Pritchard, "Crucial Years," pp. 130–131; Morse, *Chronicles*, V, 81–84.

64. Lin, *CS*, in *YPCC*, II, 149.

65. The emperor's determination to extirpate opium frequently found expression in his instructions to Lin. For example, see *YPCC*, II, 91, 94, 95; In a memorial received at court on July 8, 1839, Lin complained that the ineffectiveness of the coastal officials in driving away the intruding ships was partially due to their fear of Britain's prestige. See *IWSM*, 7:10b. On June 17, 1839, in the course of an interview, E. C. Bridgman gave Lin an account of British naval power and steam vessels. This seemed to be "unpalatable, and once or twice raised a frown on his brow." See *CR*, 8:77 (1839–1840).

66. Ch'en Li, *Tung-shu chi* (A collection of works by Ch'en Tung-shu; 1892), 5:30b.

67. This idea of Lin's is also more or less pointed out by G. W. Overdijkink in Chapter 3 of his book, *Lin Tse-hsü, Een Biographische Schets* (Leiden, 1938). H.

Kroes has a review of this work in which he summarizes Overdijkink's findings of Lin's primary policy at Canton: "Opium traffic had definitely to cease, but war was to be avoided. Being personally convinced that England did not wish a war with China, Lin believed that he could go pretty far in his demands." See *YJSS*, 3.1:118 (October 1940).

68. "Ya-p'ien tsou-an," p. 93.

69. *IWSM*, 10:10b. Teng T'ing-chen said much the same thing to the emperor in November 1838. See Wang Yen-wei, p. 26. As pointed out by T. F. Tsiang, the exhortation, the stopping of the trade, and the deprivation of the foreigners' servants and daily supplies were the effective weapons the Chinese had always resorted to in controlling foreigners. See Chiang T'ing-fu (T. F. Tsiang), "Chung-kuo yü chin-tai shih-chieh ti ta-pien-chü," p. 805.

70. Lin, *CS*, in *YPCC*, II, 181; *IWSM*, 10:5b.

71. An American trader, A. A. Low, wrote his sister, Mrs. Harriet Low Hillard, in London reporting that the hong merchants who had been expecting trouble were getting over their fears. See Elma Loines, ed., *The China Trade Post-Bag*, p. 68.

72. See Lin, "JC," pp. 8–9. In memory of their work together, Governor-General Teng composed a poem for Lin in 1844 that reveals that their early efforts in managing the maritime affairs aimed at "taming the barbarian chief"; and they frequently carried on their discussions of strategy late into the night, greatly taxing their "livers and kidneys." See Teng T'ing-chen, *Shuang-yen-chai shih-ch'ao*, in *YPCC*, II, 579.

73. Lin, "JC," p. 4; Liang T'ing-nan, *I-fen wen-chi*, *YPCC*, VI, 9.

74. Liang T'ing-nan, *I-fen chi-wen* (Shanghai, 1937), colophon by Meng Sen, p. 2. Liang T'ing-nan, *I-fen wen-chi*, in *YPCC*, VI, 9. There is a slight discrepancy in this statement among different editions of this work. While one hand-copied edition at Cornell University has "pertaining to maritime affairs," other versions state "pertaining to customs affairs." The former seems to be more appropriate in meaning and superior in style. That Liang T'ing-nan assisted Lin in his fight against opium is briefly stated in *YHKC*, 17:2. For a biographical sketch of Liang, see Hummel, I, 503–505.

75. Lin, "JC," p. 9; Hunter, *Fan-kwae*, p. 137. Lin's manner of examination was entirely un-Chinese. It was conducted with a tone of "great familiarity, and with a singular knowledge of his subject." He even managed to pick up some foreign vocabulary and often amazed his witness by the occasional use of English or Portuguese words. "Which is the largest opium dealer," he once asked a linguist, "Mr. Dent or Mr. Jardine? Is it true that Mr. Jardine is worth three millions of dollars?" The linguist replied: "No, perhaps one million more." See JM, Canton 553, Matheson to Jardine, May 1, 1839. Also see King, *Opium Crisis*, p. 18.

76. Lin, "JC," p. 9.

77. Jardine was well known to Peking. He was ordered to leave Canton by the court in 1837, but the hong merchants defended him and gave bonds that, if Jardine were later caught engaging in opium traffic, they were willing to be punished. It will be recalled that James Innes was found guilty of dealing in opium on Dec. 3, 1838, when the customs officers made a seizure of his opium immediately in front of his residence. Lin felt that the bonds given by the hong merchants could no longer be relied on. See *PP: China Corr.*, pp. 323, 324, 421; Lin, *HCL*, in *YPCC*, II, 241.

78. Lin, *HCL*, in *YPCC*, II, 240–242. J. Robert Morrison's translation of this edict is found in *PP: China Corr.*, pp. 352–355. The English version, while giving the correct Chinese date, gave a wrong Western date. On receiving this edict, the

hong merchants were very frightened. One of them said, "No have see so fashion before." Hunter, *Fan-kwae*, p. 138.

79. I have compared the official translation by Morrison, in *PP: China Corr.*, pp. 350–352, and the unofficial translation, found in American Board of Commissioners for Foreign Missions, Letters and Papers, vol. 130, item 29, no. 1, with the Chinese version in Lin, *HCL*, in *YPCC*, II, 242–244. At one place where Lin Tse-hsü adverts to the emperor's anger about the smuggling of opium, Morrison renders it: "Of this the Great Emperor having now heard, his wrath has been fearfully aroused, nor will *it* rest till the evil be utterly extirpated." It is the emperor who will not rest, not his wrath. The unofficial version is much more accurate on this point. Lin then goes on to notify the foreigners that he was especially given an imperial commissioner's *kuan-fang* (an oblong seal bestowed upon the emperor's trouble shooters), *the bearers of which had suppressed insurrections in vassal states, secured the outer frontier, and repeatedly performed meritorious services*, to come to deal with the opium problem. But Morrison incorrectly translated this passage as, "I, The High Commissioner, having my home in the maritime province of Fuhkeen, and, consequently, having early had intimate acquaintance with all the arts and shifts of the outer foreigners, *for this reason have been honoured by the Great Emperor with the full powers and privileges of 'a High Imperial Commissioner, who, having frequently performed meritorious services, is sent to settle the affairs of the outer frontier.'*" The unofficial translation is also in error.

Morrison translates the next passage: "But, reflecting that they are men from distant lands, and that they have not before been aware that the prohibition of opium is so severe, I cannot bear, *in the present plain enforcement of the laws and restrictions*, to cut them off without instructive monition." This is inaccurate. The unofficial version correctly renders it as, "but remembering that ye are foreigners from afar, and that hitherto ye may not have known that our laws are so severe, *I now clearly expound the statute to you*, not bearing to slay you without previous instructive warning." (All italics mine.)

80. Morrison also mistranslated this quotation as "has no benefit to derive from the purchase of your foreign commodities."

81. "Ya-p'ien tsou-an," p. 92.

82. *PP: China Corr.*, pp. 355, 356; Slade, pp. 38–39; Hunter, *Fan-kwae*, p. 138.

83. Slade, pp. 26, 27, 42.

84. *Ibid.*, pp. 32–33, 38.

85. *Ibid.*, pp. 34–38.

86. Lin, "JC," p. 9; Loines, *Post-Bag*, p. 68.

87. Slade, p. 42.

88. The hong merchants were: Howqua, Mowqua, Puankhequa, Samqua senior and junior, Poonhoyqua, Mingqua, Gowqua, Saoqua, Yetuck, Fontai, and Kingqua. See Slade, p. 43.

89. Slade, pp. 43–44.

90. *Ibid.*, pp. 45–46. An hour or two prior to the meeting, Howqua, the shrewd head of the hong merchants and life-long friend of Russell and Company, appeared in the company's office and requested John C. Green, chief of the house, to add 150 chests of opium to the quantity which the company intended to subscribe to the general contribution. Howqua promised to pay for this addition, a cost of $105,000, out of his own purse. Hunter, *Fan-kwae*, p. 139.

91. A. A. Low believes that the surrender of 1,036 chests was never reported to Commissioner Lin. Loines, *Post-Bag*, p. 68.

92. The firm of Dent and Company later surrendered 1,700 chests of opium to

the Chinese authority, an amount second only to that surrendered by Jardine, Matheson, 7,000 chests. Next to Dent, Russell surrendered 1,437 chests that were British property. See Morse, *Conflict*, p. 218, f.n. 17; William C. Hunter, "Journal of Occurrences at Canton during the Cessation of Trade, 1839" (MS in Boston Athenaeum), p. 4.

93. Lin, *HCL*, in *YPCC*, II, 244–245; Waley, *Opium War*, p. 35; Loines, *Post-Bag*, p. 68; *PP: China Corr.*, p. 365; Slade, p. 49.

94. Loines, *Post-Bag*, p. 69.

95. *PP: China Corr.*, pp. 365, 366.

96. Some foreigners were not entirely in sympathy with Dent, but probably did not expressly dissent from the community's feeling. See King, *Opium Crisis*, pp. 44–45. Low at the time (although he later modified his conviction) fully believed that Howqua's fears "were but too well grounded" and did not think Dent's "were so reasonable." See Loines, *Post-Bag*, p. 69.

97. Slade, pp. 50, 51.

98. *PP: China Corr.*, pp. 366, 367; Slade, p. 51. Among this group John Slade, editor of the *Canton Register*, had some command of the Chinese language. Samuel Fearon, Chinese interpreter to the General Chamber of Commerce, according to Nye, spoke Chinese fluently. It is strange that they should not have put their ability to use. See Slade, p. 42; Nye, *Peking the Goal*, p. 21; *PP: China Corr.*, pp. 365–367; Loines, *Post-Bag*, pp. 68–69; Morse, *Conflict*, p. 219; "Ya-p'ien tsou-an," p. 92.

99. Forbes, *Personal Reminiscences*, pp. 148, 349; Loines, *Post-Bag*, p. 69. At this time it became known to the foreign community that Commissioner Lin had hired a comprador and two cooks who were accustomed to foreign cuisine. This was understood to be intended for Dent should it be possible to induce him to come into the city. See JM, Canton 553, Matheson to Jardine, May 1, 1839.

100. Italics Elliot's; *PP: China Corr.*, p. 357.

101. *Ibid.*, p. 349.

102. JM, Canton 553, Matheson to Jardine, May 1, 1839; *PP: China Corr.*, p. 349.

103. *PP: China Corr.*, p. 356. Since the Union Jack could not be found at the moment, the boat's ensign was hoisted instead. Slade, pp. 52–53.

104. Hunter, "Journal," pp. 1–2.

105. *PP: China Corr.*, p. 357.

106. *A Digest of the Despatches on China with a connecting Narrative and Comments* (London, 1840), p. 81.

107. Liang T'ing-nan, *I-fen wen-chi*, in *YPCC*, VI, 11; King, *Opium Crisis*, p. 22; "Ya-p'ien tsou-an," pp. 92–93. The trade was actually stopped two days before, on March 22, when the three-day deadline was over. Five American and two British ships with full cargoes would have put out to sea on the 23rd, but were detained at Whampoa. See a letter addressed to Baring Brothers and Company by Russell and Company from Canton, dated April 10, 1839, Forbes Collection (MSS in Baker Library, Harvard University), case 1; also see Hunter, "Journal," p. 30.

108. Hunter, "Journal," p. 1; under another entry (April 14, p. 23) of Hunter's journal, however, the number of Chinese employees driven away was estimated at "over 400." See also *ibid.*, pp. 3, 5, 6, 11; *PP: China Corr.*, pp. 6–7, 11, 32, 37, 416.

109. Hunter, "Journal," pp. 5, 7–9; Loines, *Post-Bag*, p. 70; *PP: China Corr.*, p. 357.

110. The *Larne*'s gig was lent to Elliot by Blake since his own boat had been recently stolen. See FO 17/36, Capt. P. J. Blake to Naval Commander-in-Chief in

India, dated Macao, March 31, 1839. Also see Loines, *Post-Bag*, p. 71; Hunter, "Journal," p. 4, 9, 27.

111. Hunter, "Journal," pp. 2, 4, 16, 27.

112. Official figures of the number of foreigners confined in the factories are not readily available to me. It was given as two hundred by Earl Cranston and *Blackwood's Magazine*. Gideon Nye, Jr., said there were two hundred Europeans, presumably excluding the Parsees. Kuo T'ing-i agrees with Williams, saying that 275 foreigners were detained. Chiang T'ing-fu agrees with Hunter, giving it as 350. No authority was cited in any of the accounts. Pending the discovery of new evidence, I follow Hunter, for he was one of those confined. His report is not inconsistent with that of Nye, also a prisoner at the factories. See Cranston, pp. 42, 46; "War with China, and the Opium Question," *Blackwood's Edinburgh Magazine*, 47.293:372 (March 1840); Nye, *Peking the Goal*, p. 14; Kuo T'ing-i, *Chin-tai Chung-kuo shih*, II, 137; Williams, *The Middle Kingdom*, II, 500; Chiang T'ing-fu, *Chung-kuo chin-tai shih* (Chinese modern history; Hong Kong, 1954), p. 16; Hunter, "Journal," p. 24.

113. Loines, *Post-Bag*, p. 71; Hunter, "Journal," p. 5.

114. Although there were more men and boats at Whampoa, the British could probably muster no more than 250 men and 28 boats of all sorts to storm Canton; sufficient forces had to be left in Whampoa to look after the ships. The ships at Whampoa were all in "a state of defence and ready for sea." Captain Marquis of the *Reliance* was charged with the duty of commanding the fleet but he was "most earnestly and urgently enjoined" by Elliot to attempt nothing. On March 28, Elliot sent a message to Marquis saying that there need be no apprehension for the safety of British life and property. At the same time, Marquis was again reminded that in no circumstances should the boats of the British shipping move toward Canton except by a written order from Elliot. See FO 17/36, Blake to Naval Commander-in-Chief in India, dated Macao, April 1, 1839. Also see Hunter, "Journal," pp. 11–12, 17, 20, 27, 58.

115. *Ibid.*, pp. 21–22, 26, 28, 29–30, 31.

116. Loines, *Post-Bag*, p. 71.

117. Hunter, "Journal," pp. 2, 23–25; Hunter, *Fan-kwae*, pp. 143–144.

118. See JM, Canton 553, Matheson to Jardine, May 1, 1839. Also Hunter, "Journal," pp. 2, 3, 5, 13.

119. Letter from Russell and Company to Baring Brothers, dated Canton, April 10, 1839, Forbes Collection (MSS in Baker Library, Harvard University), case 1; Hunter, "Journal," p. 13.

120. Hunter, "Journal," pp. 5–6, 21, 26–28, 30; Lin, "JC," p. 12; Lin, *HCL*, in *YPCC*, II, 277, 278; *PP: China Corr.*, p. 389.

121. *PP: China Corr.*, p. 357; Lin, *HCL*, *in YPCC*, II, 245; Forbes *Personal Reminiscences*, p. 146; Hunter, "Journal," p. 1.

122. "Ya-p'ien tsou-an," p. 93; Hunter, "Journal," p. 5; *PP: China Corr.*, p. 358.

123. Nye, *Peking the Goal*, p. 15; Hunter, "Journal," pp. 6, 9, 10, 19, 27, 28, 31, 33, 34–35; Hunter, *Fan-kwae*, p. 142; Nye, *Peking the Goal*, p. 16; FO 17/36, P. J. Blake to Naval Commander-in-Chief in India, dated Macao, March 31, 1839. Also see *PP: China Corr.*, p. 358.

124. Lin, *HCL*, in *YPCC*, II, 279; FO 17/35, John Abel Smith to Sir Alexander Johnston, Sept. 10, 1839, encl.; Hunter, "Journal," p. 36; *CR*, 8:18 (1839–1840). On the 22nd, the remaining detainees were set free and four days later Elliot arrived at Macao with other British merchants. See FO 17/36, Blake to Admiral Maitland, May 31, 1839.

125. Hunter, "Journal," p. 17; King, *Opium Crisis*, p. 45; Loines, *Post-Bag*, p. 71.
126. See Appendix D.
127. "Ya-p'ien tsou-an," p. 92; Chiang T'ing-fu, "Tao-kuang ch'ao *Ch'ou-pan i-wu shih-mo*," p. 8.
128. Lin, *HCL*, in *YPCC*, II, 252–253. Elliot assailed Lin for falsely giving Elliot's intention to escape with Dent as the cause for the confinement when he wrote Palmerston on April 6, and he stated that, since the 19th, all intercourse between Canton, Whampoa, and the outside anchorages was stopped and since the 21st no passage boats had been allowed to run. See *PP: China Corr.*, p. 385. Elliot was correct. But he could also have pointed out that the Chinese servants, compradors, cooks, etc., were not ordered to leave the factories, an immediate blockade was not imposed, and other extraordinary measures were not adopted until Elliot's arrival on the evening of March 24, when reports reached the Chinese authorities alleging that Elliot had attempted to help Dent escape. JM, Canton 553, Matheson to Jardine, May 1, 1839. Also see Hunter, "Journal," p. 20; *PP: China Corr.*, p. 388.

Chapter VI. Opium Smoke and War Clouds

1. FO 17/30, Elliot to Palmerston, dated Macao, March 22, 1839.
2. *PP: China Corr.*, pp. 355–356, 360–364.
3. *Ibid.*, p. 356; FO 17/31, Elliot to Palmerston, dated Canton, March 30, 1839.
4. *PP: China Corr.*, p. 349.
5. The Chinese received this document at or shortly before 1 A.M. See Lin, *HCL*, in *YPCC*, II, 247; *PP: China Corr.*, pp. 267, 368, 371.
6. *PP: China Corr.*, pp. 367–369.
7. Hunter, "Journal," p. 11.
8. *PP: China Corr.*, pp. 367–368.
9. Lin, *HCL*, in *YPCC*, II, 247, 250; *PP: China Corr.*, pp. 387–388, 397.
10. *PP: China Corr.*, pp. 370, 372; Hunter, "Journal," p. 4.
11. Lin, *HCL*, in *YPCC*, II, 248–250. This document was not included in *PP: China Corr.*, but an English translation can be found in Shuck, pp. 100–117, and Slade, pp. 60–62.
12. The Chinese term *t'ien-tao* is translated as "the Tao of Heaven," "natural law," and "cosmic energy" in William E. Soothill and Lewis Hodous, *A Dictionary of Chinese Buddhist Terms* (London, 1937), p. 147. It is translated as "Providence" and "the way of Heaven" in Mathews' *Chinese-English Dictionary*. See Lin, *HCL*, in *YPCC*, II, 248–250; Slade, pp. 60–62.
13. Lin, *HCL*, in *YPCC*, II, 250. This proclamation was enclosed in an edict from Lin to Elliot, dated March 26, 1839. Lin asked him to translate it into English to be circulated among the foreign merchants. He also ordered the hong merchants to post a copy at the factories. See *ibid.*, p. 248. An English version of the document can be seen in Shuck, pp. 102ff.
14. Williams, *The Middle Kingdom*, II, 501.
15. The notice stated: "Now I, the said Chief Superintendent, thus constrained by paramount motives affecting the safety of the lives and liberty of all the foreigners here present in Canton, and by other very weighty causes, do hereby, in the name and on the behalf of Her Britannic Majesty's Government, enjoin and require all Her Majesty's subjects now present in Canton, forthwith to make a surrender to me, for the service of Her said Majesty's Government, to be delivered over to the Government of China, of all the opium belonging to them or British opium under their controul . . . and I . . . do now, in the most full and unreserved

manner, hold myself responsible, for and on the behalf of Her Britannic Majesty's Government, to all and each of Her Majesty's subjects surrendering the said British-owned opium into my hands to be delivered over to the Chinese Government . . .

"And it is specially to be understood that the proof of British property and value of all British opium surrendered to me agreeably to this notice, shall be determined upon principles, and in a manner hereafter to be defined by Her Majesty's Government." See *PP: China Corr.*, p. 374.

16. *Ibid.*, p. 375; Lin, "JC," p. 10.

17. Slade, pp. 42–45.

18. See Elliot's first protest of March 25, 1839, in *PP: China Corr.*, p. 367. On the evening of the 24th, shortly after his arrival, speaking to all the foreign merchants in Canton, with Howqua and Mowqua present, Elliot exclaimed, "I will remain with you to my last gasp. Thank God we have a British man of war — small indeed she is — outside, commanded by a British officer. . . . I would also observe that two American frigates are hourly expected, and I confidently rely upon the cordial support and co-operation of their captains in this emergency." Slade, p. 54. The two American frigates alluded to were the *Columbia* and the *John Adams*. See Hunter, "Journal," p. 12.

19. FO 17/36, Captain Blake to Admiral Maitland, April 1, 1839. S. W. Williams, one of the detainees, wrote that "it could not be honestly said that the lives of foreigners were in jeopardy" (*The Middle Kingdom*, II, 502–503).

20. "Chinese Affairs," *Quarterly Review*, 65.13:553 (March 1840).

21. *PP: China Corr.*, pp. 343–345.

22. Russell and Company to John M. Forbes, Canton, March 4, 1839, Forbes Collection, case 1.

23. Slade, p. 36.

24. *PP: Correspondence relative to the Actual Value of the Opium Delivered Up to the Chinese Authorities in 1839* (1843), p. 6. Russell and Company estimated that 21,000 chests from Calcutta and 30,000 chests from Bombay were scheduled to come to China, an estimate much higher than Elliot's. See Russell and Company to John M. Forbes, cited in note 22 above. The *Quarterly Review*'s remarks on Elliot's decision to deliver up the opium were quite to the point: "An immediate market for the whole quantity — the purchaser Her Majesty's Superintendent, — the paymaster the Chancellor of the Exchequer." See "Chinese Affairs," p. 555.

25. Slade, p. 59; Forbes, *Personal Reminiscences*, pp. 160, 351; Hunter, "Journal," p. 13 (April 5, 1839).

26. JM, Canton 553, Matheson to Jardine, May 1, 1839.

27. "Chinese Affairs," p. 552.

28. *PP: China Corr.*, pp. 358, 377, 380.

29. Lin, *HCL*, in *YPCC*, II, 255; *PP: China Corr.*, pp. 381, 383, 384, 386–387.

30. Lin, "JC," pp. 10–11; Hunter, "Journal," p. 12.

31. The capacity of each opium ship was from 800 to 1300 chests. See Nathan Allen, *An Essay on the Opium Trade* (Boston, 1850), p. 53; Lin, *HCL*, in *YPCC*, II, 261–263.

32. Hunter, "Journal," p. 14; *IWSM*, 6:15, 27a–b; Lin, "JC," pp. 11–16.

33. Lin, "JC," pp. 12, 15; Hunter, "Journal," p. 27; *IWSM*, 6:27b; *PP: China Corr.*, p. 428.

34. This edict was included in Lin, *HCL*, in *YPCC*, II, 265–266.

35. *Ibid.*, p. 273.

36. Lung-hsueh being too far from the Bogue, Commissioner Lin gave an order

on April 14 that opium ships should proceed to the Sha-chiao offing where the opium was to be received. See Lin, "JC," p. 12.

37. Lin was not entirely exaggerating. Forbes wrote that "some of the opium dealers actually boasted of the manner in which they had manufactured opium for Commissioner Lin!" However, he explained, this was not done to any great extent. See Forbes, *Personal Reminiscences*, p. 160.

38. In his edict to Elliot dated April 21, Lin complained that only one of these four ships arrived at Sha-chiao, and it refused to deliver its opium; the other three sailed away from Lintin toward the south. Lin's accusation was not without ground. Aside from the four ships in question, several of the opium ships that did report to surrender each had less than a hundred chests aboard. The *Bombay* surrendered 15 chests, the *Coral* 47, the *Thistle* 50, and the *Nymph* 80 chests. At the end of May, Captain Blake commented on the delivery of the opium by saying that it was "loudly clamoured" that many opium ships on the east coast "either had not been recalled, or had *private* orders not to return if they were making a better market by their present pursuits." This was confirmed by a letter of Elliot to the Earl of Aberdeen, dated Nov. 10, 1843, in which he stated: "The unquestionable fact is, that sales had become active outside towards the close of the delivery at Chuenpee, and hence the difficulty of completing my arrangement." See Lin, *HCL*, in *YPCC*, II, 275; "A List of the Names of Vessels Surrendering Opium at Chuenpee," in FO 17/32, Elliot to Palmerston, dated Macao, July 8, 1839, encl. 1, p. 55; FO 17/36, Blake to Admiral Maitland, May 30, 1839; *PP: Correspondence relative to the Difference between the Number of Chests of Opium undertaken to be Surrendered by Heerjeebhoy Rustumjee, and the Number of Chests actually Surrendered by Heerjeebhoy Rustumjee* (1845), p. 14.

39. Lin, *HCL*, in *YPCC*, II, 272–276.

40. Thom accompanied Johnston in his mission as Chinese interpreter. See Slade, p. 73.

41. Lin, *HCL*, in *YPCC*, II, 277–278; Lin, "JC," p. 13; Hunter, "Journal," pp. 31–32.

42. Lin, *HCL*, in *YPCC*, II, 278–279; Lin, "JC," p. 13.

43. The figure was derived from a total of Lin's daily account in his diary. A small portion of this amount was in bags. See Lin, "JC," pp. 12–15.

44. Lin, *HCL*, in *YPCC*, II, 279–280. *CR*, 8:14 (1839–1840), had a brief and quite accurate account of the dispute.

45. Hsueh Ch'eng-ch'ing, "Ya-p'ien chan-shih ti erh-ko hsiao-wen-t'i" (Two small problems in the history of the Opium War), "Shih-ti chou-k'an," No. 102, in *TKP* (Sept. 11, 1936), p. 11.

46. *PP: China Corr.*, pp. 375, 428.

47. *Ibid.*, p. 414; *IWSM*, 8:11b; Lin, *HCL*, in *YPCC*, II, 283–284.

48. "Ya-p'ien tsou-an," pp. 101, 102. The memorial was received by the emperor on June 10. See *IWSM*, 6:26, 27b.

49. Ch'eng Wei-hsin, "Tu Ch'en Kung-lu chu Chung-kuo chin-tai-shih" (A review of Ch'en Kung-lu's *Chung-kuo chin-tai-shih*), in Li Ting-i et al., eds., *Chung-kuo chin-tai-shih lun-ts'ung* (A collection of articles on modern Chinese history; Taipei, 1957), 1st ser., I, 249; "Ya-p'ien tsou-an," p. 99.

50. *IWSM*, 7:20, 6:14.

51. "Ya-p'ien tsou-an," p. 102.

52. Estimated by Williams (*The Middle Kingdom*, II, 503). The value of the opium surrendered was estimated at from two to three million sterling by the opium holders. See their memorial to Palmerston dated Canton, May 23, 1839, in

PP: China Corr., p. 418; Michie estimated its value at upwards of two million sterling and Warren at 2.4 million sterling. See Alexander Michie, *The Englishman in China During the Victorian Era* (London, 1900), I, 53, and Samuel Warren, *The Opium Question* (London, 1840), p. 1.

53. The dispatch was dated Canton, April 22, 1839. *PP: China Corr.*, pp. 390-391.

54. *IWSM*, 6:15b, 16.

55. "Ya-p'ien tsou-an," p. 94; *IWSM*, 6:16, 18b-20.

56. A complete copy of this memorial is included in KYLT, 2:[8-11]. The *IWSM* version (6:18b-20) is much abridged.

57. *IWSM*, 6:20a-b; "Ya-p'ien tsou-an," p. 104.

58. Lin, "JC," pp. 16-17, 18-19; "Ya-p'ien tsou-an," pp. 107-108.

59. There is a mysterious discrepancy regarding the number and dimensions of the trenches. Lin's report, dated June 13, stated that he built two trenches, each measuring approximately over 150 by 150 *ch'ih*; whereas Bridgman and King, who carefully inspected the work, gave quite different data. See *IWSM*, 7:7b; *CR*, 8:70-77 (1839-40); *Supplement to the Singapore Free Press*, July 25, 1839.

60. Lin, *CS*, in *YPCC*, II, 159; Lin, "JC," p. 19.

61. *CR*, 8:74 (1839-40).

62. *IWSM*, 7:6-9b. An English translation of this memorial is in P. C. Kuo, pp. 243-247.

63. Lin, "JC," p. 21. This memorial reached the emperor on July 28. See *IWSM*, 7:18-20. An English translation is in P. C. Kuo, pp. 247-250.

64. *IWSM*, 7:19-20b.

65. *Ibid.*, pp. 18b-19.

66. Charles Gutzlaff, *The Life of Taou-Kwang* (London, 1852), p. 160. Gutzlaff died on Aug. 9, 1851, at Hong Kong (see *ibid.*, p. vii). Gutzlaff also charged that in Commissioner Lin's time the prison of Canton was filled "with wretches falsely denounced as opium-smokers" (*ibid.*, p. 160). He did not realize that opium smoking was one thing for which a person could hardly be falsely convicted. Lin in his very early memorials during the great debate on opium pointed out that suspects should be left alone without opium for a day, from morning until midnight. Those who could stand it would be pronounced innocent; those who could not overcome the craving for the drug would be considered smokers. Thus it would not even be necessary to hold a trial. See Lin's memorial in *IWSM*, 2:25-26. Gutzlaff seemed to be too involved with the opium dealers to be objective. As previously mentioned, he accompanied Jardine's clipper *Sylph* as interpreter on a voyage to Shanghai and Tientsin to sell opium. Thereafter he continued to be of service along the coast for some years. James Innes, one of the most active opium smugglers, once wrote: "I would give a thousand dollars for three days of Gutzlaff." See Greenberg, pp. 139, 140.

67. "Chinese Affairs," p. 556.

68. *CR*, 8:70 (1839-40); *IWSM*, 7:18b.

69. *The Rupture with China, and its Causes* (London, 1840), p. 21.

70. "Chinese Affairs," p. 556.

71. Lin, "JC," pp. 18-20; Lin, *CS*, in *YPCC*, II, 160.

72. John W. Edmonds, *Origin and Progress of the War between England and China* (New York, 1841), p. 14.

73. The letter is dated Macao, Sept. 7, 1839; American Board of Commissioners for Foreign Missions, Letters and Papers, vol. 130, item 55.

74. *A Digest of the Despatches on China with connecting narrative and Comments* (London, 1840), p. 213.

75. "China," *Dublin University Magazine*, 40.89:589 (May 1840).

76. This view was presented in *Hunt's Merchants' Magazine*, 1.4:362 (October 1839).

77. See comments by A. A. Low and the *Dublin University Magazine* supporting such views in Loines, *Post-Bag*, p. 72, and "China," p. 589.

78. Elliot to Palmerston, dated Canton, April 6, 1839, *PP: China Corr.*, p. 387; Slade, p. 54.

79. *PP: China Corr.*, p. 343. To avoid the suspicion of taking Elliot's quotation out of its context, I must point out that the "traffic" discussed here means the opium smuggling on the Canton River inside the Bogue. To me it seems to be a logical conclusion of Elliot's remarks that, once the Chinese government was irked into action by the traffic inside the Bogue and took the unavoidable next step of adopting harsh measures to stop the traffic outside the Bogue (at Lintin, Nan-ao, and on the Fukien coast), these harsh measures would also be justified.

80. Slade, p. 52.

81. *PP: China Corr.*, p. 258. This instruction was worded with the typical skill of a nineteenth-century statesman. Its ostensible purpose was to aim at restraining Elliot from any action that would assist the opium smugglers in violating Chinese laws. However, Palmerston was well aware that the English smugglers, with their superior vessels and arms, could probably take care of themselves should any skirmishing take place between them and the Chinese.

82. *PP: China Corr.*, pp. 233, 309, 349, 362, 364.

83. *Ibid.*, p. 358.

84. *Ibid.*, pp. 385, 386.

85. *IWSM*, 5:17b, 6:12; "Ya-p'ien tsou-an," p. 92. The memorial reached the emperor on May 2, 1839.

86. Lin, *HCL*, in *YPCC*, II, 242, 243.

87. *PP: China Corr.*, p. 392.

88. Letter from Russell and Company to Baring Brothers and Company, dated Canton, April 10, 1839, Forbes Collection, case 1; *PP: China Corr.*, p. 418; Gutzlaff, p. 160.

89. *CR*, 8:454, 327 (1839–40). The English in this bond, though full of errors, is still intelligible, except for the part that reads, "so if there are distinguish between good and bad . . ." The Chinese version of the bond, perhaps done by one of Lin's interpreters, is clear but not in good style. According to the Chinese version, the part quoted above should mean "so that the good can be distinguished from the evil." See Lin, *HCL*, in *YPCC*, II, 331. Another bond similar to this one is in *ibid.*, p. 321.

90. *Ibid.*, pp. 323, 343.

91. *PP: China Corr.*, pp. 385, 387, 392–394, 397–398; Lin, *HCL*, in *YPCC*, II, 260, 263; Slade, p. 73.

92. *PP: China Corr.*, pp. 395–396.

93. Slade, pp. 74–78; Hunter, "Journal," pp. 18–19.

94. Hunter, "Journal," pp. 16, 18–19.

95. Letter from Russell and Company to Baring Brothers and Company, dated Canton, April 10, 1839, Forbes Collection, case 1.

96. Lin, "JC," p. 11; Nye, *Peking the Goal*, pp. 22–23; Hunter, "Journal," p. 19.

97. *PP: China Corr.*, p. 397.

98. See his memorial dated Oct. 6, 1839. Lin, *CS*, in *YPCC*, II, 184. This memorial reached the emperor on October 29. See *IWSM*, 8:22–23.

99. *PP: China Corr.*, p. 397.

100. *CR*, 8:13–14 (1839–40).

101. Hunter, "Journal," p. 29; *PP: China Corr.*, pp. 390, 401; *CR*, 8:12 (1839–40). Under the date April 22, Elliot wrote Palmerston: "Yesterday the Hong merchants brought me a direct address under the seals of the High Commissioner, the Governor, and Lieut.-Governor, reiterating the demand for the bond. I tore it up at once." He made a mistake on the date — he received the address on the 20th, not the 21st.

102. *PP: China Corr.*, pp. 385, 390, 406–407.

103. Before Elliot left Macao for Canton, he wrote the governor of Macao on March 22 requesting protection from sudden attack by the Chinese. He was assured of full protection to British lives and property, with the exception of opium traders. See *PP: China Corr.*, p. 408.

104. *Ibid.*, pp. 363, 403, 406, 411–412.

105. *CR*, 8:20–21 (1839–40); Nye, *Peking the Goal*, p. 26.

106. *PP: China Corr.*, pp. 410, 411, 417; Lin, *HCL*, in *YPCC*, II, 296; Nye, *Peking the Goal*, p. 31.

107. Lin, *HCL*, in *YPCC*, II, 297; *PP: China Corr.*, p. 417.

108. *CR*, 8:24–25 (1839–40); *PP: China Corr.*, pp. 404–405, 391, 410–411; Nye, *Peking the Goal*, pp. 29–30.

109. *IWSM*, 7:32b; Lin, *CS*, in *YPCC*, II, 176.

Chapter VII. The Coming of the War and the Fall of Lin

1. *PP: China Corr.*, pp. 387, 389, 409.

2. *Ibid.*, pp. 390, 391.

3. See his dispatch to Palmerston dated Canton, May 6, 1836, *ibid.*, pp. 405, 410.

4. FO 17/31 Elliot to Backhouse (private) May 30, 1839, partially quoted in Costin, *Great Britain and China*, p. 59.

5. "Chinese Affairs," *Quarterly Review*, p. 560.

6. JM, Canton 553, Matheson to Jardine, May 1, 1839.

7. *PP: China Corr.*, pp. 418–420. Williams' comment on this memorial was that it recapitulated the aggressive acts of the Chinese government, "but nothing was said in it of their own unlawful acts . . . no allusion to the causes of these acts of aggression." Williams, *The Middle Kingdom*, II, 504; *PP: China Corr.*, pp. 384, 391.

8. Slade, pp. 142–144.

9. Some of the publications can be found in my bibliography. Seven pamphlets were reviewed in the *Quarterly Review*, 65.130:537–581 (March 1840); "On the China and the Opium Question," *Blackwood's Edinburgh Magazine*, p. 718; "Chinese Affairs," p. 572.

10. *PP: Memorials Addressed to Mer Majesty's Government by British Merchants Interested in the Trade with China* (1840), pp. 1, 2, 3, 6, 7, 5, 10.

11. See the records of the Foreign Office during this period, e.g., FO 17/35 and 36.

12. FO 17/35, Jardine to Palmerston, Oct. 26, 1839. See also Fairbank, *Trade and Diplomacy*, I, 82.

13. FO 17/35, Jardine to Palmerston, Oct. 27, 1839.

14. FO 17/36, John Abel Smith et al. to Palmerston, Nov. 2, 1839 (appendix).

15. *PP: China Corr.*, pp. 193*–194* (distinguish from pp. 193–194); Costin, pp. 59–60.

16. FO 17/36, Palmerston to the Lords of the Admiralty (secret), Nov. 4, 1839.

Copies of this communication were sent to Captain Elliot and Sir J. Hobhouse of the India Board.

17. Quoted in Fairbank, *Trade and Diplomacy*, I, 83, and Greenberg, pp. 214–215.

18. See the interesting discussion by Mervyn Armstrong, "Palmerston and the Opium War," *Shih-hsüeh nien-pao* (Historical annual), 1.1:x (July 1929).

19. Nye, *Peking the Goal*, p. 32; Slade, pp. 112, 113, 121–122.

20. Cited in Earl Cranston, "The American Missionaries' Outlook on China, 1830–1860" (diss. Harvard University, 1930), p. 45.

21. "Chinese Affairs," pp. 558–559.

22. Lin, "JC," p. 22; Lin, *CS*, in *YPCC*, II, 177.

23. Letter of S. W. Williams, dated Macao, August 29, 1839, American Board of Commissioners for Foreign Missions, Letters and Papers, vol. 130, item 174. According to a letter from A. W. Elmslie (brother of Elliot's secretary), who was stationed in China with the navy, the affray was touched off by the sailors' throwing stones at the temple. See FO 17/35, A. W. Elmslie to William Elmslie, Jr. (in London), Sept. 3, 1839. The letter was communicated to the Foreign Office by William Elmslie. Another report from China stated: "A party of 30 sailors having landed made an unprovoked attack on a village of friendly Chinese; in which an unfortunate man was killed, and very many of both sexes were desperately wounded. An attempt was made by Capt. Elliot to hush the matter up, by a payment of about $2000 to the relatives of the deceased." See FO 17/36, Larpent to Palmerston, encl., November 16, 1839.

24. FO 17/32, Elliot to Palmerston, July 18, 1839; *PP: China Corr.*, pp. 154, 440.

25. FO 17/32, Elliot to Jardine, Matheson & Co., encl. 1 in Elliot to Palmerston, July 18, 1839; also see *PP: China Corr.*, p. 432.

26. Lin, *CS*, in *YPCC*, II, 177; *PP: China Corr.*, pp. 434, 442.

27. The grand jury consisted of a group of eminent merchants including J. H. Astell, W. Bell, George T. Braine, and James Matheson. See *Canton Press*, Aug. 17, 1839.

28. FO 17/32, Elliot to Palmerston, August 27, 1839; also see *PP: China Corr.*, pp. 433, 441.

29. Ouchterlony, *The Chinese War*, p. 21; *PP: China Corr.*, p. 433.

30. *PP: China Corr.*, pp. 231–232, 294–296, 317–318.

31. *CR*, 8:181, 214–215 (1839–40).

32. Lin, "JC," p. 26; Lin, *CS*, in *YPCC*, II, 177; *PP: China Corr.*, p. 433, 435, 436.

33. *Ibid.*, p. 437. After some investigation, Elliot did not believe the atrocity was done by order of the government; it was merely an act of the pirates. See *ibid.*, pp. 434, 435, 436.

34. Lin, *CS*, in *YPCC*, II, 178; *IWSM*, 8:5a–b.

35. Lin, "JC," p. 28.

36. Lin, *CS*, in *YPCC*, II, 183–184; *IWSM*, 8:13b.

37. *PP: China Corr.*, pp. 434, 443, 445–446.

38. *Ibid.*, p. 447; *IWSM*, 8:14b, 431.

39. *PP: China Corr.*, p. 448; *IWSM*, 8:14b.

40. FO 17/35, A. W. Elmslie to William Elmslie, Jr., Sept. 5, 1839.

41. *IWSM*, 8:15a–b; *PP: China Corr.*, pp. 446–447. It is highly doubtful that Lin, Teng, and Kuan deliberately wanted to deceive the emperor on the report of the battles. These officials depended on the lower officers for such information, and as a rule the latter often exaggerated British casualties. Lin did not mention this clash in his diary, but in mid-November he recorded several "great victories" that were not substantiated by current British accounts and were obviously untrue. These

were also reported to the emperor. If Lin did not sincerely believe in them, he would not have recorded them in his diary, which was kept for himself and was not published until 1954. Cf. *IWSM*, 8:15–22, and Lin, "JC," p. 37.

42. *IWSM*, 16b–17; *CR*, 8:427–428 (1839–40). From mid-September to the end of October, the subprefect of Macao and Elliot entered into an extensive correspondence. The demands and answers were mostly repetitions of old arguments. Elliot went as far as to agree that all British ships should undergo a thorough search by the Chinese at Sha-chiao, and he increased the reward for the conviction of the murderer of Lin Wei-hsi to two thousand dollars. But he would not agree to the signing of the bonds prescribed by Commissioner Lin, which was one of Lin's basic prerequisites for the resumption of trade. See *PP: Additional Papers relating to China*, pp. 11, 24.

43. *PP: Additional correspondence relating to China*, p. 9.

44. *CR*, 8:324 (1839–40). This agreement was said to apply only to the ships actually present in China, not to those that might arrive thereafter. However, there is no evidence in Chinese sources to corroborate the existence of such an agreement.

45. Elliot's letter to Smith stated: "I have this day received a communication from the weiyuen [deputy] and keunmin foo [subprefect of Macao], containing the violation of the agreement to conduct the trade outside the port of Canton, lately submitted directly to me under the signets of the high commissioner and governor. Their excellencies now peremptorily require the delivery of the murderer of Lin Weihe, and the entrance of the ships at Whampoa, with the signature of the bond of consent; or their departure from these coasts in three days, under menaces of destruction. This shameless proceeding of the government is obviously attributable to the entrance of the ship Thomas Coutts, and the belief of the mandarins that their possession of hostages will enable them to constrain us into the acceptance of conditions incompatible with the honour of the British crown, and the safety of the queen's subjects." *Ibid.*, p. 328.

46. *Ibid.*, p. 381.

47. *PP: Additional Correspondence*, pp. 9, 11; *CR*, 8:328 (1839–40).

48. Cranston, appendix A, pp. 300ff; *CR*, 8:78–83, 434 (1839–40); *IWSM*, 8:30b; *PP: Additional Correspondence*, p. 13.

49. *IWSM*, 9:2b, 9:4b; *The Times* (London), Nov. 12, 1840, p. 3.

50. Compare this amount with the total import of Chinese tea to England in 1837, which amounted to 30,625,206 pounds, and the average annual import of the eight-year period beginning with 1830, which was 34,449,095 pounds. See *Memorials Addressed to Her Majesty's Government by British Merchants Interested in the Trade with China*, p. 16; *The Times*, Nov. 11, 1840, p. 5; *ibid.*, Sept. 9, 1840, p. 5.

51. Forbes, *Personal Reminiscences*, pp. 149–150.

52. Letter from J. M. Forbes to Robert B. Forbes, dated Milton, December 20, 1839, Forbes Collection, V. F–8, p. 50.

53. Slade, pp. 124–126.

54. Forbes, pp. 148, 159.

55. Letter from Joseph Coolidge, Jr., to Augustine Heard, dated Canton, Dec. 13, 1839, Heard Papers (MSS in Baker Library, Harvard University), V. EM-12.

56. Hunter, *Fan-kwae*, p. 146; *CR*, 8:457 (1839–40); Forbes, p. 151.

57. Letter from Coolidge to Heard (see note 55).

58. Forbes, pp. 151, 155; Slade, p. 117.

59. *Singapore Free Press*, April 9, 1840, quoted in *The Times*, July 4, 1840; Cranston, pp. 56–57.

60. *PP: China Corr.*, p. 431; reports of Teng T'ing-chen (as governor-general of Fukien and Chekiang), in *IWSM*, 11:1–3b, 5; *The Times*, Oct. 5, 1840, p. 4.

61. *IWSM*, 11:3b–4; *CR*, 8:442, 648 (1839–40); *The Times*, Nov. 11, 1840, p. 5.

62. *The Times*, Nov. 11, 1840, p. 4; Nov. 13, 1840, p. 3.

63. JM, Chusan 1, Robert Thom to James Matheson, July 15, 1840; *The Times*, Dec. 8, 1840, p. 5; [Robert] Jocelyn, *Six Months with the Chinese Expedition; or Leaves from a Soldier's Note-Book* (London, 1841), p. 55.

64. *IWSM*, 12:9; *The Times*, Dec. 8, 1840, p. 5.

65. JM, Chusan 1. For an interesting account of some of Gutzlaff's Chinese assistants, see Waley, *Opium War*, pp. 235–243.

66. Hsia Nai, "Ya-p'ien chan-cheng-chung ti T'ien-chin t'an-p'an" (The Tientsin negotiations during the Opium War), *Wai-chiao yueh-pao* (Foreign affairs), 4.4:45 (Apr. 15, 1934); T. F. Tsiang, "China and European Expansion," p. 9.

67. Hsia Nai, "Ya-p'ien chan-cheng-chung," 4.5:120 (May 15, 1934); *IWSM*, 12:30; *The Times*, Jan. 7, 1841, p. 3; Jocelyn, pp. 110, 116.

68. Chiang T'ing-fu, "Tao-kuang ch'ao *Ch'ou-pan i-wu shih-mo*," p. 8.

69. *IWSM*, 7:20, 8:9b–10, 17–18; 9:4b–5, 18a–b; 10:34, 40b; 11:4, 9–10; 12:4b, 5b, 8, 11, 14b, 22; 14:39; 5:11b–12. For the last few years of Lin's life, see Kuo T'ing-i, *Chin-tai Chung-kuo shih-shih jih-chih*, I, 107, 109; *ibid.*, II, 145, 165, 166; *Ch'ing-shih* (History of the Ch'ing dynasty; Taipei, 1951), VI, 4547–4549.

70. Hsia Nai, "Ya-p'ien chan-cheng-chung," 4.4:49. Hsia Nai also rejected the view that the emperor was influenced by Governor-General Ch'i-shan, for when the emperor began to adopt a soft policy toward the British, Ch'i-shan was still freely advocating the stringent approach (*ibid.*, p. 50).

71. *Ch'ing-shih*, VI, 4513; Hsia Nai, "Ya-p'ien chan-cheng-chung," 4.4:53; Gutzlaff, p. 24.

72. For instance, read this comment: "We are satisfied that a very different mode of connexion is now ripe for development, and cannot be much retarded. Let it be remembered, that ninety years ago our sole connexion with India was mercantile. Army we had none, beyond a few files of musketeers for oriental pomp, and otherwise requisite as a local police. Territory we had none, beyond what was needed for our cows, pigs, and a cabbage garden. Nor had we any scheme of territorial aggrandizement in those days, beyond what was strictly necessary as a means of playing into our commercial measures, were it by the culture of indigo for instance, and other experimental attempts, or with a view to more certain lines of transit and of intercourse, unfettered by hostile custom-houses. What was it that changed that scene? A quarrel with a native prince. By his atrocities, we were forced into ambitious thoughts. It happens too often in such countries — that to murder is the one sole safeguard against being murdered; insurrection the remedy beforehand against monstrous oppression; and, not to be crushed by the wheels of the tiger-hearted despot, you must leap into his chariot, and seize the reins yourself." "Canton Expedition and Convention," *Blackwood's Edinburgh Magazine*, 50.313:687 (November 1841).

73. *PP: Additional Papers*, p. 5.

74. "Ya-p'ien tsou-an," p. 92.

75. *YPCC*, II, 569.

76. "Chinese Affairs," p. 571; "The Opium and the China Question," p. 724.

BIBLIOGRAPHY

Listed below are the principal Chinese, Japanese, and Western sources that I have consulted or cited.

WESTERN SOURCES

Address to the People of Great Britain, Explanatory of Our Commercial Relations with the Empire of China, and of the Course of Policy by Which It May be Rendered an Almost Unbounded Field for British Commerce, by a visitor to China [Mr. Gordon]. London: Smith, Elder and Co., 1836; 127 pp.

Allen, Nathan. *An Essay on the Opium Trade.* Boston: John P. Jewett and Co., 1850; 68 pp.

American Board of Commissioners for Foreign Missions, South China, 1838-1844. Letters and Papers of the Board. Deposited in Houghton Library, Harvard University.

Anglo-Chinese Calendar, 1831 and 1834 issues. Canton: Office of the Chinese Repository.

Armstrong, Mervyn. "Palmerston and the Opium War," Shih-hsueh nien-pao (Historical annual), 1.1:vi-x (July 1929).

Bernard, W. D. *Narrative of the Voyage and Services of the Nemesis from 1840 to 1843, and of the Combined Naval and Military Operations in China.* 2 vols.; London, 1844; 960 pp.

Bingham, John Elliot. *Narrative of the Expedition to China, from the Commencement of the War to the Present Period.* 2 vols.; London, 1842; 395 and 424 pp.

Bridgman, E. C. *A Chinese Chrestomathy in the Canton Dialect.* Macao, 1841; 698 pp.

Brief Observations Respecting the Pending Disputes with the Chinese, and a Proposal for Bringing Them to a Satisfactory Conclusion. London: J. Ridgway, 1840; 15 pp.

Britton, Roswell S.   The Chinese Periodical Press, 1800-1912.
   Shanghai: Kelly and Walsh, 1933.

Brunnert, H.S. and V.V. Hagelstrom.   Present Day Political Organization
   of China, tr. A. Beltchenko and E.E. Moran.   Shanghai: Kelly
   and Walsh, 1912; 572+81 pp.

Bullock, T.H.   The Chinese Vindicated, or Another View of the Opium
   Question; Being in Reply to a Pamphlet by Samuel Warren.
   London: Allen, 1840; 120 pp.

"Canton Expedition and Convention," Blackwood's Edinburgh Magazine,
   50. 313:677-688 (Nov. 1841).

Canton Press, The.   1835-1844.

Canton Register and Price Current, The.   1827-1843.

Chang Hsin-pao.   "Ya-p'ien chan-cheng" (The Opium War), in John K.
   Fairbank and Mary C. Wright, eds., "Documentary Collections
   on Modern Chinese History," Journal of Asian Studies, 17.1:60-66
   (Nov. 1957).

Chang Hsi-t'ung.   "The Earliest Phase of the Introduction of Western
   Political Science into China," Yenching Journal of Social Studies,
   5. 1:1-29 (July 1950).

Chao Feng-t'ien.   "An Annotated Bibliography of Chinese Works on the
   First Anglo-Chinese War," Yenching Journal of Social Studies,
   3. 1:61-103 (Oct. 1940).

Chen Ching-Jen (Ch'en Ch'in-jen).   "Opium and Anglo-Chinese Relations,"
   Chinese Social and Political Science Review, 19:386-437 (1935-1936).

Chen, Gideon (Ch'en Ch'i-t'ien).   Lin Tse-hsü, Pioneer Promoter of the
   Adoption of Western Means of Maritime Defense in China.   Peiping:
   Yenching University Press, 1934; 65 pp.

Ch'en Kuan-sheng (Kenneth Ch'en).   "The Growth of Geographical
   Knowledge concerning the West in China during the Ch'ing Dynasty."
   M.A. thesis, Yenching University, 1934.

------"Hai-lu," Monumenta Serica, 7:208-226 (1942).

"China," The Dublin University Magazine, 40. 89:579-594 (May 1840).

"China: Its Early History, Literature, and Language; Mistranslation
   of Chinese Official Documents; Causes of the Present War," The
   Westminster Review (American ed.), 34. 67:127-141 (Sept. 1840).

274

"Chinese Affairs," The Quarterly Review, 65.130:537-581 (Mar. 1840).

Chinese Repository, see CR.

Ch'iu, A. K'aiming. "Chinese Historical Documents of the Ch'ing Dynasty, 1644-1911," Pacific Historical Review, 2:324-336 (1932).

Chu Shih-chia. "Chinese Documents in the United States National Archives," Far Eastern Quarterly, 9.4:377-383 (Aug. 1950).

Collis, Maurice. Foreign Mud. London: Faber and Faber, Ltd., 1946; 318 pp.

"Commerce of China," Hunt's Merchants' Magazine, 3.6:465-481 (Dec. 1840).

Costin, W.C. Great Britain and China, 1833-1860. Oxford University Press, 1937; 362 pp.

CR: Chinese Repository, ed. E.C. Bridgman and S. Wells Williams. Macao or Canton, monthly; 1832-1851.

Cranston, Earl. "The American Missionaries' Outlook on China, 1830-1860." Ph.D. thesis, Harvard University, 1930; 327 pp.

Danton, George H. The Culture Contacts of the United States and China: The Earliest Sino-American Culture Contacts, 1784-1844. New York, 1931; 133 pp.

Davis, Sir John Francis. China During the War and Since the Peace. 2 vols.; London, 1852; 327 and 342 pp.

------China: A General Description of That Empire and Its Inhabitants, with the History of Foreign Intercourse down to the Events which Produced the Dissolution of 1857. New ed., rev. and enlarged; 2 vols.; London, 1857; 480 and 428 pp.

Dennett, Tyler. Americans in Eastern Asia. New York, 1922; 725 pp.

Description of the City of Canton: With an Appendix Containing an Account of the Population of the Chinese Empire, Chinese Weights and Measures, and the Imports and Exports of Canton. 2nd ed.; Canton, 1839.

De Vargas, Ph. "William C. Hunter's Books on the Old Canton Factories. Yenching Journal of Social Studies, 2.1:91-117 (July 1939).

Digest of the Despatches on China with Connecting Narrative and Comments. London, 1840; 240 pp.

Downing, C. Toogood. The Fan-Qui in China in 1836-7. 3 vols.; London, 1837; 316, 306, and 327 pp.

Eames, James Bromley. The English in China, Being an Account of the Intercourse and Relations between England and China from the Year 1600 to the Year 1843, and a Summary of Later Developments. London: Sir Isaac Pitman and Sons, 1909; 622 pp.

Edkins, J. Chinese Currency. Shanghai, 1901; 151 pp.

Edmonds, John W. Origin and Progress of the War between England and China: A Lecture Delivered before the Newburgh Lyceum, Dec. 11, 1841. New York, 1841; 24 pp.

Fairbank, John K. "Tributary Trade and China's Relations with the West," Far Eastern Quarterly, 1.2:129-149 (Feb. 1942).

------Trade and Diplomacy on the China Coast: The Opening of the Treaty Ports, 1842-1854. 2 vols.; Cambridge, Mass.: Harvard University Press, 1953; 489 and 88 pp.

Fairbank, John K. and Masataka Banno. Japanese Studies of Modern China: A Bibliographical Guide to Historical and Social-Science Research on the 19th and 20th Centuries. Rutland, Vermont, 1955; 329 pp.

------and Kwang-Ching Liu. Modern China, A Bibliographical Guide to Chinese Works, 1898-1937. Cambridge, Mass.: Harvard University Press, 1950; 608 pp.

------and S.Y. Teng. "On the Transmission of Ch'ing Documents," Harvard Journal of Asiatic Studies, 4.1:12-46 (May 1939).

------and S.Y. Teng. "On the Ch'ing Tributary System," Harvard Journal of Asiatic Studies, 6.2:135-246 (June 1941).

Fishel, Wesley R. The End of Extraterritoriality in China. Berkeley: University of California Press, 1952; 318 pp.

FO 17: Foreign Office, General Correspondence, China (key number FO 17). Filed in the Public Record Office, London.

Forbes Collection. MSS deposited in Baker Library, Harvard University.

Forbes, Robert B. Remarks on China and the China Trade. Boston, 1844; 80 pp.

------Personal Reminiscences. 3rd ed. rev.; Boston, 1892; 412 pp.

Fox, Grace. British Admirals and Chinese Pirates, 1832-1869. London: Kegan Paul, Trench, Trubner and Co. , Ltd. , 1940; 227 pp.

Fry, William Storrs. Facts and Evidence relating to the Opium Trade with China. London, 1840; 64 pp.

Gaskill, Gussie Esther. "A Chinese Official's Experiences during the First Opium War, " The American Historical Review, 39.1:82-86 (Oct. 1933).

Giles, Herbert A. A Glossary of References on Subjects Connected with the Far East. Hongkong, Shanghai, and London, 1886; 283 pp.

"Great Britain at the Commencement of the Year 1843, " Blackwood's Edinburgh Magazine, 53. 327:1-23 (Jan. 1843).

Greenberg, Michael. British Trade and the Opening of China, 1800-42. Cambridge, England: The University Press, 1951; 221 pp.

Gutzlaff, Charles. The Life of Taou-Kwang, Late Emperor of China, with Memoirs of the Court of Peking; Including a Sketch of the Principal Events in the History of the Chinese Empire during the Last Fifty Years. London, 1852; 280 pp.

Hall, John W. "Notes on the Early Ch'ing Copper Trade with Japan, " Harvard Journal of Asiatic Studies, 12. 3:444-461 (Dec. 1949).

Hall, Ronald Ascott. Eminent Authorities on China. London, 1931; 275 pp.

Hummel, Arthur W. "Correspondence regarding William C. Hunter, " Yenching Journal of Social Studies, 2. 2:294-295 (Feb. 1940).

------, ed. Eminent Chinese of the Ch'ing Period. 2 vols.; Washington, D. C.: Government Printing Office, 1943, 1944; 1103 pp.

Hunter, William C. "Journal of Occurrences at Canton during the Cessation of Trade, 1839. " MS, in Boston Athenaeum; 37 pp.

------The "Fan-Kwae" at Canton before Treaty Days, 1825-1844. London, 1882; 160 pp.

------Bits of Old China. Shanghai, 1911; 280 pp.

Hunt's Merchants' Magazine, or The Merchants' Magazine and Commercial Review. New York, 1839-1870.

Jardine, Matheson and Co. Archives. Deposited in the University
Library, Cambridge, England.

Jocelyn, Robert, Viscount. Six Months with the Chinese Expedition,
or Leaves from a Soldier's Note-Book. London, 1841; 155 pp.

Kann, Eduard. The Currencies of China: An Investigation of Silver
and Gold Transactions Affecting China, with a Section on Copper.
Shanghai: Kelly and Walsh, 1927; 562 pp.

Keeton, G.W. The Development of Extraterritoriality in China. 2 vols.;
London, 1928; 405 and 422 pp.

Kerr, J.G. "Opium and the Smoking Extract," The China Review,
12.1:41-47 (July-Aug. 1883).

[King, Charles W.] Opium Crisis: A Letter Addressed to Charles
Elliot, Esq., Chief Superintendent of the British Trade with
China. London: 1839 (letter dated Macao 29 May 1839); 82 pp.

Kuo, P.C. A Critical Study of the First Anglo-Chinese War. Shanghai:
Commercial Press, 1935; 315 pp.

Latourette, Kenneth Scott. The Great Century in Northern Africa and
Asia, A.D. 1800-1914. London, n.d.; 502 pp. Vol. 6 of his
A History of the Expansion of Christianity.

Lindsay, H. Hamilton. Is the War with China a Just One? London,
1840; 40 pp.

[------] Remarks on Occurrences in China. London, 1840; 103 pp.

Liu Shih-shun. Extraterritoriality: Its Rise and Its Decline (Studies in
History, Economics and Public Law, Vol. 118, No. 2).
Columbia University, 1925; 227 pp.

Ljungstedt, Andrew. "History of Macao, a Portuguese Settlement in
China, Comprehending the Most Remarkable Events from Its
Commencement to the Introduction of a Constitutional Government
in 1822, and Sketches of Its Foreign Relations, with Plans and
Engravings." MS in the British Museum; preface dated Macao,
November 1822.

Lockart, J.H. Stewart. The Currency of the Farther East, from the
Earliest Times up to 1895. Hong Kong, 1907; 223 pp.

Loines, Elma, ed. The China Trade Post-Bag of the Seth Low Family of Salem and New York, 1829-1873. Manchester, Maine: Falmouth Publishing House, 1953; 324 pp.

Lubbock, Alfred Basil. The China Clippers. 2nd ed.; Glasgow, 1914; 387+23 pp.

------The Opium Clippers. Boston: Lauriat Co., 1933; 392 pp.

McCulloch, John Ramsay. A Dictionary, Practical, Theoretical, and Historical, of Commerce and Commercial Navigation. New ed., corrected and improved, with a supplement; 2 vols.; London, 1854; 1484 pp.

Mackenzie, Alexander. A History of the Mathesons. 2nd ed.; London, 1900; 162 pp.

McPherson, D. Two Years in China, Narrative of the Chinese Expedition from Its Formation in April 1840 till April 1842. London, 1842; 391 pp.

Marx, Francis. Report of the East India Committee of the Colonial Society on the Causes and Consequences of the Military Operations in China. London, 1843; 109 pp.

Mason, Mary Gertrude. Western Concepts of China and the Chinese, 1840-1876. New York, 1939; 288 pp.

Matheson, James. The Present Position and Prospects of the British Trade with China. London: Smith, Elder and Co., 1836; 80 pp.

Mayers, William Frederick. The Chinese Government: A Manual of Chinese Titles, Categorically Arranged and Explained with an Appendix. 3rd ed.; Shanghai, 1897; 196 pp.

Medical Missionary Society in China, The. London: Royston and Brown, 1839.

Michie, Alexander. The Englishman in China during the Victorian Era. 2 vols.; London, 1900; 442 and 510 pp.

Morrison, Eliza. Memoirs of the Life and Labours of Robert Morrison, D.D. 2 vols.; London, 1839; 551 and 543 pp.

Morrison, John Robert. A Chinese Commercial Guide, Consisting of a Collection of Details respecting Foreign Trade in China. Canton, 1834; 2nd ed., rev. by S. Wells Williams (Macao, 1844), 279 pp.; 3rd and 4th eds. (Canton: Office of the Chinese Repository, 1848 and 1856); 5th ed., see Samuel Wells Williams.

Morse, Hosea Ballou. The Trade and Administration of the Chinese Empire. London and New York, 1908; 451 pp.

------The International Relations of the Chinese Empire: The Period of Conflict 1834-1860. Shanghai, 1910; 727 pp.

------Chronicles of the East India Company Trading to China, 1635-1834. Vols. 1-4 (Oxford, 1926), 305, 435, 388, and 427 pp.; Vol. 5 (Oxford, 1929), 212 pp.

------The Gilds of China. 2nd ed.; London and New York, 1932; 111 pp.

Munro, Neil Gordon. Coins of Japan. London, 1905; 281 pp.

"Narrative of a Voyage Round the World, during the Years 1835, 36, and 37, Including a Narrative of an Embassy to the Sultan of Muscat, and the King of Siam, by W.S.W. Ruschenberger," The Edinburgh Review, 68:46-75 (1838-1839).

Nye, Gideon Jr. Tea and the Tea Trade. 3rd ed.; New York, 1850; 56 pp.

------The Morning of My Life in China. Canton, 1873; 73 pp.

------Peking the Goal: The Sole Hope of Peace. Canton, 1873; 104 pp.

------The Opium Question and the Northern Campaigns. Canton, 1875; 108 p

O'Byrne, William R. A Naval Biographical Dictionary: Comprising the Life and Services of Every Living Officer in Her Majesty's Navy, from the Rank of Admiral of the Fleet to That of Lieutenant, Inclusive. London, 1849; 1400 pp.

"On the China and the Opium Question," Blackwood's Edinburgh Magazine, 47.296:847-853 (June 1840).

"Opium and the China Question, The," Blackwood's Edinburgh Magazine, 47.296:717-731 (June 1840).

Ouchterlony, John. The Chinese War: An Account of All the Operations of the British Forces from the Commencement to the Treaty of Nanking. 2nd ed.; London, 1844; 522 pp.

Overdijkink, G.W. Lin Tse-hsü, Een Biographische Schets. Leiden: E.J. Brill, 1938; 173 pp.

Owen, David Edward. British Opium Policy in China and India. New Haven: Yale University Press, 1934; 399 pp.

Parker, Edward Harper, tr.   Chinese Account of the Opium War.
Shanghai, 1888; 82 pp.   A translation of Wei Yuan, Sheng-wu
chi (1878 ed.), last two chapters.

Parker, Peter.   The Hospital Reports of the Medical Missionary Society
in China for the Year 1839.   Canton, 1840; 22 pp.

Parliamentary Papers, see PP.

Parshad, I. Durga.   Some Aspects of Indian Foreign Trade, 1757-1893.
London, 1932; 238 pp.

Peake, Cyrus H.   "Documents Available for Research on the Modern
History of China," American Historical Review, 38:61-67 (1932).

Pew, William A.   China's Struggle for Nationhood.   Salem, Mass.,
1927; 16 pp.

Philip, Robert.   The Life and Opinions of the Rev. William Milne, D.D.,
Missionary to China.   London: John Snow, 1840.

Phipps, John.   A Practical Treatise on the China and Eastern Trade:
Comprising the Commerce of Great Britain and India, Particularly
Bengal and Singapore, with China and the Eastern Islands.   In-
cluding Much Useful Information, and Many Interesting Particulars
Relative Thereto; with Directions, and Numerous Statements and
Tables, Adapted to the Use of Merchants, Commanders, Pursers,
and Others, Connected with the Trade of China and India.   Calcutta,
1835; 338+85 pp.

PP: Parliamentary Papers (Blue Books).

> Opium Trade.   1832; 173 pp.
>
> Papers Relative to the Establishment of a Court of Judicature
> in China.   1838; 9 pp.
>
> Correspondence Relating to China.   1840; 458 pp.
>
> Papers Relating to China.   1840; 52 pp.
>
> Additional Correspondence Relating to China.   1840; 14 pp.
>
> Additional Papers Relating to China.   1840; 12 pp.
>
> Report from the Select Committee on the Trade with China.   1840.
>
> Correspondence Relative to the Actual Value of the Opium
> Delivered up to the Chinese Authorities in 1839.   1843; 11 pp.
>
> Correspondence Relative to the Difference between the Number
> of Chests of Opium Undertaken to be Surrendered by

Heerjeebhoy Rustumjee, and the Number of Chests Actually
Surrendered by Heerjeebhoy Rustumjee. 1845; 45 pp.

Pritchard, Earl H. "Anglo-Chinese Relations during the Seventeenth
and Eighteenth Centuries," University of Illinois Studies in the
Social Sciences, 17.1-2:1-244 (March-June 1929).

------"The Crucial Years of Early Anglo-Chinese Relations, 1750-1800,"
Research Studies of the State College of Washington, 4.3-4:95-442
(Sept.-Dec. 1936).

Remer, Charles Frederick. The Foreign Trade of China. Shanghai,
1926; 269 pp.

Review of the Management of Our Affairs in China, since the Opening of
the Trade in 1834; With an Analysis of the Gov't Despatches from
the Assumption of Office by Capt. Elliot, on the 14th December,
1836, to the 22nd of March, 1839. London: Smith, Elder, and
Co., 1840; 217 pp.

Richard, L. Comprehensive Geography of the Chinese Empire and
Dependencies, tr. M. Kennelly. Shanghai, 1908; 713 pp.

Rupture with China, and Its Causes; Including the Opium Question
and Other Important Details; in a Letter to Lord Viscount
Palmerston, The, by a Resident in China. London: Sherwood,
Gilbert, and Piper, 1840; 60 pp.

Sargent, A.J. Anglo-Chinese Commerce and Diplomacy. Oxford,
1907; 332 pp.

Scott, John Lee. Narrative of a Recent Imprisonment in China after
the Wreck of the Kite. London, 1841; 131 pp.

See Chong-su. Foreign Trade of China. New York, 1919; 451 pp.

Shen Wei-tai. China's Foreign Policy, 1839-1860. New York, 1932;
197 pp.

Shuck, J. Lewis. Portfolio Chinensis, or A Collection of Authentic
Chinese State Papers Illustrative of the History of the Present
Position of Affairs in China with a Translation, Notes and
Instruction. Macao, 1840; 191 pp.

Sketch of Lord Napier's Negociations with the Authorities at Canton,
A, extracted from Asiatic Journal (Aug. 1837). London:
J. L. Cox and Sons, 1837; 16 pp.

Slade, John. Notices on the British Trade to the Port of Canton, with Some Translations of Chinese Official Papers Relative to That Trade. London: Smith, Elder, and Co. , 1830; 104 pp.

------Narrative of the Late Proceedings and Events in China. Canton Register Press, preface dated Macao, Apr. 23, 1840; 183+75 pp.

Statement of Claims of the British Subjects Interested in Opium Surrendered to Captain Elliot at Canton for the Public Service. London, 1840; 209 pp.

Staunton, Sir George Thomas. Remarks on the British Relations with China, and the Proposed Plans for Improving Them. London, 1836.

Steiner, W. H. and Eli Shapiro. Money and Banking. 3rd ed. ; New York, 1956; 855 pp.

Stelle, Charles C. "American Trade in Opium to China, 1821-39, " Pacific Historical Review, 10:57-74 (Mar. 1941).

Stephens, H. Morse. "The Administrative History of the British Dependencies in the Further East, " American Historical Review, 4. 2:246-272 (Jan. 1899).

Stifler, Susan Reed. "Language Students of the East India Company's Canton Factory, " Journal of the North China Branch of the Royal Asiatic Society, 69:46-82 (1938).

Swisher, Earl. China's Management of the American Barbarians: A Study of Sino-American Relations, 1841-1861, with Documents. New Haven, 1951; 844 pp.

Teng, S. Y. Chang Hsi and the Treaty of Nanking, 1842. Chicago: University of Chicago Press, 1944; 191 pp.

Teng, S. Y. and J. K. Fairbank. China's Response to the West. 2 vols. ; Cambridge, Mass.: Harvard University Press, 1954; 296 and 84 pp.

Thelwall, Rev. A. S. The Iniquities of the Opium Trade with China. London, 1839; 178 pp.

Tilley, John A. C. and Stephen Gaselee. The Foreign Office. London and New York: G. P. Putnam's Sons, Ltd. , 1933; 335 pp.

Times, The. London, 1838-1841.

Tripathi, Amales. Trade and Finance in the Bengal Presidency, 1793-1833. Bombay, Calcutta, and Madras: Orient Longmans, 1956; 289 pp.

Tsiang, T. F. (Chiang T'ing-fu). "The Government and the Co-Hong of Canton, 1839," Chinese Social and Political Science Review, 15.4:602-607 (Jan. 1932).

------"China and European Expansion," Politica (London), 2.5:1-18 (Mar. 1936).

Turner, F. S. British Opium Policy and Its Results to India and China. London, 1876; 308 pp.

Wagel, Srinivas R. Chinese Currency and Banking. Shanghai: North-China Daily News and Herald, Ltd., 1915; 457 pp.

Waley, Arthur. The Opium War through Chinese Eyes. London: George Allen and Unwin, 1958; New York: Macmillan Company, 1959; 257 pp.

"War with China, and the Opium Question," Blackwood's Edinburgh Magazine, 47.293:368-384 (Mar. 1840).

Warren, Samuel. The Opium Question. London, 1840; 130 pp.

Webster, Sir Charles. The Foreign Policy of Palmerston, 1830-41: Britain, the Liberal Movement and the Eastern Question. 2 vols.; London, 1951; 914 pp.

Wharton, Francis. "East India, and the Opium Trade," Hunt's Merchants' Magazine, 4.1:9-22 (Jan. 1841).

Williams, Samuel Wells. The Middle Kingdom: A Survey of the Geography, Government, Education, Social Life, Arts, Religion, etc., of the Chinese Empire and its Inhabitants. 2 vols.; London, 1848 and 1883; 1204 pp.

------The Chinese Commercial Guide, Containing Treaties, Tariffs, Regulations, Tables, etc., Useful in the Trade to China and Eastern Asia; With an Appendix of Sailing Directions for Those Seas and Coasts. 5th ed.; Hong Kong: A Shortrede and Co., 1863; 266 pp.; earlier eds., see John Robert Morrison.

Wood, Herbert John. "Prologue to War: Anglo-Chinese Conflict 1800-1834." Ph.D. thesis, University of Wisconsin, 1938; 471+25 pp.

Wu Wen-tsao. The Chinese Opium Question in British Opinion and Action. New York, 1928; 190 pp.

A Ying 阿英 , comp. Ya-p'ien chan-cheng wen-hsueh chi 鴉片戰
　　爭文學集 (A collection of Opium War literature). 2 vols.;
　　Peking, 1957; 1010 pp.

Chang Chung-fu 張忠紱. "Ya-p'ien chan-cheng-ch'ien Ch'ing-t'ing
　　pan-li wai-chiao chih chi-kuan yü shou hsü" 鴉片戰爭前清
　　廷辦理外交之機關與手續 (The office and pro-
　　cedure for dealing with diplomatic affairs of the Ch'ing dynasty
　　before the Opium War); Wai-chiao yueh-pao 外交月報
　　(Foreign affairs), 2.2:1-7 (Feb. 1933).

Chang Te-ch'ang 張德昌. "Ch'ing-tai ya-p'ien chan-cheng ch'ien
　　chih Chung-Hsi yen-hai t'ung-shang" 清代鴉片戰爭前
　　之中西沿海通商 (Maritime trade between China and
　　the West before the Opium War in the Ch'ing dynasty); Ch'ing-
　　hua hsueh-pao 清華學報 (Tsing Hua journal), 10.1:97-145
　　(1935).

Ch'en Ch'i-t'ien 陳其田 (Gideon Chen). Shan-hsi p'iao-chuang
　　k'ao-lueh 山西票莊考略 (A brief historical study of the
　　Shansi banks). Shanghai: Commercial Press, 1937; 198 pp.

Ch'en Ch'iu 陳鏊. "Ya-p'ien chan-cheng Chung-wen shu-mu chieh-
　　t'i" 鴉片戰爭中文書目解題 (An annotated bibliography
　　of Chinese works on the Opium War); Shih-hsueh nien-pao 史
　　學年報 (Historical annual), 3.2:174-177 (Dec. 1940).

Ch'en K'ang-ch'i 陳康祺. Lang-ch'ien chi-wen 郎潛紀聞
　　(Memoirs of a retired gentleman). 16 chüan in 12 ts'e;
　　preface 1880.

Ch'en Li 陳澧. Tung-shu chi 東塾集 (A collection of works by Ch'en Tung-shu). 6 chüan; 1892.

Ch'en Lu 陳陸. "Ya-p'ien chan-cheng yü Chung-kuo chün-ch'i" 鴉片戰爭與中國軍器 (The Opium War and Chinese weapons); Chung-ho yueh-k'an 中和月刊 (Chung-ho monthly), 1.8:76-92 (Aug. 1940).

Ch'eng Wei-hsin 程維新. "Tu Ch'en Kung-lu chu Chung-kuo chin-tai-shih" 讀陳恭祿著中國近代史 (A review of Ch'en Kung-lu's Chung-kuo chin-tai-shih); in Li Ting-i et al., eds., Chung-kuo chin-tai-shih lun-ts'ung, I, 237-250.

Chiang Hsiang-nan 蔣湘南. Ch'i-ching-lou wen-ch'ao 七經樓文鈔 (Collected works of Chiang Hsiang-nan). 1920 ed.

Chiang-shang chien-sou, see Hsia Hsieh.

Chiang T'ing-fu (T. F. Tsiang) 蔣廷黻. "Ch'i-shan yü ya-p'ien chan-cheng" 琦善與鴉片戰爭 (Ch'i-shan and the Opium War); Ch'ing-hua hsueh-pao, 6.3:1-26 (Oct. 1931).

------"Chung-kuo yü chin-tai shih-chieh ti ta-pien-chü" 中國與近代世界的大變局 (China and the great changes of the modern world); Ch'ing-hua hsueh-pao, 9.4:783-827 (Oct. 1934).

------"Tao-kuang ch'ao Ch'ou-pan i-wu shih-mo chih shih-liao ti chia-chih" 道光朝籌辦夷務始末之史料的價值 (The value of the Ch'ou-pan i-wu shih-mo of the Tao-kuang reign); Ch'ing-hua chou-k'an 清華周刊 (Tsing Hua weekly), 37.9:5-14 (1936).

------Chung-kuo chin-tai shih 中國近代史 (Chinese modern history). Changsha: Commercial Press, 1938; reprinted 1954 in Hong Kong by Li-ta ch'u-pan she 立達出版社; 126 pp.

------, comp. Chin-tai Chung-kuo wai-chiao shih-liao chi-yao 近代中國外交史料輯要 (Selected materials on modern Chinese diplomatic history). 2 vols.; Shanghai: Commercial

Press, 1932-1934; 413 and 584 pp.

Ch'ien Chia-chü (Chein Chea-Chu) 千家駒. "I-ko li-shih shih-shih ti hsin-k'an-fa" 一個歷史事實的新看法 (The Opium War seen from a new angle); Chung-shan wen-hua chiao-yü-kuan chi-k'an 中山文化教育館季刊 (Quarterly review of the Sun Yat-sen Institute for Advancement of Culture and Education), 2.3:789-799 (1935).

------"Tung-yin-tu kung-ssu ti chieh-san yü ya-p'ien chan-cheng" 東印度公司的解散與鴉片戰爭 (The dissolution of the East India Company and the Opium War); Ch'ing-hua chou-k'an, 37.9-10:61-81 (1936).

Ching-pao 京報 (Peking gazette).

Ch'ing-shih 清史 (History of the Ch'ing dynasty), ed. Chang Ch'i-yun 張其昀 et al. 8 vols.; Taipei: National War College in association with the Institute of Chinese Culture, 1961.

Ch'ing-shih kao, see CSK.

Ch'ing-shih lieh-chuan 清史列傳 (Biographical series of the History of the Ch'ing dynasty). 80 chüan; Shanghai: Chung Hua Book Co., 1928.

Ch'ing-tai wai-chiao shih-liao 清代外交史料 (Documents on the foreign relations of the Ch'ing dynasty). Peiping: Palace Museum, 1931-1933. Chia-ch'ing period (1796-1820), 6 ts'e; early Tao-kuang period (1821-1835), 4 ts'e.

"Ch'ing Tao-kuang ch'ao kuan-shui an" 清道光朝關稅案 (Documents on the customs duties of the Tao-kuang period); Shih-liao hsün-k'an 史料旬刊 (Historical materials published thrice monthly), No. 31. Peiping: Palace Museum, 1931.

Chou Chi-hua 周際華. "Ts'ung-cheng-lu (Hai-ling)" 從政錄 (海陵) (Records during term of office as magistrate of T'ai-

chou, Kiangsu; in chüan 2 of Chia-yin-t'ang hui-ts'un 家蔭堂
彙存 (Collected works of Chou Chi-hua; 7 chüan in 8 ts'e,
1839, reprinted 1858).

Ch'ou-pan i-wu shih-mo, see IWSM.

Chu Yun 朱橒, comp. Yueh-tung ch'eng-an ch'u-pien 粵東成案
初編 (Criminal and civil cases decided in the province of
Canton, first series). 38 chüan and a supplementary chüan;
printed by the provincial government, 1832.

Chung-kuo shih-hsueh lun-wen so-yin 中國史學論文索引
(An index to articles on history), comp. Department of History,
Peking University, and the Institute of History, the Academy
of Science. Vol. 1, Peking, 1957; 421 pp.

CSK: Ch'ing-shih kao 清史稿 (Draft history of the Ch'ing dynasty),
comp. Chao Erh-hsün 趙爾巽. 536 chüan; preface 1927.

CSL: Ta-Ch'ing li-ch'ao shih-lu 大清歷朝實錄 (Veritable
records of successive reigns of the Ch'ing dynasty. Photo-
offset ed. by Manchoukuo Kuo-wu-yuan (Manchukuo Council of
State Affairs), 1937; 4485 chüan.

Etō Shinkichi 衛藤瀋吉. "Ahen sensō izen ni okeru Eikoku shōnin
no seikaku" 阿片戰爭以前における英國商人の
性格 (Activities of the British "country traders" in China
before the Opium War); Tōyō bunka kenkyūjo kiyō 東洋文化研
究所紀要 (Bulletin of the Institute for Oriental Culture),
3:5-80 (June 1952).

Fan Wen-lan 范文瀾. Chung-kuo chin-tai shih 中國近代史
(Modern Chinese history), Vol. 1. Rev. ed.; Peking: Hsin-hua,
1949; 543 pp.

Hatano Tarō 波多野太郎, comp. "Saikin Chūgoku rekishi gaku
rombun yōmoku" 最近中國歷史學論文要目

288

(A list of more important recent articles on Chinese history);
in Yokohama daigaku ronsō 橫濱大學論叢 (Bulletin of the
Yokohama City University Society), Vol. 3, No. 3 (1951).

Hsia Hsieh 夏燮 (pseud. Chiang-shang chien-sou 江上蹇叟).
Chung-Hsi chi-shih 中西紀事 (A record of Sino-Western
affairs). 24 chüan in 8 ts'e; first preface Tao-kuang 30, 12th
month (1851), second preface to rev. ed. 1859, last preface 1865.

Hsia Nai 夏鼐 (pseud. Tso-min 作民). "Pai-nien ch'ien ti Chung-
Ying i-mu ch'ung-t'u" 百年前的中英一幕衝突
(The Anglo-Chinese conflict of 1834); Kuo-wen chou-pao 國聞
週報 (National news weekly), 11.16:[31-38] (1934).

------"Ya-p'ien chan-cheng-chung ti T'ien-chin t'an-p'an" 鴉片戰
爭中的天津談判 (The Tientsin negotiations during the
Opium War); Wai-chiao yueh-pao, 4.4:43-56 (Apr. 15, 1934);
ibid., 4.5:95-123 (May 15, 1934).

------"Tao-kuang ch'ao Ch'ou-pan i-wu shih-mo ting-wu i-tse" 道光
朝籌辦夷務始末訂誤一則 (The correction of certain
mistakes in Ch'ou-pan i-wu shih-mo for the Tao-kuang period);
Ch'ing-hua chou-k'an, 39.7:605-612 (1936).

Hsiao I-shan 蕭一山. Ch'ing-tai t'ung-shih 清代通史 (General
history of the Ch'ing period). 2 vols.; Shanghai, 1928; 929 pp.

Hsieh Ch'ing-kao 謝清高. Hai-lu 海錄 (A maritime record).
2 chüan; preface ca. 1820 by Yang Ping-nan 楊炳南; reprinted
at least six times between 1870 and 1936.

Hsieh Hsing-yao 謝興堯. "Ya-p'ien chan-ch'ien chih Chung-Ying
wai-chiao" 鴉片戰前之中英外交 (Diplomatic
relations between Great Britain and China before the Opium
War); I-ching pan-yueh k'an 逸經半月刊 (Semi-monthly
of modern history), 15:4-10 (1936).

Hsueh Ch'eng-ch'ing 薛澄清. "Ya-p'ien chan-shih ti erh-ko hsiao-
        wen-t'i" 鴉片戰史的二個小問題 (Two small problems
        in the history of the Opium War); "Shih-ti chou-k'an" 史地周
        刊 (Historical and geographical weekly), No. 102, in Ta-kung pao
        大公報 (Sept. 11, 1936), p. 11.

Hsü Ch'iu 許球. "Ch'ing chin ya-p'ien shu" 請禁鴉片疏 (A
        memorial requesting the prohibition of opium). Incomplete
        text in Hsia Hsieh, Chung-Hsi chi-shih, reprinted in Ya-p'ien
        chan-cheng, I, 475; English tr. in Chinese Repository, 3:390-398
        (1834-1835).

Hsü K'uan-hou 徐寬厚. "Ya-p'ien huo-hua ch'u-shih" 鴉片禍華
        初史 (The early history of the opium evil in China); "Shih-
        ti chou-k'an," No. 124, in Ta-kung pao (Feb. 19, 1937), p. 3.

Hsü Nai-chi 許乃濟. "Hsü-t'ai-ch'ang tsou-i" 許太常奏議
        (Memorials of Hsü Nai-chi). 1 chüan; MS in Library of Nanking;
        one memorial reprinted in Ya-p'ien chan-cheng, I, 471-474.

Hsü Shih-ch'ang 徐世昌. Ta-Ch'ing chi-fu hsien-che chuan 大清
        畿輔先哲傳 (Biographies of eminent statesmen of the
        Ch'ing dynasty). 40+6 chüan in 22 ts'e; Tientsin, n.d.

Huang Chueh-tzu 黃爵滋. "Huang-shao-ssu-k'ou tsou-kao" 黃少
        司冦奏稿 (Memorials of Huang Chueh-tzu). 20 chüan;
        MS deposited in National Library of Peking; included in part
        in Ya-p'ien chan-cheng, I, 477-504.

IWSM: Ch'ou-pan i-wu shih-mo 籌辦夷務始末 (A complete
        account of our management of barbarian affairs. Photolitho-
        graphic reproduction, Peiping, 1930. Tao-kuang period (1836-
        1850), 80 chüan, presented to the throne 1856.

Jen Tsung-chi 任宗濟. "Tao-kuang ch'ao chin-yen chih ching-chi pei-ching" 道光朝禁烟之經濟背景 (The economic background of the opium prohibition during the Tao-kuang period); "Ching-chi chou-k'an" 經濟周刊 (Economic weekly), No. 127, in Ta-kung pao (Aug. 21, 1935), p. 3.

Kao Shu-k'ang 高叔康. "Shan-hsi p'iao-hao ti ch'i-yuan chi ch'i ch'eng-li ti nien-tai" 山西票號的起源及其成立的年代 (The origin and date of establishment of the Shansi banks); Shih-huo 食貨 (Journal of Chinese economic history), 6.1:24-35 (July 1, 1937).

Kuan Jui-wu 關瑞梧. "I-wu shih-mo wai ya-p'ien chan-hou Chung-Ying i-ho shih-liao shu-chien" 夷務始末外鴉片戰後中英議和史料數件 (A few documents not included in the Ch'ou-pan i-wu shih-mo concerning Anglo-Chinese negotiations after the Opium War); Shih-hsueh nien-pao, 1.3:183-194 (1931).

Kuan T'ien-p'ei 關天培. Ch'ou-hai ch'u-chi 籌海初集 (Papers relating to the preparation of maritime defense). 4 chüan; preface ca. 1841.

Kuang-chou fu-chih, see Shih Ch'eng.

Kuang-tung-sheng wai-hai chan-ch'uan tso-fa 廣東省外海戰船作法 (Instructions for constructing warships for the Canton waters). 40 chüan; 1800?.

Kubota Bunzō 窪田文三. Shina gaikō tsūshi 支那外交通史 (A comprehensive history of Chinese foreign relations). Tokyo, 1928; 506 pp.

"K'uei-yung liu-tu," see KYLT.

Kung Tzu-chen 龔自珍. Ting-an ch'üan-chi 定盦全集 (Complete works of Kung Tzu-chen). Ssu-pu pei-yao ed.; 12 chüan; Shanghai, 1933.

Kuo T'ing-i (Kuo Ting-yee) 郭廷以 . Chin-tai Chung-kuo shih 近代 中國史 (Modern Chinese history). 2nd ed.; 2 vols.; Shanghai: Commercial Press, 1947; 635 and 636 pp.

------Chin-tai Chung-kuo shih-shih jih-chih 近代中國史事日誌 (Modern China chronology). 2 vols.; Taipei: Institute of Modern History, Academia Sinica, 1963.

KYLT: "K'uei-yung liu-tu" 潰癰流毒 (The bursting carbuncle and the spreading poison). MS in the Library of Congress; 6 chüan, unpaginated.

Li Huan 李桓 , ed. Kuo-ch'ao ch'i-hsien lei-cheng ch'u-pien 國朝 耆獻類徵初編 (Ch'ing biographies systematically arranged). 732 chüan in 300 ts'e; Siangyin (Hsiang-yin), Hunan, 1884-1890; index by rhymes.

Li Kuei 李圭 . Ya-p'ien shih-lueh 鴉片史略 (A brief account of the opium question). 2 chüan; reprinted by National Peking Library, 1931; reprinted by Shen-chou kuo-kuang-she 神州國 光社 in Chung-kuo nei-luan wai-huo li-shih ts'ung-shu 中國 内亂外禍歷史叢書 (An historical series on China's domestic disorder and foreign invasion; 1936), ts'e 12; reprinted in T'ao K'ang-te, Ya-p'ien chih chin-hsi, pp. 104-194; included in Ya-p'ien chan-cheng, VI, 203-249.

Li Ting-i 李定一 et al., eds. Chung-kuo chin-tai-shih lun-ts'ung 中國 近代史論叢 (A collection of articles on modern Chinese history), 1st ser., Vol. 1. Tapei, 1956; 304 pp.

Li Yuan-tu 李元度 , ed. Kuo-ch'ao hsien-cheng shih-lueh 國朝先 正事略 (Biographies of leading personages of the Ch'ing dynasty). 60 chüan; 1866.

Liang Chia-pin 梁嘉彬 . Kuang-tung shih-san-hang k'ao 廣東十 三行考 (A study of the thirteen hongs at Canton). Shanghai:

Commercial Press, 1937; 414 pp.

Liang Shao-hsien 梁紹獻, ed. Nan-hai hsien-chih 南海縣志 (Gazetteer of Nan-hai district). 26 chüan; 1872.

Liang T'ing-nan 梁廷枏. I-fen chi-wen 夷氛記聞 (An account of the barbarian invasion). 5 chüan; Peiping, 1937, original preface 1874; 132 pp.

------I-fen wen-chi 夷氛聞記 (An account of the barbarian invasion). 5 chüan; reprinted in Ya-p'ien chan-cheng, VI, 1-104. With minor variations, this is identical with Liang's I-fen chi-wen. The Wason Collection in the Cornell University Library has two hand-copied versions of the work.

------, ed. Yueh hai-kuan chih, see YHKC.

Lieh Tao 列島, comp. Ya-p'ien chan-cheng shih lun-wen chuan-chi 鴉片戰爭史論文專集 (A collection of articles on the Opium War). Peking, 1958; 380 pp.

Lin Tse-hsü 林則徐. HCL: Hsin-chi-lu 信及錄 (Faithful records). 1929; reprinted by Shen-chou kuo kuang she in Chung-kuo nei-luan wai-huo li-shih ts'ung-shu, ts'e 28 (1936); reprinted in Ya-p'ien chan-cheng, II, 229-364.

------"Lin Tse-hsü chih Shen Ting-fu han" 林則徐致沈鼎甫函 (A letter to Shen Ting-fu from Lin Tse-hsü); Ya-p'ien chan-cheng, II, 570-571.

------"JC": "Lin Tse-hsü jih-chi" 林則徐日記 (Diaries of Lin Tse-hsü). Printed from the original for the first time in Ya-p'ien chan-cheng, II, 1-85.

------CS: Lin Wen-chung-kung cheng-shu 林文忠公政書 (The political writings of Lin Tse-hsü). 37 chüan; 1886; partially reprinted in Ya-p'ien chan-cheng, II, 131-227.

Lo Erh-kang 羅爾綱. "Ya-p'ien chan-cheng ch'ien-hou Chung-kuo ti li-chih ho chün-pei" 鴉片戰爭前後中國的吏治和

單備 (Government and defense in China during the era of the Opium War); "Shih-ti chou-k'an," No. 25, in Ta-kung pao (Mar. 8, 1935), p. 11.

Lo Po-tan 羅伯聃 (Robert Thom). I-shih mi-chuan 意拾秘傳 (Chinese translation of Aesop's Fables). 4 chüan; chüan 2 dated 1838.

------Hua-Ying t'ung-yung tsa-hua 華英通用雜話 (Chinese and English vocabulary, Pt. 1), chüan 1. Canton, 1843; 80 pp.

Lu K'un 盧坤, Ch'en Hung-ch'ih 陳鴻墀, et al., comps. Kuang-tung hai-fang hui-lan 廣東海防彙覽 (Maritime defense in Kwangtung). 42 chüan; n.d.

Meng Ch'ing-lin 孟慶霖. "Ya-p'ien chan-cheng chih tung-chi" 鴉片戰爭之動機 (The causes of the Opium War); Chung-ho yueh-k'an, 1.12:50-60 (Dec. 1940).

Miao Ch'i-ch'ang 繆其昌. "Chung-Ying ch'u-tz'u chiao-chan chih yen-chiu chi ch'i wen-hsien" 中英初次交戰之研究及其文獻 (A review of P.C. Kuo, A Critical Study of the First Anglo-Chinese War); in T'u-shu chi-k'an 圖書季刊 (Quarterly bulletin of Chinese bibliography, Chinese ed.), 2.3:184-186 (1935).

Miao Ch'üan-sun 繆荃孫, ed. Hsu pei-chuan-chi 續碑傳集 (Ch'ing biographies from the Tao-kuang period through the Kuang-hsü period). 88 chüan in 24 ts'e; Soochow: Kiangsu Provincial Printing Office, 1910.

Nan-hai hsien-chih, see Liang Shao-hsien.

Pao Cheng-ku 鮑正鵠. Ya-p'ien chan-cheng 鴉片戰爭 (The Opium War). Shanghai, 1954; 140 pp.

Pao Shih-ch'en 包世臣 . An-wu ssu-chung 安吳四種 (Collected
   works of Pao Shih-ch'en). 36 chüan; 1846, reprinted 1888.

P'eng Hsin-wei 彭信威 . Chung-kuo huo-pi shih 中國貨幣史
   (A history of Chinese currency). 2 vols.; Shanghai, 1954; 636 pp.

P'eng Tse-i 彭澤益 . "Ch'ing-tai Kuang-tung yang-hang chih-tu ti
   ch'i-yuan" 清代廣東洋行制度的起源 (The origin
   of the hong system at Canton in the Ch'ing dynasty); Li-shih yen-
   chiu 歷史研究 (Historical studies), 1:1-24 (1957).

Sa Shih-wu 薩士武 . "Ya-p'ien chan-i Hsia-men yü-ti tsa-k'ao" 鴉片
   戰役廈門禦敵雜考 (The defense of Amoy during the Opium
   War); "Shih-ti chou-k'an," No. 127, in Ta-kung pao (Jan. 29, 1937),
   p. 3.

------"Pu-ch'ung Lin Wen-chung-kung nien-p'u ti liang-chung shih-liao"
   補充林文忠公年譜的兩種史料 (Two collections of
   source materials supplementing Lin Wen-chung-kung nien-p'u); "Shih-
   ti chou-k'an," No. 127, in Ta-kung pao (Mar. 12, 1937), p. 3.

Sakoda Naruo 迫田稔夫 . "Rin Soku-jo ni okeru kinen shisō no hatten
   ni tsuite" 林則徐における禁烟思想の發展に
   ついて (On the development of Lin Tse-hsü's thought against
   the opium traffic); Kadai shigaku 鹿大史學 (Kagoshima University
   history studies), 5:1-15 (1957).

Shao-t'ang chü-shih, see Wang Chih-ch'un.

Shen Yen-ch'ing 沈衍慶 . Huai-ch'ing i-kao 槐卿遺稿 (Collected
   works of Shen Yen-ch'ing). 6 chüan; 1862.

Shih Ch'eng 史澄 , ed. Kuang-chou fu-chih 廣州府志 (Gazetteer
   of Kuang-chou prefecture). 163 chüan in 60 ts'e; comp. 1879,
   printed by Yueh-hsiu academy 粵秀書院 , 1879.

Shimoda Reisuke 下田禮佐. "Ahen sensō made, ahen sensō izen ni okeru ahen bōeki" 阿片戰爭まで—阿片戰爭以前に於ける阿片貿易 (The opium trade before and up to the Opium War); Chiri ronsō 地理論叢 (Geographical studies; Kyoto), 8:93-120 (1936).

Ta-Ch'ing li-ch'ao shih-lu, see CSL.

T'ai-p'ing shan-jen 太平山人. "Tao-kuang ch'ao yin-huang wen-t'i" 道光朝銀荒問題 (The problem of the silver shortage in Tao-kuang's reign); Chung-ho yueh-k'an, 1.8:61-75 (Aug. 1940).

Tanaka Masayoshi 田中正美. "Rin Soku-jo no gōrishugi to sono genkai" 林則徐の合理主義とその限界 (Lin Tse-hsü's rationalist policy and its limitations); Rekishigaku kenkyū 歴史學研究 (Journal of historical studies), 190:29-38 (Dec. 1955).

T'ang Hsiang-lung 湯象龍. "Tao-kuang ch'ao yin-kuei wen-t'i" 道光朝銀貴問題 (Outflow of silver in the Tao-kuang period); She-hui k'o-hsueh tsa-chih 社會科學雜誌 (Quarterly review of social sciences), 1.3:1-31 (Sept. 1930).

"Tao-kuang-ch'ao wai-yang t'ung-shang an" 道光朝外洋通商案 (Documents on foreign trade in the Tao-kuang period); Shih-liao hsün-k'an, Nos. 4-6, 8-11, 13, 15, 17, 19, 21, 23, 25 (1930-1931).

"Tao-kuang shih-i-nien ch'a-chin ya-p'ien-yen an" 道光十一年查禁鴉片煙案 (Documents on the suppression of opium in Tao-kuang, eleventh year); Shih-liao hsün-k'an, Nos. 3-6, 9 (1930-1931).

T'ao K'ang-te 陶亢德, ed. Ya-p'ien chih chin-hsi 鴉片之今昔 (Opium, its present and past). Shanghai, 1937; 194 pp.

T'ao Yuan-chen 陶元珍. "Tu 'Ch'i-shan yü ya-p'ien chan-cheng'" 讀琦善與鴉片戰爭 (On reading "Ch'i-shan and the

Opium War"); "Ta-kung pao t'u-shu fu-k'an" 大公報圖書副
刊 (Ta-kung pao literary supplement), No. 77, in Ta-kung pao
(May 2, 1935), p. 3.

Teng T'ing-chen 鄧廷楨 . Shuang-yen-chai ch'üan-chi 雙硯齋全
集 (The complete works of Teng T'ing-chen). 12 ts'e; 1919.

------"Teng T'ing-chen kuan-yü ya-p'ien chan-cheng ti shu-hsin" 鄧
廷楨關於鴉片戰爭的書信 (Ten letters of Teng
T'ing-chen concerning the Opium War); in Ya-p'ien chan-cheng,
II, 583-590. The original letters, all written in 1840, are in the
Institute of Modern History, Chinese Academy of Science.

THL: Tung-hua ch'üan-lu 東華全錄 (Complete record of the
Tung-hua [gate]), comp. Wang hsien-ch'ien 王先謙 .
252 ts'e; editor's preface 1884; Tao-kuang period, 60 chüan
in ts'e 147-164.

Thom, Robert, see Lo Po-tan.

Ting Ming-nan 丁名楠 et al. "Ti-i-tz'u ya-p'ien chan-cheng--wai-
kuo tzu-pen-chu-i ch'in-lueh Chung-kuo ti k'ai-tuan" 第一
次鴉片戰爭—外國資本主義侵略中國的開端
(The first Opium War--the beginning of foreign capitalist
aggression against China); in Chung-kuo k'o-hsueh-yuan li-shih
yen-chiu-so ti-san-so chi-k'an 中國科學院歷史研究
所第三所集列 (Monograph series of the Third Branch,
Institute of Historical Studies, Chinese Academy of Science),
1:114-152 (Peking, 1955).

Tōyō shiryō shūsei 東洋史料集成 (A collection of source materials
on Chinese history, ed. Sekai rekishi jiten henshū iinkai
Tōyō shi bukai 世界歷史事典編集委員會東洋史部會
(Section on Oriental History, Editorial Committee, Encyclopedia
of World History). Tokyo, 1956.

Tso-min, see Hsia Nai.

Tung-hua ch'üan-lu, see THL.

Ueda Toshio 植田捷雄. "Ahen sensō ron" 阿片戰爭論
(A treatise on the Opium War); Kokusaihō gaikō zasshi 國際法
外交雜誌 (Journal of international law and diplomacy),
42.1:22-47 (Jan. 1943); ibid., 42.2:135-158 (Feb. 1943); ibid.,
42.3:237-270 (Mar. 1943).

Ueda Toshio, Banno Masataka, et al., comps. Chūgoku gaikō bunsho
jiten 中國外交文書辭典 (A glossary of Chinese diplomatic
documents). Tokyo, 1954; 139 pp.

Wan Ssu-nien 萬斯年. "Ya-p'ien chan-cheng shih-tai Hua-pei ching-
chi shih-liao ti hsin-fa-chien" 鴉片戰爭時代華北經
濟史料的新發見 (Newly discovered materials on the
economic history of North China during the period of the Opium
War); T'u-shu chi-k'an, 2.3:149-158 (1935).

Wang Chih-ch'un 王之春. Kuo-ch'ao jou-yuan chi 國朝柔遠記
(Record of the ruling dynasty's graciousness to strangers).
20 chüan; 1891, also 1892, 1895, and 1896.

------, under pseud. Shao-t'ang chü-shih 芍唐居士. Fang-hai
chi-lueh 防海紀畧 (A brief record of maritime defense).
2 chüan; Shanghai, 1895. Largely identical with Wei Yuan's
"I-sou ju-k'ou chi."

Wang Ming-lun 王明倫. "Ya-p'ien chan-cheng ch'ien Yun-nan
t'ung-k'uang-yeh chung ti tzu-pen-chu-i meng-ya" 鴉片戰爭
前雲南銅礦業中的資本主義萌芽 (The early
growth of capitalism in the Yunnan copper-mining industry
before the Opium War); Li-shih yen-chiu, 3:39-46 (1956).

Wang Shu-an 王柕庵. "Shih-san-hang yü Ch'ü Ta-chün Kuang-chou
chu-chih-tz'u" 十三行與屈大均廣州竹枝詞

(The thirteen hongs and Ch'ü Ta-chün's ballad of Canton);
Li-shih yen-chiu, 6:22 (1957).

Wang Yen-wei 王彦威. "Yang-wu shih-mo ta-lueh" 洋務始末
大略 (An account of China's foreign affairs); Chung-kuo hsueh-
pao 中國學報 (Chinese studies), 1:17-36 (1912).

Wei Ch'i 魏耆. Shao-yang Wei-fu-chün shih-lueh 邵陽魏府君
事略 (A brief biography of my father, Wei Yuan of Shao-yang).
1 chüan; printed in the Kuang-hsü period; included in Ya-p'ien
chan-cheng, VI, 436-446.

Wei Chü-hsien 衛聚賢. "Shan-hsi p'iao-chuang chih ch'i-yuan" 山
西票莊之起源 (The origins of the Shansi banks);
Chung-yang yin-hang yueh-pao 中央銀行月報 (Central
Bank monthly), 4.6:1243-45 (June 1935).

------Shan-hsi p'iao-hao shih 山西票號史 (A history of the
Shansi banks). Chungking, 1944; 386 pp.

Wei Ying-ch'i 魏應麒. Lin Wen-chung-kung nien-p'u 林文忠公年譜
(A chronological biography of Lin Tse-hsü). Shanghai, 1935; 200 pp.

------Lin Tse-hsü 林則徐 (A brief sketch of the life of Lin Tse-hsü).
Chungking, 1945; 98 pp.

Wei Yuan 魏源. Sheng-wu chi 聖武記 (A record of imperial
military exploits). 14 chüan; preface to first ed. 1842.

------Hai-kuo t'u-chih 海國圖志 (An illustrated gazetteer of
the maritime countries). 50 chüan (1844); later eds., 60 chüan
(1847), 100 chüan (1852), reprint (1876).

------Tao-kuang yang-sou cheng-fu chi 道光洋艘征撫記
(Record of the pacification of the foreign ships in the Tao-kuang
period). Included in 1846 and later eds. of his Sheng-wu chi and
some other works; almost identical with his "I-sou ju-k'ou chi."

------"I-sou ju-k'ou chi" 夷艘入寇記 (Account of the invasion by
barbarian vessels); in Ya-p'ien chan-cheng, VI, 105-136.

MS deposited in Peking University Library; several versions
of this work under slightly different titles, and all in manuscript,
circulated widely just after the Opium War.

Wu Chia-pin 吳嘉賓. Ch'iu-tzu-te-chih-chih wen-ch'ao 求自得之
室文鈔 (The collected works of Wu Chia-pin). 12 chüan
in 4 ts'e; 1866.

Ya-p'ien chan-cheng, see YPCC.

"Ya-p'ien tsou-an" 鴉片奏案 (A collection of memorials concerning
opium). MS deposited in the Library of Peking; printed for the
first time in Ya-p'ien chan-cheng, II, 87-130.

Yano Jin'ichi 矢野仁一. "Kō Shaku-ji oyobi Rin Soku-jo no ahen
sōgi ni tsuite" 黄爵滋及び"林則徐の鴉片奏議
に就いて (On the memorials discussing the opium question
submitted by Huang Chueh-tzu and Lin Tse-hsü); in Takase
Hakushi Kanreki kinen Shinagaku ronsō 高瀬博士還曆
記念支那學論叢 (Collected essays in Chinese studies
celebrating the sixtieth birthday of Dr. Takase), pp. 757-771.
Kyoto, 1928.

------Kinsei Shina gaikōshi 近世支那外交史 (Modern Chinese
diplomatic history). Tokyo: Kōbundō 弘文堂, 1935.

------Ahen sensō to Honkon アヘン戰爭と香港 (The Opium War
and Hong Kong). Tokyo: Kōbundō, 1939; 316 pp.

Yao Wei-yüan 姚薇元. Ya-p'ien chan-cheng shih-shih-k'ao 鴉片
戰爭史實考 (A study of the Opium War). Shanghai, 1955;
a reprint of the 1942 Kweiyang ed.

YHKC: Yueh hai-kuan chih 粵海關志 (Gazetteer of the Maritime
Customs of Kwangtung), ed. Liang T'ing-nan. 30 chüan;
ca. 1840.

YPCC: Ya-p'ien chan-cheng 鴉片戰爭 (The Opium War), ed.
Ch'i Ssu-ho 齊思和, Lin Shu-hui 林樹惠, and Shou Chi-yü
壽紀瑜. 6 vols.; Shanghai, 1954; 3757 pp.

Yueh hai-kuan chih, see YHKC.

Yü Ch'ang-hui 俞昌會, comp. Fang-hai chi-yao 防海輯要
(Essentials of maritime defense). Chüan shou 卷首 and
18 chüan in 10 ts'e; 1842.

Yü Cheng-hsieh 俞正燮. Kuei-ssu lei-kao 癸巳類稿 (A
selection of Yü Cheng-hsieh's writings and investigations);
in An-hui ts'ung-shu 安徽叢書, 3rd ser. (1934). 15 chüan;
1st preface 1833.

Yü En-te 于恩德. Chung-kuo chin-yen fa-ling pien-ch'ien shih
中國禁煙法令變遷史 (History of the changes in
Chinese antiopium laws). Shanghai: Chung-hua Book Co.,
1934; 332 pp.

Yü Hung-kan 余宏淦. Yen-hai hsien-yao t'u-shuo 沿海險要
圖說 (The strategic places of the Chinese coast, with maps).
Shanghai, 1903.

a-fu-jung 阿芙蓉

Amoy 廈門

An-ch'en-wan (Anson's Bay) 安臣灣

Anunghoy, see Ya-niang-hsieh

Ao-men hsin-wen lu 澳門新聞錄 (the Canton Press)

Ao-men ping-t'ou 澳門兵頭 (governor of Macao)

Ao-men tsa-lu 澳門雜錄 (the Canton Register)

Ao-men t'ung-chih 澳門同知 (subprefect of Macao)

Ao-men yueh-pao 澳門月報 (the Chinese Repository)

Bohea hills, see Wu-i

Canh Hung 景興

Chang Ch'ao-fa 張朝發

Chang-chou (Lungki) 漳州

Chang Nan-shan 張南山

Chang Shih-ch'eng 張師誠

Chang Yuan 章沅

Ch'ang-chou-kang 長州岡

ch'ang-sui 長隨

Chao-an (Chaoan) 詔安

Chao-ch'ing 肇慶 (Koyiu 高要)

Ch'ao-chou (Chaochow) 潮州

Chapu 乍浦

Chen-hai (Chinhai) 鎮海

Chen-k'ou 鎮口

chen-tu 鴆毒

Ch'en Hsi 陳喜

Ch'en Hung-ch'ih 陳鴻墀

Ch'en Ts'ang-ch'i 陳藏器

Cheng Shih-ch'ao 鄭士超

cheng-ta chou-tao 正大周到

"Chi Hai-shen wen" 祭海神文

chi-hsi yung-ch'u, ken-chu tuan-chueh 積習永除，根株斷絕

Chi-lien (John C. Green) 記連

Chi-lin chiang-chün 吉林將軍

chi-mi 羈縻

Chi-ning 濟寧

Ch'i-hsien (Kihsien) 祁縣

Ch'i Kung 祁𤥂

Ch'i-shan 琦善

chia-ch'ang fan-ts'ai 家常飯菜

Chia-lü-chih (T. R. Colledge) 加律治

Chiang Ta-piao 蔣大彪
Chiang Yu-hsien 蔣攸銛
Chieh-hsiu (Kiehsiu) 介休
chieh-kuan t'ing 接官亭
Chien-sha-tsui (Tseënshatsuy) 尖沙嘴
ch'ien-chuang 錢莊
ch'ien-ku 錢穀
Ch'ien-shan-chai 前山寨
Chih Ch'eng Hsin 志成信
Chin 金
Chin-hsing-men (Kum Sing Mun, Kumsing-moon Harbor) 金星門
chin-hua (Turkey opium) 金花
chin-wen 今文
ch'in-ch'ai ta-ch'en 欽差大臣
Chinchew, see Ch'üan-chou
Ching (Charles W. King) 喨 (京, 哩)
ching-shang 敬上
ching-shih chih-yung chih-hsueh 經世致用之學
ch'ing-ch'e tu-yü 輕車都尉
Chinhai, see Chen-hai
Chinkiang 鎮江
Chiu-chou (Macao Roads) 九洲
ch'iu-t'ao huang-ti chao-hsueh shen-yuan 求討皇帝昭雪申寃

Chou Chi-hua 周際華
Chou T'ien-chueh 周天爵
ch'ou 丑
Chu Tsun 朱嶟
ch'uan-p'ai 傳牌
Ch'uan-pi (Chunpee, Chuenpe) 穿鼻
Chuanchow, see Ch'üan-chou
Chuang-ch'in-wang I-tou (Prince Chuang) 莊親王奕竇
Chuang Ts'un-yü 莊存與
chueh-ting-i 決定義
Chuenpe, see Ch'uan-pi
Chung-hsi chi-shih 中西紀事
Chunhou, see Chen-k'ou
Chunpee, see Ch'uan-pi
Chusan (Chushan) 舟山
Ch'ü-chiang 曲江 (Kükong, Shaochou 韶州)
Ch'ü Ta-chün 屈大均
Ch'üan-chou (Chinchew, Chuanchow) 泉州
chün-min-fu (Keun Min Foo; subprefect of Macao) 軍民府 ; see also Ao-men t'ung-chih
Cohong, see kung-hang

erh-shih-ssu ch'u t'ou-jen 二十四處頭人

fan-ch'ai (ouvidor [Chief justice] of Macao) 番差

Fan-pa-ch'en (Magdalimus
　　Jacobus Senn van Basel,
　　Dutch consul) 番吧啞
Fatshan (Nan-hai, Namhoi) 佛山
Feng-ch'eng (Fengcheng) 豐城
feng-su jen-hsin 風俗人心
Fo-kang 佛岡
Fo-shan, see Fatshan
Foochow (Hou-kuan) 福州
fu 賦
Fu-kuo-kung P'u-hsi (Imperial
　　Duke P'u-hsi) 輔國公溥喜

Gia Long 嘉隆
Gia Long Thong Bao 嘉隆通寶
Gowqua, see Hsieh Ao-kuan

Ha-feng-a 哈豐阿
Hai-chu p'ao-t'ai (Dutch Folly)
　　海珠砲台
Hai-fang shu-chü 海防書局
Han (the storeship Ruparell) 含
Han Chao-ch'ing 韓肇慶
Hang-Chia-Hu circuit 杭嘉湖道
Hantong, see Wantong
Heng-tang, see Wantong
Heungshan, see Hsiang-shan
Ho Lao-chin (Ho Lao-kin) 何老近
Ho Lao-kin, see Ho Lao-chin
Ho-shen 和珅
Ho T'ai-ch'ing 何太青

Hou-kuan (Foochow) 侯官
Howqua, see Wu Hao-kuan
Hsi-yang i-mu (Portuguese governor
　　of Macao) 西洋夷目
Hsia Hsieh 夏燮
Hsiang-k'ang 祥康
Hsiang-shan (Heungshan) 香山
Hsiao-ch'üan ch'eng-huang-hou
　　孝全成皇后
Hsiao-lü-sung (Manila) 小呂宋
hsiao-t'u (a generic term for
　　Malwa, Turkey, and Persian
　　opium) 小土
Hsieh Ao-kuan 謝鰲官 (Gowqua,
　　alias Hsieh Yu-jen 謝有仁)
Hsieh Kuo-t'ai 謝國泰
Hsieh Yu-jen, see Hsieh Ao-kuan
Hsin-an (Sunoan) 新安
Hsin-hui (Sunwui) 新會
hsin-shan (Persian opium) 新山 ;
　　see also hung-jou
hsing luan-pang, yung chung-tien
　　刑亂邦，用重典
hsing-ming 刑名
Hsiung Ching-hsing 熊景星
Hsueh-hai t'ang 學海堂
hsü-chang sheng-shih 虛張聲勢
Hsü Ch'iu 許球
Hsü Kuang 徐廣
Hsü Nai-chi 許乃濟

304

Hsü Shih-lin 徐士林
Hsüan-na-li 軒拿厘
Hsüan-nan shih-she 宣南詩社
hsün-ch'uan 巡船
hu-chia hu-wei 狐假虎威
Hu-Kuang 湖廣
Hu-men (Bocca Tigris, the Bogue) 虎門
hu-pu 戶部
Hua-lin-chih (Framjee) 化林治
Hua-mo (W. S. Wetmore) 滑摩
Hua-shih (the storeship Ariel) 花時
Huang Chueh-tzu 黃爵滋
Huang Chung-mo 黃中模
Hui-an (Hweian) 惠安
Hui-chou (Waiyeung) 惠州
Hung Hsiu-ch'üan 洪秀全
hung-jou (Persian opium) 紅肉; see also hsin-shan
hung-p'ai 紅牌
Hweian, see Hui-an

I K'e-chung 儀克中
i-kuan (the factories) 夷館
I-liang 怡良
I-li-pu 伊里布
I-lü (Captain Charles Elliot) 義律
I-p'i-li (Ilbery) 依庇厘
i-shou-wei-chan, i-i-tai-lao 以守為戰，以逸待勞

jen-chen pan-li 認真辦理
jen chi cheng-fa 人即正法
Jih Sheng Ch'ang (a draft bank) 日昇昌
Jih Sheng Ch'ang (a dye shop) 日昇長
Ju-yuan 乳源
Juan Yuan (Yuen Yuen) 阮元

K'ai-pao pen-ts'ao 開寶本草
kan-chieh 甘結
Kan-ei tsū-hō 寬永通寶
Kan River 贛江
kang-chiao 港腳
Kao I-yung 高宜勇
Kao Shu-k'ang 高叔康
keng-tzu 庚子
Keun Min Foo, see chün-min fu
Kiehsiu, see Chieh-hsiu
Kihsien, see Ch'i-hsien
Koyiu, see Chao-ch'ing
ku-ni (Benares opium) 沽泥; see also ku-yen
ku-yen (Benares opium) 沽烟; see also ku-ni
k'uai-hsieh 快蟹
kuan-feng-shih 觀風試
Kuan T'ien-p'ei 關天培
"Kuang-chou chu-chih-tz'u" 廣州竹枝詞

305

Kuang-hsieh (Kwang Heep; Canton police commandant) 廣協

kuei-hsü-i 歸墟義

Kum Sing Mun, see Chin-hsing men

kun-tse 棍賣

kung-hang (Cohong) 公行

kung-pan-t'u (Bengal opium) 公班土 ; see also wu-t'u, kung-yen

kung-so (Consoo) 公所

Kung Tzu-chen 龔自珍

Kung-yang chuan 公羊傳

kung-yen (Bengal opium) 公烟 ; see also kung-pan-t'u

Kuo Kuei-ch'uan 郭桂船

Kuo-shih-li (Wu-shih-la; Charles Gutzlaff) 郭士立

Kuo T'ai-ch'eng 郭泰成

Kükong, see Ch'ü-chiang

Kwang Heep, see Kuang-hsieh

Lankeet, see Lung-hsueh

Lantao, see Ta-hsü-shan

Lao-wan-shan (Ladrone Islands) 老萬山

Li Chao-lo 李兆洛

Li-chieh (the storeship Jane) 喇嗒

Li Hsien 李賢

Li Hung-chang 李鴻章

Li Hung-pin 李鴻賓

Li-shih (the storeship Mermaid) 利是

Li Shih-chen 李士楨

Li Tseng-chieh 李曾階

Li Tun-yeh 李敦業

Liang Chia-pin 梁嘉彬

Liang En-sheng 梁恩升

Liang T'ing-nan 梁廷枏

Lieh-te 獵德

Lien-chou 連州

Lien-kuo (Denmark) 嗹國

Lien-shih* (the Esperanca, Captain Linstedt) 嗹吐

"Lin Ch'ing-t'ien" 林青天

Lin Wei-hsi (Lin Weihe) 林維喜

Lin Weihe, see Lin Wei-hsi

ling-shih 領事

Ling-ting (Lintin) 零丁

Lintin, see Ling-ting

Liu Feng-lu 劉逢祿

Liu Han 劉翰

Liu Jung-ch'ing 劉榮慶

Liu K'ai-yü 劉開域

Lo-ch'ang (Lokchong) 樂昌

---

*It was the Chinese practice in this period to refer to Western ships by the names of their captains.

306

Lo-fo (J. P. van Loffelt, acting French consul) 羅弗

Lo Po-tan (Robert Thom) 羅伯聃

Lokchong, see Lo-ch'ang

Lu Chi-kuang, see Lu Mao-kuan

Lu K'un 盧坤

Lu Mao-kuan 盧茂官 (Mowqua, alias Lu Chi-kuang 盧繼光)

Lu Ta-yueh 盧大鉞

Lun Ch'ao-kuang 倫朝光

Lung-ch'i (Lungki, Chang-chou) 龍溪

Lung-hsueh (Lankeet) 龍穴

Lungki, see Lung-ch'i

Lü Lao-pei (William John Lord Napier) 律勞卑

ma-chan ("merchant") 馬占, 孖氈

ma-ch'ien ch'u-chien mi-nang-hua 馬前初見米囊花

Ma-ko 媽閣

Ma-t'a-lun (Sir Frederick Maitland) 嗎哒噜

Ma-ti-ch'en (James Matheson) 吗哒唓

Ma-wen-chih (Bomanjee, a Parsee merchant) 嗎文治

mao 卯

Mei-lien (the Wellesley, Captain Maitland) 嘆蓮

Mei-ling-kuan 梅嶺關

Meng-mai (Bombay) 孟買

mi-nang 米囊

Ming-shih 明史

Ming-ya-la (Bengal) 明雅喇

Mowqua, see Lu Mao-kuan

Mu-chang-a 穆彰阿

mu-yu 幕友

Namhoi, see Nan-hai

Namoa, see Nan-ao

Namyong, see Nan-hsiung

Nan-an 南安

Nan-ao (Namoa) 南澳

Nan-hai (Namhoi, Fatshan) 南海

Nan-Han shu 南漢書

Nan-hsiung (Namyung) 南雄

Nan-huan chieh 南環街

Nan-k'ang 南康

Nanping (Yen-p'ing) 南平

Nan-wan 南灣

nei-wu-fu 內務府

Niang-ma-ko 娘媽閣

Ning-chin 寧津

p'a-lung 扒龍

Pai-ho, see Pei-ho

pai-p'i (Malwa opium) 白皮 ; see also pai-t'u

pai-t'u (Malwa opium) 白土 ; see also pai-p'i

pan-t'ing (bum-boats) 辦艇

P'an-yü 番禺 (Panyü, Suntso
新造)

p'ang-i 旁義

Panyü, see P'an-yü

Pao An-t'ai 保安泰

pao-chia 保甲

Pao-hsing 寶興

Pao Shih-ch'en 包世臣

Pei-chih-wen (Rev. E. C. Bridgman)
啤(唎)啥吱

Pei-ho 白河

Pen-ts'ao shih-i 本草拾遺

P'eng-nien 彭年

P'eng Tse-i 彭澤益

P'i-li (the sloop Larne, Captain
Blake) 嘶叻

p'iao-chuang 票莊

Pien (Baynes) 邊

pien-i hsing-shih 便宜行事

Pien-sun (Captain Benson of the
Morrison) 咭噠

pin, see ping

p'in-hsueh chien-yu 品學兼優

ping (pin) 稟

P'ing-yao (Pingyao) 平遙

po-pi 波畢

pu-k'o-sheng-shu 不可勝數

pu-kuan mao-i 不管貿易

P'u-hsi, see Fu-kuo-kung P'u-hsi

Quang Trung 光中

Samqua, see Wu Shuang-kuan

San-ma-ti-ch'en (Donald Matheson?)
三孖地臣

San-pa 三巴

San-pa-men 三巴門

san-pan 三板

San-yu-lou 三友樓

Sha-chiao (Shakok, Sandy Head,
Sandy Point, Shakeo) 沙角

Shakeo, see Sha-chiao

shang-yin 上癮

Shao-chou, see Ch'ü-chiang

Shen Chen-pang 沈鎮邦

Shen Yen-ch'ing 沈衍慶

shih-jen chiu-yin 十人九癮

Shih-na (Peter Wanton Snow, U.S.
consul) 士那 (吐哪)

Shih-tan-fo (Stanford, an English
merchant) 士丹弗

shih-yao 食妖

shu-ch'ien-wan liang 數千萬兩

shu-pan 書辦

shui-shih-ying 水師營

Shuntak (Shun-te) 順德

Soochow (Wuhsien) 蘇州

ssu 巳

Su Ch'e 蘇轍

Su-ch'in-wang Ching-min 肅親
王敬敏

308

Su-leng-e 蘇楞額
Su Tung-p'o 蘇東坡
Suchow (Tungshan) 徐州
Sung River 松江
Sunoan, see Hsin-an
Suntso, see P'an-yü
Sunwui, see Hsin-hui
Swatow 汕頭

ta-chien 大鐾
Ta-hsü-shan (Lantao) 大嶼山
Ta-huang-chiao River 大黃滘支河
ta-k'uai jen-hsin 大快人心
ta-nan-i 答難義
ta-pan (tai-pan, taepan) 大班
Ta-p'eng hai (Mirs Bay) 大鵬海
Ta-p'eng ying (Tapang, or Ta-p'eng, Squadron) 大鵬營
Ta-p'i-shih (John Francis Davis) 達庇時
ta-pien ch'eng-fa, pu-ch'eng shih-t'i 大變成法，不成事體
Ta-ta-p'i (Dadabhoy, a Parsee merchant) 打打披
ta-t'u (Bengal and Benares opium) 大土
taepan, see ta-pan
tai-pan, see ta-pan
T'ai-chou 泰州
T'ai-ku (Taiku) 太谷

tan-chia-ch'uan 蛋家船
Tan-ma-ko-shih (the Thomas Coutts) 担麻葛士
Tan-ma-shih (the brig Algerine, Captain Kingcome) 担嗎吐
Tan-ti-la (the storeship Nymph) 丹地喇
Tan-yeh-li (Daniell, an English merchant) 單耶厘
Tang-lang (the Royal Saxon) 當郎
Tang Tingching, see Teng T'ing-chen
T'ao Yung 陶鏞
Te-chi-la-shih (the Cambridge, Captain Douglas) 嗼嗯喇吐
Te-k'e-chin-pu 德克金布
te-t'i chou-tao 得體周到
Teng T'ing-chen 鄧廷楨
Teng Ying 鄧瀛
T'eng-wang-ko 滕王閣
t'i-tu 提督
tien-shih 典史
Tien-ti (Lancelot Dent) 顚地
T'ien-hou-kung 天后宮
t'ien-tao 天道
Tinghai 定海
To-la-na (Warren Delano) 多喇哪
t'o-ku kai-chih 託古改制

309

Tsaemow, see Ts'ai Mao

Ts'ai Mao (Tsaemow, Old Tom) 蔡懋

Tsan-tsu-chih-li 嘈啐啮喱 (Captain Lord John Churchill, died on H. M. S. Druid, June 3, 1840)

Ts'an-hsün 參遜 or Tsun-ch'en 噂臣 (A. R. Johnston)

Ts'ao Chih 曹植

Tseënshatsuy, see Chien-sha-tsui

Tseng Kuo-fan 曾國藩

Tseng Sheng 曾勝

Tso-che-ma-ti-sha (Governor Adriao Accacio Da Silveira Pinto ?) 嗽嚧嗎哋唦

Tsun-ch'en, see Ts'an-hsün

tsung-kuan (consul) 總管

tsung-ping 總兵

Tu-lu-chi (Turkey) 都魯機

tun-ch'uan 躉船 ; see also ya-p'ien-tun

T'ung-ku-wan (Tongkoo, Tong Koo, or Toongkoo Bay, Urmstone's Harbor) 銅鼓灣

T'ung-Yung circuit 通永道

Waiyeung (Hui-chou) 惠陽

Wan-an (Wanan) 萬安

Wan-la (Captain Warner of the Thomas Coutts) 彎喇

wan-pu-te-i 萬不得已

Wang Chen-kao 王振高

Wang Ch'ing-lien 王青蓮

Wang-hsia 望廈

Wang-mai (Bombay) 望買

Wang Yueh 王玥

Wantong (Heng-tang, Hantong) 橫檔

wei 未

Wei-ch'en (the storeship Hercules) 威臣

Wei-li (the storeship Austen) 威喇

wei-li-to (procurador or vereador) 委嚟多

Wei T'ai Hou 蔚泰厚

Wei Yuan 魏源

wei-yuan 委員

wen wu hsün-p'u 文武巡捕

Wenchow (Wen-chou) 温州

Wu Han 吳涵

Wu Hao-kuan 伍浩官 (Howqua, alias Wu Shao-jung 伍紹榮)

Wu-i (Bohea hills) 武夷

Wu Lan-hsiu 吳蘭修

Wu Shao-jung, see Wu Hao-kuan

Wu-shih-la, see Kuo-shih-li

Wu Shuang-kuan 吳爽官 (Samqua, alias Wu T'ien-heng 吳天恒)

Wu T'ien-heng, see Wu Shuang-
    kuan
wu-t'u (Bengal opium) 烏土 ;
    see also kung-pan-t'u
Wuhsien (Wu-hsien) 吳縣

ya-hang 牙行
Ya-niang-hsieh (Anunghoy)
    亞娘鞋
ya-p'ien-tun 鴉片蔓 ; see also
    tun-ch'uan
"Ya-p'ien-yen fu" 鴉片烟賦
Yang-ch'eng 羊城
yang-huo hang 洋貨行
Yang-ma-ti-ch'en (Alexander
    Matheson ?) 央孖地臣
yang-shang 洋商
Yao 猺
yao-k'ou 窰口
Yeh Heng-shu 葉恒樹

Yen-p'ing (Nanping) 延平
yin-chien 引見
Yin-i-shih (James Innes) 咽義吐
yin-shui 引水
Ying-chi-li (Robert Inglis) 英記利
Ying-lung 英隆
ying-su 鶯 (罌) 粟
yu-k'o 游客
yuan-chih 遠職
Yuan Te-hui 袁德輝
Yuan Yü-lin 袁玉麟
Yueh hai-kuan-pu 粵海關部
Yueh-hsiu 粵秀
Yueh-hua 越華
yun-ssu 運司
yü 諭
Yü-ch'ien 裕謙
Yü-k'un 豫堃
Yü Pao-ch'un 余保純

311

INDEX

Abercromby Robertson, mutiny, 198
Agency houses, 13, 14. *See also* Country trade; names of individual firms
Ahin (linguist), 155–156
Ahtone (linguist), 155–156
Alanci (linguist), 155–156
Alantsae (linguist), 168
Algerine (brig), 107, 109
Alligator (warship), 209
Alpha, opium seized on board the, 106
Amherst, Lord (William Pitt), 10
Amherst mission, 12
Amoy, 2, 193
Andromache (frigate), 56
Annam, 45
Antiopium statute, 97
Anunghoy, 204
Argyle incident, 66–67
Asee (Yeh Heng-shu), 20
Astell, John H., 53, 199, 200
Auckland, Lord (George Eden), 102, 190
Aurelia (opium ship), 27, 30
Austin (opium ship), 26
Austria, China trade, 1, 6, 136

Benares opium, 22, 23, 104
Bengal Herald, 95
Bengal opium, 21
Benson, Capt., 174
Bimetallic currencies, 46
Bjornstjerna, Count, 48–49
Blackburn, 192–193
Black Joke (schooner), 199–200
Blackwood, Capt. P., 55
Blackwood's Edinburgh Magazine, 49, 94, 215–216, 272n72
Blake, Capt. P. J., 158, 161, 162, 177–178
Board of Revenue, 5
Bocca Tigris (the Bogue), 115
Bogue, the, 6, 59, 204
Bombay Chamber of Commerce, 192
Bombay incident, 108–109
Bond issue, 143, 179–186, 204, 207
Braine, G. T., 147
Bridgman, Rev. E. C., 11, 136, 174–175
Brightman, E. W., 61
Bristol, 192–193
British East India Company. *See* East India Company
British firms, protest factory confinement, 192–193
Brokerage organizations (*yao-k'ou*), 32, 90, 128
Bum-boats (*pan-t'ing*), 105
Burrell, Brig.-Gen. George, 209

Cabreta Point (Chi-ching-t'ou), 7
Cambridge, 202, 203

Canton: Western trade at, 2, 6, 8–9, 62; defenses, 58–60; British blockade (1840), 209. *See also* Country trade; China; names of individual nations
Canton factories: description, 8; confinement, 144, 151–158, 229–230, 263n112
Canton Press, 138
Canton Press Price Current, 111
Canton Register: sinophobic attitude, 47, 82, 98, 248–249n46; on British China policy, 61–62, 63, 67, 83, 87, 99, 175, 248–249n46; as organ for free traders, 63, 82, 249n60
Capel, Rear-Adm. Thomas Bladen, 102
Carnatic, 196
Chang Ch'ao-fa, Brigade-General, 209
Chang-chou (Lungki, Lung-ch'i), 33
Chang Nan-shan, 140
Chang Shih-ch'eng, 121
Chang Yuan, 40
Ch'ang-chou-kang, 60
Chao-an, 33
Ch'ao-chou, 33
Chen-hai (Chinhai), 209
Chen-k'ou, 171, 173
Ch'en Ch'i-t'ien, 37
Ch'en Hung-ch'ih, 88
Ch'en Ts'ang-ch'i, 16
Cheng Shih-ch'ao, 19
Chi-ching-t'ou (Cabreta Point), 7
Chi-ning, 122
Ch'i-hsien (Kihsien), 37
Ch'i Kung, 58, 88
Ch'i-shan, 93, 96, 211, 212
Chia-ch'ing Emperor, 17, 19, 20, 95, 121
Chiang Hsiang-nan, 35
Chiang Ta-piao, 130
Chien-sha-tsui clash. *See* Lin Wei-hsi affair
Ch'ien-lung Emperor, 3, 140
Ch'ien-shan-chai, 200, 201
Chin-wen ("modern text") school, 123
China: foreign trade, 2, 6, 8–9, 32, 36–37, 62, 206–208 (*see also* Bond issue; names of individual nations); tributary diplomacy, 2, 11, 12, 65, 138–140, 214; cultural antipathy to West, 10, 11; legal concepts clash with West's, 12, 184, 186; antiopium edicts (1729–1839), 17, 19, 20, 97, 98, 219–221; monetary system and problems, 39–46, 234n32, 243n86, 244n-87; official corruption and opium problem, 46–48, 116, 172, 176; effects of Opium War, 216–217. *See also* Opium trade
Ch'in-ch'ai ta-ch'en (imperial high commissioner), 120
Chinchew. *See* Ch'üan-chou
Chinhai (Chen-hai), 209
Chinese Repository, 31–32, 175

Ching-shang, 76
Ching-shih chih-yung chih-hsueh, 123
Chinnery, George, 8, 235n37
Chopboats, 153
Chou Chi-hua, 96
Chou, Duke of, 127
Chou T'ien-chueh, 33
Chu Tsun, 89–90, 91–92, 117
Chusan Islands, 28, 193, 209–210
Ch'uan-pi, 168, 204
Ch'uan-pi engagement, 205–206
Chuang, Prince, 94
Chuang Ts'un-yü, 123
Chuenpee. *See* Ch'uan-pi
Ch'ü-chiang, 33
Ch'üan-chou (Chinchew), 2, 23, 33, 47–48
Cleveland (Ki-le-wun), 112
Cohong, 4. *See also* Hong merchants; names
    of individual merchants
Colledge, Dr. T. R., 61
Colonel Young (opium ship), 24–25
Columbia (frigate), 265n18
Comprador, 6, 7
Confucius, 258n49
Consoo House, 144, 146, 149, 150, 153, 154,
    183, 185, 198
Conway (warship), 209
Conyngham, Lennox, 68
Copper coinage. *See* China, monetary system
Coral (opium ship), 29
Corruption. *See* China, official corruption
Costin, W. C., 117
Country trade: role in balancing England's
    China trade, 4, 41, 42; dependence on
    opium, 244n88
Cumsha, 6
Custom-finding test, 129–130

Daniell, James F. N., 144
Davidson, W. S. 21
Davis, John Francis, 52, 57, 62–63
Delano, Warren, 183, 207
Denmark, China trade, 1, 136
Dent, Lancelot: in coastal smuggling trade,
    27; helps force Napier's backdown, 61;
    under attack as opium smuggler, 90, 98,
    148–151, 158, 171; in negotiations over
    Lin's demands, 144–147.
Dent affair, legal aspects, 150
Dent and Company, 21, 27, 191, 197, 207,
    261n92. *See also* Country trade
Detention of foreign community at Canton,
    141–160
De Quincey, Thomas, 17
Douglas, Capt. 202–203
Downing, Toogood, 34
Dublin Magazine, 176, 251n25

East India Company: China trade monopoly,
    1, 12, 51, 132; Select Committee, 3, 20,
    48; and opium production and trade, 18,
    21–22, 48, 237n6; and silver drain from
    China, 43. *See also* Great Britain; India

Edicts, antiopium. *See* China, antiopium
    edicts
Edinburgh Review, 30
Elliot, Capt. Charles: ambivalence on opium
    trade, 49, 106, 177–179; and *Argyle* inci-
    dent, 66–67; private correspondence with
    Foreign Office during Robinson's tenure,
    68–69; advocacy of moderate course, 68–
    69, 71, 81, 160, 214; early career and
    family background, 69, 253n59; appointed
    chief superintendent and conflict with
    Teng (1836–37), 69, 70, 73, 74, 76–77,
    103–104; and British naval visits to
    China, 78, 79, 102, 105; actions through
    Dec. 1838 and ban of inner-river smug-
    gling, 79, 103, 114–115, 255–256n104;
    hopes for opium legalization, 87, 89, 91,
    249n56; on rigor of prohibition enforce-
    ment, 101, 117, 118; on *Bombay* incident,
    109; in Ho Lao-chin affair, 113; on extra-
    territoriality, 138, 139; and 1839 crisis,
    144, 157, 160, 162–163, 187–188, 230,
    264n128, 265n18; and Dent affair, 150–
    151; orders opium surrender, 164–165,
    167, 264–265n15; misinterprets Lin's mo-
    tives, 172; and bond issue, 181–187; call
    for British military intervention, 189–191;
    on indemnity issue, 192; and Lin Wei-hsi
    affair, 196–199, 271n45; and Kowloon
    clash, 202–203; on Americans remaining
    in Canton, 206, 208
Elliot, Adm. George, 210
Elmslie, A. W., 203, 270n23
Elmslie (Elliot's secretary), 76, 204
English East India Company. *See* East India
    Company
Extraterritoriality: conflict between Chinese
    and Western views, 138–140, 186, 197;
    Palmerston denies inherent right of, 198;
    issue, as direct cause of war, 214

Factory Street, 113
Fairbank, John K., 4–5
Fairy (opium ship), 26, 29, 240n43
Fairy Queen affair, 67
Falcon (opium ship), 26
Fast crabs (smug boats), 32–33, 103, 116
Fearon, Samuel, 11, 150, 183, 262n98
Feng-ch'eng, 125
Flint, James, 140
Fo-kang, 163
Foochow, 2, 193
Forbes, John M., 206–207
Forbes, Robert, 166, 183, 206–207, 208
Foreign opium traders, 176, 191, 192. *See
    also* Opium trade; names of individual
    traders
Fort William, 197, 199
Free (private) traders: clash with China's
    containment policy, 14; extent by 1834,
    81; dissension within, 81–84. *See also*
    China; Foreign merchants; Great Britain;
    India; Opium trade; names of individuals
    and firms

George the Fourth, 162, 229–230
Gibb, T. A., 67
Gold-silver ratio. See China, monetary system
Gordon, H. G.: on importance of opium trade to Britain and India, 42–43; under attack as opium dealer, 90, 91, 98
Governor Findlay (opium ship), 26, 28
Gowqua, 148–150
"Grand chop," 7
Grant, Capt. Alexander, 30
Great Britain: China trade, 1, 41, 131–132, 179, 224–228 (see also Bond issue; China; India; Opium trade); and Industrial Revolution, 13; and opium trade, 48–50, 77, 132, 222–223; China trade as opening for colonial ambitions, 179, 272n72; military relations with China, 209. See also Elliot; Maitland mission; Opium War
Green, John C., 144, 146, 207
Greenberg, Michael, 132
Gresham's Law, 45–46
Grey, 207
Gutzlaff, Rev. Charles: official service in China, 11, 29, 66–67, 202, 209, 210; interpreter for opium smugglers, 23, 24, 27, 95, 267n66; early life and role in China, 26–27; China Opened (1838), 66; in 1839–40 crisis, 175, 180, 202, 209, 210, 267n66; Thom's low opinion of, 210; on opium traffic, 239n31, n32; death, 267n66

Hai-fang shu-chü, 142
Han Chao-ch'ing, 47, 130
Harriet (opium ship), 26
Hart, Robert, 35
Heerjeebhoy, 156
Hellas (opium ship), 29
High commissioner, title, 120
Hill, Dr., 137
Ho Lao-chin, 112–113
Ho T'ai-ch'ing, 88
Hog Lane, 113
Holland, 1
Hong Kong, 162, 193, 202, 205
Hong merchants: origin, 4, 233n18; government exactions, 14; debts to foreigners and bankruptcies, 14, 237n72; incompetence in public affairs as cause for Anglo-Chinese conflict, 14, 214; as middlemen, 53, 76–77, 91, 114, 142–143, 144–148, 155; Chinese government's strictures against, 90, 142–143; names, 261n88
Hooghly, 21
Hoppo: establishment, 4, 5; corrupt reputation, 10, 38, 82; role in opium suppression, 20, 104, 125–126; origin of term, 234n23. See also Yü-k'un
Ho-shen, 46–47
Hou-kuan (Foochow), 121
Howqua: estimate of fortune, 5; insecurity of position, 20, 145–146, 148–150, 155; as mediator, 55, 72–73, 78, 81, 113, 148–150, 168, 181, 183, 185, 207, 261n90;

and Lin's letter to Victoria, 137; and Dent affair, 148–150; suffering during factory confinement, 155; and opium surrender, 168, 261n90; and bond issue, 181, 183, 185, 207
Hsia Hsieh, 96
Hsia Nai, 213
Hsiang-k'ang, 36
Hsiao-ch'üan, Empress (Niuhuru), 88, 250n14
Hsiao I-shan, 213
Hsieh Kuo-t'ai, Maj., 131
Hsü Chi-yü, 240–241n55
Hsü Ch'iu, 89–90, 91–92, 117
Hsü Kuang, 130
Hsü Nai-chi, 85–89, 94
Hsü Shih-lin, 121
Hsüan-nan poetry club, 122, 126
Hsueh-hai t'ang, Canton, 87
Huang, Chueh-tzu, 40, 92, 97, 126
Huang Chung-mo, 40
Hui-chou, 33
Hung Hsiu-ch'üan, 216
Hunter, William C.: praises Canton trade, 9; on foreigners' contempt for Chinese officials, 82; on Ho Lao-chin affair, 112–113; 255n100; describes Lin, 125–126; and Lin's letter to Victoria, 137; on factory confinement and opium confiscation, 153, 155–156, 158, 163, 166, 184; early career, 258–259n51
Hunt's Merchants' Magazine, 30
Hyacinth (warship), 208

I-liang, 107, 125–126, 133–134, 180, 196
I-li-pu, 93
Imogene (frigate), 56
Imperial audience (yin-chien), 130
Imperial Household Department (nei-wu-fu), 5
Indemnity issue, 191–193
India: role in Sino-British trade, 41, 42–43; and opium trade, 132, 192, 237–238n6. See also East India Company
Inglis, Robert, 149, 150, 191
Innes, James: coastal smuggling, 23; Chinese seizure of opium, 79, 112, 171, 254n94; under attack as opium smuggler, 90, 143; expulsion, 98, 114
International relations, traditional Chinese concept of, 2. See also China, tributary diplomacy

Jamesina (opium ship), 23
Japan, 45
Jardine, Matheson and Company: nature of business during 1830s, 13; coastal smuggling, 23–26, 27–28; use of American agents, 207; amount of opium surrendered, 262n92
Jardine, William: early career, 13; as leader of coastal smuggling, 26, 27–28; defends character of opium merchants, 49; in Napier crisis, 55, 57, 63; on legalization

rumors, 87; under attack as opium smuggler, 90, 98, 142–143, 260n75, n77; views on opium and religion, 95; on rigors of enforcement of antiopium laws, 101, 102, 111; on 1837 opium-price decline, 104; as lobbyist in England for opium compensation and war, 191, 193–194; popularity among Canton traders, 250n68
Jardine (opium ship), 26
Jauncey, Capt. F., 28
Jih Sheng Ch'ang. See Shansi banks
John Adams (frigate), 265n18
John Biggar (opium ship), 23–24
Johnston, A. R., 148, 167–169, 170
Juan Yuan, 20, 87, 88, 190
Ju-yuan, 33
Juliet, 7
Just, Leonard, 106

Kaifeng, 212
K'ai-pao pen-ts'ao, 16
Kan River, 124, 125
K'ang-hsi Emperor, 12
Kao I-yung, 60
Kao Shu-k'ang, 37
Keeson-chow (Kiaochow), 193
Kiaochow, 193
Ki-le-wun (Cleveland), 112
Kihsien (Ch'i-hsien), 37
King, Charles W.: on American opium trade, 31; witnesses opium destruction, 135, 174–175; in factory confinement, 146, 183; vindication of Teng's honesty, 252n52
Kowloon clash, 202–203
Kronberg (brig), 23, 26
Kuan T'ien-p'ei, Adm.: appointed chief of Canton water forces, 62; and Maitland mission, 108, 110; and Bombay incident, 109; and Lin, 126, 141, 173; and opium surrender, 168; and ch'uan-pi engagement, 204–206
Kükong (Ch'ü-chiang), 33
Kung-hang (Cohong), 4. See also Hong merchants
Kung Tzu-chen, 122, 123; letter to Lin, 126–128, 140
Kung-yang interpretation, 123
Kuo Kuei-ch'uan, 141
Kuo T'ai-ch'eng, 38

Lady Hays (opium ship), 26
Lady Hughes incident, 12, 139, 197
Lankeet (Lung-hsueh), 168
Larne (sloop), 109, 154, 161, 177
Leeds, 192–193
Leslie (Dent's partner), 149
Li Chao-lo, 123
Li Hsien, Col., 109, 110
Li Hung-chang, 217, 242n70
Li Hung-pin, 36, 47, 51, 52–53
Li Tseng-chieh, 60, 62
Li Tun-yeh, 168
Liang En-sheng, 130

Liang T'ing-nan, 101, 141–142
Lieh-te, fort of, 59
Lin Tse-hsü: mission hindered by language and cultural barriers, 10, 131–132; on moral and economic facets of opium trade, 35, 37, 40, 260n75; suppression of Chinese involved in opium, 47, 128–131; success of memorial on prohibition, 93, 97; appointed imperial commissioner, 94, 120; famous statement against opium, 96; Taokuang Emperor's high opinion, 120; limits on power in Canton, 121, 127; distinction of early career, 121–124; as scholar and student of alien cultures, 123, 131–132, 140, 257n15; later career and death, 124, 212–213; trip to Canton, 124–125; description, 126; basic strategy in Canton, 126, 128, 213–214; letters to Queen Victoria, 134–138; denies extraterritoriality claims, 138–139; military strategy and desire to avoid conflict, 140, 141; edict to foreign merchants, 143–144; moves against Dent, 148–150; factory confinement, 151–158, 159; and surrender of opium, 156–157, 163–164, 167–172, 265–266n36–38; destruction of opium, 172–176; rashness of methods, 176, 215; and bond issue, 179–186; British accusations of corruption, 192, 267n66; attempts to restore trade, 195; and Lin Wei-hsi affair, 196–199; visit to Macao, 200–201; memorials on Kowloon and Ch'uan-pi clashes, 203, 205, 270n41; as scapegoat, 210, 212; contribution as patriot and prophet, 215, 217
Lin Wei-hsi affair, 13, 196–199, 202, 204, 205, 214, 270n23, 271n42, n45
Lindsay, H. H., 191
Linguists: functions and fees, 6, 7; role during detention, 155–156
Lintin Island: as opium depot, 21, 32, 106, 165; Chinese threat to cut off supplies, 105
Liu Feng-lu, 123
Liu Han, 16
Liu Jung-ch'ing, 36
Liu K'ai-yü, 168
Liverpool, 192–193
Lo-ch'ang, 33
London, reactions to detention, 192–193
Lord Amherst (opium ship), 28, 30
Louisa (Elliot's cutter), 109, 202, 203
Low, A. A., 260n71
Lu K'un: and Napier crisis, 51, 52–53, 55, 56, 60; early career, 58; strengthening of Canton defenses, 58–60; and legalization drive, 88
Lu Ta-yueh, 109, 110
Lun Ch'ao-kuang, 130
Lung-ch'i (Chang-chou), 33
Lung-hsueh, 168
Lungki (Chang-chou), 33

Ma-ko fort, 201

Macao, 107, 136, 171; in 1839 crisis, 186–188, 199–202
Macartney mission, 12, 13
McKay, Capt. William, 23–24, 26, 29
McCulloch, John, 36, 116
Macvicar, John, 207
Magniac, Charles, 20, 21
Magniac, Hollingworth, 21, 238n7, 244n88
Magniac Smith and Company, 191
Maitland, Rear-Adm. Sir Frederick L.: mission to China, 78, 103, 107–111, 177, 194; diplomatic aspects of mission, 78, 109, 194; failure to end opium prohibition, 110; on *Bombay* incident, 254n78
Malwa opium, 19, 21, 22, 23, 104
Manchester, 192–193
Mangalore, 196, 197
Mao Tse-tung, 216
Maria (opium ship), 29
Maritime Defense Publishing Bureau (Hai-fang shu-chü), 142
Marjoribanks, Charles, 62
Marquis, Capt., 113, 165, 263n114
Matheson, Alexander, 63, 171, 191
Matheson, Donald, 171
Matheson, James: early career, 13, 21; returns to England as lobbyist (1834), 83; in 1839 crisis, 144–147, 156, 171; on Lin's and Elliot's tactics, 160, 166; on dullness of 1839 trade, 165; advice to lobbyists, 191–192
Mei-ling Pass, 125
Merwanjee, 90, 98
Ming-shih, 17
"Modern text" (*chin-wen*) school, 123
Morrison, John Robert: interpreter and translator of Chinese, 11, 180, 236n48, 259n59; Elliot's secretary, 76, 78; and Dent affair, 149; incorrect translations, 261n79, n80
Morrison, Robert, 11, 53, 164
Morse, H. B., 9, 94
Moss, Mark, 199–200
Mowqua, 55, 148–150, 181, 183
Mu-chang-a, 94, 213

Namhoi, magistrate of, 128, 149, 163, 183, 185
Namhung (Nan-hsiung), 33
Namoa, 26, 33. *See also* Nan-ao
Nan-an, 125
Nan-ao (Namoa), 26, 33, 130, 169
Nan-Han shu, 142
Nan-hsiung, 33
Nan-huan Street, Macao, 200
Nan-wan fort, 201
Nanking, Treaty of (1842), 3
"Napier fizzle," significance, 62
Napier, Lord William John: struggle to avoid submission to Chinese protocol, 12, 53, 54–55, 56–57; appointment to China post, 51; early career and objects of mission, 52; suggests formation of chamber of commerce, 54; disregard of instructions,

57; retreat to Macao and death, 61; main reason for failure, 61; Lin ascribes death to divine retribution, 164
New China Street, 153
Niang-ma-ko Temple, 200
Ningpo, 2, 193
Nye, Gideon, Jr., 113, 207, 244n87

Old China Street, 153
Old Tom (linguist), 155–156
Olyphant, D. W. C., 31
Omega (opium ship), 29
Opium: early references to in China, 16; Chinese tariff revenue, 17, 128; price in China, 19, 21, 22, 104, 208, 241n59, 253n72; suppression campaigns in China, 30, 116, 128–131 (*see also* China; Lin Tse-hsü; Teng T'ing-chen); legalization movement, 85–89, 91–92, 94, 117, 190; indemnity issue, 191–193
— Chinese confiscation (1839): Lin's terms for surrender, 156–157; used as pretext for war by British, 161; surrender of, 165–172; amount disputed, 171, 266–267n52; disposal of, 172–176; foreign approval of destruction, 175–176
— Chinese edicts against. *See* China, anti-opium edicts
— Consumption: introduction and early use in China, 16; physical effects, 17; effect on China's economy and morality, 32; spread in China, 34–36; unreliability of records, 35; among soldiers and officials, 36; medical opinion on effects, 94; Western journalistic opinion on effects, 94, 95; Chinese condemnation, 95–96, 143, 241–242n67, n70
— Trade: growth and extent, 19, 35, 77, 104, 208, 240–241n55; world importance, 30; Western press concern over, illegality, 30, 246n119; effect on Chinese commerce, 32, 36–37; distribution network in China, 33; as cause of specie drain, 39–46; Lin's admonitions to Victoria, 135; as direct cause of war, 214. *See also* East India Company; names of countries
Opium War: as clash between two cultures, 15; Elliot's shift of trade to Macao, 188; Kowloon clash, 202; formal beginning, 209; direct causes, 214; Western press warnings, 215–216; long-range impact on China, 216–217
Orwell, 162
Ostenders, 1
Ouchterlony, Lt. John, 34

Palmerston, Lord Henry John Temple: and *Fairy* incident, 29; bypasses Robinson for Canton information, 68; pressure on Elliot to seek political recognition, 71–72, 73, 76, 77, 80, 160; negotiates Portuguese recognition of Elliot's position, 75; orders naval visits to China, 103; policy of non-interference with opium smuggling, 106, 116–117, 177, 268n81; and Ho Lao-chin affair, 114; and Lin's letter to Victoria, 138; yields to domestic pressures for war, 192–194; denies inherent right of extra-territoriality, 198; letter to Chinese emperor (1840), 210

Panyü, magistrate of, 128, 163, 183, 185

Pao An-t'ai, 130

Pao-chia system, 129

Pao-hsing, 96

Pao Shih-ch'en, 34, 125

Parker, Peter, 137, 195

Parsees, 158

Patna opium, 19, 22, 23, 104

Pearl (schooner), 202, 203

Pen-ts'ao shih-i, 16

Petitions by foreigners, 8. See also *Pin*

Pidgin English, 235–236n47

Pilotage, 6

Pin (*ping*); significance of use by foreigners, 70; Palmerston's objections, 72, 76; Elliot's attempts to avoid, 79, 80, 108

P'ing-yao, 37, 38

Pinto, Don Adriao Accacio de Silveira, 186–187

Poppy, introduction into China, 16

Port clearance (grand chop), 7

Portugal: China trade, 1, 17–18, 21; status in Macao, 136; in 1839–40 crisis; 186–187, 199–202, 203

Propagandists (*yu-k'o*), 127

Prussia, 1, 6, 136

P'u-hsi, Imperial Duke, 94

Quarterly Review: on American stake in opium trade, 31; doubts evil effects of opium, 94; on 1839 crisis, 165, 166–167, 175; on dangers of inland war with China, 215

Quemoy, 193

Raleigh (sloop), 29

Rattlesnake (troopship), 209

Receiving ships, 32. See also Lintin Island

Red Rover (opium ship) 26

Rees, Capt. John: in coastal smuggling, 23, 24–25, 28, 29; correspondence with Jardine, 30, 87, 101

Reliance, 113, 158, 162

Revenue, Board of, 5

Rhubarb, 131, 134, 135

Robinson, Sir George Best: becomes Davis' second in command, 62; early career in China, 64; policy as chief superintendent, 64–69, 249n47; and *Fairy Queen* affair, 67

Royal Saxon, 205

Russell and Company: importance in opium trade, 31; withdraws from opium trade, 118–119; in 1839 crisis, 153, 157, 165, 180, 184; as agent for British firms (1840), 206, 207

Russia, 216

Rustomjee, Dadabhoy, 90, 98, 144, 171

Ryan, James, 207

Samqua, 183

Sandy Head, 167, 169, 171

San-pa Gate, fort, 200, 201

Schroff, 234n32

Scrambling dragons, 32. See also Fast crabs

Secret societies and opium trade, 33

Security merchant system, 4

Sha-chiao (Sandy Head), 167, 169, 171

Shanghai, 193

Shansi banks and opium trade, 37–39, 242n73, n79, 243n81

Shao-chou, 125

Shen Chen-pang, 131

Shen Yen-ch'ing, 96

Silk, 135

Silver, 44, 45. See also China, monetary system

Singapore Free Press, 175

Slade, John, 150, 156, 234n31, 262n98

Smith, Capt. Henry, 204, 205–206

Smith, John Abel, 193, 194

Smug boats, 32–33. See also Fast crabs

Snow, Peter Wanton, 183, 184

Soochow, 34

Spain, 136, 245n104

Su Ch'e, 16

Su-leng-e, 40

Su, Prince, 95–96

Su Tung-p'o, 16

Sunda, 137

Superintendent of Maritime Customs for Kwangtung. See Hoppo; Yü-k'un

Surat, 6

Suy-Hong, 113

Sweden, 1, 136

Sylph (opium ship), 23, 95

Ta-chien, 76

Ta-huang-chiao River, 60

Tai-pan, 51, 65, 70

T'ai-ku, 37, 38

Taiping rebellion, 213

Tao-kuang Emperor: determination to extirpate opium traffic, 36, 93–94, 95, 179–180; dynastic decline during reign, 43, 82; disavowal of *Bombay* incident hidden from, 110; changing attitude toward Lin, 123, 136, 210, 212, 213

T'ao Yung, 16

Tartar general, 110, 173

Te-k'e-chin-pu, 107

Tea, 3, 131, 134, 135

Tea boats, 153

Teng T'ing-chen: antiopium work, 47, 91, 96, 98, 103, 104, 111, 115, 133–134, 162–163, 180, 187; appointed governor-general, 70; protocol conflict with Elliot, 72, 74, 76–77, 78, 80; and legalization movement, 86–87, 88, 250n13; early career, 99–100; honesty questioned, 100,

101, 252n52; and Maitland mission, 107, 111; talents and achievements compared to Lin's, 123, 129; reception of Lin, 125–126; and Lin Wei-hsi affair, 196; visits Macao, 200–201; and Ch'uan-pi engagement, 205; defense of Fukien and exile, 211, 212
Teng Ying, 172–173
T'eng-wang-ko, 125
Thom, Robert: interpreter and translator, 11; in 1839 crisis, 150, 168, 170, 254–255n94; and battle of Tinghai, 209–210; later career, 236n49
Thomas Coutts, 138, 181, 204
Thomas Perkins, 112
T'ien-hou-kung, 150
T'ien-tao (Providence), 163, 264n12
Tiger fort, 108
Times, The (London), 210, 229–230, 250–251n14
Tindal, Hassan, 199–200
Tinghai, battle of, 209–210
Tongkoo Bay, 107, 177, 205
Tributary system. *See* China, tributary diplomacy
Troughton, 103
Ts'ao Chih, 96
Tseng Kuo-fan, 217
Tseng Sheng, 58
Tsiang T'ing-fu, 210
Tso-chuan, allusion by Lin, 259n62
T'ung-ku-wan. *See* Tongkoo Bay
Turkey opium, 23, 238n19
Turner, Richard, 90, 98

United States: opium trade, 31, 42, 238n19; bimetallic currency, 46; Lin's notion of its government, 136; China trade, 206–208. *See also* King; Russell and Company

Van Basel, Senn, 183, 184
Victoria, Queen of England, 134–138

Volage, 201, 202, 204, 205, 208

Wabash incident, 20
Wang Chen-kao, 130
Wang Ch'ing-lien, 99
Wang-hsia, 200
Wang-Yueh, 85
Warner, Capt., 138, 181, 204
Water Witch, 27
Weddell, Capt. J., 138
Wei T'ai Hou. *See* Shansi banks
Wei Yuan, 122, 123
Wellesley (warship), 107, 109, 110, 209
Wellington, Duke of (Arthur Wellesley), 49, 61, 83
Wen-chou, 33
Wetmore, W. S., 144–147, 183, 207
Whampoa, 6, 60
Whiteman, John C., 61, 90, 98
Williams, S. Wells, 164, 196
Wu Lan-hsiu, 88

Yang-ch'eng academy, 130
Yao-k'ou (brokerage organizations), 32, 90, 128
Yeh Heng-shu, 20
Yellow River, shift of, 212
Yen Hsi-shan, 242n70
Yen-p'ing, 33
Ying-lung, 173
Young Tom (linguist), 155–156
Yü (command), 78
Yü-ch'ien, 212
Yü-k'un, 125–126, 141. *See also* Hoppo
Yü Pao-ch'un, 173
Yuan-chih, 70
Yuan Te-hui, 137, 258–259n51
Yuan Yü-lin, 92
Yueh-hai-kuan chih, 141–142
Yueh-hsiu academy, 130
Yueh-hua academy, 88, 126, 130
Yung-cheng Emperor, 2